THE WAY WE NEVER WERE

The Way We Never Were

American Families and the
Nostalgia Trap

STEPHANIE COONTZ

BasicBooks
A Division of HarperCollins*Publishers*

Library of Congress Cataloging-in-Publication Data

Coontz, Stephanie.
  The way we never were : American families and the nostalgia trap /
Stephanie Coontz.
    p. cm.
  Includes bibliographical references and index.
  ISBN 0-465-00135-1
  1. Family—United States—History—20th century. 2. United States—
Social conditions. 3. Nostalgia. I. Title.
HQ535.C643 1992   91–59009
306.85'0973—dc20   CIP

Designed by Ellen Levine

92 93 94 95 SWD/HC 9 8 7 6 5 4 3 2

Contents

Preface

THIS book began as a conventional chronological account of American family life from 1900 to 1990, a sequel to my previous book, *The Social Origins of Private Life: A History of American Families, 1600–1900*. Since publication of that book, I have received numerous speaking requests from nonacademic audiences—hospital ethics committees concerned about how to define families, psychologists' and social workers' associations, church groups, Rotary clubs, and labor organizations. In each case, people were seeking a way to assess the conflicting messages they were receiving (and often feeling) about the changing forms and functions of American families. Gradually, I began to see that one contribution I could make to their debates was to place the urgent concerns I heard at these meetings in some sort of historical perspective.

At first, I unconsciously tried to incorporate this project into my original outline. The result was a mess—detailed historical chronologies interspersed with occasional comments on the applicability of some past event to modern family dilemmas. Susan Armitage, director of American Studies at Washington State University, first suggested that the prospectus for a sequel to my previous work now contained within it quite a different book on various myths about past family life. Simultaneously, a number of op-ed editors at various newspapers challenged me to demonstrate the contemporary relevance of family history in more accessible form. Accordingly, I reorganized the book to highlight particular myths and stereotypes, especially those most directly applicable to current debates about family life and gender roles.

I received help in recasting my topic from many sources. My editor at Basic Books, Steve Fraser, provided incisive comments to keep my writing focused. A dedicated group of colleagues and friends from many disciplines and occupations met regularly to help me decide how to organize my discussion: I would like to thank Priscilla Bowerman, Peta Henderson, Jeanne Hahn, Charles Pailthorp, Larry Mosqueda, Jim Ascher, Suzette McCann, and Kathleen O'Shaunessy for their extraordinary commitment of time and energy. I also received helpful advice and criticism from Nancy Hartsock, Steven Rose, Susan Strasser, Russell Lidman, David Marr, Nancy Holmstrom, York Wong, Alan Nasser, Jill Severn, Leo and Sherry Frumkin, Ted Brackman, Gonzalo Munevar, Brian Price, Greg Weeks, Sarah Williams, and Charlotte Raynor.

My research assistant, Paul Ortiz, worked for starvation wages tracking down books and articles, checking footnotes, collecting data, and giving me the benefit of his critical reading of each chapter. Paul Schipper helped me complete many notes in the copyediting stage, as did several of the library staff at the University of Hawaii in Hilo, where I was on exchange at the time. Michael Simmons and John Finnan extricated me from numerous computer crises. I received generous help from successive secretarial teams: Adelle Smith, Peggy Davenport, Cindy Fry, Lupe Valadez, and Mary Hansen, and especially Pam Udovich, who typed and printed my final revisions. The Evergreen State College kindly provided me with a sponsored research grant as well as allowed me an unpaid leave to complete the book, and its library staff were unstinting in their help.

Finally, I would like to thank my family—nuclear, extended, blended, and fictive—who have never confused being "untraditional" with being uncommitted and who have supported me in many ways during the writing of this book. I am especially grateful to my son, Kristopher, for his patience, good cheer, and common sense.

Introduction

PESSIMISTS argue that the family is collapsing; optimists counter that it is merely diversifying. Too often, both camps begin with an ahistorical, static notion of what "the" family was like before the contemporary period. Thus we have one set of bestsellers urging us to reaffirm traditional family values in an era of "family collapse" and another promising to set us free from traditional family traps if we can only turn off "old tapes" and break out of old ruts. In this book, I am less inclined to identify some recent qualitative change in family patterns that people should repudiate or embrace. I am not going to recite a litany of ways in which modern families have "abandoned traditional commitments," failed their children, or "lost their moral compass." Nor, however, will I offer soothing words about achieving "self-actualization," making divorce a "growth experience," or celebrating the "new family pluralism." I hope to contribute to a more nuanced appraisal of where American families have come from and the challenges they face as they approach the year 2000.

When schoolchildren return from vacation and are asked to list the good things and the bad things about their summer, their lists tend to be equally long. Over the year, however, if the exercise is repeated, the good list grows longer and the bad shorter until by the end of the year the children are describing not actual vacations but idealized images of Vacation.

So it is with families. The actual complexity of our history—even of our own personal experience—gets buried under the weight of an idealized image. On both a personal and a social level, when things are going well, we credit our successful adherence to the family ideal, forgetting the conflicts, ambivalences, and departures from the "norm." When things are going poorly, we look for the "dysfunctional" elements of our family life, blaming our problems on "abnormal" experiences or innovations.

I hope to expose many of our "memories" of traditional family life as myths. Families have always been in flux and often in crisis; they have never lived up to nostalgic notions about "the way things used to be." But that doesn't mean the malaise and anxiety people feel about modern families are delusions, that everything would be fine if we would only realize that the past was not all it's cracked up to be. Proving that there was no "golden age" of the family is in one sense a debater's point that rightfully leaves most audiences unsatisfied. Even if things were not always right in families of the past, it seems clear that some things have newly gone wrong.

Some of the most disturbing problems are those involving youth. More than 20 percent of American children live in poverty—one in eight children under age twelve actually goes hungry; almost 100,000 are homeless on any given night. America's record in vaccinating children age two and under is worse than that of any country in the Western Hemisphere, except Bolivia and Haiti; the United States ranks twenty-first in the world in infant mortality. "We're still number one" in homicide rates, though. Every day, 135,000 children take a gun to school; every fourteen hours, a child younger than age five is murdered; in Chicago's inner city, 74 percent of the children have witnessed a shooting, stabbing, or robbery. Homicide has now replaced motor-vehicle accidents as the leading cause of death among children below the age of one. The violent-death rate of teenagers rose from 62.4 per 100,000 in 1984 to 69.7 in 1988, an increase of 12 percent. The teen suicide rate has quadrupled since 1950.[1]

In a recent national poll, one in seven Americans claimed to have been sexually abused as a child, while one in six reported being physically abused. One out of every ten newborns has been exposed to some kind of illicit drug, and teachers are bracing themselves for what happens when crack-affected babies reach school age. Each year, there are 30,000 pregnancies among young women under the age of fifteen. U.S. children rank behind those of most of America's industrial competitors in school achievement tests: The high school dropout rate in America is 27 percent, compared to 5 percent in Japan and 2 percent in Russia.[2]

Our murder rate is four times higher than Europe's; our rape rate is seven times higher. However, as the U.S. Surgeon General notes, "The home is actually a more dangerous place for American women than the city streets." Each day, four women are killed by their male partners; in 1989, more women were abused by their husbands than got married in the same period.[3]

The precise links between these depressing figures and recent family changes are not always clear, but it is logical to posit some connection. Family life seems more fragile than ever. The rate of divorce tripled between 1960 and 1982, then leveled off at a point where 50 percent of first marriages, and 60 percent of second ones, are likely to end in divorce within forty years. Between 1960 and 1986, the proportion of teenage mothers who were unmarried rose from 15 percent to 61 percent, while the total number of children growing up with only one parent doubled, to a full quarter of all children under age eighteen. Twenty-five percent of the people polled in a recent national inquiry into American morality said that for $10 million they would abandon their entire family; a large number of people are evidently willing to do the same thing for free, judging from the astonishing statistics on how few noncustodial fathers spend time with their children after divorce.[4]

Not all the changes affecting American families are negative, but even innovations of which most people approve create uncomfortable predicaments. Most women want to retain the gains they have made in jobs, education, and law, but working women are burdened with a second shift at home and haunted by images such as those so prevalent during the Gulf War, in which female soldiers were almost invariably shown kissing their infants good-bye. Few Americans want to return to the days of segregated gender roles and legal inequality, but they are not sure how to build male-female intimacy in the midst of continuing inequities, the complicated dynamics of sexual harassment and mistrust, and the extremes of isolated self-sufficiency on the one hand and co-dependency on the other.

Most Americans welcome the expanded tolerance for alternative family forms and reproductive arrangements, although they are perplexed by the difficult boundary disputes that accompany new family definitions. Courts have been asked to decide what happens to fertilized ova if the partners split up and to rule whether sperm donors or surrogate mothers have higher rights. It is surely wrong to consider a woman who agrees to become a surrogate mother nothing more than a "carrier" for the fetus, but isn't the woman who made plans to receive that baby for nine months also an expectant mother? What about child-custody disputes between lesbian or gay partners? Do paternal grandparents have any right to visit their grandchildren if their daughter-in-law has custody and forbids the relationship to continue? How does a divorced woman relate to the "wife-in-law" she gains when her husband remarries, a woman who may actually take more care of her children on visitation weekends than her ex-husband does?

Contrary to the doomsday scenario, there have been undeniable gains associated with the democratization of family relations, the expansion of women's options outside the family and men's responsibilities within it, the erosion of ethnocentric and moralistic norms about what a proper family must be and do, and the new tolerance for unconventional family relations. But these gains have been accompanied by unanticipated and difficult new inequalities. While divorce has been a vital option for many, family dissolution often impoverishes women and children and, at least in our current social context, puts some youth "at risk." Even though many families as well as individual women benefit from women's new work opportunities, child care by profit-making companies, state agencies, and unregulated homeworkers all have major drawbacks. There seems to be an erosion of commitment to social obligations in general, and to children in particular, within America. There are no easy answers to such problems.

But, then again, there never were. Women and children bore the brunt of poverty within "traditional" two-parent families just as surely, if less visibly, as they do in modern female-headed households: Budget studies and medical records reveal that women and children in poor families of the past were far more likely to go without needed nutrients than were male heads of families. "Poverty has always been feminized," comments economist Claudia Goldin.[5]

Twenty percent of American children live in poverty today: At the turn of the century the same proportion lived in orphanages, not because they actually lacked both parents, but because one or both parents simply could not afford their keep. As late as 1960, after ten years of low divorce rates, one in three children lived in poverty. Modern statistics on child-support evasion are appalling, but prior to the 1920s, a divorced father did not even have a legal child-support obligation to evade. Until that time, children were considered assets of the family head, and his duty to support them ended if he was not in the home to receive the wages they could earn. As for child abuse, it has far too long and brutal a history to be blamed on recent family innovations.[6]

While overpermissiveness may create problems among some modern youth, overwork was responsible for the prevalence of delinquency and runaways in the late nineteenth century. Today's high school dropout rates are shocking, but as late as the 1940s, less than half the youths entering high school managed to finish, a figure much smaller than today's. Violence is reaching new highs in America, but before the Civil War, New York City was already considered the most dangerous place to live in the world; the United States has had the highest homicide rates in the industrial world for almost 150 years.[7]

Alcohol and drug abuse, similarly, were widespread well before modern rearrangements of gender roles and family life. In the 1820s, per capita consumption of alcohol was almost three times higher than it is today, and there was a major epidemic of opium and cocaine addiction in the late nineteenth century. "On a per capita basis, narcotic abuse was certainly as bad and probably worse" then as it is today. Many middle-class women were addicted to patent medicines that contained powerful drugs; pharmacists routinely dispatched young messenger boys to people's homes with vials of morphine.[8]

I am not arguing that the more things change, the more they remain the same. There have been many transformations in family life and social relations in American history, but they have been neither as linear nor as unitary as many accounts claim. Some changes have resulted in gains for one kind of family and losses for another, or gains for one family member and losses for another. Alternatively, things that seemed like gains in one context were experienced as losses in another. However, the historical record is clear on one point: Although there are many things to draw on in our past, there is no one family form that has ever protected people from poverty or social disruption, and no traditional arrangement that provides a workable model for how we might organize family relations in the modern world.

To say that no easy answers are to be found in the past is not to close off further discussion of family problems, but to open it up. To find *effective* answers to the dilemmas facing modern families, we must reject attempts to "recapture" family traditions that either never existed or existed in a totally different context. Only when we have a realistic idea of how families have and have not worked in the past can we make informed decisions about how to support families in the present or improve their future prospects.

This book examines the myths and half-truths that surround our understanding of American families, both past and present. In most cases, I organize each chapter around one widespread myth or stereotype about family change rather than giving a more conventional linear account of how families evolved into their present form. Detailed endnotes and a select bibliography provide references for those who wish to pursue any topic in greater depth.

Not all myths are bad, of course. People need shared stories and rituals to bring them together and reinforce social solidarity. But myths that create unrealistic expectations about what families can or should do tend to erode solidarities and diminish confidence in the problem-solving abilities of those whose families "fall short." Many of the myths I treat in this book are white, middle-class myths, both because middle-class individuals are the predominant mythmakers in our society and because the media tends to project fragments of the white, middle-class experience into universal "trends" or "facts." I show how these myths distort the diverse experiences of other groups in America and argue that they don't even describe most white, middle-class families accurately.

The most common reaction to a discordance between myth and reality is guilt. Even as children, my students and colleagues tell me, they felt guilty because their families did not act like those on television. Perhaps the second most common reaction is anger—a sense of betrayal or rage when you and your family cannot live as the myths suggest you should be able to do. My hope is that this book can help people put some of that guilt or anger aside and develop more compassion both for those who are still trying to live up to the myths and for those who are struggling, whether more or less successfully, to adjust their family norms and behaviors to modern realities.

In chapter 1, I discuss a few common myths about family forms and features in past times, showing the difficulty of making blanket generalizations about how families have evolved, much less about whether they have been getting better or worse. I then turn to myths about specific family types or traits. Chapter 2, for example, argues that the "Leave It to Beaver" ideal was a new invention of the 1950s, not an example of tradition, and that families of the period were both more diverse and less idyllic than we sometimes think.

Some people believe that the trouble with modern families is their abandonment of the traditional gender divisions that used to allow men to concentrate on breadwinning and women on childraising. Sociologist David Popenoe defines the "traditional nuclear family" as based on "a sharp division of labor...with the female as full-time housewife and the male as primary provider and ultimate authority."[9] In chapter 3, I discuss the contradictions inherent in this division of labor, which tried to resolve the tensions of liberal individualism by assigning ambition to men and altruism to women, expecting love to bridge the chasm. In chapter 4, I argue that even with such a division of labor, families were seldom economically or emotionally self-reliant.

Not until the late nineteenth century did people elevate the nuclear family to their central source of loyalty, obligation, and personal satisfaction. In chapter 5, I suggest that, far from forming the traditional basis of civic responsibility, this ideal represented a rejection of older obligations beyond the family. Chapter 6 traces the complex relation between family privacy and state intervention, showing that families have never been immune from outside interference and that our modern standards of family privacy are, ironically, largely a product of state intervention.

In chapter 7, I question the links that are often drawn between feminism, women's increasing labor-force participation, and the growth of an acquisitive, materialistic mentality. Chapter 8 details the main changes that have occurred in marriage, sex, reproduction, intergenerational relations, and the life course; and chapter 9 takes on the myth that children can be raised properly only in traditional families. Chapter 10 attempts to correct some of the stereotypes that distort public discussion of black family life in America. In chapter 11, I take a new look at the "crisis of the family," arguing that modern family dilemmas stem from a general crisis of economic, social, and political reproduction that cannot be solved by a return to traditional values.

The epilogue offers a note of hope. Although it may seem overwhelming to see family problems as only one symptom of a much larger social crisis, it is in some ways encouraging. It means, for example, that people have not suddenly and inexplicably "gone bad." They are struggling with serious dilemmas and, though many make poor choices or cannot carry out their highest ideals, are generally trying to do their best. There is evidence that we can help families do better and that we can do so now.

1

•••

The Way We Wish We Were:

Defining the Family Crisis

WHEN I begin teaching a course on family history, I often ask my students to write down ideas that spring to mind when they think of the "traditional family." Their lists always include several images. One is of extended families in which all members worked together, grandparents were an integral part of family life, children learned responsibility and the work ethic from their elders, and there were clear lines of authority based on respect for age. Another is of nuclear families in which nurturing mothers sheltered children from premature exposure to sex, financial worries, or other adult concerns, while fathers taught adolescents not to sacrifice their education by going to work too early. Still another image gives pride of place to the couple relationship. In traditional families, my students write—half derisively, half wistfully—men and women remained chaste until marriage, at which time they extricated themselves from competing obligations to kin and neighbors and committed themselves wholly to the marital relationship, experiencing an all-encompassing intimacy that our more crowded modern life seems to preclude. As one freshman wrote: "They truly respected the marriage vowels"; I assume she meant *I-O-U*.

Such visions of past family life exert a powerful emotional pull on most Americans, and with good reason, given the fragility of many modern commitments. The problem is not only that these visions bear a suspicious resemblance to reruns of old television series, but also that the scripts of different shows have been mixed up: June

Cleaver suddenly has a Grandpa Walton dispensing advice in her kitchen; Donna Stone, vacuuming the living room in her inevitable pearls and high heels, is no longer married to a busy modern pediatrician but to a small-town sheriff who, like Andy Taylor of "The Andy Griffith Show," solves community problems through informal, old-fashioned common sense.

Like most visions of a "golden age," the "traditional family" my students describe evaporates on closer examination. It is an ahistorical amalgam of structures, values, and behaviors that never coexisted in the same time and place. The notion that traditional families fostered intense intimacy between husbands and wives while creating mothers who were totally available to their children, for example, is an idea that combines some characteristics of the white, middle-class family in the mid-nineteenth century and some of a rival family ideal first articulated in the 1920s. The first family revolved emotionally around the mother-child axis, leaving the husband-wife relationship stilted and formal. The second focused on an eroticized couple relationship, demanding that mothers curb emotional "overinvestment" in their children. The hybrid idea that a woman can be fully absorbed with her youngsters while simultaneously maintaining passionate sexual excitement with her husband was a 1950s invention that drove thousands of women to therapists, tranquilizers, or alcohol when they actually tried to live up to it.

Similarly, an extended family in which all members work together under the top-down authority of the household elder operates very differently from a nuclear family in which husband and wife are envisioned as friends who patiently devise ways to let the children learn by trial and error. Children who worked in family enterprises seldom had time for the extracurricular activities that Wally and the Beaver recounted to their parents over the dinner table; often, they did not even go to school full-time. Mothers who did home production generally relegated child care to older children or servants; they did not suspend work to savor a baby's first steps or discuss with their husband how to facilitate a grade-schooler's "self-esteem." Such families emphasized formality, obedience to authority, and "the way it's always been" in their childrearing.

Nuclear families, by contrast, have tended to pride themselves on the "modernity" of parent-child relations, diluting the authority of grandparents, denigrating "old-fashioned" ideas about childraising, and resisting the "interference" of relatives. It is difficult to imagine the Cleavers or the college-educated title figure of "Father Knows

Best" letting grandparents, maiden aunts, or in-laws have a major voice in childrearing decisions. Indeed, the kind of family exemplified by the Cleavers, as we shall see in chapter 2, represented a conscious *rejection* of the Waltons' model.

The Elusive Traditional Family

Whenever people propose that we go back to the traditional family, I always suggest that they pick a ballpark date for the family they have in mind. Once pinned down, they are invariably unwilling to accept the package deal that comes with their chosen model. Some people, for example, admire the discipline of colonial families, which were certainly not much troubled by divorce or fragmenting individualism. But colonial families were hardly stable: High mortality rates meant that the average length of marriage was less than a dozen years. One-third to one-half of all children lost at least one parent before the age of twenty-one; in the South, more than half of all children aged thirteen or under had lost at least one parent.[1]

While there are a few modern Americans who would like to return to the strict patriarchal authority of colonial days, in which disobedience by women and children was considered a small form of treason, these individuals would doubtless be horrified by other aspects of colonial families, such as their failure to protect children from knowledge of sexuality. Eighteenth-century spelling and grammar books routinely used *fornication* as an example of a four-syllable word, and preachers detailed sexual offenses in astonishingly explicit terms. Sexual conversations between men and women, even in front of children, were remarkably frank. It is worth contrasting this colonial candor to the climate in 1991, when the Department of Health and Human Services was forced to cancel a proposed survey of teenagers' sexual practices after some groups charged that such knowledge might "inadvertently" encourage more sex.[2]

Other people searching for an ideal traditional family might pick the more sentimental and gentle Victorian family, which arose in the 1830s and 1840s as household production gave way to wage work and professional occcupations outside the home. A new division of labor by age and sex emerged among the middle class. Women's roles were redefined in terms of domesticity rather than production, men were labeled "breadwinners" (a masculine identity unheard of in colonial days), children were said to need time to play, and gentle maternal guidance supplanted the patriarchal authoritarianism of the past.

But the middle-class Victorian family depended for its existence on the multiplication of other families who were too poor and powerless to retreat into their own little oases and who therefore had to provision the oases of others. Childhood was prolonged for the nineteenth-century middle class only because it was drastically foreshortened for other sectors of the population. The spread of textile mills, for example, freed middle-class women from the most time-consuming of their former chores, making cloth. But the raw materials for these mills were produced by slave labor. Slave children were not exempt from field labor unless they were infants, and even then their mothers were not allowed time off to nurture them. Frederick Douglass could not remember seeing his mother until he was seven.[3]

Domesticity was also not an option for the white families who worked twelve hours a day in Northern factories and workshops transforming slave-picked cotton into ready-made clothing. By 1820, "half the workers in many factories were boys and girls who had not reached their eleventh birthday." Rhode Island investigators found "little half-clothed children" making their way to the textile mills before dawn. In 1845, shoemaking families and makers of artificial flowers worked fifteen to eighteen hours a day, according to the New York *Daily Tribune*.[4]

Within the home, prior to the diffusion of household technology at the end of the century, house cleaning and food preparation remained mammoth tasks. Middle-class women were able to shift more time into childrearing in this period only by hiring domestic help. Between 1800 and 1850, the proportion of servants to white households doubled, to about one in nine. Some servants were poverty-stricken mothers who had to board or bind out their own children. Employers found such workers tended to be "distracted," however; they usually preferred young girls. In his study of Buffalo, New York, in the 1850s, historian Lawrence Glasco found that Irish and German girls often went into service at the age of eleven or twelve.[5]

For every nineteenth-century middle-class family that protected its wife and child within the family circle, then, there was an Irish or a German girl scrubbing floors in that middle-class home, a Welsh boy mining coal to keep the home-baked goodies warm, a black girl doing the family laundry, a black mother and child picking cotton to be made into clothes for the family, and a Jewish or an Italian daughter in a sweatshop making "ladies'" dresses or artificial flowers for the family to purchase.

Furthermore, people who lived in these periods were seldom as enamored of their family arrangements as modern nostalgia might suggest. Colonial Americans lamented "the great neglect in many parents and masters in training up their children" and expressed the "greatest trouble and grief about the rising generation." No sooner did Victorian middle-class families begin to withdraw their children from the work world than observers began to worry that children were becoming *too* sheltered. By 1851, the Reverend Horace Bushnell spoke for many in bemoaning the passing of the traditional days of household production, when the whole family was "harnessed, all together, into the producing process, young and old, male and female, from the boy who rode the plough-horse to the grandmother knitting under her spectacles."[6]

The late nineteenth century saw a modest but significant growth of extended families and a substantial increase in the number of families who were "harnessed" together in household production. Extended families have never been the norm in America; the highest figure for extended-family households ever recorded in American history is 20 percent. Contrary to the popular myth that industrialization destroyed "traditional" extended families, this high point occurred between 1850 and 1885, during the most intensive period of early industrialization. Many of these extended families, and most "producing" families of the time, depended on the labor of children; they were held together by dire necessity and sometimes by brute force.[7]

There was a significant increase in child labor during the last third of the nineteenth century. Some children worked at home in crowded tenement sweatshops that produced cigars or women's clothing. Reformer Helen Campbell found one house where "nearly thirty children of all ages and sizes, babies predominating, rolled in the tobacco which covered the floor and was piled in every direction."[8] Many producing households resembled the one described by Mary Van Kleeck of the Russell Sage Foundation in 1913:

In a tenement on MacDougal Street lives a family of seven—grandmother, father, mother and four children aged four years, three years, two years and one month respectively. All excepting the father and the two babies make violets. The three year old girl picks apart the petals; her sister, aged four years, separates the stems, dipping an end

of each into paste spread on a piece of board on the kitchen table; and
the mother and grandmother slip the petals up the stems.[9]

Where children worked outside the home, conditions were no
better. In 1900, 120,000 children worked in Pennsylvania mines and
factories; most of them had started work by age eleven. In Scranton,
a third of the girls between the ages of thirteen and sixteen worked
in the silk mills in 1904. In New York, Boston, and Chicago,
teenagers worked long hours in textile factories and frequently died
in fires or industrial accidents. Children made up 23.7 percent of the
36,415 workers in southern textile mills around the turn of the century. When reformer Marie Van Vorse took a job at one in 1903, she
found children as young as six or seven working twelve-hour shifts.
At the end of the day, she reported: "They are usually beyond speech.
They fall asleep at the tables, on the stairs; they are carried to bed
and there laid down as they are, unwashed, undressed; and the inani-
mate bundles of rags so lie until the mill summons them with its im-
perious cry before sunrise."[10]

By the end of the nineteenth century, shocked by the conditions in
urban tenements and by the sight of young children working full-
time at home or earning money out on the streets, middle-class
reformers put aside nostalgia for "harnessed" family production and
elevated the antebellum model once more, blaming immigrants for
introducing such "un-American" family values as child labor. Reformers advocated adoption of a "true American" family—a restricted, exclusive nuclear unit in which women and children were
divorced from the world of work.

In the late 1920s and early 1930s, however, the wheel turned yet
again, as social theorists noted the independence and isolation of the
nuclear family with renewed anxiety. The influential Chicago School
of sociology believed that immigration and urbanization had weakened the traditional family by destroying kinship and community
networks. Although sociologists welcomed the increased democracy
of "companionate marriage," they worried about the rootlessness of
nuclear families and the breakdown of older solidarities. By the time
of the Great Depression, some observers even saw a silver lining in
economic hardship, since it revived the economic functions and social importance of kin and family ties. With housing starts down by
more than 90 percent, approximately one-sixth of urban families had
to "double up" in apartments. The incidence of three-generation
households increased, while recreational interactions outside the

home were cut back or confined to the kinship network. One news-paper opined: "Many a family that has lost its car has found its soul."[11]

Depression families evoke nostalgia in some contemporary ob-servers, because they tended to create "dependability and domestic inclination" among girls and "maturity in the management of money" among boys. But, in many cases, such responsibility was in-separable from "a corrosive and disabling poverty that shattered the hopes and dreams of...young parents and twisted the lives of those who were 'stuck together' in it." Men withdrew from family life or turned violent; women exhausted themselves trying to "take up the slack" both financially and emotionally, or they belittled their hus-bands as failures; and children gave up their dreams of education to work at dead-end jobs.[12]

From the hardships of the Great Depression and the Second World War and the euphoria of the postwar economic recovery came a new kind of family ideal that still enters our homes in "Leave It to Beaver" and "Donna Reed" reruns. In the next chapter, I will show that the 1950s were no more a "golden age" of the family than any other period in American history. For now, I will argue that our re-curring search for a traditional family model denies the diversity of family life, both past and present, and leads to false generalizations about the past as well as wildly exaggerated claims about the present and the future.

The Complexities of Assessing Family Trends

If it is hard to find a satisfactory model of the traditional family, it is also hard to make global judgments about how families have changed and whether they are getting better or worse. Some general-izations about the past are pure myth. Whatever the merit of recur-ring complaints about the "rootlessness" of modern life, for instance, families are *not* more mobile and transient than they used to be. In most nineteenth-century cities, both large and small, more than 50 percent—and often up to 75 percent—of the residents in any given year were no longer there ten years later. People born in the twenti-eth century are much more likely to live near their birthplace than were people born in the nineteenth century.[13]

This is not to say, of course, that mobility did not have different effects then than it does now. In the nineteenth century, claims historian Thomas Bender, people moved from community to community, taking advantage, as we shall see in chapter 4, of nonfamilial networks and institutions that integrated them into new work and social relations. In the late twentieth century, people move from job to job, following a career path that shuffles them from one single-family home to another and does not link them to neighborly networks beyond the family. But this change is in our community ties, not in our family ones.[14]

A related myth is that modern Americans have lost touch with extended-kinship networks or have let parent-child bonds lapse. In fact, more Americans than ever before have grandparents alive, and there is good evidence that ties between grandparents and grandchildren have become stronger over the past fifty years. In the late 1970s, researchers returned to the "Middletown" studied by sociologists Robert and Helen Lynd in the 1920s and found that most people there maintained closer extended-family networks than in earlier times. There had been some decline in the family's control over the daily lives of youth, especially females, but "the expressive/emotional function of the family" was "more important for Middletown students of 1977 than it was in 1924." More recent research shows that visits with relatives did *not* decline between the 1950s and the late 1980s.[15]

Today 54 percent of adults see a parent, and 68 percent talk on the phone with a parent, at least once a week. Fully 90 percent of Americans describe their relationship with their mother as close, and 78 percent say their relationship with their grandparents is close. And for all the family disruption of divorce, most modern children live with at least *one* parent. As late as 1940, 10 percent of American children did not live with either parent, compared to only one in twenty-five today.[16]

What about the supposed eclipse of marriage? Neither the rising age of those who marry nor the frequency of divorce necessarily means that marriage is becoming a less prominent institution than it was in earlier days. Ninety percent of men and women eventually marry, more than 70 percent of divorced men and women remarry, and fewer people remain single for their entire lives today than at the turn of the century. One author even suggests that the availability of divorce in the second half of the twentieth century has allowed some women to try marriage who would formerly have remained single all their lives. Others argue that the rate of hidden marital separation in the late nineteenth century was not much less than the rate of visible separation today.[17]

Studies of marital satisfaction reveal that more couples reported their marriages to be happy in the late 1970s than did so in 1957, while couples in their second marriages believe them to be much happier than their first ones. Some commentators conclude that marriage is becoming less permanent but more satisfying. Others wonder, however, whether there is a vicious circle in our country, where no one even tries to sustain a relationship. Between the late 1970s and late 1980s, moreover, reported marital happiness did decline slightly in the United States. Some authors see this as reflecting our decreasing appreciation of marriage, although others suggest that it reflects unrealistically high expectations of love in a culture that denies people safe, culturally approved ways of getting used to marriage or cultivating other relationships to meet some of the needs that we currently load onto the couple alone.[18]

Part of the problem in making simple generalizations about what is happening to marriage is that there has been a polarization of experiences. Marriages are much more likely to be ended by divorce today, but marriages that do last are described by their participants as happier than those in the past and are far more likely to confer such happiness over many years. It is important to remember that the 50 percent divorce rate estimates are calculated in terms of a forty-year period and that many marriages in the past were terminated well before that date by the death of one partner. Historian Lawrence Stone suggests that divorce has become "a functional substitute for death" in the modern world. At the end of the 1970s, the rise in divorce rates seemed to overtake the fall in death rates, but the slight decline in divorce rates since then means that "a couple marrying today is more likely to celebrate a fortieth wedding anniversary than were couples around the turn of the century."[19]

A similar polarization allows some observers to argue that fathers are deserting their children, while others celebrate the new commitment of fathers to childrearing. Both viewpoints are right. Sociologist Frank Furstenberg comments on the emergence of a "good dad–bad dad complex": Many fathers spend more time with their children than ever before and feel more free to be affectionate with them; others, however, feel more free simply to walk out on their families. According to 1981 statistics, 42 percent of the children whose father had left the marriage had not seen him in the past year. Yet studies show steadily increasing involvement of fathers with their children as long as they are in the home.[20]

These kinds of ambiguities should make us leery of hard-and-fast pronouncements about what's happening to the American family. In many cases, we simply don't know precisely what our figures actually mean. For example, the proportion of youngsters receiving psychological assistance rose by 80 percent between 1981 and 1988. Does that mean they are getting more sick or receiving more help, or is it some complex combination of the two? Child abuse reports increased by 225 percent between 1976 and 1987. Does this represent an actual increase in rates of abuse or a heightened consciousness about the problem? During the same period, parents' self-reports about very severe violence toward their children declined 47 percent. Does this represent a real improvement in their behavior or a decreasing willingness to admit to such acts?[21]

Assessing the direction of family change is further complicated because many contemporary trends represent a reversal of developments that were themselves rather recent. The expectation that the family should be the main source of personal fulfillment, for example, was not traditional in the eighteenth and nineteenth centuries, as we shall see in chapter 5. Prior to the 1900s, the family festivities that now fill us with such nostalgia for "the good old days" (and cause such heartbreak when they go poorly) were "relatively undeveloped." Civic festivals and Fourth of July parades were more important occasions for celebration and strong emotion than family holidays, such as Thanksgiving. Christmas "seems to have been more a time for attending parties and dances than for celebrating family solidarity." Only in the twentieth century did the family come to be the center of festive attention and emotional intensity.[22]

Today, such emotional investment in the family may be waning again. This could be interpreted as a reestablishment of balance between family life and other social ties; on the other hand, such a trend may have different results today than in earlier times, because in many cases the extrafamilial institutions and customs that used to socialize individuals and provide them with a range of emotional alternatives to family life no longer exist.

In other cases, close analysis of statistics showing a deterioration in family well-being supposedly caused by abandonment of tradition suggests a more complicated train of events. Children's health, for example, improved dramatically in the 1960s and 1970s, a period of extensive family transformation. It ceased to improve, and even slid backward, in the 1980s, when innovative social programs designed to relieve families of some "traditional" responsibilities were repealed. While infant mortality rates fell by 4.7 percent a year during the 1970s, the rate of decline decreased in the 1980s, and in both 1988 and 1989, infant mortality rates did not show a statistically significant decline. Similarly, the proportion of low-birth-weight babies fell during the 1970s but stayed steady during the 1980s and had even increased slightly as of 1988. Child poverty is lower today than it was in the "traditional" 1950s but much higher than it was in the nontraditional late 1960s.[23]

Wild Claims and Phony Forecasts

Lack of perspective on where families have come from and how their evolution connects to other social trends tends to encourage contradictory claims and wild exaggerations about where families are going. One category of generalizations seems to be a product of wishful thinking. As of 1988, nearly half of all families with children had both parents in the work force. The two-parent family in which only the father worked for wages represented just 25 percent of all families with children, down from 44 percent in 1975. For people overwhelmed by the difficulties of adjusting work and schools to the realities of working moms, it has been tempting to discern a "return to tradition" and hope the problems will go away. Thus in 1991, we saw a flurry of media reports that the number of women in the work force was headed down: "More Choose to Stay Home with Children" proclaimed the headlines; "More Women Opting for Chance to Watch Their Children Grow."[24]

The cause of all this commotion? The percentage of women aged twenty-five to thirty-four who were employed dropped from 74 percent to 72.8 percent between January 1990 and January 1991. However, there was an exactly equal decline in the percentage of men in the work force during the same period, and for both genders the explanation was the same. "The dip is the recession," explained Judy Waldrop, research editor at *American Demographics* magazine, to anyone who bothered to listen. In fact, the proportion of *mothers* who worked increased slightly during the same period.[25]

This is not to say that parents, especially mothers, are happy with the pressures of balancing work and family life. Poll after poll reveals that both men and women feel starved for time. The percentage of women who say they would prefer to stay home with their children if they could afford to do so rose from 33 percent in 1986 to 56 percent in 1990. Other polls show that even larger majorities of women would trade a day's pay for an extra day off. But, above all, what these polls reveal is women's growing dissatisfaction with the failure of employers, schools, and government to pioneer arrangements that make it possible to combine work and family life. They do not suggest that women are actually going to stop working, or that this would be women's preferred solution to their stresses. The polls did not ask, for example, how *long* women would like to take off work, and failed to take account of the large majority of mothers who report that they would miss their work if they did manage to take time off. Working mothers are here to stay, and we will not meet the challenge this poses for family life by inventing an imaginary trend to define the problem out of existence.

At another extreme is the kind of generalization that taps into our worst fears. One example of this is found in the almost daily reporting of cases of child molestation or kidnapping by sexual predators. The highlighting of such cases, drawn from every corner of the country, helps disguise how rare these cases actually are when compared to crimes committed within the family.

A well-publicized instance of the cataclysmic predictions that get made when family trends are taken out of historical context is the famous *Newsweek* contention that a single woman of forty has a better chance of being killed by a terrorist than of finding a husband. It is true that the proportion of never-married women under age forty has increased substantially since the 1950s, but it is also true that the proportion has *decreased* dramatically among women over that age. A woman over thirty-five has a *better* chance to marry today than she did in the 1950s. In the past twelve years, first-time marriages have increased almost 40 percent for women aged thirty-five to thirty-nine. A single woman aged forty to forty-four still has a 24 percent probability of marriage, while 15 percent of women in their late forties will marry. These figures would undoubtedly be higher if many women over forty did not simply pass up opportunities that a more desperate generation might have snatched.[26]

Yet another example of the exaggeration that pervades many analyses of modern families is the widely quoted contention that "parents today spend 40 percent less time with their children than did parents in 1965." Again, of course, part of the problem is where researchers are measuring from. A comparative study of Muncie, Indiana, for example, found that parents spent much more time with their children in the mid-1970s than did parents in the mid-1920s. But another problem is keeping the categories consistent. Trying to track down the source of the 40 percent decline figure, I called demographer John P. Robinson, whose studies on time formed the basis of this claim. Robinson's data, however, show that parents today spend about the same amount of time caring for children as they did in 1965. If the total amount of time devoted to children is less, he suggested, I might want to check how many fewer children there are today. In 1970, the average family had 1.34 children under the age of eighteen; in 1990, the average family had only .96 children under age eighteen—a decrease of 28.4 percent. In other words, most of the decline in the total amount of time parents spend with children is because of the decline in the number of children they have to spend time with![27]

Now I am not trying to say that the residual amount of decrease is not serious, or that it may not become worse, given the trends in women's employment. Robinson's data show that working mothers spend substantially less time in primary child-care activities than do nonemployed mothers (though they also tend to have fewer children); more than 40 percent of working mothers report feeling "trapped" by their daily routines; many routinely sacrifice sleep in order to meet the demands of work and family. Even so, a majority believe they are *not* giving enough time to their children. It is also true that children may benefit merely from having their parents available, even though the parents may not be spending time with them.

But there is no reason to assume the worst. Americans have actually gained free time since 1965, despite an increase in work hours, largely as a result of a decline in housework and an increasing tendency to fit some personal requirements and errands into the work day. And according to a recent Gallup poll, most modern mothers think they are doing a better job of communicating with their children (though a worse job of house cleaning) than did their own mothers and that they put a higher value on spending time with their family than did their mothers.[28]

Negotiating Through the Extremes

Most people react to these conflicting claims and contradictory trends with understandable confusion. They know that family ties remain central to their own lives, but they are constantly hearing about people who seem to have *no* family feeling. Thus, at the same time as Americans report high levels of satisfaction with their *own* families, they express a pervasive fear that other people's families are

falling apart. In a typical recent poll, for example, 71 percent of respondents said they were "very satisfied" with their own family life,
but more than half rated the overall quality of family life as negative:
"I'm okay; you're not."[29]

This seemingly schizophrenic approach does not reflect an essentially intolerant attitude. People worry about families, and to the extent that they associate modern social ills with changes in family life,
they are ambivalent about innovations. Voters often defeat measures
to grant unmarried couples, whether heterosexual or homosexual,
the same rights as married ones. In polls, however, most Americans
support tolerance for gay and lesbian relationships. Although two-
thirds of respondents to one national poll said they wanted "more
traditional standards of family life," the same percentage rejected the
idea that "women should return to their traditional role." Still larger
majorities support women's right to work, including their right to
use child care, even when they worry about relying on day-care centers too much. In a 1990 *Newsweek* poll, 42 percent predicted that
the family would be worse in ten years and exactly the same percentage predicted that it would be better. Although 87 percent of people
polled in 1987 said they had "old-fashioned ideas about family and
marriage," only 22 percent of the people polled in 1989 defined a
family solely in terms of blood, marriage, or adoption. Seventy-four
percent declared, instead, that family is any group whose members
love and care for one another.[30]

These conflicted responses do not mean that people are hopelessly
confused. Instead, they reflect people's gut-level understanding that
the "crisis of the family" is more complex than is often asserted by
political demagogues or others with an ax to grind. In popular commentary, the received wisdom is to "keep it simple." I know one television reporter who refuses to air an interview with anyone who uses
the phrase "on the other hand." But my experience in discussing
these issues with both the general public and specialists in the field is
that people are hungry to get beyond oversimplifications. They don't
want to be told that everything is fine in families or that if the economy improved and the government mandated parental leave, everything would be fine. But they don't believe that every hard-won victory for women's rights and personal liberty has been destructive of
social bonds and that the only way to find a sense of community is to
go back to some sketchily defined "traditional" family that clearly involves denying the validity of any alternative familial and personal
choices.

Americans understand that along with welcome changes have

come difficult new problems; uneasy with simplistic answers, they are willing to consider more nuanced analyses of family gains and losses during the past few decades. Indeed, argues political reporter E. J. Dionne, they are *desperate* to engage in such analyses.[31] Few Americans are satisfied with liberal and feminist accounts that blame all modern family dilemmas on structural inequalities, ignoring the moral crisis of commitment and obligation in our society. Yet neither are they convinced that "in the final analysis," as David Blankenhorn of the Institute for American Values puts it, "the problem is not the system. The problem is us."[32]

Despite humane intentions, an overemphasis on personal responsibility for strengthening family values encourages a way of thinking that leads to moralizing rather than mobilizing for concrete reforms. While values are important to Americans, most do not support the sort of scapegoating that occurs when all family problems are blamed on "bad values." Most of us are painfully aware that there is no clear way of separating "family values" from "the system." Our values may make a difference in the way we respond to the challenges posed by economic and political institutions, but those institutions also reinforce certain values and extinguish others. The problem is not to berate people for abandoning past family values, nor to exhort them to adopt better values in the future—the problem is to build the institutions and social support networks that allow people to act on their best values rather than on their worst ones. We need to get past abstract nostalgia for traditional family values and develop a clearer sense of how past families actually worked and what the different consequences of various family behaviors and values have been. Good history and responsible social policy should help people incorporate the full complexity and the tradeoffs of family change into their analyses and thus into action. Mythmaking does not accomplish this end.

2

•••

"Leave It to Beaver" and "Ozzie and Harriet":

American Families in the 1950s

OUR most powerful visions of traditional families derive from images that are still delivered to our homes in countless reruns of 1950s television sit-coms. When liberals and conservatives debate family policy, for example, the issue is often framed in terms of how many "Ozzie and Harriet" families are left in America. Liberals compute the percentage of total households that contain a breadwinner father, a full-time homemaker mother, and dependent children, proclaiming that fewer than 10 percent of American families meet the "Ozzie and Harriet" or "Leave It to Beaver" model. Conservatives counter that more than half of all mothers with preschool children either are not employed or are employed only part-time. They cite polls showing that most working mothers would like to spend more time with their children and periodically announce that the Nelsons are "making a comeback," in popular opinion if not in real numbers.[1]

Since everyone admits that nontraditional families are now a majority, why this obsessive concern to establish a higher or a lower figure? Liberals seem to think that unless they can prove the "Leave It to Beaver" family is on an irreversible slide toward extinction, they cannot justify introducing new family definitions and social policies. Conservatives believe that if they can demonstrate the traditional family is alive and well, although endangered by policies that reward two-earner families and single parents, they can pass measures to revive the seeming placidity and prosperity of the 1950s, associated in many people's minds with the relative stability of marriage, gender roles, and family life in that decade. If the 1950s family existed today, both sides seem to assume, we would not have the contemporary social dilemmas that cause such debate.

At first glance, the figures seem to justify this assumption. The 1950s was a profamily period if there ever was one. Rates of divorce and illegitimacy were half what they are today; marriage was almost universally praised; the family was everywhere hailed as the most basic institution in society; and a massive baby boom, among all classes and ethnic groups, made America a "child-centered" society. Births rose from a low of 18.4 per 1,000 women during the Depression to a high of 25.3 per 1,000 in 1957. "The birth rate for third children doubled between 1940 and 1960, and that for fourth children tripled."[2]

In retrospect, the 1950s also seem a time of innocence and consensus: Gang warfare among youths did not lead to drive-by shootings; the crack epidemic had not yet hit; discipline problems in the schools were minor; no "secular humanist" movement opposed the 1954 addition of the words *under God* to the Pledge of Allegiance; and 90 percent of all school levies were approved by voters. Introduction of the polio vaccine in 1954 was the most dramatic of many medical advances that improved the quality of life for children.

The profamily features of this decade were bolstered by impressive economic improvements for vast numbers of Americans. Between 1945 and 1960, the gross national product grew by almost 250 percent and per capita income by 35 percent. Housing starts exploded after the war, peaking at 1.65 million in 1955 and remaining above 1.5 million a year for the rest of the decade; the increase in single-family homeownership between 1946 and 1956 outstripped the increase during the entire preceding century and a half. By 1960, 62 percent of American families owned their own homes, in contrast to 43 percent in 1940. Eighty-five percent of the new homes were built in the suburbs, where the nuclear family found new possibilities for privacy and togetherness. While middle-class Americans were the prime beneficiaries of the building boom, substantial numbers of white working-class Americans moved out of the cities into affordable developments, such as Levittown.[3]

Many working-class families also moved into the middle class. The number of salaried workers increased by 61 percent between 1947 and 1957. By the mid-1950s, nearly 60 percent of the population had what was labeled a middle-class income level (between $3,000 and $10,000 in constant dollars), compared to only 31 percent in the "prosperous twenties," before the Great Depression. By 1960, thirty-one million of the nation's forty-four million families owned their own home, 87 percent had a television, and 75 percent possessed a car. The number of people with discretionary income doubled during the 1950s.[4]

For most Americans, the most salient symbol and immediate beneficiary of their newfound prosperity was the nuclear family. The biggest boom in consumer spending, for example, was in household goods. Food spending rose by only 33 percent in the five years following the Second World War, and clothing expenditures rose by 20 percent, but purchases of household furnishings and appliances climbed 240 percent. "Nearly the entire increase in the gross national product in the mid-1950s was due to increased spending on consumer durables and residential construction," most of it oriented toward the nuclear family.[5]

Putting their mouths where their money was, Americans consistently told pollsters that home and family were the wellsprings of their happiness and self-esteem. Cultural historian David Marc argues that prewar fantasies of sophisticated urban "elegance," epitomized by the high-rise penthouse apartment, gave way in the 1950s to a more modest vision of utopia: a single-family house and a car. The emotional dimensions of utopia, however, were unbounded. When respondents to a 1955 marriage study "were asked what they thought they had sacrificed by marrying and raising a family, an overwhelming majority of them replied, 'Nothing.'" Less than 10 percent of Americans believed that an unmarried person could be happy. As one popular advice book intoned: "The family is the center of your living. If it isn't, you've gone far astray."[6]

The Novelty of the 1950s Family

In fact, the "traditional" family of the 1950s was a qualitatively new phenomenon. At the end of the 1940s, all the trends characterizing the rest of the twentieth century suddenly reversed themselves: For the first time in more than one hundred years, the age for marriage and motherhood fell, fertility increased, divorce rates declined, and women's degree of educational parity with men dropped sharply. In a period of less than ten years, the proportion of never-married persons declined by as much as it had during the entire previous half century.[7]

At the time, most people understood the 1950s family to be a new invention. The Great Depression and the Second World War had reinforced extended family ties, but in ways that were experienced by most people as stultifying and oppressive. As one child of the Depression later put it, "The Waltons" television series of the 1970s did not show what family life in the 1930s was really like: "It wasn't a big family sitting around a table radio and everybody saying goodnight while Bing Crosby crooned 'Pennies from Heaven.'" On top of Depression-era family tensions had come the painful family separations and housing shortages of the war years: By 1947, six million American families were sharing housing, and postwar family counselors warned of a widespread marital crisis caused by conflicts between the generations. A 1948 *March of Time* film, "Marriage and Divorce," declared: "No home is big enough to house two families, particularly two of different generations, with opposite theories on child training."[8]

During the 1950s, films and television plays, such as "Marty," showed people working through conflicts between marital loyalties and older kin, peer group, or community ties; regretfully but decisively, these conflicts were almost invariably "resolved in favor of the heterosexual couple rather than the claims of extended kinship networks,...homosociability and friendship." Talcott Parsons and other sociologists argued that modern industrial society required the family to jettison traditional productive functions and wider kin ties in order to specialize in emotional nurturance, childrearing, and production of a modern personality. Social workers "endorsed nuclear family separateness and looked suspiciously on active extended-family networks."[9]

Popular commentators urged young families to adopt a "modern" stance and strike out on their own, and with the return of prosperity, most did. By the early 1950s, newlyweds not only were establishing single-family homes at an earlier age and a more rapid rate than ever before but also were increasingly moving to the suburbs, away from the close scrutiny of the elder generation.

For the first time in American history, moreover, such average trends did not disguise sharp variations by class, race, and ethnic group. People married at a younger age, bore their children earlier and closer together, completed their families by the time they were in their late twenties, and experienced a longer period living together as a couple after their children left home. The traditional range of acceptable family behaviors—even the range in the acceptable number and timing of children—narrowed substantially.[10]

The values of 1950s families also were new. The emphasis on producing a whole world of satisfaction, amusement, and inventiveness within the nuclear family had no precedents. Historian Elaine Tyler May comments: "The legendary family of the 1950s...was not, as common wisdom tells us, the last gasp of 'traditional' family life with deep roots in the past. Rather, it was the first wholehearted effort to create a home that would fulfill virtually all its members' personal needs through an energized and expressive personal life."[11]

Beneath a superficial revival of Victorian domesticity and gender distinctions, a novel rearrangement of family ideals and male-female relations was accomplished. For women, this involved a reduction in the moral aspect of domesticity and an expansion of its orientation toward personal service. Nineteenth-century middle-class women had cheerfully left housework to servants, yet 1950s women of all classes created makework in their homes and felt guilty when they did not do everything for themselves. The amount of time women spent doing housework actually *increased* during the 1950s, despite the advent of convenience foods and new, labor-saving appliances; child care absorbed more than twice as much time as it had in the 1920s. By the mid-1950s, advertisers' surveys reported on a growing tendency among women to find "housework a medium of expression for...[their] femininity and individuality."[12]

For the first time, men as well as women were encouraged to root their identity and self-image in familial and parental roles. The novelty of these family and gender values can be seen in the dramatic postwar transformation of movie themes. Historian Peter Biskind writes that almost every major male star who had played tough loners in the 1930s and 1940s "took the roles with which he was synonymous and transformed them, in the fifties, into neurotics or psychotics." In these films, "men belonged at home, not on the streets or out on the prairie,...not alone or hanging out with other men." The women who got men to settle down had to promise enough sex to compete with "bad" women, but ultimately they provided it only in the marital bedroom and only in return for some help fixing up the house.[13]

Public images of Hollywood stars were consciously reworked to show their commitment to marriage and stability. After 1947, for example, the Actors' Guild organized "a series of unprecedented speeches...to be given to civic groups around the country, emphasizing that the stars now embodied the rejuvenated family life unfolding in the suburbs." Ronald Reagan's defense of actors' family values was especially "stirring," noted one reporter, but female stars, unlike Reagan and other male stars, were obliged to *live* the new values as well as propagandize them. Joan Crawford, for example, one of the brash, tough, independent leading ladies of the prewar era, was now pictured as a devoted mother whose sex appeal and glamour did not prevent her from doing her own housework. She posed for pictures mopping floors and gave interviews about her childrearing philosophy.[14]

The "good life" in the 1950s, historian Clifford Clark points out, made the family "the focus of fun and recreation." The ranch house, architectural embodiment of this new ideal, discarded the older privacy of the kitchen, den, and sewing room (representative of separate spheres for men and women) but introduced new privacy and luxury into the master bedroom. There was an unprecedented "glorification of self-indulgence" in family life. Formality was discarded in favor of "livability," "comfort," and "convenience." A contradiction in terms in earlier periods, "the sexually charged, child-centered family took its place at the center of the postwar American dream."[15]

On television, David Marc comments, all the "normal" families moved to the suburbs during the 1950s. Popular culture turned such suburban families into capitalism's answer to the Communist threat. In his famous "kitchen debate" with Nikita Khrushchev in 1959, Richard Nixon asserted that the superiority of capitalism over communism was embodied not in ideology or military might but in the comforts of the suburban home, "designed to make things easier for our women."[16]

Acceptance of domesticity was the mark of middle-class status and upward mobility. In sit-com families, a middle-class man's work was totally irrelevant to his identity; by the same token, the problems of working-class families did not lie in their economic situation but in their failure to create harmonious gender roles. Working-class and ethnic men on television had one defining characteristic: They were unable to control their wives. The families of middle-class men, by contrast, were generally well behaved.[17]

Not only was the 1950s family a new invention; it was also a historical fluke, based on a unique and temporary conjuncture of economic, social, and political factors. During the war, Americans had saved at a rate more than three times higher than that in the decades before or since. Their buying power was further enhanced by America's extraordinary competitive advantage at the end of the war, when every other industrial power was devastated by the experience. This privileged economic position sustained both a tremendous expansion of middle-class management occupations and a new honeymoon between management and organized labor: During the 1950s, real wages increased by more than they had in the entire previous half century.[18]

The impact of such prosperity on family formation and stability was magnified by the role of government, which could afford to be generous with education benefits, housing loans, highway and sewer construction, and job training. All this allowed most middle-class Americans, and a large number of working-class ones, to adopt family values and strategies that assumed the availability of cheap energy, low-interest home loans, expanding educational and occupational opportunities, and steady employment. These expectations encouraged early marriage, early childbearing, expansion of consumer debt, and residential patterns that required long commutes to work—all patterns that would become highly problematic by the 1970s, as we shall see in chapters 8 and 11.

A Complex Reality: 1950s Poverty, Diversity, and Social Change

Even aside from the exceptional and ephemeral nature of the conditions that supported them, 1950s family strategies and values offer no solution to the discontents that underlie contemporary romanticization of the "good old days." The reality of these families was far more painful and complex than the situation-comedy reruns or the expurgated memories of the nostalgic would suggest. Contrary to popular opinion, "Leave It to Beaver" was not a documentary.

In the first place, not all American families shared in the consumer expansion that provided Hotpoint appliances for June Cleaver's kitchen and a vacuum cleaner for Donna Stone. A full 25 percent of Americans, forty to fifty million people, were poor in the mid-1950s, and in the absence of food stamps and housing programs, this poverty was searing. Even at the end of the 1950s, a third of American children were poor. Sixty percent of Americans over sixty-five had incomes below $1,000 in 1958, considerably below the $3,000 to $10,000 level considered to represent middle-class status. A majority of elders also lacked medical insurance. Only half the population had savings in 1959; one-quarter of the population had no liquid assets at all. Even when we consider only native-born, white families, one-third could not get by on the income of the household head.[19]

In the second place, real life was not so white as it was on television. Television, comments historian Ella Taylor, increasingly ignored cultural diversity, adopting "the motto 'least objectionable programming,' which gave rise to those least objectionable families, the Cleavers, the Nelsons and the Andersons." Such families were so completely white and Anglo-Saxon that even the Hispanic gardener in "Father Knows Best" went by the name of Frank Smith. But contrary to the all-white lineup on the television networks and the streets of suburbia, the 1950s saw a major transformation in the ethnic composition of America. More Mexican immigrants entered the United States in the two decades after the Second World War than in the entire previous one hundred years. Prior to the war, most blacks and Mexican-Americans lived in rural areas, and three-fourths of blacks lived in the South. By 1960, a majority of blacks resided in the North, and 80 percent of both blacks and Mexican-Americans lived in cities. Postwar Puerto Rican immigration was so massive that by 1960 more Puerto Ricans lived in New York than in San Juan.[20]

These minorities were almost entirely excluded from the gains and privileges accorded white middle-class families. The June Cleaver or Donna Stone homemaker role was not available to the more than 40 percent of black women with small children who worked outside the home. Twenty-five percent of these women headed their own households, but even minorities who conformed to the dominant family form faced conditions quite unlike those portrayed on television. The poverty rate of two-parent black families was more than 50 percent, approximately the same as that of one-parent black ones. Migrant workers suffered "near medieval" deprivations, while termination and relocation policies were employed against Native Americans to get them to give up treaty rights.[21]

African Americans in the South faced systematic, legally sanctioned segregation and pervasive brutality, and those in the North were excluded by restrictive covenants and redlining from many benefits of the economic expansion that their labor helped sustain. Whites resisted, with harassment and violence, the attempts of blacks to participate in the American family dream. When Harvey Clark tried to move into Cicero, Illinois, in 1951, a mob of 4,000 whites spent four days tearing his apartment apart while police stood by and joked with them. In 1953, the first black family moved into Chicago's Trumbull Park public housing project; neighbors "hurled stones and tomatoes" and trashed stores that sold groceries to the new residents. In Detroit, *Life* magazine reported in 1957, "10,000 Negroes work at the Ford plant in nearby Dearborn, [but] not one Negro can live in Dearborn itself."[22]

More Complexities: Repression, Anxiety, Unhappiness, and Conflict

The happy, homogeneous families that we "remember" from the 1950s were thus partly a result of the media's denial of diversity. But even among sectors of the population where the "least objectionable" families did prevail, their values and behaviors were not entirely a spontaneous, joyful reaction to prosperity. If suburban ranch houses and family barbecues were the carrots offered to white middle-class families that adopted the new norms, there was also a stick.

Women's retreat to housewifery, for example, was in many cases not freely chosen. During the war, thousands of women had entered new jobs, gained new skills, joined unions, and fought against job discrimination. Although 95 percent of the new women employees had expected when they were first hired to quit work at the end of the war, by 1945 almost an equally overwhelming majority did not want to give up their independence, responsibility, and income, and expressed the desire to continue working.[23]

After the war, however, writes one recent student of postwar reconstruction, "management went to extraordinary lengths to purge women workers from the auto plants," as well as from other high-paying and nontraditional jobs. As it turned out, in most cases women were not permanently expelled from the labor force but were merely downgraded to lower-paid, "female" jobs. Even at the end of the purge, there were more women working than before the war, and by 1952 there were two million more wives at work than at the peak of wartime production. The jobs available to these women, however, lacked the pay and the challenges that had made wartime work so satisfying, encouraging women to define themselves in terms of home and family even when they were working.[24]

Vehement attacks were launched against women who did not accept such self-definitions. In the 1947 bestseller, *The Modern Woman: The Lost Sex,* Marynia Farnham and Ferdinand Lundberg described feminism as a "deep illness," called the notion of an independent woman a "contradiction in terms," and accused women who sought educational or employment equality of engaging in symbolic "castration" of men. As sociologist David Riesman noted, a woman's failure to bear children went from being "a social disadvantage and sometimes a personal tragedy" in the nineteenth century to being a "quasi-perversion" in the 1950s. The conflicting messages aimed at women seemed almost calculated to demoralize: At the same time as they labeled women "unnatural" if they did not seek fulfillment in motherhood, psychologists and popular writers insisted that most modern social ills could be traced to domineering mothers who invested too much energy and emotion in their children. Women were told that "no other experience in life…will provide the same sense of fulfillment, of happiness, of complete pervading contentment" as motherhood. But soon after delivery they were asked, "Which are you first of all, Wife or Mother?" and warned against the tendency to be "too much mother, too little wife."[25]

Women who could not walk the fine line between nurturing motherhood and castrating "momism," or who had trouble adjusting to "creative homemaking," were labeled neurotic, perverted, or schizophrenic. A recent study of hospitalized "schizophrenic" women in the San Francisco Bay Area during the 1950s concludes that institutionalization and sometimes electric shock treatments were used to force women to accept their domestic roles and their husbands' dictates. Shock treatments also were recommended for women who sought abortion, on the assumption that failure to want a baby signified dangerous emotional disturbance.[26]

All women, even seemingly docile ones, were deeply mistrusted. They were frequently denied the right to serve on juries, convey property, make contracts, take out credit cards in their own name, or establish residence. A 1954 article in *Esquire* called working wives a "menace"; a *Life* author termed married women's employment a "disease." Women were excluded from several professions, and some states even gave husbands total control over family finances.[27] There were not many permissible alternatives to baking brownies, experimenting with new canned soups, and getting rid of stains around the collar.

Men were also pressured into acceptable family roles, since lack of a suitable wife could mean the loss of a job or promotion for a middle-class man. Bachelors were categorized as "immature," "infantile," "narcissistic," "deviant," or even "pathological." Family advice expert Paul Landis argued: "Except for the sick, the badly crippled, the deformed, the emotionally warped and the mentally defective, almost everyone has an opportunity [and, by clear implication, a duty] to marry."[28]

Families in the 1950s were products of even more direct repression. Cold war anxieties merged with concerns about the expanded sexuality of family life and the commercial world to create what one authority calls the domestic version of George F. Kennan's containment policy toward the Soviet Union: A "normal" family and vigilant mother became the "front line" of defense against treason; anticommunists linked deviant family or sexual behavior to sedition. The FBI and other government agencies instituted unprecedented state intrusion into private life under the guise of investigating subversives. Gay baiting was almost as widespread and every bit as vicious as red baiting.[29]

The Civil Service Commission fired 2,611 persons as "security risks" and reported that 4,315 others resigned under the pressure of investigations that asked leading questions of their neighbors and inquired into the books they read or the music to which they listened. In this atmosphere, movie producer Joel Schumacher recalls, "No one told the truth....People pretended they weren't unfaithful. They pretended that they weren't homosexual. They pretended that they weren't horrible."[30]

Even for people not directly coerced into conformity by racial, political, or personal repression, the turn toward families was in many cases more a defensive move than a purely affirmative act. Some men and women entered loveless marriages in order to forestall attacks about real or suspected homosexuality or lesbianism. Growing numbers of people saw the family, in the words of one husband, as the one "group that in spite of many disagreements internally always will face its external enemies together." Conservative families warned children to beware of communists who might masquerade as friendly neighbors; liberal children learned to confine their opinions to the family for fear that their father's job or reputation might be threatened.[31]

Americans were far more ambivalent about the 1950s than later retrospectives, such as "Happy Days," suggest. Plays by Tennessee Williams, Eugene O'Neill, and Arthur Miller explored the underside of family life. Movies such as *Rebel Without a Cause* (1955) expressed fears about youths whose parents had failed them. There was an almost obsessive concern with the idea that the mass media had broken down parental control, thus provoking an outburst of "delinquency and youthful viciousness." In 1954, psychiatrist Fredric Wertham's *Seduction of the Innocents* warned: "The atmosphere of crime comic books is unparalleled in the history of children's literature of any time or any nation." In 1955, Congress discussed nearly 200 bills relating to delinquency. If some of these anxieties seem almost charmingly naïve to our more hardened age, they were no less real for all that.[32]

Many families, of course, managed to hold such fears at bay—and it must be admitted that the suburbs and small towns of America were exceptionally good places for doing so. Shielded from the multiplying problems and growing diversity of the rest of society, residents of these areas could afford to be neighborly. Church attendance and membership in voluntary associations tended to be higher in the suburbs than in the cities, although contact with extended kin was less frequent. Children played in the neighborhoods and cul-de-sacs with only cursory warnings about strangers.[33]

In her autobiographical account of a 1950s adolescence, Susan Allen Toth remembers growing up "gradually" and "quietly" in a small town of the period: "We were not seared by fierce poverty, racial tensions, drug abuse, street crimes." Perhaps this innocence was "constricting," she admitted, but it also gave a child "shelter and space to grow." For Toth, insulation from external problems meant that growing up was a process of being "cossetted, gently warmed, transmuted by slow degrees."[34]

For many other children, however, growing up in 1950s families was not so much a matter of being protected from the harsh realities of the outside world as preventing the outside world from learning the harsh realities of family life. Few would have guessed that radiant Marilyn Van Derbur, crowned Miss America in 1958, had been sexually violated by her wealthy, respectable father from the time she was five until she was eighteen, when she moved away to college.[35] While not all family secrets were quite so shocking, author Benita Eisler recalls a common middle-class experience:

As college classmates became close friends, I heard sagas of life at home that were Gothic horror stories. Behind the hedges and driveways of upper-middle-class suburbia were tragedies of madness, suicide, and—most prevalent of all—chronic and severe alcoholism....

The real revelation for me was the role played by children in…keeping up appearances. Many of my new friends had been pressed into service early as happy smiling fronts, emissaries of family normalcy, cheerful proof that "nothing was really wrong" at the Joneses.[36]

Beneath the polished facades of many "ideal" families, suburban as well as urban, was violence, terror, or simply grinding misery that only occasionally came to light. Although Colorado researchers found 302 battered-child cases, including 33 deaths, in their state during one year alone, the major journal of American family sociology did not carry a single article on family violence between 1939 and 1969. Wife battering was not even considered a "real" crime by most people. Psychiatrists in the 1950s, following Helene Deutsch, "regarded the battered woman as a masochist who provoked her husband into beating her."[37]

Historian Elizabeth Pleck describes how one Family Service Association translated this psychological approach into patient counseling during the 1950s. Mrs. K came to the Association because her husband was an alcoholic who repeatedly abused her, both physically and sexually. The agency felt, however, that it was simplistic to blame the couple's problems on his drinking. When counselors learned that Mrs. K refused her husband's demands for sex after he came home from working the night shift, they decided that they had found a deeper difficulty: Mrs. K needed therapy to "bring out some of her anxiety about sex activities."[38]

We will probably never know how prevalent incest and sexual abuse were in the 1950s, but we do know that when girls or women reported incidents of such abuse to therapists, they were frequently told that they were "fantasizing" their unconscious oedipal desires. Although incest cases were common throughout the records of case-workers from 1880 to 1960, according to historian Linda Gordon's study of these documents, the problem was increasingly redefined as one of female "sex delinquency." By 1960, despite overwhelming evidence to the contrary, experts described incest as a "one-in-a-million occurrence." Not until the 1970s, heartened by a supportive women's movement, were many women able to speak out about the sexual abuse they had suffered in silent agony during the 1950s; others, such as Marilyn Van Derbur, are only now coming forward.[39]

Less dramatic but more widespread was the existence of significant marital unhappiness. Between one-quarter and one-third of the marriages contracted in the 1950s eventually ended in divorce; during that decade two million legally married people lived apart from each other. Many more couples simply toughed it out. Sociologist Mirra Komarovsky concluded that of the working-class couples she interviewed in the 1950s, "slightly less than one-third [were] happily or very happily married."[40]

National polls found that 20 percent of all couples considered their marriages unhappy, and another 20 percent reported only "medium happiness." In the middle-class sample studied by Elaine Tyler May, two-thirds of the husbands and wives rated their marriages "decidedly happier than average," but an outside observer might well have scaled this back to a percentage much like Komarovsky's, for even the happiest couples reported many dissatisfactions and communication problems. "The idea of a 'working marriage' was one that often included constant day-to-day misery for one or both partners."[41]

A successful 1950s family, moreover, was often achieved at enormous cost to the wife, who was expected to subordinate her own needs and aspirations to those of both her husband and her children. In consequence, no sooner was the ideal of the postwar family accepted than observers began to comment perplexedly on how discontented women seemed in the very roles they supposedly desired most. In 1949, *Life* magazine reported that "suddenly and for no plain reason" American women were "seized with an eerie restlessness." Under a "mask of placidity" and an outwardly feminine appearance, one physician wrote in 1953, there was often "an inwardly tense and emotionally unstable individual seething with hidden aggressiveness and resentment."[42]

Some women took this resentment out on their families. Surely some of the bizarre behaviors that Joan Crawford exhibited toward her children, according to her daughter's bitter remembrance, *Mommie Dearest,* flowed from the frustration of being forced into a domestic role about which she was intensely ambivalent. Other women tried to dull the pain with alcohol or drugs. Tranquilizers were developed in the 1950s in response to a need that physicians explicitly saw as female: Virtually nonexistent in 1955, tranquilizer consumption reached 462,000 pounds in 1958 and soared to 1.15 million pounds merely a year later. Commentators noted a sharp increase in women's drinking during the decade, even though many middle-class housewives kept their liquor stash hidden and thought no one knew that they needed a couple of drinks to face an evening of family "togetherness."[43]

But not even "the four b's," as the mother of a colleague of mine used to label her life in the 1950s—"booze, bowling, bridge, and boredom"—could entirely conceal the discontents. In 1956, the *Ladies' Home Journal* devoted an issue to "The Plight of the Young Mother." When *McCall's* ran an article entitled "The Mother Who Ran Away" in the same year, the magazine set a new record for readership. A former editor commented: "We suddenly realized that all those women at home with their three and a half children were miserably unhappy." By 1960, almost every major news journal was using the word *trapped* to describe the feelings of the American housewife. When *Redbook's* editors asked readers to provide them with examples of "Why Young Mothers Feel Trapped," they received 24,000 replies.[44]

Although Betty Friedan's bestseller *The Feminine Mystique* did not appear until 1963, it was a product of the 1950s, originating in the discontented responses Friedan received in 1957 when she surveyed fellow college classmates from the class of 1942. The heartfelt identification of other 1950s women with "the problem that has no name" is preserved in the letters Friedan received after her book was published, letters now at the Schlesinger Library at Radcliffe.[45]

Men tended to be more satisfied with marriage than were women, especially over time, but they, too, had their discontents. Even the most successful strivers after the American dream sometimes muttered about "mindless conformity." The titles of books such as *The Organization Man*, by William Whyte (1956), and *The Lonely Crowd*, by David Riesman (1958), summarized a widespread critique of 1950s culture. Male resentments against women were expressed in the only partly humorous diatribes of *Playboy* magazine (founded in 1953) against "money-hungry" gold diggers or lazy "parasites" trying to trap men into commitment.[46]

Contradictions of the 1950s Family Boom

Happy memories of 1950s family life are not all illusion, of course— there were good times for many families. But even the most positive aspects had another side. One reason that the 1950s family model was so fleeting was that it contained the seeds of its own destruction, a point I will explore further in chapter 7. It was during the 1950s, not the 1960s, that the youth market was first produced, then institutionalized into the youth culture. It was through such innocuous shows as "Howdy Doody" and "The Disney Hour" that advertisers first discovered the riches to be gained by bypassing parents and appealing directly to youth. It was also during this period that advertising and consumerism became saturated with sex.[47]

In the 1950s, family life was financed by economic practices that were to have unanticipated consequences in the 1970s. Wives and mothers first started to work in great numbers during the 1950s in order to supplement their families' purchasing power; expansion of household comforts came "at the cost of an astronomical increase of indebtedness." The labor-management accord of the 1950s helped erode the union movement's ability to oppose the takebacks and runaway shops that destroyed the "family wage system" during the 1970s and 1980s.[48]

Family and gender strategies also contained some time bombs. Women who "played dumb" to catch a man, as 40 percent of Barnard College women admitted to doing, sometimes despised their husbands for not living up to the fiction of male superiority they had worked so hard to promote. Commitment to improving the quality of family life by manipulating the timing and spacing of childbearing led to the social acceptability of family planning and the spread of birth-control techniques. Concentration of childbearing in early marriage meant that growing numbers of women had years to spare for paid work after the bulk of their child-care duties were finished. Finally, 1950s families fostered intense feelings and values that produced young people with a sharp eye for hypocrisy; many of the so-called rebels of the 1960s were simply acting on values that they had internalized in the bosom of their families.[49]

Teen Pregnancy and the 1950s Family

Whatever its other unexpected features, the 1950s family does appear, at least when compared to families in the last two decades, to be a bastion of "traditional" sexual morality. Many modern observers, accordingly, look back to the sexual values of this decade as a possible solution to what they see as the peculiarly modern "epidemic" of teen pregnancy. On closer examination, however, the issue of teen pregnancy is a classic example of both the novelty and the contradictions of the 1950s family.

Those who advocate that today's youth should be taught abstinence or deferred gratification rather than sex education will find no 1950s model for such restraint. "Heavy petting" became a norm of dating in this period, while the proportion of white brides who were pregnant at marriage more than doubled. Teen birth rates soared, reaching highs that have not been equaled since. In 1957, 97 out of every 1,000 girls aged fifteen to nineteen gave birth, compared to only 52 of every 1,000 in 1983. A surprising number of these births were illegitimate, although 1950s census codes made it impossible to identify an unmarried mother if she lived at home with her parents. The incidence of illegitimacy was also disguised by the new empha sis on "rehabilitating" the white mother (though not the black) by putting her baby up for adoption and encouraging her to "start over"; there was an 80 percent increase in the number of out-of-wedlock babies placed for adoption between 1944 and 1955.[50]

The main reason that teenage sexual behavior did not result in many more illegitimate births during this period was that the age of marriage dropped sharply. Young people were not taught how to "say no"—they were simply handed wedding rings. In fact, the growing willingness of parents to subsidize young married couples and the new prevalence of government educational stipends and home ownership loans for veterans undermined the former assumption that a man should be able to support a family before embarking on marriage. Among the middle class, it became common for young wives to work while their husbands finished school. Prior to the 1950s, as David Riesman wrote of his Depression-era classmates, it would not "have occurred to us to have our wives support us through graduate school."[51]

Contemporary teenage motherhood, as we shall see in chapter 8, in some ways represents a *continuation* of 1950s values in a new economic situation that makes early marriage less viable. Of course, modern teen pregnancy also reflects the rejection of some of those earlier values. The values that have broken down, however, have little to do with sexual restraint. What we now think of as 1950s sexual morality depended not so much on stricter sexual control as on intensification of the sexual double standard. Elaine Tyler May argues that sexual "repression" gave way to sexual "containment." The new practice of going steady "widened the boundaries of permissible sexual activity," creating a "sexual brinksmanship" in which women bore the burden of "drawing the line," but that line was constantly changing. Popular opinion admitted, as the *Ladies' Home Journal* put it in 1956, that "sex suggestiveness" was here to stay, but insisted that it was up to women to "put the brakes on."[52]

This double standard led to a Byzantine code of sexual conduct: "Petting" was sanctioned so long as one didn't go "too far" (though this was an elastic and ambiguous prohibition); a woman could be touched on various parts of her body (how low depended on how serious the relationship was) but "nice girls" refused to fondle the comparable male parts in return; mutual stimulation to orgasm was compatible with maintaining a "good" reputation so long as penetration did not occur.

The success of sexual containment depended on sexual inequality. Men no longer bore the responsibility of "saving themselves for marriage"; this was now exclusively a woman's job. In sharp contrast to the nineteenth century, when "oversexed" or demanding men were considered to have serious problems, it was now considered "normal" or "natural" for men to be sexually aggressive. The "average man," advice writers for women commented indulgently, "will go as far as you let him go." When women succeeded in "holding out" (a phrase charged with moral ambiguity), they sometimes experienced problems "letting go," even after marriage; when they failed, they were often reproached later by their husbands for having "given in." The contradictions of this double standard could not long withstand the period's pressures for companionate romance: By 1959, a more liberal single standard had already gained ground among older teenagers across America.[53]

The Problem of Women in Traditional Families

People who romanticize the 1950s, or any model of the traditional family, are usually put in an uncomfortable position when they attempt to gain popular support. The legitimacy of women's rights is so widely accepted today that only a tiny minority of Americans seriously propose that women should go back to being full-time housewives or should be denied educational and job opportunities because of their family responsibilities. Yet when commentators lament the collapse of traditional family commitments and values, they almost invariably mean the uniquely female duties associated with the doctrine of separate spheres for men and women.

Karl Zinsmeister of the American Enterprise Institute, for example, bemoans the fact that "workaholism and family dereliction have become equal-opportunity diseases, striking mothers as much as fathers." David Blankenhorn of the Institute for American Values expresses sympathy for the needs of working women but warns that "employed women do not a family make. The goals of women (and of men, too) in the workplace are primarily individualistic: social recognition, wages, opportunities for advancement, and self-fulfillment. But the family is about collective goals…, building life's most important bonds of affection, nurturance, mutual support, and long-term commitment."[54]

In both statements, a seemingly gender neutral indictment of family irresponsibility ends up being directed most forcefully against women. For Blankenhorn, it is not surprising that *men's* goals should be individualistic; this is a parenthetical aside. For Zinsmeister, the problem with the disease of family dereliction is that it has spread to women. So long as it was confined to men, evidently, there was no urgency about finding a cure.

The crisis of commitment in America is usually seen as a problem associated with women's changing roles because women's family functions have historically mediated the worst effects of competition and individualism in the larger society. Most people who talk about balancing private advancement and individual rights with "nurturance, mutual support, and long-term commitment" do not envision any serious rethinking of the individualistic, antisocial tendencies in our society, nor any ways of broadening our sources of nurturance and mutual assistance. Instead, they seek ways—sometimes through repression, sometimes through reform—of rebuilding a family in which women can continue to compensate for, rather than challenge, the individualism in our larger economy and polity. The next chapter explores the reliance of American individual*ism* on the subordination of women's individual*ity* and the contradictions that has produced in our historical understanding of love and family life.

3

....

"My Mother Was a Saint":
Individualism, Gender Myths, and the Problem of Love

SURVEYING the erosion of 1950s family patterns at the beginning of the 1970s, economist George Gilder warned that the decline in marriage rates threatened the stability of Western civilization: The single man "is disposed to criminality, drugs and violence. He is irresponsible about his debts, alcoholic, accident prone, and venereally diseased. Unless he can marry, he is often destined to a Hobbesian life—solitary, poor, nasty, brutish, and short."[1]

More recent conservative writers—and even a few feminist ones—are equally adamant that American culture requires women to counteract male individualism. Allan Carlson, president of the Rockford Institute on the Family, argues that for capitalism to avoid self-destruction, the family must be walled off from competitive pressures, by government intervention if necessary. Conservative lecturer Connie Marshner warns that "capitalism cannot stand by itself." The very success of private enterprise in producing choice threatens capitalism's existence: "Having freedom of preference means that *preference formation becomes a crucial task of society*"; only families based on male breadwinning and female childrearing can shape preference formation in a way that preserves both economic self-reliance and interpersonal obligation.[2]

Allan Bloom's bestseller, *The Closing of the American Mind* (1987), linked the decline of traditional Western philosophy and liberal thought to the erosion of the family as "the intermediary...that gave men and women unqualified concern for at least some others." The "ambitious, warlike, protective, possessive character" of men is vital to the Western tradition, he maintained, but it was formerly offset by women's commitment to nurturing, caregiving, and altruism. Feminists, however, forcibly rearranged these roles, freeing women from their duty to protect men from their own natures. For Bloom, the reopening of the (white male) American mind cannot be accomplished without the reenclosure of women in traditional gender roles.[3]

Authors such as those just mentioned want to return to a traditional family that antedates the 1950s family by more than one hundred years, reviving the Victorian notion of separate spheres for men and women. In the nineteenth-century middle-class family, a much more rigid division of labor between men and women prevailed than in the 1950s: Women were legally excluded, for example, from the vote, from professional training, and from most colleges. In the absence of a consumer culture and the modern mass media, the Victorian domestic family was much more resistant to materialism, consumerism, and sexual eroticism. There was no distinct youth culture, and the "panty raids" that convulsed otherwise apathetic college towns in the 1950s would have been inconceivable. The Victorian "cult of True Womanhood" did not open the door to self-gratification by touting the family as the source of personal happiness; instead, it sternly associated the family with the development of both "individual and collective character."[4]

Within this family, women and men faced no contradictory messages about their roles. Mothers were considered the moral guardians of civilization itself. Men had no doubt that they themselves were both the protectors and the representatives of their families in relation to the outside world as well as the ultimate source of authority in the household.

According to some authors, this "natural" division of gender roles was the cornerstone of the *real* traditional family. It produced a sentimental, almost sacred, domestic sphere whose long-term commitments and nurturing balanced the pursuit of self-interest in the public arena. Recent social problems, they argue, stem from a self-defeating superegalitarianism that denies men's and women's differing needs and abilities and desanctifies family relations.

In fact, however, such gender roles and family ideals are far from natural and have not always existed. It is worth noting that the word *family* originally meant a band of slaves. Even after the word came to apply to people affiliated by blood and marriage, for many centuries the notion of family referred to authority relations rather than love ones. The sentimentalization of family life and female nurturing was historically and functionally linked to the emergence of competitive individualism and formal egalitarianism for men. In chapter 7, I will explore the reasons that the Victorian division of gender roles broke down in the twentieth century. In this chapter, I will demonstrate that female domesticity and male individualism developed together, as an alternative to more widely dispersed social bonds, emotional ties, and material interdependencies. Consequently, attempting to reimpose domesticity on women without rethinking the role of individualism in our economy and polity would only re-create the same tensions that undermined the Victorian family in the first place.[5]

To illustrate the intimate, if often inconsistent, relation between competitive individualism and family sentimentality, I will briefly summarize the evolution of Western liberal thought and market principles since the Enlightenment. A growing preoccupation with personal equality, individual self-reliance, and objective contractual rights made it very hard for theorists to incorporate positive notions of interdependence or neediness into their ideal models of socioeconomic and political arrangements. Instead, liberal theory projected all dependence onto women and children, relocating interdependence in "natural" gender and age relations: men's protection of women and children and women's personal nurturing qualities.

Political and economic relationships came to be organized around the contractual rights of equal, independent individuals; only gender and family relationships remained organized around personal needs, individual differences, and dependence. This led to a growing divergence between politics, law, and economics—the site of competition and objective laws, men's arenas—and interpersonal relations—the site of altruism and subjectivity, women's arenas. It also created a polarization between public rights and private needs that eventually hampered people's ability to develop a responsible approach to either.

Originally, male and female principles, public and private relations, were supposed to balance and complement each other. But as several philosophers have recently pointed out, the Western tradition gradually came to view independence and concern for others as mutually exclusive traits. Caring for others was confined to women, and personal autonomy was denied them; personal autonomy was reserved for men, and caring for others was either denied them or penalized. Within the home, women cared for the personal needs of their families; outside the home, elaborate and consciously feminine

rituals allowed lower-class women to express needs in terms of child-
ish helplessness and upper-class women to express caring in terms of
moralistic mothering. For men, however, dependency became a negative, disgraceful quality in public; neediness could be expressed
only in the bosom of the family.[6]

Social Dependence and Interdependence in Other Cultures

The Anglo-American notion that dependence on others is immature,
weak, shameful, or uniquely feminine is foreign to most cultures. In
the world view of these societies, independence is antisocial; expressing one's neediness, even codifying it, is the route to social har-
mony and personal satisfaction for both men and women. The
Japanese, for example, have a noun *amae*, which means reliance on
the goodwill or indulgence of another, and a verb *amaru*, which
means essentially to ask for such indulgence. Although increasingly
there is a disapproving connotation attached to these words, it is not
culturally stigmatized to emphasize one's dependence on others.
Modern American parents teach their children that they can be anything they want to be; in ancient Greece, such overweening confidence in the individual's ability to shape his or her own fate was
the sin of hubris, and it brought the protagonists of many Greek
tragedies to bitter ends.

In most precapitalist societies, economic, social, and political interactions were not separable from personal relations. No individual
operated independently of the kin group or the local community.
Consequently, definitions of self were always contextual, because the
self did not pick and choose relations with others; it emerged out of
these relations and remained dependent on them. Independence was
feared, not cherished. A person's entitlements and obligations, similarly, were not deduced from abstract principles of equal rights but
from highly particularistic personal relationships. (It is striking how
many of these descriptions still apply to women. Some psychologists
argue that women's moral standards differ from men's in precisely
this regard, since those standards are derived from personal relationships and concrete responsibilities rather than from abstract rights.
This probably has less to do with intrinsically female "ways of knowing" than with the fact that women's lives have remained far more

rooted in personalistic, nonmarket interactions than have men's.)[7]

The notion that love was, or should be, a purely personal relationship between two individuals, and the primary source of sustained commitments, was equally foreign to most precapitalist cultures. Social customs recognized both the inevitability of dependence and the necessity of dispersing it across society, beyond separate couples or even extended-family networks. Gift giving was one such custom; it established a relationship that was alternately one-sided and therefore more permanent than an "even" relationship in which accounts are always settled so that one party can leave at any time.

Our values tell us to "even things up" as quickly as possible, to discharge our debts and obligations, and to recover the "natural" state of individual independence. Once Americans pass the age of childhood, there are few things that distress us more than receiving a holiday gift, however small, from someone for whom we do not have a gift in return. We find it equally disturbing to give or receive a gift that is "worth" less than that of the other party in the exchange. Our notions of fairness and justice revolve around giving as good as we get and getting as much as we give.

Among the San people of the Kalahari Desert in Africa, by contrast, giving an immediate return for any offering implies a profound insult, for such an act suggests that one is unwilling to be indebted to others, uninterested in bearing the burden of obligation that helps a relationship last. Rather, the recipient waits a decent amount of time and eventually returns a gift that is slightly larger, putting the original donor under future obligation. Elsewhere, institutions such as the Kula exchange networks of the Trobriand Islanders in the Pacific and the funeral ceremonies of early Native Americans extended this reciprocity over much greater distances and periods of time. As the Melanesians put it: "Our feasts are the movement of a needle which sews together the parts of our reed roofs, making of them a single roof, a single word."[8]

In these societies, gift giving is not an individual act of love or even an outcome of family solidarity; it is a social and political way of establishing ties and duties that extend beyond family borders. Acceptance of a gift does not impugn one's manhood or confirm one's femininity. The obligation and responsibility involved in receiving any gift are recognized by all, yet bestowal of a gift is emphatically not a personal bargain. Among the Trobrianders, for example, a man suspected of giving gifts to his Kula partner in order to force a comparable return is "labeled with the vile phrase: he barters."[9]

Organizing social relations through reciprocity involves a delicate balance. It is unacceptable to give a gift with the sole motive of getting something in return, yet it is unthinkable to accept a gift without understanding that it sets up conditions for future behavior; it is an equally antisocial act to refuse a gift and the obligation that gift entails. The difficulty of maintaining this balance may explain why some languages—German, for example—came to refer to gifts and poison with the same word. Personal relations of dependency, deference, and commitment may be stable and humane in some cultures, but they have produced tremendous abuses in others.[10]

The Dark Side of Interdependence: Dependency and Subjugation

As social, political, and economic inequalities emerged in various ancient societies, at different times and in different ways, reciprocity *with* others was often transformed into permanent obligations *from* others. Such was the situation in Europe during the period immediately preceding settlement of the New World. The ideology of gift giving and interdependence remained, but most of the population was subordinated to noble families who ruled through military and religious intimidation, imposing a permanent dependence on the lower classes and extracting from them deference and obligations that were one-sided and open-ended: These obligations included the duty to produce surplus for the rulers, provide them with intimate personal services (sometimes including sex), furnish extra food when they decided to throw a feast, and wait at their tables.[11]

The world view of the European nobility and absolutist monarchies was corporate, interdependent, anti-individualistic—and extremely repressive. The notion of the "Great Chain of Being," which held that all classes were connected in a hierarchical but organic whole, left no room for the comparatively modern concept that the poor are responsible for their own condition and therefore undeserving of charity or sympathy; but it also left no room for the possibility that they might improve their lot. In Gothic cathedrals, the Great Chain of Being was epitomized in huge carved pillars that depicted saints and fine lords standing on the backs of kneeling peasants.

Freedom Struggles and the Rise of Individual Contract Rights

Naturally enough under these conditions, struggles to overthrow the stranglehold of such rulers tended to be directed *against* interpersonal dependencies, overarching obligations, and entangling commitments. European dissidents, from the sixteenth century on, aimed to reduce the authority of extended-kinship networks, neighbors, social superiors, and the state. By the seventeenth century, the revolutionary language of equal rights set abstract laws above local customs, impartial procedures above rulers' caprices, market exchanges above reciprocity, and nuclear family prerogatives above the claims of kin and neighbors. Precise contracts with clear limits replaced ambiguous personal relationships requiring ongoing negotiation and compromise.

The emergence of Enlightenment ideology, Protestant religion, and capitalist production opened up new opportunities for resisting subjugation. Enlightenment philosophy held that humans were rational beings whose self-interest could lead them to civic virtue without coercion or religious mystification by rulers. (There was serious question, though, as to whether slaves, women, the lower classes, Native Americans, and the Irish were fully human.) Protestant ideology made individual conscience the final arbiter of moral behavior. Theorists of the emerging market economy argued that under free competition, the self-interest of small producers would interact with consumer choice to yield greater productivity and prosperity for all. In the political realm, supporters of republicanism or democracy attacked the paternalism and deference by which monarchs and aristocracies had ruled, insisting that a moral society could be built only by those who freed themselves from economic and political dependence on such elites. As Thomas Jefferson put it: "Dependence begets subservience and venality, suffocates the germ of virtue, and prepares fit tools for the designs of ambition."[12]

The links between Enlightenment philosophy, Protestantism, antimonarchical revolutions, and market relations are multistranded and a subject of endless academic debate. Here, however, it is necessary to note only that none of these strands was separable from the rise of capitalism and the development of liberal ideology. Liberal ideology, in its original sense, was a doctrine that linked the concept of freedom to the pursuit of self-interest in a competitive market, postulating that men—I use the word advisedly—were rational egoists who could accurately assess that their long-term interest required the de-velopment of civic government and law.

The triumph of contractual relations excluded philanthropy and moral concerns from economic behavior but elevated the importance of keeping commitments. The ideology of equal rights banished per-sonal ties and pity from political transactions but demanded impar-tiality from those who enforced or regulated such transactions. Al-though a contract could no longer be broken by appealing to higher moral laws, changed circumstances, community custom, or personal sympathy, it could also not be evaded or weakened by distance in space or time. Thus, although liberal capitalism eroded the sense that elites were responsible for dependents, it at least initially increased the reach of social networks, because the social contract was said to apply to all.[13]

The Dark Side of Independence: Freedom and Fragmentation

But the rise of individualism had another side. As many observers feared, deliverance from corporate restraints could mean destruction of all traditional limits to personal self-seeking. In the seventeenth century, the poet John Donne linked economic individualism and equal-rights ideology to the Copernican Revolution, which destroyed the old certitudes of the Ptolemaic universe. The new philosophy, he argued, elevated individualism to the center of the moral universe, undermining the sense of organic unity with God, nature, and other human beings:

'Tis all in peeces, all coherence gone;
All just supply and all Relation:
Prince, Subject, Father, Sonne are things forgot,
For every man alone thinkes he hath got
To be a Phoenix, and that then can bee
None of that kinde, of which he is, but hee. [14]

Donne argued against the excesses of self-reliance, warning that "No man is an *Iland*, intire of it selfe; every man is a peece of the *Con-tinent*, a part of the *maine*." Yet by 1652, a widely published pamphlet asserted the opposite: "Every man is an island; and hath somewhat which he may call his own, and which he not only lawfully may, but out of duty to God ought to defend...against all other men."[15]

By 1719, Daniel Defoe had turned the island into a central metaphor for the human condition. The shipwrecked hero of *Robinson Crusoe* has an experience opposite to those in older literary treatments of isolation or banishment: His humanity does not disintegrate in isolation but is made stronger and more pure. Crusoe finds both personal maturity and economic fortune when he is deprived of his social crutches and forced to pit himself, unaided, against nature. The final payoff for his years of isolated labor eventually requires aid from others, but he gains that aid by, in effect, enslaving Friday, to whose labor he has a right because he saved his life. *Robinson Crusoe*, one of the more popular books in Anglo-American literature during the eighteenth and nineteenth centuries, provided an object lesson in self-reliance and liberal morality for millions of readers.[16]

In 1651, Thomas Hobbes had pronounced his famous assessment of the natural outcome of individual competitiveness: "a Warre of every one against every one." Later theorists, such as John Locke and Adam Smith, presented a more benign view of individualism, in part because they modified it by emphasizing obligations between the genders: They assumed, unlike Hobbes, that men and women were unequal in the state of nature, which at least removed half the human race from the war. But Hobbes's extremism highlighted the central ambiguity of classical liberalism: It "can mean equal effective freedom of all to use and develop their capacities," writes philosopher C. B. Macpherson, yet it can simultaneously "mean freedom of the stronger to do down the weaker by following market rules."[17]

Liberal theory assumed that people had free will and a basic equality of potential; therefore, whatever they were willing to give in a contract was, by definition, a fair bargain, providing that no force or trickery was involved. The tradition that contracts should be reviewed for their larger justice or morality was undermined, because whatever the parties agreed to was their own business.[18]

By assuming the equality of bargaining individuals, moral theorist Ruth Smith and historian Deborah Valenze argue, liberalism reduced morality "to questions of legal and political procedures"; justice became focused "on due process, not on substantive ends."[19] In some ways this was a step forward. The early impact of liberalism was to substitute regular laws and predictable rules for the arbitrary decisions of rulers. Not until the late nineteenth century were moral considerations completely excluded from economic and political transactions, despite the growing inability of legal theory to find a positive place for them in its precepts.

Most Enlightenment and liberal thinkers gave only limited endorsement to individualism and privatism, insisting that these traits must be modified by universal reason. Hence the emphasis on education in Enlightenment philosophy: not, originally, as a means to personal mobility and economic success, as parents tend to justify education today, but as a way of reconciling individual liberty with social cohesion. Early political economists believed that critical reason, nurtured by careful education, would lead "enlightened" individuals to reject shortsighted definitions of self-interest. In eighteenth-century thought—including that of Adam Smith, the supposed father of laissez-faire economics—"enlightened self-interest" meant not "taking care of number one" but supporting the extension of mass education, vigorously opposing financial speculation, and fully accepting political obligations. Laws, regulations, and due process provisions were seen as *enhancing* individual rights by providing a secure framework for social cooperation, competition, and negotiation.[20]

But since most theorists of rational egoism deduced rationality from people's ability to calculate and pursue their own needs, there was a strong instrumental aspect to definitions of reason and, especially in the nineteenth century, a tendency to drop the word *enlightened* in discussions of how to protect self-interest. As humans came to be defined as solitary island dwellers rather than as gregarious collaborators, regulation of social and economic intercourse came to be considered an unwarranted interference with the individual's right to pursue self-interest. Liberty ceased to be conceptualized as a particular set of social *relationships* among humans, protected by careful regulation. It became, instead, an entirely individual quality or personality trait, independent of social relationships and therefore to be defended *against* regulation.[21]

Increasingly, freedom was defined negatively, as lack of dependence, the right not to be obligated to others. Independence came to mean immunity from social claims on one's wealth or time. Sociologist Robert Bellah and his collaborators analyze the dilemma that was inherent in the new ideology and that has become increasingly severe as traditional community counterweights to individualism have disappeared: "Freedom is perhaps the most resonant, deeply held American value.…Yet freedom turns out to mean being left alone by others, not having other people's values, ideas or styles of life forced upon one." But "if the entire world is made up of individuals, each endowed with the right to be free of others' demands, it becomes hard to forge bonds of attachment to, or cooperation with other people, since such bonds would imply obligations that necessarily impinge on one's freedom." In such conditions, the self on which one must rely becomes like that of Robinson Crusoe—"a socially unsituated self," an island, a self "for which [one] owes nothing to society." Notions of self-reliance that originally referred to the collective achievements of a community or a class may be reduced to the conceit of the self-made man. The progress of individualism, it turns out, shades easily into fragmentation.[22]

The language of contractual rights was a powerful tool of protest against coercion from above, but it did not address the human need for interdependence. As welfare scholar Michael Ignatieff points out: "Rights language offers a rich vernacular for the claims an individual may make on or against the collectivity, but it is relatively impoverished as a means of expressing individuals' needs *for* the collectivity."[23]

Indeed, the focus on individual rights raised the possibility that contract negotiations would penetrate every corner of personal life and reduce all obligations to those that could be codified in "objective" bargains—a tendency we have certainly seen in recent decades, even within our most intimate personal relations. By the late eighteenth century, it was clear that liberal theory had a serious problem in setting limits to the pursuit of self-interest. Accordingly, both philosophers and ordinary citizens looked for one arena of life that might sustain interdependent relations and soften the effects of untrammeled individual competition; with remarkable unanimity, they found it in the sexual division of labor.

Rational Egoism for Men, Irrational Altruism for Women

The precondition for "freeing" men from traditional obligations, hierarchies, and interdependencies to become individualistic economic and political actors was a magnification of women's moral obligations and personal dependencies, both in the family and beyond it. Social historian Philippe Aries argues that with the rise of Enlightenment philosophy and the manufacturing system, previously "diffuse" obligations and emotions were increasingly concentrated in the family. At the same time, women's work was more clearly demarcated from men's, and middle-class women in particular were increasingly excluded from former occupations. They were assigned to domesticity inside the home and voluntary religious or charity work outside it.[24]

Self-reliance and independence worked for *men* because *women* took care of dependence and obligation. In other words, the liberal theory of human nature and political citizenship did not merely leave women out: It worked precisely because it was applied exclusively to half the population. Emotion and compassion could be disregarded in the political and economic realms only if women were assigned these traits in the personal realm. Thus the use of the term *individualistic* to describe men's nature became acceptable only in the same time periods, social classes, and geographic areas that established the cult of domesticity for women. The cult of the Self-Made Man required the cult of the True Woman.[25]

For both men and women, this meant specialization in one set of behaviors, skills, and feelings at the cost of suppressing others. By the early nineteenth century, Alexis de Tocqueville observed that America had "applied to the sexes the great principle of political economy which governs the manufactures of our age, by carefully dividing the duties of man from those of women so that the great work of society may be better carried on." As Bellah argues: "The ethic of achievement articulated by men was sustained by a moral ecology shaped by women."[26]

Liberal politics and capitalist markets expunged particularistic ties, social obligations, and personal dependencies from their general operating principles (though it took much longer to expel them from daily transactions, especially at the local level). They redefined these behaviors as *family* functions and relocated them in love relations. As part of the same process, the liberal family tried to banish instrumental motives, impersonal standards, and competitive organizing principles from its own midst. A sentimentalism that was newly considered inappropriate in business and politics was now deemed the *only* appropriate foundation of family life, which was supposed to be based on "affective individualism," rather than on the combination of instrumentalism and corporatism that had prevailed earlier.[27]

By the nineteenth century, the family was widely regarded as the one place where interdependence, noncalculative reciprocity, and gift giving prevailed, the arena in which people learned to temper public ambition or competition with private regard for others. As one American commentator described it:

We go forth into the world…and the heart is sensible to a desolation of feeling; we behold every principle of justice and honor, disregarded, and good sacrificed to the advancement of personal interest; and we turn from such scenes with a painful sensation, almost believing that virtue has deserted the abodes of men; again, we look to the *sanctuary* of *home;* there…disinterested love is ready to sacrifice everything at the altar of affection.[28]

It is important to note that despite this rhetoric, the family was not in real life the sole counterweight to "the advancement of personal interest" in the early period of liberalism. The political movements that grew out of the great democratic revolutions of the seventeenth and eighteenth centuries, and the need for cooperation involved in getting a new economic system off the ground, drew people into many collective activities and associations beyond the family. Family ties were not initially conceptualized as an alternative to such associations but were expected to work together with economic and political institutions in a system of checks and balances that reconciled liberty with duty, self-interest with altruism, and male principles with female ones. In the next chapter, I will show that cooperation beyond the family remained central to most people's experiences. Chapter 5 demonstrates that it was not until the 1870s and 1880s that family morality became a *substitute* for social cohesion rather than a new source for it.

Nevertheless, an important dynamic was set in motion quite early, and many contemporary dilemmas of love and individualism can be traced back to it: The general tendency of liberal capitalism was to polarize people's thinking between "objective," universal principles in the public sphere and "subjective," particularistic relationships in the private one. Increasingly, people pressed their claims in public life on the basis of generic, abstract rights that were designed to apply to all people equally, whatever their unique circumstances or qualities. In personal life, by contrast, people sought to meet their needs by calling on the intimate, exclusive, particular bonds of love.

The Growing Importance of Love

Once people are defined as essentially self-reliant and independent, due nothing by virtue of their common dependencies but earning rewards solely for their individual efforts and achievements, then families and love affairs become the only place for the noncontractual giving of services, the exchange of gifts. Idealization of family as the site of altruism seems to have grown in direct proportion to the spread of individualism and market principles in the rest of society. Love became a unique relationship because it established an arena of life in which calculative rationality and cost-benefit analysis were not supposed to occur.

Women began to romanticize love and nurturing as female qualities that compensated for, or even outweighed, men's political power and economic resources. Men began to romanticize women as givers of services and emotions that could not be bought on the open market or claimed as political tribute but seemed to flow from generosity and self-sacrifice rather than from calculation or exchange. One obvious problem was that as long as women were economically dependent on men, their "gifts" were the price they paid for food, shelter, and protection. Men were uneasily aware of the material considerations that contaminated a wife's gift giving and altruism; that is why men's greatest veneration of female self-sacrifice was often reserved for mothers and why deference to mothers has historically been compatible with contempt for other women. But at least in the courtship phase, male sentimentalization of femininity was generally applied to lovers as well.

Romance, as John Berger puts it in his novel *G*, "is an elaborate state of anticipation" for gifts that cannot be claimed but must be bestowed and will be bestowed only so long as you are special to your lover for what you *need*, not what you achieve. In romance, unlike anywhere else in liberal society, an adult is rewarded for expressing dependence. Most children, Berger points out, are allowed to be dependent in relation to everyone. They are surrounded with the rights of dependence "(their right to indulgence, to consolation, etc.): and so they cannot fall in love." But if a child comes to feel

> that happiness is not something that can be assured and promised but is something that each has to try and find for himself, if he is aware of being essentially alone, then he may find himself anticipating pure, gratuitous and continual gifts offered by another and the state of that anticipation is the state of being in love.[29]

Such a child has become a modern, liberal adult somewhat earlier than is generally approved. For adults in an individualistic society, and perhaps, too, for growing numbers of children in recent years, love becomes the only bridge between the scattered human islands of independence and self-interest.

This tendency of capitalist and republican ideology to romanticize family life and gender differentiation was reinforced by the crisis of political obligation in the liberal state, which could no longer claim divine right to absolute obedience yet increasingly disavowed its right to enforce cooperation for some greater good. Social contract theory accords the state legitimacy only for as long as it provides security of individuals' lives and property. Why, then, should citizens sacrifice their lives and property to defend the state? As states adopted liberal values and organizing principles, they were forced to justify their demands on citizens less in terms of collective or communitarian goals than in terms of the necessity "to defend *private* interests and discharge *private* obligations." The most emotionally compelling of those private obligations was protection of men's dependents. Thus wars were increasingly explained as being fought for hearth and home, most especially "to protect our women."[30]

Gender obligations, family affections, and romantic love, then, became the ultimate bulwark against the tendency of contractual individualism to slide into a total denial of obligation and interdependence. They were the repositories for interpersonal dependencies, emotional needs, mutual assistance, and informal reciprocities that were being ejected from economic contracts and political transactions. And yet, ironically, gender obligations, love, and family also played a central role in reproducing economic and political individualism.

Family obligations were an important spur to exertion and competition in the market. Adam Smith's discussion of "the invisible hand" of capitalism, for example, assumed that it was men's responsibilities to their wives and children that gave them the incentive to work for increased production and prosperity. Similarly, an American writer advised men in 1840: "If you are in business, get married, for the married man has his mind fixed on his business and his family, and is more likely of success."[31]

Love of family, moreover, could justify almost any kind of behavior toward strangers. For more than one hundred years, "I did it all for you" has been a legitimate male defense against a woman's tentative objections to any of his actions in business or politics. It also seems to have been a way that men put a moral gloss on behaviors or life choices that otherwise might make them uncomfortable. Autobiographies of early capitalist entrepreneurs demonstrate that there was a close connection between intense family sentiment and competitive business ambitions. The nineteenth-century American industrialist Benjamin Franklin Newell, for instance, recalled how his mother's protectiveness and altruism within the family had stimulated his search for self-reliance and success in the market:

> How well do I remember in the late hours of the night...she would come to my bedside, and kneeling with overflowing heart pour out her soul in prayer that God would preserve her darling boy from the snares so thick around him....How many times I wished that I were older, and had some good work so that I could support her.[32]

This convoluted link between personal ambition and family sentiment has been a recurring theme in the reminiscences of self-made men, suggesting that they have not been insensible to the moral ambiguities and psychic costs of individualism. Even the toughest players of political or economic hardball seem somehow to believe that their violations of social or civic norms pale beside their devotion to their families. "Nobody will ever write a book probably about my mother," Richard Nixon told reporters in his final press conference, justifying his term as president despite the Watergate incident that forced him to resign. "My mother was a saint."[33]

I recently led a discussion on the family with a group of male computer consultants who seemed quite conscious of the ways that family sentimentality helped them deal with the moral dilemmas of a competitive, self-seeking economy. Again and again, they described the discomfort of negotiating independent contracts in the absence of set salaries. What made them feel okay about demanding high fees, holding out for more concessions from the other side, or even taking jobs that seemed distasteful to them, most agreed, was the idea that they needed the money for their families. "Every time I started to see the other guy's side of the argument," explained one, "I kept thinking of how much I could do for my kids if I got the fee I wanted."[34]

It is interesting to note that while earlier generations of men tended to justify aggressive economic behavior by reference to the needs of mothers and wives, recent cohorts tend to cite their children's needs. Perhaps men have adjusted their psychological defense mechanisms to reflect the fact that grown women are no longer as dependent as they were formerly and therefore can no longer legitimize—or be held responsible for—the choices men make in the competitive world.

Ultimately, however, whether it is mother, wife, or child who keeps a man going, or whether a woman focuses her self-sacrifice on parent, husband, or child, the simultaneous connection and contrast between nurturing within the family and competition outside it leads to a profound sense of loneliness. "Once you leave home," parents regularly warn their children, "nobody owes you a thing." "It's a jungle out there," says the stereotypical male provider when his wife and kids meet him at the door. Thus, as Robert Bellah and his collaborators write, the ideal of the self-reliant individual is "passed from parent to child through ties that bind us together in solitude as well as love."[35]

The Family, Masculine and Feminine Identity, and the Contradictions of Love

How can commitment and dependence be sustained in one part of society when they are devalued in another? Contrary to popular opinion, this dilemma is not of recent origin. No sooner did society draw a sharp distinction between a private life based on interdependence and a public life based on individual pursuit of self-interest than the problem arose of how to maintain a proper balance between the two. For liberal social theorists, there was but one answer: The mutual reliance between individualism and interdependence could be preserved only by first sharpening the division of labor between men and women, then by emphasizing the ways that men and women required each other, the *incompleteness* of one without the other. In eighteenth-century Europe and early-nineteenth-century America, a striking rearrangement of gender identities and stereotypes occurred. To men were assigned all the character traits associated with competition: ambition, authority, power, vigor, calculation, instrumentalism, logic, and single-mindedness. To women were assigned all the traits associated with cooperation: gentleness, sensitivity, expressivism, altruism, empathy, personalism, and tenderness.[36]

Historian Barbara Welter has summed up the definition of "True Womanhood" that emerged in America in the first few decades of the nineteenth century: "piety, purity, submissiveness, and domesticity. Put them all together and they spelled mother, daughter, sister, wife—woman." As mother, daughter, sister, and wife, woman cared for son, father, brother, and husband. Yet in order to give this care, she also depended on the economic support of such men. Thus, as political scientist Virginia Sapiro notes, women were defined as dependents because everyone else was dependent on them. As men shed their social identities and embraced individualism and self-reliance, collectivism and dependence were frequently *imposed* on women.[37]

Even today, the most fervent supporters of independence in the economy and polity apply their moral values and theoretical concepts to only half of the population. Charles Murray, a well-known opponent of welfare dependency, argues that "economic independence—standing on one's own abilities and accomplishments—is of paramount importance in determining the quality of a family life." But he clearly confines this notion to men. One of the objections of Murray and his followers to welfare, indeed, is that it gives women "a meaningful alternative to the financial support available through marriage"—in other words, it makes a woman less dependent on a husband.[38]

Liberal capitalism's organization of both society and family, then, depended on a rigid division of labor by gender that denied women the assertiveness that was supposedly the basis of contract rights and denied men the empathy that was supposedly the basis of companionate marriage. The chasm between male individualism and female altruism was to be bridged by love. But there were several problems with this arrangement.

One problem was that the powerful legal, political, and economic principles of liberal theory—liberty, equality, fraternity, and the rights of man—could claim universality only by ignoring women and the family. Accordingly, there was a deafening silence about women and the family both in political theory and in popular tracts about private enterprise. Political theorist Susan Okin points out that most Anglo-American theories of justice—not to mention most arrangements of work and education—have been about men who have wives at home.[39]

Stories written to teach youngsters the values of liberal society, similarly, tended to ignore families. In Horatio Alger's novels about the self-made man, for example, the fathers of his protagonists were generally dead; the mothers were weak and ineffectual. From L. Frank Baum's Oz books to the Nancy Drew mysteries, the most enduring children's characters have lacked at least one parent, while the most popular American heroes, in literature, comics, and West-ern movies, have avoided marriage. Men learn their roles and values best in places women cannot go. For women, the only place to dis-cover role models, practical advice, and emotional support for their tasks in democratic society has been the romance novel.

For some women, of course, and some men as well, the contrast between liberalism's claim to universality and its denial of individual rights to women was an insupportable contradiction. Fond fathers who educated their daughters in republican principles awakened de-sires and frustrations that led such women to demand the rights of citizenship. Nineteenth-century feminist Elizabeth Cady Stanton drew the opposite conclusion from most liberal theorists on the basis of her *acceptance* of their assumptions about human nature:

> The isolation of every human soul and the necessity of self-depen-dence must give each individual the right to choose his own sur-roundings. The strongest reason for giving woman all the opportuni-ties...for the full development of her faculties, her forces of mind and body...is the solitude and personal responsibility of her own individ-ual life...as an individual she must rely on her self.[40]

The doctrine of republicanism provided little justification for *forc-ing* women not to rely on themselves; it could only suggest that in re-ality they would be much happier if they did not—and would be more likely to find true love. But would they really? The doctrine of separate spheres gave men and women fewer and fewer areas of com-patibility just as their relations were becoming more and more de-pendent on love. Even as women longed for the perfect romance and the ideal intimacy of true love, they increasingly felt that they could communicate deeply only with other women, who shared their per-sonality traits and experiences. Historian Nancy Cott suggests that the contradictions between separate spheres and romance had cre-ated a "marriage trauma" for many women by the early decades of the nineteenth century.[41]

Men, too, might fantasize about the ideal of the opposite sex but be daunted by the reality of the alien creature they were actually sup-posed to marry. In 1850, Donald Mitchell's *Reveries of a Bachelor* rhapsodized about the "glow of feeling" that emanated from the very word *home* but raised a misgiving that undoubtedly occurred to many men and women during this period. "I wonder," he mused, "if a married man with his sentiment made actual is, after all, as happy as we poor fellows, in our dreams?"[42]

There were other contradictions in the notion of love as the unity of opposites. If women sometimes chafed at their dependence, men often resented their obligations. A whole genre of humor was built around male resistance to women's attempts, in Huck Finn's words, to "sivilize" men. Sometimes the humor turned hostile. From the Davy Crockett stories of the early nineteenth century to men's survivalist tracts today, some men have defined maleness in misogynistic terms and claimed the wilderness as their natural preserve. The tendency of liberal states to justify war on the basis of "protecting our women" has often led men to wonder whether those women were worth the sacrifice. Historian Susan Gubar has noted recurrent themes in literature written during the Second World War of female ingratitude, male resentment of women's helplessness, and men's hostile determination to collect the sexual "rewards" due them for their labors on women's behalf.[43]

Conflicted feelings about both love and the "opposite sex" were built in to the liberal division of labor by gender. Jean-Jacques Rousseau, for example, one of the first philosophers to sentimentalize both individual self-reliance and female dependency, was radically ambivalent about love. While love derived its intensity from individualism, it also created a dependency that undermined individualism. The male lover tries to find a partner who represents the highest embodiment of female virtue and beauty. To be worthy of her, he must meet the highest ideals of male virtue and beauty. The paradox is this: What makes each individual unique in the other's eyes is that each represents the best of a *stereotype;* what makes love complete is when each lover most fully conforms to the proper gender role.[44]

As Berger puts it, the lover searches "for one single person to represent all that he is not, to confront him as his other half and his opposite" and thus to "make the world complete for him."[45] But he must also make the world complete for her by being all that she is not. In consequence, philosopher Elizabeth Rapaport explains:

> The lover is dependent, entirely, terribly dependent on his beloved for something he needs, the reciprocity of his love...[but] He will only be loved if she finds him pre-eminent. He must present himself in the guise in which she would see her beloved. This leads to a false presentation of the self and the chronic fear of exposure and loss of love.[46]

Women, of course, face the same problem: The more successfully they attract a lover to their ideal gender qualities, the more they must suppress those aspects of their personality that do not fit the ideal. Each person loses his or her *own* half in the process of finding "the other half."

In the world of separate spheres, both men and women need love, but they seek and experience it very differently. For men who subscribe to the values of bourgeois individualism, love introduces an uncomfortable contradiction into their personal sense of autonomy and rationality. It is "a mysterious and irrational force irreconcilable with their otherwise highly rational, respectable existence." Men tend to see love as not susceptible of conscious or rational control, as a force that hits with little warning and may pass just as suddenly— somewhat like a summer storm. (Indeed, it would be difficult to understand how men could make a *rational* decision to fall in love with a person who embodies all the traits that men are taught to hold in contempt in every other sphere of their lives.) While some men are captivated by this one socially acceptable chance to abandon rationality and calculation, and therefore fall in love over and over again, for most men the ideal is to get out of the storm, to resolve the uncertainty, to be able to stop doing this foreign, threatening, and above all *distracting* emotional work.[47]

For women who accept their role in the liberal division of labor, however, love is both a rational choice and a pursuit that requires conscious, calculating behavior. Maleness represents a world of achievement, autonomy, and effectiveness. It is highly desirable to gain access to someone who represents that world, but it is also dangerous, because there is always the chance that a man will treat a woman the way he treats the rest of the world, as a prize to conquer and then leave behind. The woman must control her own emotional storms, harnessing both her own and her lover's feelings to achieve definite ends. The excitement of romance novels, suggests literary critic Ann Snitov, lies both in the danger attached to falling in love with a "real man" and in the triumph of getting him to make an exception for one woman in his adversarial approach to life.[48]

For a woman, the process of falling in love is not so much a loss of control as it is a socially acceptable way of exploring her own powers, challenging herself, finding the simultaneous transcendence and self-absorption that men find in work. But even at the height of love, and especially after marriage, women find nothing "mysterious" about feelings. Emotions are women's work; the home is the place where most of that work takes place.[49]

Among the many misunderstandings and tensions that these gender differences produce are two that have recently aroused considerable political and legal controversy—for example, in the confirmation hearings for Judge Clarence Thomas and in the well-publicized feuds of various prominent couples over financial settlements after a breakup. Since women have historically been expected to do the work of managing emotions, many have learned to read men, to interpret their nonverbal signals and ambiguous remarks, anticipating what men want or need and what will be unwelcome to them. Men have not been trained to interpret female signals with the same sensitivity, but rather to expect that women will reinterpret, make allowances for, translate into "prettier" form, or simply absorb men's remarks and behaviors. This is a fundamental issue in sexual harassment. Some men deny any responsibility to read women's signals; others are honestly confused about how they can learn to tell what is acceptable and what is not. In either case, women insist, men must recognize that their older definitions of normal male-female interactions were based on the assumption that men bore no responsibility for fine-tuning relationships—and that this has to change.

In many recent financial disputes, by contrast, we see what happens when women do not take responsibility for evaluating just what they are *giving* in a relationship and what they are *giving up*. This can lead women into a bitter kind of bookkeeping about what they have "given" in their job as wife or lover. When the relationship dies, a woman may be shocked to find how little monetary worth is accorded the work she has done in the guise of gift giving.[50]

The same gender divisions that lead to idealization of love and romance, then, can create serious misunderstandings and conflicts in heterosexual love relations. Even when a couple manages to establish harmonious family commitments, the stereotypes on which these commitments rest often make life outside the family even more harsh for individuals who do not or cannot conform to gender expectations. The more women are defined in terms of an ideal myth, for example, the more possible it is for men to ignore or actively abuse women who do not meet that ideal. Thus in the nineteenth century, the cult of True Womanhood was perfectly compatible with the exploitation of female slaves and factory workers. In the twentieth century, a recurring theme in rape and sexual harassment cases has been the notion that if a woman has ever departed from ideal behavior in any way, she has no real "womanhood" to be violated or offended. The wives and mothers of rapists almost invariably, and usually in good faith, defend them as the soul of chivalry—at least toward women who conform to the prevailing myths.

Gender stereotypes about men create binds for them as well. One of the reasons that the majority of the homeless are men, and in turn that the homeless receive so little sympathy, is that men who cannot sustain an independent existence in the competitive world, like women who do not exhibit a dependent existence in the family, are often considered unworthy of sympathy or aid. As Peter Marin, researcher on homelessness, points out: "An irony asserts itself: Simply by being in need of help, men forfeit the right to it."[51]

Ultimately, these stereotypes are destructive even for those who *do* live up to them—or down to them, as the case may be. A noted psychiatrist points out that until very recently, most theories of family "normalcy" have been based on highly gender-biased criteria. One study that sought to distinguish the characteristics of dysfunctional and successful families, for example, defined "adequate" families—which they also termed "normal"—as those that produced men who functioned well in their work and social relations. But the women in such families, they noted, were typically "overwhelmed with responsibility," "psychosomatically ill," and "sexually dissatisfied." The researchers, finding that most American families fell into the "adequate" range, concluded that "The Family is alive and well." By this definition, of course, a normal family is composed of a healthy husband and a sick wife.[52]

From a different perspective, it is becoming clear, families based on a rigid gender division of labor have led to equally serious disabilities for males, by denying them access to intimacy except through women. This is one reason that men, but not women, are often much healthier when they are married and why their health, unlike women's, deteriorates after experiencing divorce or widowhood. Recently, seeking a substitute for the unconditional love they fear women will no longer give or they no longer believe they have the right to demand, many men have begun to reexamine their relationships with their fathers to find an alternative source of nurturance—often, they come up with nothing. In a men's group retreat attended by one of my students, each man was asked to set up an imaginary meeting with his father and tell the father what was uppermost on his mind. The woods echoed with three refrains: "Don't ever hit me again," "Please tell me you're proud of me," and "You never told me that you loved me."[53]

Myths of the Victorian Family

Defenders of Victorian gender roles will say that these problems have surfaced only in recent years. Despite all the tensions and contradictions of nineteenth-century families, most men and women hid their resentment or pain well enough to stay married. A return to "traditional gender roles" and a reconstruction of firm boundaries between the family and the outside world, many argue, would at least avoid the bitter disputes we see today over how men and women ought to behave toward each other.

There are two flaws in this analysis. The first is that the sexual division of labor in the nineteenth-century middle-class family, as we saw in chapter 1, depended on the existence of African-American, immigrant, and working-class families with very different age and gender roles. Sentimentalization of middle-class family life justified terrible exploitation of those other families.

The second flaw is that even for the privileged minority who lived in proper Victorian families, the gendered division of labor discussed above was *not* confined to the family. Prior to the twentieth century, the principle that individualism in society should be balanced only by solidarity in the family was more honored in the breach than in the observance. Society implicitly recognized the contradictions involved in expecting husband and wife to fill all the emotional needs and social dependencies that were being expelled from formal political and economic institutions. Consequently, there were many culturally approved ways of defusing the tensions of heterosexual love and finding other ways to balance individualism and altruism.

Victorian middle-class families were not the centers of male-female intimacy that twentieth-century commentators generally imagine. They were built on passionate female bonds that frequently took precedence over relations within the nuclear family. While the husband-wife relationship was often conventional and reserved, people routinely endorsed intimacies among women that would be thought scandalous by many in today's supposedly more broad-minded society. In a typical diary, for example, a woman might accord her husband only a few lines but rhapsodize for pages over her love for a school friend. If the friend came to visit, the husband would be banished to the parlor while the two women spent the night "embracing," "pinching" each other, and exchanging confidences.

Perfectly respectable Victorian women wrote to each other in terms such as these: "I hope for you so much, and feel so eager for you…that the expectation once more to see your face again, makes me feel hot and feverish." They recorded the "furnace blast" of their "passionate attachments" to each other, extolled each other's "sweet, soft lips" and "lily-white hands," and counted the hours until they could lie in bed, "caressing" each other again. They carved their initials into trees, set flowers in front of one another's portraits, danced together, kissed, held hands, and endured intense jealousies over rivals or small slights.[54]

Today, if a woman died and her son or husband found such diaries or letters in her effects, he would probably destroy them in rage or humiliation. In the nineteenth century, these sentiments were so respectable that surviving relatives often published them in elegies or donated the diaries and letters to libraries.

Romantic friendships also existed among some men. Although these were confined to a short period, arising in the late teens and ending at marriage, they often included physical caresses as well as emotional intimacy, and this behavior seems to have been considered well within the range of normality. Not until the late 1800s was there a clear demarcation of a distinct homosexual male subculture from an earlier homosocial one, and not until the early 1900s did ardent woman-to-woman bonds begin to be considered deviant.[55]

The idea that all of one's passionate attachments should go toward a member of the opposite sex was absent in the sex-segregated Victorian family, despite its rhetoric about the centrality of love. And no sooner did this idea begin to dominate family relations than its inherent instability revealed itself. Acceptance that the couple relationship should be the sole source of emotional and erotic intimacy made an unsatisfactory relationship increasingly unbearable. *Great Expectations,* as the title of one book on early-twentieth-century divorce suggests, led to major disappointments. By 1889, the United States had the highest divorce rate in the world; since then, the divorce rate and the sales of romance novels have risen side by side.[56]

Many modern Americans are ready to discard the myth that nuclear families ever have been or should be emotionally self-sufficient, especially if that self-sufficiency has to be constructed on rigid gender roles. A myth that dies much harder is the notion that whatever the other problems of traditional families, at least they were economically self-sufficient. The gendered division of labor might not always have been satisfying, most people admit, and it was often unfair to women—but at least it produced a unit held together by hard work, family loyalty, and a fierce determination to be beholden to no one else. The self-reliant family is the moral centerpiece of both liberal capitalism and the ideology of separate spheres for men and women; it is what brings otherwise forward-looking people to long for at least a partial revival of Victorian morality. Yet this family, too, as the next chapter demonstrates, is a historical myth.

4

....

We Always Stood on Our Own Two Feet:
Self-reliance and the American Family

"THEY never asked for handouts," my grandfather used to say whenever he and my grandmother regaled me with stories about pioneer life in Puget Sound after George Washington Bush and Michael T. Simmons defied the British and founded the first American settlement in the area. But the homesteaders didn't turn down handouts either during that hard winter of 1852, when speculators had cornered almost all the already low supply of wheat. Fortunately, Bush refused to sell his grain for the high prices the market offered, reserving most of what he did not use himself to feed his neighbors and stake them to the next spring's planting.

The United States' successful claim to Puget Sound was based on the Bush-Simmons settlement. Ironically, once Bush had helped his community become part of the Oregon territory, he became subject to Oregon's exclusionary law prohibiting African Americans from residing in the Territory. His neighbors spearheaded passage of a special legislative bill in 1854, exempting Bush and his family from the law. Bush's descendants became prominent members of what was to become Washington state, and the story of Bush's generosity in 1852 has passed into local lore.[1] Neither my grandparents' paternalistic attitudes toward blacks nor their fierce hatred of charity led them to downplay how dependent the early settlers had been on Bush's aid, but the knowledge of that dependence did not modify their insistence that decent families were "beholden to no one."

When I was older, I asked my grandfather about the apparent contradiction. "Well," he said, "that was an exception; and they paid him back by getting that bill passed, didn't they? It's not like all these people nowadays, sitting around waiting for the government to take care of them. The government never gave us anything, and we never counted on help from anybody else, either." Unless, of course, they were family. "Blood's thicker than water, after all," my grandparents used to say.

My grandparents are not the only Americans to allow the myth of self-reliance to obscure the reality of their own life histories. Politicians are especially likely to fall prey to the convenient amnesia that permits so much self-righteous posturing about how the "dependent poor" ought to develop the self-reliance and independence that "the rest of us" have shown. Sen. Phil Gramm, for example, co-author of the 1985 Gramm-Rudman-Hollings balanced budget amendment, is well known for his opposition to government handouts. However, his personal history is quite different from his political rhetoric.

Born in Georgia in 1942, to a father who was living on a federal veterans disability pension, Gramm attended a publicly funded university on a grant paid for by the federal War Orphans Act. His graduate work was financed by a National Defense Education Act fellowship, and his first job was at Texas A&M University, a federal land-grant institution. Yet when Gramm finally struck out on his own, the first thing he did was set up a consulting business where he could be, in his own words, "an advocate of fiscal responsibility and free enterprise." From there he moved on to Congress, where he has consistently attempted to slash federal assistance programs for low-income people.[2]

Self-reliance is one of the most cherished American values, although there is some ambiguity about what the smallest self-reliant unit is. For some it is the rugged individualist; for most it is the self-sufficient family of the past, in which female nurturing sustained male independence vis-à-vis the outside world. While some people believe that the gender roles within this traditional family were unfair, and others that they were beneficial, most Americans agree that prior to federal "interference" in the 1930s, the self-reliant family was the standard social unit of our society. Dependencies used to be cared for within the "natural family economy," and even today the healthiest families "stand on their own two feet."[3]

The fact is, however, that depending on support beyond the family has been the rule rather than the exception in American history, despite recurring myths about individual achievement and family enterprise. It is true that public aid has become less local and more impersonal over the past two centuries, a process described in chapter

6, but Americans have been dependent on collective institutions beyond the family, including government, from the very beginning.

A Tradition of Dependence on Others

The tendency of Americans to overestimate what they have accomplished on their own and deny how much they owe to others has been codified in the myth that the colonists came on an "errand into the wilderness" and built a land of plenty out of nothing. In reality, however, the abundant concentrations of game, plants, and berries that so astonished Eastern colonists were not "natural"; they had been produced by the cooperative husbandry and collective land-use patterns of Native Americans. In the Northwest, the valuable Douglas fir forests and plentiful herds of deer and elk found by early settlers existed only because Native American burning practices had created sustained-yield succession forests that maximized use of these resources without exhausting them.[4]

Even after they confiscated the collective work of others, though, European settlers did not suddenly form a society of independent, self-reliant families. Recent research in social history demonstrates that early American families were dependent on a large network of neighbors, church institutions, courts, government officials, and legislative bodies for their sustenance. It is true that in colonial days, the poor or disabled were generally cared for in families, but not, normally, in their *own* families. Families who did not have enough money to pay their passage to America or establish their own farms were split up, with their members assigned to be educated, fed, and trained for work in various propertied households. Elderly, ill, or orphaned dependents were taken care of in other people's families, and city officials gave allowances in money or kind to facilitate such care. The home-care system, however, soon buckled under the weight of population growth and increasing economic stratification. By the mid-eighteenth century, governments had begun to experiment with poorhouses and outdoor relief.[5]

It was not a colonial value to avoid being beholden to others, even among the nonpoor. Borrowing and lending among neighbors were woven into the very fabric of life. The presence of outstanding accounts assured the continuing circulation of goods, services, and social interactions through the community: Being under obligation to others and having favors owed was the mark of a successful person. Throughout the colonies, life was more corporate than individualistic or familial. People operated within a tight web of obligation, debt, dependence, "treating," and the calling in of favors.[6]

As America made the transition to a wage-earning society in the 1800s, patterns of personal dependence and local community assistance gave way to more formal procedures for organizing work and taking care of those who were unable to work, either temporarily or permanently. But the rise of a generalized market economy did not lessen dependency, nor did it make the family more able to take care of its own, in any sector of society.

Within the upper classes, family partnerships, arranged marriages, dowries, and family loans no longer met the need for capital, recruitment of trusted workers, and exploration of new markets. The business class developed numerous extrafamilial institutions: mercantile associations; credit-pooling consortia; new legal bodies for raising capital, such as corporations or limited liability partnerships; and chambers of commerce. Middle-class fraternal organizations, evangelical groups, and maternal associations also reached beyond kinship ties and local community boundaries to create a vast network of mutual aid organizations. The first half of the nineteenth century is usually called not the age of the family but the age of association.[7]

For the working class throughout the nineteenth century, dependence was "a structural," almost inevitable, part of life. Among workers as well, accordingly, blood was not always thicker than neighborhood, class, ethnicity, or religion. Black, immigrant, and native-born white workers could not survive without sharing and assistance beyond family networks.[8]

Working-class and ethnic subcommunities evolved around mutual aid in finding jobs, surviving tough times, and pooling money for recreation. Immigrants founded lodges to provide material aid and foster cooperation. Laborers formed funeral aid societies and death or sick benefit associations; they held balls and picnics to raise money for injured workers, widows, or orphans, and took collections at the mills or plant gates nearly every payday. Recipients showed the same lack of embarrassment about accepting such help as did colonial families. Reformer Margaret Byington, observing working-class life at the end of the nineteenth century, noted that a gift of money to a fellow worker who was ill or simply down on his luck was "accepted...very simply, almost as a matter of course." Among the iron-and steelworkers of Pittsburgh, "Innumerable acts of benevolence passed between the residents of the rows and tenements,...rarely remarked upon except for their absence." Some workers' cultures revolved around religious institutions, some around cooperative societies or militant unionism—but all extended beyond the family. Indeed, historian Michael Katz has found that in parts of early-twentieth-century Philadelphia, "Neighbors seemed more reliable and willing to help one another than did kin."[9]

Among Catholic populations, godparenting was one way of institutionalizing such obligations beyond the family. In traditional Mexican and Mexican-American communities, for example, rites of baptism cut across divisions between rich and poor, Native American, mestizo, and Spanish. Godparents became *comadres* or *copadres* with the biological parents, providing discipline and love as needed. They were morally obliged to give financial assistance in times of need or to take on full parental responsibilities if the biological parents should die. Irish and Italian districts had similar customs. Some Native American groups had special "blood brother" rituals; the notion of "going for sisters" has long and still thriving roots in black communities.[10]

Yet even ties of expanded kinship, class, neighborhood, and ethnicity were never enough to get many families by. Poor Americans, for example, have always needed support from the public purse, even if that support has often been inadequate. Indeed, notes one welfare historian, the history of dependence and assistance in America is marked by "the early and pervasive role of the state. There has never been a golden age of volunteerism."[11]

By the end of the nineteenth century, neither poorhouses, outdoor relief, nor private charity could cope with the dislocations of industrial business cycles. As late as 1929, after nearly a decade of prosperity, the Brookings Institute found that the "natural family economy" was not working for most Americans: Three-fifths of American families earned $2,000 or less a year and were unable to save anything to help them weather spells of unemployment or illness. The Great Depression, of course, left many more families unable to make it on their own.[12]

Even aside from times of depression, the inability of families to survive without public assistance has never been confined to the poor. Middle-class and affluent Americans have been every bit as dependent on public support. In fact, comparatively affluent families have received considerably *more* public subsidy than those in modest circumstances, while the costs of such subsidies have often been borne by those who derived the least benefit from them.

To illustrate the pervasiveness of dependence in American family history, I will examine in greater detail the two main family types that are usually held up as models of traditional American independence: the frontier family, archetype of American self-reliance, and the 1950s suburban family, whose strong moral values and work ethic are thought to have enabled so many to lift themselves up by their bootstraps. In fact, these two family types probably tie for the honor of being the most heavily subsidized in American history, as well as for the privilege of having had more of their advantages paid for by minorities and the lower classes.

Self-reliance and the American West

Our image of the self-reliant pioneer family has been bequeathed to us by the *Little House on the Prairie* books and television series, which almost every American has read or seen. What is less well known is that these stories, based on the memoirs of Laura Ingalls Wilder, were extensively revised by her daughter as an ideological attack on government programs. When Wilder's daughter, Rose Wilder Lane, failed to establish a secure income as a freelance writer in the 1930s, she returned to her family home in the Ozarks. Here, historian Linda Kerber reports, "Lane announced that she would no longer write so that she would not have to pay taxes to a New Deal government." However, "she *rewrote* the rough drafts of her mother's memoirs,...turning them into the *Little House* books in which the isolated family is pitted against the elements and makes it—or doesn't—with no help from the community."[13]

In reality, prairie farmers and other pioneer families owed their existence to massive federal land grants, government-funded military mobilizations that dispossessed hundreds of Native American societies and confiscated half of Mexico, and state-sponsored economic investment in the new lands. Even "volunteers" expected federal pay: Much of the West's historic "antigovernment" sentiment originated in discontent when settlers did not get such pay or were refused government aid for unauthorized raids on Native American territory. It would be hard to find a Western family today or at any time in the past whose land rights, transportation options, economic existence, and even access to water were not dependent on federal funds. "Territorial experience got Westerners in the habit of federal subsidies," remarks Western historian Patricia Nelson Limerick, "and the habit persisted long after other elements of the Old West had vanished."[14]

It has been an expensive habit, in more ways than one. The federal government spent $15 million on the Louisiana Purchase in 1803 and then engaged in three years of costly fighting against the British in order to gain more of Florida. In the 1830s, state governments funded outright or financially guaranteed three-fourths of the $200 million it cost to build canals linking the Atlantic seaboard trading centers with new settlements around the Great Lakes and the Ohio and Mississippi rivers. The government got a bargain in the 1830s when it forced the Cherokees to "sell" their land for $9 million and then deducted $6 million from that for the cost of removing them along "The Trail of Tears," where almost a quarter of the 15,000 Native Americans died. Acquiring northern Mexico was even more expensive: The war of annexation cost $97 million; then, as victor, the United States was able to "buy" Texas, California, southern Arizona, and New Mexico from Mexico for only an additional $25 million.

The land acquired by government military action or purchase, both funded from the public purse, was then sold—at a considerable loss—to private individuals. The Preemption Act of 1841 allowed settlers to buy land at $125 an acre, far below the actual acquisition cost; in 1854, the Graduation Act permitted lands that had been on the market for some time to be sold for even less. The Homestead Act of 1862 provided that a settler could buy 160 acres for $10 if the homesteader lived on the land for five years and made certain improvements. The federal government also gave each state 30,000 acres to help finance colleges that could improve agricultural education and techniques. These land-grant colleges made vital contributions to Western economic expansion.

Even after this generous, government-funded head start, pioneer families did not normally become self-sufficient. The stereotypical solitary Western family, isolated from its neighbors and constantly on the move, did exist, but it was also generally a failure. Economic success in nineteenth-century America, on the frontier as well as in the urban centers, was more frequently linked to persistence and involvement in a community than to family self-reliance or the restless "pioneering spirit."[15]

As historian John Mack Farragher describes frontier life in Sugar

Creek, Illinois, between 1820 and 1850, for example, "self-sufficiency" was not a family quality but "a community experience....Sharing work with neighbors at cabin raisings, log rollings, hayings, husking, butchering, harvesting or threshing were all traditionally communal affairs." The prairie was considered common land for grazing, and a "'borrowing system' allowed scarce tools, labor and products to circulate to the benefit of all." As one contemporary explained to prospective settlers: "Your wheel-barrows, your shovels, your utensils of all sorts, belong not to yourself, but to the public who do not think it necessary even to *ask* a loan, but take it for granted." This community, it must be stressed, was not necessarily egalitarian: One traveler characterized Illinois as "heaven for men and horses, but a very different place for women and oxen." But "mutuality" and "suppression of self-centered behavior," not rugged individualism or even the carving out of a familial "oasis," were what created successful settlements as America moved West, while the bottom line of westward expansion was federal funding of exploration, development, transportation, and communication systems.[16]

In the early twentieth century, a new form of public assistance became crucial to Westerners' existence: construction of dams and other federally subsidized irrigation projects. During the Depression, government electrification projects brought pumps, refrigeration, and household technology to millions of families who had formerly had to hand pump and carry their water and who had lacked the capacity to preserve or export their farm produce. Small farmers depended on the government to slow down foreclosures and protect them from the boom and bust of overproduction, soil exhaustion, and cutthroat competition.[17]

Without public subsidies, the maintenance of independent family farms would have been impossible. Yet even with all this help from government and neighbors, small family enterprises did not turn out to be the major developers of the West. Their dependence on government subsidization, it turned out, produced a political constituency and ideological cover for policies that channeled much greater benefits to wealthy individuals and corporations. Of the billion acres of western land distributed by the end of the century, for example, only 147 million acres became homesteads, and even many of these ended up in speculators' hands. Sociologists Scott and Sally McNall estimate that "probably only one acre in nine went to the small pioneers." One hundred and eighty-three million acres of the public domain were given to railroad companies, generally in alternating square-mile sections to a depth of ten miles on either side of the line. These federal giveaways, not family enterprise, were what built most major western logging companies. Environmental historian John Opie and rural geographer Imhoff Vogeler argue that for 200 years, federal policy has promoted the myth of the independent family farm at the same time it has encouraged waste or misuse of land and water and subsidized huge, though not necessarily efficient, agribusinesses. Yet trying to solve such inequity by simply cutting federal subsidies, as in the 1990 Farm Bill, flies in the face of 200 years of experience: The existence of family farms and diversified agriculture has always depended on public subsidy.[18]

Self-Reliance and the Suburban Family

Another oft-cited example of familial self-reliance is the improvement in living standards experienced by many Americans during the 1950s. The surge in homeownership at that time, most people believe, occurred because families scraped together down payments, paid their mortgages promptly, raised their children to respect private property, and always "stood on their own two feet." An entire generation of working people thereby attained middle-class status, graduating from urban tenements to suburban homeownership, just as Lucille Ball and Desi Arnaz did in their television series.

The 1950s suburban family, however, was far more dependent on government handouts than any so-called "underclass" in recent U.S. history. Historian William Chafe estimates that "most" of the upward mobility at this time was subsidized in one form or another by government spending. Federal GI benefits, available to 40 percent of the male population between the ages of twenty and twenty-four, permitted a whole generation of men to expand their education and improve their job prospects without foregoing marriage and children. The National Defense Education Act retooled science education, subsidizing both American industry and the education of individual scientists. In addition, the surge in productivity during the 1950s was largely federally financed. More than $50 billion of government-funded wartime inventions and production processes were turned over to private companies after the war, creating whole new fields of employment.[19]

Even more directly, suburban homeownership depended on an

unprecedented enlargement of federal regulation and financing. The first steps were taken in the Great Depression, when the Home Owners Loan Corporation (HOLC) set up low-interest loans to allow people to refinance homes lost through foreclosure. The government began to underwrite the real estate industry by insuring private homeownership lenders, loaning directly to long-term buyers, and subsidizing the extension of electricity to new residential areas. But the real transformation of attitudes and intervention came in the 1950s, with the expansion of the Federal Housing Authority and Veterans' Administration loans.

Before the Second World War, banks often required a 50 percent down payment on homes and normally issued mortgages for only five to ten years. In the postwar period, however, the Federal Housing Authority (FHA), supplemented by the GI Bill, put the federal government in the business of insuring and regulating private loans for single-home construction. FHA policy required down payments of only 5 to 10 percent of the purchase price and guaranteed mortgages of up to thirty years at interest rates of just 2 to 3 percent on the balance. The Veterans Administration asked a mere dollar down from veterans. At the same time, government tax policies were changed to provide substantial incentives for savings and loan institutions to channel their funds almost exclusively into low-interest, long-term mortgages. Consequently, millions of Americans purchased homes with artificially low down payments and interest rates, courtesy of Uncle Sam.[20]

It was not family savings or individual enterprise, but federal housing loans and education payments (along with an unprecedented expansion of debt), that enabled so many 1950s American families to achieve the independence of homeownership. Almost *half* the housing in suburbia depended on such federal financing. As philosopher Alan Wolfe points out: "Even the money that people borrowed to pay for their houses was not lent to them on market principles; fixed-rate mortgages, for example, absolved an entire generation from inflation for thirty years."[21]

Yet this still understates the extent to which suburbia was a creation of government policy and federal spending. True, it was private real estate agents and construction companies who developed the suburban projects and private families who bought the homes. But it was government-funded research that developed the aluminum clapboards, prefabricated walls and ceilings, and plywood paneling that composed the technological basis of the postwar housing revolution.

And few buyers would have been forthcoming for suburban homes without new highways to get them out to the sites, new sewer systems, utilities services, and traffic control programs—all of which were not paid for by the families who used them, but by the general public.

In 1947, the government began a project to build 37,000 miles of new highway. In 1956, the Interstate Highway Act provided for an additional 42,500 miles. Ninety percent of this construction was financed by the government. The prime beneficiaries of this postwar road-building venture, which one textbook calls "the greatest civil engineering project of world history," were suburbanites. Despite arguments that road building served "national interests," urban interstates were primarily "turned into commuter roads serving suburbia."[22]

Such federal patronage might be unobjectionable, even laudable—though hardly a demonstration of self-reliance—if it had been available to all Americans equally. But the other aspect of federal subsidization of suburbia is that it worsened the plight of public transportation, the inner cities, poor families in general, and minority ones in particular.

Federal loan policies systematized and nationalized the pervasive but informal racism that had previously characterized the housing market. FHA redlining practices, for example, took entire urban areas and declared them ineligible for loans. Government policy also shifted resources from urban areas into suburban construction and expansion. At the same time, postwar "urban renewal" and highway construction reduced the housing stock for urban workers. Meanwhile, the federal government's two new mortgage institutions, the Federal National Mortgage Association (Fannie Mae) and the Government National Mortgage Association (Ginnie Mae), made it possible for urban banks to transfer savings out of the cities and into new construction in the South and West—frequently, again, into suburban developments. By the 1970s, for example, savings banks in the Bronx invested just 10 percent of their funds in the borough and only 30 percent elsewhere in the entire state.[23]

In the 1950s and 1960s, while the general public financed roads for suburban commuters, the streetcars and trolleys that served urban and poor families received almost no tax revenues and thus steadily deteriorated, with results we are paying for today. In the nineteenth century, American public transport had been one of the better systems in the world, and one of the most used. In 1890, streetcar ridership in the United States was four times as great as that in Europe on a per capita basis. As late as 1953, a million and a half people traveled by rail each day. But expansion of the highway system undercut this form of public transport as well. Between 1946 and 1980, government aid to highways totaled $103 billion, while railroads received only $6 billion.[24]

We should not overestimate the accessibility of earlier public transport to lower-income families—in the third quarter of the nineteenth century, most people walked to work—nor should we forget the pollution and overcrowding of streets filled with horse-drawn vehicles. Yet the fact remains that government transportation policy systematically fostered improvements in private rather than public conveyances, favoring suburban development over the revitalization of urban life. By the end of the 1950s, Los Angeles epitomized the kind of city such policies produced. Once served by an efficient and widely used mass-transit system, the city was carved up by multilane freeways, overpasses, and viaducts. By the end of the decade, two-thirds of central Los Angeles had been paved over to make room for cars.[25]

The Myth of Self-reliant Families: Public Welfare Policies

The government subsidies discussed earlier, despite their ill effects on the cities and the poor, mobilized resources much more efficiently than older informal support networks had done, encouraging family formation, residential stability, upward occupational mobility, and high educational aspirations among those who received them. There is thus no intrinsic tendency of government subsidies per se to induce dependence, undermine self-esteem, or break down family ties, even though these charges are almost invariably leveled against one kind of subsidy: welfare for the poor.

During the 1960s, exposés such as Michael Harrington's *The Other America* (1962), as well as protests by poor people, stimulated attempts to ameliorate poverty and dampen social unrest. Along with reforms that lessened racial discrimination in welfare policies, the new government initiatives against poverty resulted in a substantial increase in the welfare rolls and a major extension of social insurance benefits during the 1960s and 1970s.[26]

It is important to note that the most dramatic growth in government social expenditures since the 1960s has been in social insurance programs, such as worker's compensation, disability, and Medicare. Most benefits from these programs go to members of the white middle class. Although the programs are very important for the poor they do reach, even at the height of the Great Society antipoverty initiative, between 1965 and 1971, 75 percent of America's social welfare dollars were spent on the nonpoor. The proportion going to the poor has decreased substantially since then.[27]

Yet in the late 1970s, as economic conditions tightened, a growing number of commentators began to argue that both the financial and the family afflictions of Americans existed because government had abandoned traditions of self-reliance and adopted overly generous subsidy programs for the poor. Ignoring the historical dependence of pioneer and suburban families on public support, as well as the continued reliance of industry on government handouts, some analysts asserted that the problems of poor families originated in the very fact that they received assistance at all.

Probably the most widely quoted of these commentators was Charles Murray, who wrote *Losing Ground: American Social Policy, 1950–1980.* Murray's arguments relied on the fact that "latent poverty" (the amount of poverty before any government welfare payments) declined rapidly during the 1950s and early 1960s, a period when government subsidies or transfer payments to the poor grew only slowly. During the late 1960s and the 1970s, the rate of government social welfare expenditures increased, yet in this period latent poverty ceased to decline and eventually began to grow again. Asserting a causal connection between these trends, Murray argued that poverty decreased in the early period because government welfare payments remained modest, while poverty increased in the later period as a result of the increase in government payments. The Great Society initiatives of Lyndon Johnson seduced the poor into dependence, eroded their commitment to self-reliance, family values, and the work ethic, and actually increased the poverty the programs were designed to alleviate. Welfare subsidies contained so many "disincentives" to marriage and work that they ensnared recipients in a tangled skein of dependence, demoralization, immorality, and self-destruction: "Cut the knot," Murray urged, "for there is no way to untie it." He advocated elimination of all social programs aimed at the poor, with the exception of unemployment insurance for the working-age population.[28]

The phenomenal publicity and approval generated by Murray's book had more to do with the way it tapped into powerful cultural myths about self-reliance and dependency than with any connection to empirical evidence. It is true that the expansion of the economy between 1950 and 1965—itself partly a result of government subsidies—led to rising real wages, which, of course, meant a steady decrease in pretransfer poverty. But total poverty remained much higher in the 1950s than in the Great Society period. In 1964, after fourteen years of unprecedented economic growth, the poverty rate was still 19 percent; in 1969, after five years of relatively modest government welfare programs, it was down to 12 percent, a low that has not been seen since the social welfare cutbacks began in the late 1970s. In 1965, 20 percent of American children still lived in poverty; within five years, that had fallen to 15 percent. Between 1959 and 1969, the black poverty rate was reduced from 55.1 percent to 32.2 percent.[29]

The economy weakened at the end of the 1960s, for reasons that had nothing to do with the minuscule amount of the gross national product being spent on welfare, but this makes the actual effectiveness of government assistance programs even more impressive. Despite the slowdown in economic growth, the most dramatic improvements for the poor came after the institution of new subsidy programs in the late 1960s. Even though infant mortality had been reduced very little prior to 1965, for example, it was cut in half between 1965 and 1980, during the period when Medicaid and other government-subsidized health programs were established. The gap in nutrition between low-income and other Americans had remained high throughout the 1950s and early 1960s. It narrowed significantly only between the mid-1960s and the late 1970s, as a direct result of the expansion of food stamp and school lunch programs. As late as 1963, 20 percent of Americans below the poverty line had *never* been examined by a physician; by 1970, this was true of only 8 percent of the poor.[30]

Despite stagnant real wages in the 1970s, economists Sheldon Danziger and Peter Gottschalk point out, poverty reductions continued for groups who still received government assistance. It was in groups whose subsidies declined or stagnated that poverty grew. The fastest-growing government social welfare programs during the 1970s, and the largest in absolute terms, were those directed toward the elderly; they were so effective that they wiped out the historical tendency for elders to be the poorest sector of the population.[31]

According to opponents of government aid to the poor, though, the material benefits of social welfare programs are simply not worth the social and psychological costs. Murray and others charge that relief grants and subsidies have created devastating changes in family structure and work patterns among the poor over the past two decades. Their claims conjure up ominous images of able-bodied men deserting their families so that they can sleep around without having to support their kids, and teenage girls popping out babies so that they can stay home, live off welfare, eat junk food, and watch television instead of work.

There *has* been an acceleration of urban deterioration, social decay, and family breakup in the past two decades, a process discussed in chapters 10 and 11. But the claim that rising welfare subsidies caused this is not upheld by the facts. Although both single-mother families and the rolls of Aid to Families with Dependent Children (AFDC) have expanded since the mid-1950s, for example, these trends should be understood as separate responses to other socioeconomic and cultural changes, for there is no causal relationship between welfare benefits and single-parent families. Economists William Darity and Samuel Myers found that in any specific geographic area or time period from 1955 to 1972, the higher the welfare benefits, the *lower* were the rates of female headship and welfare participation. Since 1972, the correlations Murray made so much of have ceased to prevail even at the most general level. Between 1972 and 1980, the number of children living in female-headed households rose from 14 percent to almost 20 percent, but the number in AFDC homes held constant at about 12 percent. In the same period, the number of black children in female-headed families rose by nearly 20 percent, but the number in AFDC homes actually fell by 5 percent.[32]

The image of teenage girls having babies to receive welfare checks is an emotion-laden but fraudulent cliché. If the availability of welfare benefits causes teen pregnancy, why is it that other industrial countries, with far more generous support policies for women and children, have far lower rates of teen pregnancy?[33]

Welfare benefits do seem to increase the likelihood of unmarried teen mothers moving away from their parents' households, hence increasing the *visibility* of these mothers, but they bear little or no relation to actual birth rates for unmarried women. Harvard economists David Ellwood and Mary Jo Bane compared unmarried women who would be eligible for welfare if they had an illegitimate child with unmarried women who would not be eligible: Even by confining their analysis to states that gave the most generous welfare benefits to single mothers, they found no difference in the rates of illegitimacy between the groups. Mississippi, with the lowest welfare and food stamp benefits for AFDC mothers in the entire country (only 46 percent of the federal poverty guidelines), has the second-highest percentage of out-of-wedlock births in the country; states with higher AFDC benefits than the national average tend to have *lower* rates of illegitimacy than the national average.[34]

Sociologist Mark Rank finds that "welfare recipients have a relatively low fertility rate" and that the longer a woman remains on welfare, whatever her age, the less likely she is to keep having babies. Mothers on AFDC have only one-fourth the number of births while they are on welfare as do mothers who are not on welfare.[35]

Also, there is no clear evidence that welfare benefits encourage marital breakup, although here the findings are more mixed. Some studies have demonstrated a link between higher welfare payments and marital dissolution, but others have found only modest or insignificant correlations. In March 1987 the General Accounting Office released a report summarizing more than one hundred studies completed since 1975. The report concluded that "research does not support the view that welfare encourages two-parent family breakup" or that it significantly reduces the incentive to work. While researcher Robert Moffitt's 1990 review of welfare studies found some effects of welfare programs on marriage rates, it also showed that welfare explains neither the long-term decline in marriage rates nor the most recent increases in female headship.[36]

Finally, the availability of welfare benefits and the size of grants cannot be shown to create a family cycle of dependency. A recent study of child poverty and welfare rates in both 1970 and 1980 found that "high-benefit states tend to have a relatively lower proportion of their children in poverty than low-benefit states." Census data from 1988 show that half the people on the welfare rolls in any month are off within a year. Two-fifths of those who leave eventually return for another spell, yet their total length of time on welfare still averages out to only two years or less. Only a small minority remain on the rolls for extended periods, and despite anecdotes about "welfare queens," this is not because payments are generous: The combined value of AFDC payments and food stamps is below the minimum poverty level in all but two states and one other county in America; nationally, the median worth of both benefits is only 73 percent of the poverty level. Most recipients live hand to mouth, sometimes going hungry near the end of the month or losing their housing if the welfare check is delayed for any reason. In light of this, if welfare benefits do encourage women to leave their husbands, this is a comment more on how bad their marriages must be than on how attractive the alternative of welfare is.[37]

Obviously, there are serious problems with welfare policies and practices, but we cannot analyze these problems realistically if we cling to the myth that only the poor have ever been dependent on government aid, forgetting the near-universality of families' dependence on public assistance in American history. Few people would accuse government subsidies to middle- and working-class home-owners of destroying the recipients' work ethic, demoralizing their families, or wrecking the economy. When it comes to the poor, welfare researchers Richard Cloward and Frances Fox Piven suggest: "It is not receiving benefits that is damaging to recipients, but rather the fact that benefits are so low as to ensure physical misery and an out-cast social status." Political scientist Robert Goodin reports: "Psychological studies show that aid which is given anonymously, which protects the autonomy of the recipient, and which allows him opportunities to reciprocate all have positive rather than negative effects upon the recipient—among them, encouraging subsequent attempts at self-help on his part."[38]

Certainly there are debates to be held about welfare subsidies and practices. The extent to which expanded health coverage has been accompanied by ballooning hospital and specialists' charges deserves scrutiny. So do policies that penalize welfare recipients for working or saving by reducing the amount of their grants accordingly. The fact that AFDC payments to mothers do not have much impact on work-force participation may be positive from the point of view of the work ethic but negative in terms of the work mothers are forced to take and the inadequate child care they must use. Perhaps we should link payments in this case to *not* working. On the other hand, experiments with the negative income tax show that direct subsidies to youths below the age of twenty-one *do* have substantial effects on work-force participation. Perhaps here we should assist poor youth, given their high unemployment rates, but by providing educational scholarships or jobs rather than direct grants.[39]

There are some situations, though, when it might make more sense to award direct cash grants. The Urban Affairs Center at Northwestern University, for example, recently calculated the total spending on poverty-related programs in Cook County, Illnois, during 1984, including salaries to welfare workers, doctors, social workers, psychologists, and security officers. Dividing the total ($4.8 billion) by the number of poor people in the county in that year (781, 330), urban affairs professor John McKnight found that it averaged out to $6,209 per person, or $18,600 a year for a family of three. However, the poor received only one-third of this in actual financial assistance, since social service functionaries consumed two-thirds of the total.[40]

To sustain the myth that only "abnormal" or "failed" families require public assistance, policymakers tend to smuggle into the budget the subsidies on which most families rely. Direct expenditures to the poor are debated to the last penny, accompanied by either agonized soul-searching or angry bombast about why the poor are unable to fend for themselves. But the same politicans unconcernedly vote for massive middle-class entitlement programs that are disguised as "earned" benefits (social security, for example) or slipped in as "off-budget" items whose costs are seldom tallied up until it is too late. Tax expenditures, for example, totaled $310 *billion* in fiscal year 1989, yet this massive government subsidy did not trigger the tax revolts and political upsets that have occurred over more readily comprehensible direct expenditures equaling only a tiny fraction of this sum.* As one economist points out:

> A dollar spent on housing, health care, or capital investment through the tax code has the same effects on the allocation of resources and the distribution of income as a dollar in direct spending for the same purposes. Yet, because tax expenditures are hidden and do not affect calculations of the "size of government" as measured by the ratio of outlays to GNP, they receive far less scrutiny than regular budget accounts.[42]

One way that both direct expenditures and tax subsidies for non-poor families are disguised is by attaching them, however tenuously, to an already existing work history, income level, or other personal characteristic. Or, instead of funding social services directly, the government may give tax breaks to families who purchase them privately. Such policies convey the false impression that the subsidies

---

*Recent agitation over funding for the National Endowment for the Humanities is a case in point: Federal spending on the arts in America amounts to less than 0.1 percent of the national budget, or less than is spent annually on the Pentagon's military band program; tax deductions for advertising that exploits sex to sell products cost the treasury billions of dollars each year.[41]

are somehow caused by, paid for, or *due* to the recipients because of
their individual achievements. They also tend to tie the amount of
public aid families and individuals receive to the amount of income
or advantages they already have. Thus, even widely distributed tax
deductions, such as the dependent child deduction so important to
most working families, are set up in ways that aid the rich more than
anyone else. The worth of a deduction depends on a person's tax
bracket, so two children are "worth" twice as much to a family in the
top bracket as they are to a family in more modest circumstances.
For families too poor to pay taxes, of course, such deductions are totally meaningless.

The effect of distributing public subsidies through private income-
boosting channels rather than through general social spending is that
interest group lobbies become dominant in determining which families or sectors of the population receive subsidies. While businesses,
unions, and retirement associations can form effective lobbies for the
subsidies they desire, certain groups, such as children, have very little clout in these battles. They do not have the means to organize as
interest groups or the private resources to take advantage of incentives, tax deductions, and so forth. This is one reason that, from
1978 to 1987, after adjusting for inflation, federal expenditures on
the elderly grew by 52 percent, while those directed to children fell
by 4 percent. Subsidies for children should not be taken from subsidies to the elderly, as some propose; however, "no other country has
so large an age bias to its poverty rates nor so wide an age tilt to its
allocation of resources." "What we've done in this country in the past
few decades," comments economist Sylvia Hewitt, "is socialize the
cost of growing old and privatize the cost of childhood."[43]

Subsidizing Family Housing: Hidden Inequities, Unintended Consequences, and Cost Overruns

Government housing expenditures provide an excellent illustration
of the inequities and unintended consequences of indirect, hidden
handouts to families. Critics of welfare have been quick to seize on
recent scandals at the Department of Housing and Urban Development (HUD), suggesting that the HUD fiasco resulted from government interference in the free housing market. The fact is, however,
that much of the corruption at HUD stemmed from the *reluctance* of

government to get directly involved in providing housing. Publicly owned housing accounts for only 1 percent of the U.S. housing market (compared to 37 percent in France and 46 percent in England). Instead, most housing expenditures for the poor go to private, profit-making companies in the form of "incentives" to build desired kinds of homes—producing not a welfare state but a "franchise state."[44]

Profit-making franchises, of course, tend to deliver goods to the highest bidder. When bigger profits are to be found building luxury homes rather than ones for low-income families, government has to up the ante to make it worthwhile for developers to stay in the low-income market. As government moved away from direct financing of public housing after 1965 and as urban areas grew increasingly impoverished, federal agencies multiplied their financial "incentives" to private realtors, speculators, and developers, hoping to bribe them into building or improving low-income housing. Most of the influence peddling, high-priced lobbying, and scandalous rakeoffs in HUD projects thus violated no laws but were simply the messy residue of greasing a wheel that was never constructed to turn in the direction of the poor. The wheel still has failed to turn, however: Throughout the 1980s, private housing developments built with government assistance were increasingly turned over to high-income private investors, and the affordable housing stock shrank.[45]

Meanwhile, in fiscal year 1988, while direct spending for low-income housing assistance was $13.9 billion, federal tax subsidies for homeowners were *four times as high,* totaling $53.9 billion. Households with incomes of $50,000 or more, less than 20 percent of the population in 1988, received 52.2 percent of all federal housing subsidies, or three times as much as the poorest 20 percent of American households.[46]

In addition to the inequitable distribution of housing subsidies, their indirect, privatized nature has had the unintended consequence of exacerbating suburban sprawl and destroying farmlands. Access to recreational facilities and open space, for example, are important components of family living standards, yet the government has spent far less money on building parks or preserving forests than on subsidizing people's private home building near open space. Allowing people to deduct mortgage interest and real estate taxes from their gross income but taxing them directly for open space or park purchases encourages homeowners to seek private solutions to overcrowding and pollution, moving to new suburbs as they lose the nearby unimproved lots that used to substitute for neighborhood

parks. This subsidization of *personal* living standards ignores the social costs of private gain. As early as the 1950s economist John Kenneth Galbraith pointed out that postwar capitalism had produced an
extraordinary contrast between "private opulence and public
squalor." He described Americans as driving luxury cars through
blighted cities to picnic on immaculately packaged food beside pol-
luted streams. The cars might be roomy, but the schools, hospitals,
and prisons were overcrowded; the privately purchased food might
smell enticing, but the publicly funded sanitation facilities left a foul
stench in the air.[47]

Most Americans can no longer drive away from urban problems to
their own little pieces of fresh air, clean water, and open space, because our subsidy policies have created a suburban sprawl un-
matched in other industrial nations. By the beginning of the 1970s,
for the first time, more Americans lived in suburbs than in any other
location; by the mid-1980s, twice as many people were employed in
manufacturing in the suburbs as in the central cities. Transportation
problems have become vastly more complex as older linear routes
from suburbs to central workplaces have ceased to serve the majority
of commuters, who travel not from suburb to city but "helter-skelter
to a variety of suburban work locations." Sixty-seven percent of employed suburban residents commute to a suburban workplace—69
percent of them drive to work alone, with only 11 percent using car-
pools and 4 percent using public transportation.[48]

These unintended consequences of subsidizing suburban families
have destroyed many of the benefits that families hoped to gain by
moving to suburbia in the first place. Households that gained extra
pocket money by evading taxes for city sewers and garbage now face
failing septic systems, skyrocketing garbage-disposal costs, and even
problems of toxic waste. Traffic jams and pollution alerts are no
longer confined to the cities. The tremendous decentralization of
roads, services, government, and police makes it difficult to deal with
multiuse zoning, new rental complexes, industrial parks, and the increasing mix of income and occupational levels in suburban workplaces and neighborhoods. "Local political boundaries...balkanize
metropolitan areas into more than 20,000 units of government,"
many of which are constantly at each other's throats.[49]

Today, there is growing pressure to shift resources to such public
goals as preserving open space and fighting pollution. But America's
historical reliance on subsidizing private purchases of life's amenities
has set up a vicious cycle, in which families that know they will have

to pay for their own medical care, transportation, recreation, and education resent any deduction from their finances for taxes or levies.

This miserly attitude is not simply a character flaw: It is the product of a hundred years of experience. By the end of the nineteenth century, America already had a distinctive syndrome wherein people who were employed had higher pay and more luxuries than their European counterparts, yet they had less leisure time, higher job casualty rates, worse garbage collection, fewer public parks, and less access to hospital accommodation. Such lack of investment in social capital forces each family to think first of its own savings, its own standard of living, and its own competitive position. Consequently, people fear that increased taxation, even for goals they support, will diminish their personal capacity to circumvent problems they have no historical confidence in government to solve. Thus families disgusted with the results of unplanned growth also vote down attempts to regulate it, reasoning that they can sell their home to a newcomer at a better price without regulation and then be able to retreat to an "unspoiled" area somewhere else.[50]

Even the savings and loan (S&L) crisis is partly attributable to the indirect methods by which American families have been subsidized and to our refusal to question the myth of family "self-reliance." Greedy speculators, corrupt politicians, and indulgent regulators certainly enlarged the crisis in the 1980s, but they were responding to *prior* insolvency problems. *Many of the problems of the S&Ls originated in losses on low-interest home mortgages.* It was attempts to recoup such losses that led to risky loans, financial hanky-panky, and eventually fraud.[51]

The decision of government to get involved in insuring home mortgages had seemed painless in the 1950s; as an "off-budget expenditure" neither its short-term costs nor its long-term consequences were given serious consideration. But government's encouragement of banks to commit themselves to long-term mortgages at below-market rates was a risk that grew even faster than homeownership, and the implicit liability of the Federal Savings and Loan Insurance Corporation (FSLIC) "was not financed as it accrued." Things were made even worse when the laws requiring S&Ls to be nonprofit institutions were repealed. By the late 1970s, the S&Ls were carrying huge portfolios of low-interest loans, to the benefit of millions of home buyers but to the detriment of their balance sheets. At this point, new federal legislation allowed small investors easier access to high-yielding money funds. The S&Ls had to increase interest outlays to depositors in order to compete with these funds, but they still lost millions of customer dollars to money-market mutual funds and other investments paying significantly higher returns.[52]

As *Newsweek* analysts Steven Waldman and Rich Thomas point out, Congress then faced a choice: either "shrink the industry or let it fly free in the winds of deregulation." One reason that Congress failed to consider the first option was fear of the political consequences of curtailing the home loan industry. Politicians were unwilling to bite the bullet and admit that free enterprise and family savings were not financing the homeownership that was the pride of postwar America. Rather than vigorously rethink the insurance system, they relaxed regulation to allow the S&Ls to experiment with ever-riskier schemes to attract new depositors: "The passbook savings that had provided almost 90 percent of home loans as recently as the mid-1960s accounted for only 25 percent by 1980." Congress also "issued government notes that made troubled banks appear solvent," without counting these in the budget deficit, and granted other off-budget favors, allowing banks to postpone the day of reckoning for their inability to make homeownership loans a paying proposition.[53]

The day of reckoning has now arrived, and we are paying for our refusal to seriously debate family subsidy policies not only in the almost unimaginable price of the S&L bailout, but also in the growing inaccessibility of housing. Nationally, the rise in single-family home prices has greatly outstripped the rise in income, more than tripling in twenty years. Rents also have soared, rising 14 percent faster than the overall cost of living, and even more at the low end of the market, where people have the least leeway in their budgets. The shortage of low-cost rentals means that a majority of poor renters pay more than 50 percent—sometimes as much as 70 percent—of their income on housing. A 1991 study concluded that "millions of Americans are living on the brink of homelessness." However, only 29 percent of poor-renter households live in public housing or receive any kind of rent subsidy, whether federal, state, or local.[54]

While the 1991 budget restored funding for some 10,000 new public housing units, the remaining inequities are striking testimony to the problems of our hidden subsidy policies. The *Wall Street Journal* reports, for example, that when the government sold the S&Ls it had seized in 1988, "buyers got a full plate of tax benefits and other assistance." One financier's holding company, for example, paid $315 million for five banks "and walked away with $1.7 *billion* in tax benefits."[55]

Debating Family Policy: Why It's So Hard

Attempts to sustain the myth of family self-reliance in the face of all the historical evidence to the contrary have led policymakers into theoretical convolutions and practical miscalculations that are reminiscent of efforts by medieval philosophers to maintain that the earth, not the sun, was the center of the planetary system. In the sixteenth century, leading European thinkers insisted that the sun and all the planets revolved around the earth, much as Americans insist that our society revolves around family self-reliance. When evidence to the contrary mounted, defenders of the Ptolemaic universe postulated all sorts of elaborate planetary orbits, changes of direction, and even periodic loop-de-loops in order to reconcile observed reality with their cherished theory. Similarly, rather than admit that all families need public support, we have constructed ideological loop-de-loops that explain away each instance of dependence as an "exception," an "abnormality," or even an illusion. We have distributed public aid to families through convoluted bureaucratic orbits that have become impossible to track; and in some cases—most notably in the issue of subsidized homeownership—the system has become so cumbersome that it threatens to collapse around our ears.

Today, for example, economist Isabel Sawhill points out, purchases of new homes "absorb more than 100 percent of personal savings in the United States, compared to less than 25 percent as recently as 1970. Encouraging such purchases drains savings away from investments in the modernization of factories and equipment." Sawhill suggests that we either provide people with direct grants for purchases, a practice that would quickly expose how many of our housing subsidies go to the rich, or remove housing subsidies entirely and use them to reduce the deficit and/or increase low-income housing.[56]

We urgently need a debate about the best ways of supporting families in modern America, without blinders that prevent us from seeing the full extent of dependence and interdependence in American life. As long as we pretend that only poor or abnormal families need outside assistance, we will shortchange poor families, overcompensate rich ones, and fail to come up with effective policies for helping families in the middle.

Family economic policy is not the only issue that could be debated more productively if we discarded the myth of the self-sufficient family. Many contemporary analysts explain almost every modern social, political, and cultural ill by the fact that individuals have supposedly abandoned the family as the basic unit of commitment, welfare, and morality. The decay of America's most cherished institutions, according to these commentators, has occurred because people have ceased to place the family at the center of their moral universe and to rely on family values for guidance in their political lives. As Rockford Institute President Allan Carlson puts it, America's founders

> understood the family to be the social unit that reconciled liberty with order, that kept the individual's interests in balance with the interests of community and posterity. We have already paid a huge price for forgetting that lesson, a price that ranges from high levels of crime to environmental degradation. The proper response, at both the policy and personal levels, is *a turn toward home*.[57]

In the next chapter, I will argue that this solution has been tried before and found wanting. In the late nineteenth century, the ideals of economic and emotional family self-sufficiency that had begun to evolve in the eighteenth century were decisively severed from their original connection to larger principles of civic virtue, enlightened self-interest, and a gender division of labor whose social responsibilities extended beyond the family. Debates about political ethics and societal responsibilities became compressed into polemics about personal morality and family relations—a process that we have recently seen taken to painful extremes in election campaigns and partisan political disputes. The "turn toward home" did not solve, but actually exacerbated, the social problems in the Gilded Age of the 1870s and 1880s. A similar dynamic occurred with the rediscovery of traditional family values in what may be called the "second Gilded Age" of the 1970s and 1980s.

5

Strong Families, the Foundation of a Virtuous Society:

The Family and Civic Responsibility

BY the end of the 1980s, there was widespread consensus that the past two decades had seen an erosion of civic commitment and social responsibility in America. It had been an "age of excess," people agreed, a time of acquisitiveness, self-gratification, and individual irresponsibility. Selfishness had run rampant—Wall Street financiers had defrauded small investors, high-flying developers had plundered the Department of Housing and Urban Development, middle-class parents had been too busy with careers to help their children with their homework, and urban teens had committed murder to get a pair of jogging shoes.

Annual surveys by the American Council on Education reported that the number of college students who believed financial affluence to be essential had increased from 45 percent in 1967 to more than 70 percent in 1987, while the proportion who considered it important to develop a meaningful philosophy of life fell from 84 percent to 40 percent. By 1989, a national poll found that only 24 percent of young Americans considered improving their community an important goal; 72 percent said that their main purpose in life was "being successful in job or career." In another poll, 67 percent of Americans asserted that "children do not have an obligation to their parents regardless of what their parents have done for them." Conversely, more and more cars sported bumper stickers declaring that "We're spending our children's inheritance."[1]

For many observers, the social irresponsibility, political alienation, and "me-first" hedonism of the period could be traced to the collapse of a traditional family morality that once held economic self-interest in check and imbued the young with the values of "responsible citizenship." Ever since the late nineteenth century, when President Theodore Roosevelt warned that the nation's future rested on "the right kind of home life," politicians have argued that civic virtue begins at home. As President Ronald Reagan put it in 1984: "Strong families are the foundation of society."[2]

A counterpoint to the materialism and self-absorption of the 1970s and 1980s, accordingly, was the call to revive commitment and responsibility through a "rediscovery" of family values. In 1979, John Howard of the Rockford Institute laid out the basic argument: Only in a family can a child learn to accommodate "his desires to the inherent requirements of the family group, and to comprehend and embrace as desirable and useful the concepts of duty, commitment, humility, authority, magnanimity, integrity and all the other elements of emotional maturity." The survival of "a responsible free society" depends on strengthening "the ties and obligations, the sacrifices and rewards of family life."[3]

This theme was not limited to conservatives. Betty Friedan, founder of the National Organization for Women (NOW), argued that women had to strengthen not only family life but also women's special values, in order to improve public policy; liberal Democrats and union activists increasingly identified themselves with a profamily platform. By 1990, "60 Minutes" commentator Andy Rooney spoke for many on both ends of the political spectrum in blaming America's social ills on "bad parents." Growing numbers of such parents, he charged, were producing kids "who feel no responsibility toward their family, their neighbors, or their country."[4]

In 1988, there was a brief flurry of hope that things had begun to turn around. "The Eighties Are Over," announced magazines such as *Newsweek* and *Advertising Age,* pointing to the sobering effect of the AIDS epidemic and the 1987 stock market crash or citing the renewed sentimentality about babies in popular movies. Author Tom Wolfe, chronicler of the rich and famous, hazarded the opinion that "it will no longer be as chic to flaunt wealth," while trendspotter Faith Popcorn predicted that people would embrace "family-oriented life styles," stay home to watch television, and even put on a little weight. *Good Housekeeping* magazine announced that it had discovered "the biggest social movement since the 1960s"—a move "toward the home and the family and traditional values." "My mother," crooned a female voice in a radio spot for the magazine. "My mother was convinced the center of the world was 36 Maplewood Drive. Her idea of a good time was Sunday dinner….I'm beginning to think my mother really knew what she was doing."[5]

As it turned out, the epitaph for 1980s excess was slightly premature. In August 1989, Gayfryd Steinberg, wife of New York financier Saul Steinberg, threw her husband a birthday party with an estimated cost of a million dollars. It featured Oriental rugs spread on the lawns of their country estate, ten tableaux vivants of famous paintings, such as Rembrandt's *Danae,* and identical twins dressed as mermaids frolicking in the swimming pool. A few weeks later Malcolm Forbes flew 700 guests to Tangiers for his own birthday extravaganza, which included 600 belly dancers, a 274-man honor guard, and 271 servants to wash the roasted lamb grease off revelers' hands.[6]

But for much of the country, the "Lifestyles of the Rich and Famous" had palled. "Family is big," commented *Newsday* in an end-of-year review of 1989 themes in popular culture. "So is tradition. Domesticity. Nesting." In 1990 and 1991, pop-sociologists reprised their obituaries for the "age of excess"; after all, they pointed out, upscale restaurants were serving down-home foods such as meat loaf and mashed potatoes. *Good Housekeeping* took out full-page ads in newspapers and other magazines to announce that the 1990s would be the "Decade of Decency." Other publications heralded the arrival of the "nurturing nineties" or the "we decade." Faith Popcorn averred that business was now embarrassed by the "glitz blitz" of the 1980s and would be "making responsible decisions for society." It was hard to pick up a magazine without reading that yuppies tired of materialism had abandoned networking for the joys of cocooning. Wire-service features were titled "More Americans Opt for the Simple Life," "Baby Boomers Dropping Out of Fast Track," and "The Age of the Yuppie Is Dying." Even advertisements for four-wheel-drive vehicles promised to deliver a "kinder, gentler America." At the end of 1991, a *USA Today* cover story declared that "Conspicuous Consumption Is Déclassé."[7]

The main evidence for these optimistic projections was the "rediscovery of family values" indicated in national polls, the popularity of books such as *The Power of the Family,* and the revival of magazines such as *Traditional Home.* Some cable television channels began to exist almost entirely on reruns of "The Donna Reed Show," "Leave It to Beaver," "My Three Sons," and "Father Knows Best." In the movie

industry, announced *USA Weekend* magazine, "Family Fare Is Hot."
Newsweek pointed out that in advertising circles, the Donald Trump
image no longer sold goods: "Like so many icons of the age of excess, it seems the power-broker image is going the way of Gordon
Gekko. Advertising's new male icon for the '90s? Dear old Dad."
Best-selling authors told inspiring anecdotes about people who got
off the fast track and into the joys of family. Some observers noted
that as baby boomers had families of their own, they even tended to
return to church. *Time* magazine summed it up in 1991: "Tired of
trendiness and materialism, Americans are rediscovering the joys of
home life, basic values, and things that last."[8]

A few skeptics suggested that the return to church of many 1990s
families was more a new form of child care and recreation than a fervent moral rededication. Advertisers admitted that commercials fea-
turing domestic fathers did not reflect substantive change in male
roles as much as they tapped into women's wishful thinking: "Nothing pleases a woman like an ad with a father and a cute child." The
rich did not cut back on spending, just on conspicuous spending: As
one ad agency executive noted, "stealth wealth" was the new thing.
But for many observers, the rediscovery of family raised the possibility that America would begin once more to create "responsible, honest, producing" members of society.[9]

At last, it seemed, America was accepting the proposition Ronald
Reagan had laid out in his 1986 State of the Union address: "Private
values must be at the heart of public policies." As Andy Rooney put
it, after listing the kinds of things needed to create a decent family
life—eating dinner together, for example, and parents who read to
their children: "If every child had these things while he or she was
growing up, there would be nothing to worry about for the future of
the world."[10]

Private Values versus Public Values

But the idea that private values and family affections form the heart
of public life is not at all traditional. It represents a sharp break with
Enlightenment thought and the early republican tradition, which
held that public values—the transformation of private interests into
contractual obligations and political compacts—were qualitatively
different from and superior to private values of love and personal

nurturance. "Every man in a republic," declared educator and physician Benjamin Rush, "is public property." John Adams argued that the foundation of a virtuous republic must be "a positive Passion for the public good....Superior to all private Passions." The passion to have a baby or spend more time with one's family was not high on the founders' list of public virtues.[11]

As we saw in chapter 3, Enlightenment thought stressed the role of "enlightened self-interest" in *transforming* private preoccupations into civic responsibility. Liberal theorists conceptualized men's pursuit of self-interest in more individualistic and competitive terms, but they balanced it by women's altruism, which they did not initially confine to the private nuclear family. Women were thought to have a general social responsibility for fostering morality, not merely a family one; men were expected to take overall responsibility for women and children (at least of their own class and race), not dedicate themselves solely to their own wife and kids.

The notion that enhancing private family morality could substitute for forging public values and societal bonds developed comparatively late in American history. Far from being a source of social commitment and responsibility, this chapter suggests, such a notion helped erode those traits. The "turn toward home" that some people offer as a basis for societal renewal was first proposed a little more than one hundred years ago, in a period that bears a striking resemblance to our own. It inaugurated a personalistic approach to morality that eventually intensified the very individualism that modern proponents of "home life and basic values" believe themselves to be rejecting.

The mid-1870s to the early 1890s, like the mid-1970s to the early 1990s, saw reckless self-seeking and conspicuous consumption among the rich, growing insecurity for workers, and a middle-class retreat from previous engagement in social reform. At the same time, the first Gilded Age, like the second, produced a new idealization of private life, along with impassioned efforts to "improve" other people's personal and familial morals. Yet the triumph of the nuclear family ideal and the spread of private morality in the late nineteenth century did not counteract the political and economic inequities of the day. Instead, it justified abstention from social reform and toleration of economic injustice.

As enlightened self-interest gradually gave way to immediate self-interest in the economy and polity, the nuclear family was made the sole repository for standards of decency, duty, and altruism. In this role, I shall argue, private family relations became less a preparation ground or supporting structure for civic responsibility than a *substitute* for such responsibility. And in the long run, even commitment within the family began to buckle, since it was detached from its foundation in larger infrastructures of political responsibility, social activism, and collective obligation. The private family, in this sense, was a halfway house on the road to modern "me-first" individualism.

Traditional Restraints on American Individualism

In chapter 3, I discussed the growing reliance on gender differences, love, and family life in the early modern period, as a counterweight to economic individualism. Initially, though, idealization of gender differences and family bonds coexisted with many collective or community restraints on self-interest outside the family. Until at least the second half of the nineteenth century, there were many other deterrents to individual self-seeking besides the nuclear family.

Antebellum religion, for example, set clear limits to the spread of unfettered competition and calculative egoism. The strict determinism of Puritanism faded in the late eighteenth century; by the mid-nineteenth century, Protestant evangelists had rejected predestination, arguing that the individual was responsible for his or her own fate. Although this could lead to a more condemnatory attitude toward the poor, it did not sanction unrestrained individual ambition; indeed, it encouraged strict standards of personal responsibility for converting those who might be saved—and the initial optimism of evangelicalism put the vast majority of people in that category. Evangelical sects may have condoned withdrawal from traditional social hierarchies, but at least initially they demanded increased effort in voluntary social duties. The most ardent moral reform activists and members of antislavery societies, for example, were often from evangelical backgrounds—though they generally broke from these backgrounds as they became more committed to political and social action.[12]

Secular beliefs also limited self-seeking. Enlightenment traditions combined with the political radicalization of the American Revolution to create a strong concern for promoting equality, cooperation, and community. Most urban craftsmen, rural farmers, and republican political leaders agreed with Noah Webster that "equality of property" is "the very soul of a republic." Thomas Jefferson, for example, devised numerous schemes to preserve small farmers; James Madison desired to "reduce extreme wealth towards a state of mediocrity" and to remove "unnecessary opportunities" for accumulation. Right up through the Civil War, American legal and political thought assumed that business corporations could be chartered only to serve "the general welfare" or "convenience of the public" and must subordinate "private interests" or profit-seeking to those ends.[13]

Prior to the Civil War, there was no question in people's minds that a public morality, distinct from private probity and equally or more important, was a central component of identity. In the Jeffersonian tradition, public engagement was considered the primary badge of personal character; *honor* and *virtue* were political words, not sexual ones. They designated an individual's "civic altruism," especially a man's willingness to take on political responsibilities. To describe someone as a "private" person was unflattering; a preoccupation with private morality and happiness, no matter how upright, had antisocial connotations. "When Jefferson spoke of pursuing happiness," journalist and author Garry Wills reminds us, he was not referring to a subjective or private state of mind, far less to a retreat into the family. "He meant a public happiness which is measurable."[14]

Self-reliance, similarly, "had a clearly collective context in the biblical and republican traditions. It was as a *people* that we had acted [and should strive to act] independently and self-reliantly." Self-reliance was not a civic virtue itself, merely a precondition: Only a person "free from domination by any landlord, employer, or political patron" could be expected to debate public policy intelligently rather than slavishly obeying the dictates of superiors. Both upper-class and artisan definitions of manhood in the early republic stressed public service as well as personal autonomy. Active involvement in politics and community affairs, as well as solidarity with others of the same class, was an essential ingredient of individualism in its early form.[15]

The "anti-institutionalism" of antebellum America, which later generations have confused with rejection of government or community restraints, grew out of a widespread belief in the perfectability of man and the possibility of cooperation. Far from being a Social Darwinist call for a struggle of the "fittest" against "inferior" members of society, anti-institutionalism was merely an expression of confidence that humans were intelligent and moral enough to construct a democratic society without being directed by a social or religious "elect."[16]

Essayist and poet Ralph Waldo Emerson was perhaps the most extreme proponent of American individualism prior to the Civil War, but even his notion of self-reliance was qualitatively different from later versions: It was antimaterialistic and militantly antislavery; it led to an admiration for the abolitionist John Brown as a man who "loves an idea better than all [material] things in the world." Emerson's most recent biographer contends that later attempts to paint Emerson as a proponent of economic competitiveness were "blatant corruptions of his ideals."[17]

These ideological limits to individualism were enforced by material conditions. Well into the nineteenth century, economic and social life remained particularistic, locally oriented, and dependent on personal ties. As philosopher Alan Wolfe points out, markets originally developed out of face-to-face relations of solidarity and cooperation. Although "they tend to destroy what makes them work" in their transition from the local level to a unitary, standardized system, their initial effect is to mobilize interpersonal networks and increase local solidarities. Numerous social histories demonstrate that such collaboration increased in America during the first half of the nineteenth century. Not until the 1870s did agricultural producers fully commit to the primacy of market motives over community demands in their production. Only in the last quarter of the nineteenth century, argue two recent economic historians of Western industrialization, did separate, local markets merge into one standardized, impersonal market that was "taken for granted" as the primary organizing feature of economic life.[18]

Even the division of labor between men and women in antebellum America was not immediately identified with a split between public and private life. Private life, moreover, was not yet equated with the family. In Enlightenment thought, public and private passions, equally necessary, interacted in an intricate dynamic of "checks and balances" rather than existing in opposition or isolation. In the early nineteenth century, as we have seen, male and female differences came to comprise yet another system of checks and balances, but each part of this system incorporated some elements of public and private life, and a woman's responsibility for home life was not originally confined to her own family.[19]

Although the ideology of domesticity was later to justify a retreat into family privacy, initially it brought women out of their homes into maternal associations, moral reform societies, charity organizations, missionary work, evangelical proselytizing, and temperance groups. These voluntary associations emerged "where the segregation of work and home, public and private life, and men's and women's spheres was incomplete." Despite strict prohibitions on female participation in electoral politics, the original notion of domesticity made it socially acceptable—even morally obligatory—for women to play a leading role in public moral discussion. "In some ways," historian Mary Ryan comments, "the term mother's empire symbolizes the extent of women's social jurisdiction during the antebellum era better than the word family."[20]

The idea that the family could handle sole or even primary responsibility for checking selfish individualism and creating virtuous citizens, in other words, was *not* a traditional American value. By the 1850s, it is true, there was a growing sense among some proponents of domesticity that the "true home" should be "isolated" and its love "exclusive." There was also a clear tendency to reduce women's moral responsibilities to those connected with family duties. But prior to the war, these trends were inhibited by the heavy involvement of other supporters of domesticity in antislavery and other reform movements.[21]

Only after the Civil War did the conservatizing strains of the 1850s win general acceptance among the middle class and the values of domesticity become confined to nuclear families. Only then was women's "moral ecology" reduced to the family's own backyard. The doctrine of the private family as the center of morality and personal identity, a critical redefinition and contraction of older concepts, was established by a middle class that had retreated from larger ethical concerns. Its prominence in both the first and the second Gilded Age suggests that concentration on private values may be a symptom of socioeconomic and moral fragmentation, not a remedy for it.

In both the 1870s to 1880s and the 1970s to 1980s, sentimentalization of private life coincided with a destruction of limits to unrestrained wealth-seeking and political ambition. The retreat into privatism in the first Gilded Age was more family-oriented than the retreat into privatism in the second Gilded Age, but those who seek to counter modern individualism by reviving the family-based morality of the earlier period have misunderstood its nature. Cultivation of private family life represented a repudiation of larger social and political obligations and accelerated the social atomization that has produced modern extremes of individualism.

The First Gilded Age: Emergence of a New Conservatism

The Gilded Age of the mid-1870s to mid-1890s resembles the period since the mid-1970s in some intriguing ways. After the intense idealism of the 1860s, most middle-class individuals entered a phase of political disengagement and economic reorientation that required them to disavow old alliances and beliefs. Turning away from social activism, many people focused on their personal lives and material ambitions. It would be only a partial exaggeration to argue that this era provided a foretaste of what we would later call the yuppie phenomenon, including the recent rediscovery of the joys of "cocooning."

In the 1860s, idealistic middle-class Northerners had played a leading role in social reform; they had high expectations about the kind of society that would be established once the evils of slavery were eradicated. The Civil War, however, although it ended slavery, did not produce the results for which optimists had hoped. "Instead of purging the nation once and for all of self-seeking, materialism, and corruption, the war opened the floodgates for the greatest tide of personal and political selfishness the nation had ever seen." It also led to a consolidation of state power in the service of wealthy industrial interests.[22]

By 1877, the government's new political and economic priorities were clearly established. Federal troops were withdrawn from the South, leaving blacks and radical Republicans at the mercy of the Ku Klux Klan and other terrorist organizations, but these troops were used for the first time in labor disputes, to break the Great Railroad Strike and the St. Louis General Strike. Even though there was an expansion of state aid to business and a strengthening of the state's repressive apparatus, public relief fell into disrepute, and the Supreme Court ruled that government resources could not be used to protect black Americans against discrimination. Anti-institutionalism was dead, but so was perfectionism: The state would intervene to foster industrial production and social order yet would leave questions of civil rights, social justice, and poverty strictly alone.[23]

At the top of the social scale there was a wave of financial speculation and a surge in the numbers and visibility of the super-rich. Between fifty and sixty millionaires existed in America prior to the Civil War; by the 1890s, there were 4,047. Economist Robert Gallman estimates that the share of wealth held by the top .031 percent of the population rose from 6.9 percent in 1840 to between 7.2 percent and 7.6 percent in 1850, and then (despite a temporary leveling

caused by the disappearance of property in slaves) jumped to between 14.3 percent and 19.1 percent in 1890. The top 5 percent of
the population increased their share of national income by 4 to 8
percentage points during the Gilded Age. The second Gilded Age
saw a similar "plutographic revolution," though this time it produced decamillionaires and billionaires.[24]

At the same time, poverty spread among workers and farmers
from the 1870s to the 1890s, just as it did one hundred years later.
Spells of unemployment became more frequent; child labor increased. In Pittsburgh, there was a 75 percent rise in rates of accidental death among steelworkers. Housing and health conditions in
urban tenements deteriorated. Mortgage debt grew two-and-a-half
times faster than agricultural wealth, while government deflationary
policies, historian Lawrence Goodwyn notes, favored "banker-
creditors" but weighed heavily on the nation's "producer-debtors."
African Americans were driven out of skilled trades. The Oriental exclusion movement grew virulent, and in some Western cities, the entire Asian population was forcibly expelled.[25]

The dominant ideology became much more harsh than it was previously. Social Darwinism preached that millionaires exemplified the
"survival of the fittest." The poor were labeled "unfit," a drag on the
race. To preserve the unfit in any way was to court disaster. "Nature's
cure for most social and political diseases is better than man's," argued the president of Columbia University, as did his successors in
the 1970s and 1980s, George Gilder and Charles Murray.[26]

In 1870, the Reverend Russell Conwell wrote the first draft of his
famous lecture, "Acres of Diamonds," which he delivered more than
6,000 times during the next twenty-five years and which in print
form reached an audience of millions. "I say that you ought to get
rich," he told his followers, "and it is your duty to get rich." Conversely, "there is not a poor person in the United States who was not
made so by his own shortcomings, or by the shortcomings of some
one else. It is all wrong to be poor, anyhow." Or, as Conwell's theo-
logical successors put it in the 1980s, "just claim what you need." "If
you let a hurricane or a tornado destroy your property, it's your own
fault."[27]

The 1980s attack on welfare also was foreshadowed in the first
Gilded Age. After the Civil War, writes historian George Fredrickson,
charity organizations tried "to prevent 'irresponsible' expressions of
pity and compassion from...interfering with the struggle for existence." Charitable money should go to libraries, works of art, or the
provision of advice, they argued, not material aid to the poor, be-

cause a "gift" of any kind was inherently corrupting. A single cord of wood, declared one reformer in 1887, could "ruin the best family in Boston." The industrialist Andrew Carnegie told of an acquaintance who once gave twenty-five cents to a beggar: "the quarter-dollar given that night will probably work more injury than all the money will do good which its thoughtless donor will ever be able to give in true charity."[28]

I do not want to overstate the similarities between the two periods. Among the many differences is the fact that in the 1870s and 1880s, growing economic inequalities and insecurities were at least attached to an expansion of industrial capacity and real production that paved the way for improvements in workers' real wages, something sadly lacking in the second Gilded Age. Repression against unionists, African Americans, and other minorities was much more violent in the first Gilded Age, although working-class resistance also was more militant. There was a widespread agrarian movement; strong third parties existed in several regions; the state was much weaker; and national corporations were not yet fully consolidated. In both periods, though, there was an orgy of wealth-seeking among the rich, an intensification of economic distress among the poor, and a retreat of the middle class from previous involvement in social reform.

There were some oppositional currents, of course, as there always are. In the first Gilded Age, as in the second, thousands of people continued to grapple with larger moral issues, and a significant minority attempted to ameliorate social ills. Women's clubs got involved in reform projects; temperance workers sometimes stopped denouncing drunkards long enough to consider the societal conditions that led people to drink; Helen Hunt Jackson's *Century of Dishonor* spurred indignation at the treatment of American Indians; workers organized; the Populist movement grew in rural areas; African Americans formed self-help groups; and some religious communities began to preach the "social gospel."

But the bulk of the middle class turned its back on reform. The depression of 1873 to 1877, for example, like its counterpart one hundred years later, shifted the attention of most middle-class Americans toward maintaining their own financial status. Afterward, as economic insecurity increased in the working class, some middle-class people also slipped downward in the reshuffling of occupations. Traditional routes to middle-class proprietorship and self-employment declined. Yet simultaneously, falling prices, expansion of cheap immigrant and child labor, abolition of the wartime income tax, and new mass production stimulated by the war all allowed the middle class, and a few skilled workers as well, access to consumer luxuries that a few years earlier had been confined to the rich. Pay rates rose in several new, expanding middle-class professions, and new opportunities for making and spending money appeared for those with a relatively small initial advantage in capital.

As in the 1980s, the middle class of the 1880s was kept busy maneuvering through a rapidly changing economy. Caught between the stick of economic dislocation and the carrot of expanding consumerism, it was not inclined to take assertive political action or to look with favor on workers' attempts to raise wages and win the eight-hour day. Not until the late 1890s did the middle class participate in a revival of mass action around women's suffrage, make new alliances with workers and immigrants, and begin to move in the direction of Progressive Era reform.

In the short run, most middle-class Americans rejected pressures from working people, blacks, and immigrants for additional reform. E. L. Godkin, editor of *The Nation,* expressed the viewpoint of the postwar middle-class "reformer":

> His father was occupied in assailing monstrous and palpable evils, and getting the government into the hands of the many; the son has...no abuse of any magnitude to attack....His work is to adjust the relations of the individuals of the great crowd to each other, so that they may be enabled to lead a quiet, and comfortable, and free life.[29]

The "quiet, and comfortable, and free life" for most middle-class Americans was one in which they could establish personal economic security and retreat from the social disorder of rapid industrialization. In the postwar period, the middle class, an inchoate group in the antebellum years, consolidated itself into a distinct, self-conscious, and exclusive entity. There was a sharp increase in residential segregation, both in the expanding suburbs and in the older, formerly more integrated districts of the cities. Many local histories show that the moral community linking the middle class to other classes had fragmented by the end of the 1880s. Fraternal societies ceased to play their original role of bringing together a community of producers to reinforce "a collective identity based upon workplace solidarity." They increasingly oriented themselves away from substantive political activities toward rituals that bolstered middle-class masculine identity or served psychological "tribalization" functions.[30]

Church membership grew steadily over the period, but the focus of religion narrowed. Fundamentalism tended to replace evangelicalism, and revivalism turned more conservative. Mainstream religious figures "withdrew progressively from [political] involvement....They confined their social message to calls for order and law and their ethical appeals to calls for repentance from private vice and change to personal holiness."[31]

In the 1850s, the Reverend Horace Bushnell had represented a minority voice within evangelical circles in his insistence that building Christian families was better than encouraging "romantic notions" for the "reorganization of society." After the Civil War, other religious leaders joined Bushnell in discouraging reform and validating the pursuit of economic success in the here and now. Bishop William Lawrence of Massachusetts declared that "Godliness is in league with riches." Wealth, asserted Bushnell, was "a reward and honor which God delights to bestow upon an upright people."[32]

However, few middle-class Americans were prepared to justify their social disengagement entirely in terms of unvarnished self-interest. Many felt a nagging sense of guilt about their abandonment of older community norms, and a revulsion for the excesses of the rich, which, as in the 1980s, had an unprecedented visibility. Businessmen and politicians plundered the public treasury. The rich abandoned earlier inhibitions about flaunting their wealth and proceeded to spend in ways that invite comparison with those of Forbes and Steinberg. Montana mining baron Marcus Daly constructed a lavish hotel that he kept fully staffed so that even when there were no other guests, he could eat in solitary splendor in a dining room built to hold 500. At one Newport Beach society party, sandboxes lined the tables and guests were given trowels to dig in them for buried precious stones, which they were then allowed to take home. The self-display of Leona Helmsley or Donald Trump was surely equaled by H. A. W. Tabor of Colorado, who insisted that the portrait of Shakespeare in the magnificent opera house he built for Denver be replaced with his own, demanding, "What the hell has Shakespeare ever done for Denver?" President Hayes and his wife were said to have spent $15,000 on a new dinner set for the White House—at a time when 85 percent of industrial workers earned less than $800 a year.[33]

The New Focus on Family Morality

Middle-class Americans, seeking a way of distancing themselves from such extravagant behavior without abandoning their resistance to change from below, found an answer in a "turn toward home." Anticipating Phyllis Schlafly's contention that America is a two-class society, divided not between rich and poor but between those who hold decent family values and those who do not,[34] middle-class spokesmen lumped the upper and lower classes together as lacking proper family values. The rich and the poor, they argued, were immersed in materialism and self-gratification, whereas the middle class worked for family betterment.

Conwell's defense of seeking wealth, for example, was in part justified by condemning those who already had wealth. Too often, he told his approving audiences, a rich father and mother raised their son as a "weak, little lily-fingered sissy sort of a boy" who could not even get around town without a chauffeur to drive him. Horatio Alger, similarly, always contrasted his plucky heroes with pretentious, aristocratic snobs who thought they were too good for hard work.[35]

Such caricatures allowed the middle class to differentiate itself from the "amoral" rich without feeling any duty to oppose their actions or construct an alternative political morality. They also nicely sidestepped the complaints of the poor, since they condemned or satirized only the most extreme examples of upper-class avarice—and then equated these with the "materialism" of the poor.

Contemporary exposés of Leona Helmsley, Donald Trump, Michael Milken, and other such easy targets have a similar effect. Phillips has argued that the popularity of Tom Wolfe's 1987 *Bonfire of the Vanities* reflected a revulsion against the values of the 1980s. Perhaps so, but it was a revulsion that, like its 1880s precursors, promoted a self-righteous, conservative, antipolitical response. In each period, popular social commentary allowed "decent" people to define themselves in opposition to both the dependent or criminal poor and the idle or profligate rich. In comparison, of course, the honest, hard-working "middling sort" who minds his own business and takes care of his own family need engage in no self-criticism. He can only congratulate himself on his freedom from vice—unless, of course, he is so stupid as to give a quarter to a beggar or, in Wolfe's version, allow demagogues from the underclass to make him feel guilty.

Middle-class Americans elevated family values and private rectitude into the defining features of Gilded Age morality. Aside from attempts to convince rich and poor to adopt virtuous family values, they largely abstained from social reform, asserting that private morality and family life represented a higher and purer duty than did political or social activism, which was said to be inevitably tainted by the need for compromise and expediency. As sociologist Richard Sennett points out, once the family became "a moral yardstick with which to measure the public realm," public life began to be seen as morally inferior.[36]

Many religious leaders renounced politics entirely, consigning moral and ethical issues exclusively to the private realm. "To them," writes religious historian Martin Marty, "religion had to do with sequestered and segregated areas of life. The personal, the 'spiritual,' the familial, and that having to do with private life comprised the whole." Postwar revivalists told people not to attach "undue importance" to the "connection of Christians one to another." Personal "manners," "individual growth," and family building counted for more than community organization or social reforms.[37]

Domesticity also became more private and less political in the second half of the nineteenth century. The militancy of moral reform societies faded; women's claims to moral superiority came to center more on personal comportment and less on religious commitment or social work. After the Civil War, public representations of women ceased to personify civic virtue (as in older images of the Goddesses of Liberty and Justice) and dramatized instead women's domestic functions. Virtue lost its earlier political meaning and became reduced to an assessment of whether a woman was likely to remain sexually chaste until marriage or be faithful to her husband afterward; character came to describe a man's personal traits, especially his behavior toward his family. Indeed, in a remarkable reversal of republican ideology, the man or woman who pursued larger moral concerns might even be labeled selfish. Conwell contemptuously dismissed a man who referred to himself at a Philadelphia prayer meeting as "one of God's poor": "I wonder what his wife thinks about that?"[38]

The Limits of Family Morality

The attempt by Gilded Age Americans to carve out a moral oasis in the family was very similar to the reaction of many modern people appalled by the materialism of the 1970s and 1980s. Then, as now, however, it did not create a "Decade of Decency."

First, adoption of personal morality and middle-class family values did not solve the problems of the poor. Farm families worked harder and harder only to fall further and further behind. Forty percent of industrial workers in the late nineteenth century lived below the poverty level; another 45 percent hovered just above it. Most working-class families in the late nineteenth century, like growing numbers in the late twentieth, could not rely solely on a male breadwinner, whatever their personal desires for domesticity; they required more than one income to survive. Since the housework of women was still essential to family survival, it was children rather than wives who worked, and I have already noted the appalling conditions that child laborers faced.[39]

Second, the elevation of family life to the center of morality sanctioned a rising degree of consumerism and selfishness within the middle class, by distinguishing its legitimate spending from the "irresponsible" dissipation of others. Russell Conwell assumed that people who earned money would spend it first on purchasing a family home. This achievement made the middle-class man morally better than the upper-class one, who could only "say to his wife, 'My mother gave me that, my mother gave me that, and my mother gave me this,' until his wife wishes she had married his mother." Purchase of a home also made middle-class Americans morally better than the poor, "for they that own their own homes are made more honorable and honest and pure, and true and economical and careful, by owning the home."[40]

It was only a small step from this kind of reasoning to the conclusion that building a comfortable home life was the most morally worthwhile act one could undertake. The popular preacher Henry Ward Beecher gradually shifted his message after the Civil War from emphasis on the corruptions of wealth and urban life to a defense of private domesticity. Beecher castigated railroad workers for not accepting the 10 percent to 20 percent wage cut proposed by the railroad magnates in 1877, thundering that "the man who cannot live on good bread and water is not fit to live," but he was much more indulgent toward middle-class material aspirations. The family table, he claimed, was "a kind of altar, a place sacred and so to be made as complete in its furnishings as may be." Spending money on the family home would inspire "little children, the poor, laborers, common people of all kinds" to improve their own lot.[41]

Recognizing that some of his former colleagues in the antislavery and reform movements might have "serious scruples" about repudiating wider social obligations to the "body politic," Beecher offered this ingenious reassurance to his middle-class audience:

The family is the *digesting organ* of the body politic. *The very way to feed the community is to feed the family.* This is the point of contact for each man with the society in which he lives. Through the family chiefly we are to act upon society. Money contributed there is contributed to the whole. [Emphasis added.][42]

A whole generation seems to have taken his words quite literally—judging from my grandmother's repeated injunctions to "think of the starving children of China" and clean my plate.

The Seamy Side of Family Moralism

Once morality became centered on private behavior and family standards, even the discovery of poverty at the end of the 1880s led more to moral muckraking than to serious efforts at social reform or political action. The 1887 autobiography of a retired police chief invited readers to "go with me in imagination and see the wicked character" of the city's slums; one hundred years later the *Wall Street Journal*'s front page enticed readers with details of "How a Florida Mother Needing Cash for Crack Handed Over Her Baby." Contemporary "cocooning" was anticipated by Gilded Age families retreating from the terrors of what Jacob Riis called "How the Other Half Lives." "Families cuddle the joys of the fireside when spurred by tales of dire lone agony," wrote the novelist Stephen Crane, whose early journalistic career was built on his ability to impart vivid detail to such tales. It is hard to escape the impression that there was something slightly salacious in the cuddling together of middle-class Americans who read these exposés, just as it is hard to believe Kitty Kelley's claim that the gossip and sexual innuendo in her unauthorized biography of Nancy Reagan were intended to reveal the "hypocrisy" of a couple who presided over "an era of greed and avarice with no moral compass."[43]

Moral reformer Anthony Comstock, who led the fight for criminalization of birth control and abortion, wrote sensational accounts of "gambling saloons,…poolrooms, low theatres, and rumholes." In addition to entrapping doctors by pretending to be a desperate, poverty-stricken father in need of birth control or an abortion for his wife, Comstock collected "immoral" books, photographs, and "articles made of rubber" with a zeal that bordered on obsession. "In one case," reports historian Robert Bremner, "Comstock, his assistant, a reporter, and a plainclothes policemen visited a house of prostitution and paid five dollars each to view a performance entitled 'Busy Fleas.' They must have wanted their money's worth because it was not until the conclusion of the dance that they arrested the performers."[44]

Personal moralism about sex and family was quite compatible with public or social amorality. Congressman James G. Blaine helped push through Comstock's bill prohibiting birth-control advertisements from being sent through the mail, but no ethical niceties prevented him from working as a railroad lobbyist and financial speculator while Speaker of the House of Representatives. After he handed down a decision benefiting the Little Rock & Fort Smith Railroad, the grateful company allotted him bond sales that netted a commission of $200,000. One hundred years later, others combined private moralism with public irresponsibility. Charles Keating, of S&L scandal fame, for example, took time out from financial wheeling and dealing to found the antipornography group Citizens for Decent Literature.[45]

But more than hypocrisy or voyeurism was at work here. The new emphasis on family relations and private morality led easily to scapegoating and victim blaming. Poverty and hunger were attributed not to unemployment or low wages but to lack of middle-class family norms; slums were said to be caused by people's lack of a decent respect for family privacy. The triumph of family moralism thus coincided with an "outburst of nativism" and racism.[46]

In 1889, for example, the historian Philip Bruce published *The Plantation Negro as a Freeman*, to both scholarly and popular acclaim. Bruce argued that the problems of black Americans were not due to poverty, discrimination, or racism, but to defects in their family and personal lives. He charged that black parents raised their children without discipline or moral precepts, producing boys with an "unsteady and roving disposition" and "licentious" girls who shamelessly bore illegitimate babies. Or, as columnist Georgie Ann Geyer put it, almost exactly one hundred years later, "the real civil rights problems" of America are "the lack of black male moral authority, the massive number of illegitimate births and the absence of any inculcation of inner control by parents."[47]

When moral muckraking did lead to action, it was often repressive in nature. The parallels between the 1880s and the 1980s are particularly striking here. In each case, romanticization of the family was accompanied by self-righteous, even vindictive, attitudes toward those unable to live up to the idealized image. The discovery of child abuse in the 1870s was a response to a serious problem and led to some important reforms, but abuse was defined so loosely that it often allowed the "child savers" to victimize families whose only fault was being poor or having different values than those of the middle class. Reformers in the 1870s and 1880s argued that it was better to break families apart than offer them charity, because families who received assistance would breed a vicious circle of poverty and dependence. Another reason to break up families was the "immorality" of their parents—a condition for which their poverty was often sufficient evidence.[48]

In the late 1980s and early 1990s as well, identification of the family as the main source of morality frequently led to punitive responses toward parents who failed to live up to the ideal. In 1989, California passed a law providing that parents who fail to control their children's criminal activities could be sentenced to a year in jail and a $2,500 fine. In 1991, New Hampshire decided that parents whose children produce pornography could be charged with a felony. Dermott, Arkansas, enacted an ordinance threatening parents with display in a public stockade and publication of their pictures in the local paper with the caption "Irresponsible Parent." A law in Mississippi made parents of truants liable to a year in jail and a $1,000 fine. Some states began to experiment with programs that denied checks to welfare families whose teenagers missed school.[49]

In Florida, Washington, Illinois, and California, prosecutors brought felony charges against women for harming their fetuses by taking illegal substances when pregnant. Women in South Carolina were tested for cocaine in the maternity ward; if they tested positive, they were turned in to the police and arrested in their hospital beds. When one pregnant woman in Wyoming finally left her abusive husband in 1990, the police took photographs of her bruises, sent her to the hospital, and then arrested her on charges of felony child abuse because she tested positive for alcohol. A number of states have jailed women because authorities estimated that they would not otherwise seek prenatal care.[50]

Serious public policy dilemmas are raised by these cases, but treating them solely as personal, moral, or maternal failures does not take us very far in our thinking. There was, for instance, a catch-22 for many modern mothers, just as there was for those accused of child neglect one hundred years earlier. By the end of the 1980s, growing numbers of pregnant women could not *find* prenatal care. To punish women for not getting prenatal care when we do not recognize public responsibility for providing it is uncomfortably close to the turn-of-the-century practice of penalizing poor mothers for not giving their children the benefits of affluence. Jennifer Johnson, the first woman convicted of a crime after giving birth to a baby who tested positive for drugs, had sought treatment for her addiction while pregnant and been turned away.[51]

In both periods, then, abstract idealization of family and mother-hood coexisted with condemnation of real families and mothers in their imperfect day-to-day existence. An emphasis on private moral-ity led to punishment more often than to prevention, to revenge in-stead of to relief.

But the problems associated with a societal morality based on pri-vate family values extend further than this. Elevation of the family to the center of moral dialogue set in motion a dynamic that impover-ished public life and political discourse, eventually leading to a con-fusion of personality traits with political convictions and a replace-ment of political debates with scandal-mongering.

Family Idealization and the Collapse of Public Life

As long as the idioms of love and family were engaged in a dialogue with those of politics, education, and economics, as in the republican era, notions of fraternity, justice, sisterhood, responsibility, and kin-ship could move back and forth between the two spheres, enriching both. Fraternity could be a model for revolution or antislavery work; sisterhood could inspire charity; conversely, liberty and justice could be claimed for the private sphere without fear that this would wipe out obligation and particularity. But, gradually, the two dialects di-verged, until by the late nineteenth century a totally different lan-guage was used for each. As private family language monopolized the moral vocabulary that formerly had been utilized by a wide range of institutions, discussions of public life became more abstract and di-vorced from everyday experience.

Historian Daniel Rodgers comments on the characteristic "dis-tance" between America's public words, "pitched so far above the af-fairs of daily life, and its liberating words, so close to the skin of the individual self." We have a wealth of names for individual needs and desires and a powerful set of symbols for abstract unity, such as the flag or the Founding Fathers. What Americans have "found much harder to come by [are] clear ways in which to talk about the common bonds and responsibilities of public life." Our vocabulary is "skeletally thin in everyday, middle-level phrases for common, collective action."[52]

It was during the first Gilded Age, with its hardening of the liberal division between political or economic self-interest and family morality, that Americans began to lose their ways of discussing the ethics of policies, institutions, associations, networks, and interactions that operate somewhere in between family love and dog-eat-dog competition. Numerous observers have commented on the shrinking political universe in America during and after the election of 1896, as questions of economic justice and social morality were crowded off the political agenda by personal issues and abstract patriotic posturing. The same year also marked the beginning of the American trend toward declining participation in elections, a trend in striking contrast to the experience of other industrial democracies.[53]

The Gilded Age, then, saw a notable reduction in the conceptual and linguistic tools available for public discourse. During the 1970s and 1980s, there was a similar contraction of morality to personal, individualistic terms. By 1989, when young Americans were asked to describe a good citizen, the overwhelming majority said it was someone who was personally generous and caring; only 12 percent thought good citizenship meant voting or other political involvement—a substantial decline from the figures in the late 1960s and early 1970s.[54]

When the dominant political language cannot express issues of responsibility, commitment, and morality, the only vocabulary for discussing social obligations and needs comes to be the language of love. But this language, as we saw in chapter 3, expresses an individual's obligations to one person only; in the language of love, three's a crowd. Thus the fine old word *intercourse,* which means communication, conversation, or discourse, is now reserved primarily as a synonym for *sex.* Audiences are likely to titter when someone uses the word in its original meaning.

Gradually, in both periods, Americans abandoned the discussion of needs and dependencies that were less than universal but more than dyadic. Today, for example, if we are not owed something as a right in the public world or offered it out of love in the private world, most of us are stymied. We do not have concrete ways of exploring what should be expected of "the policemen, schoolteachers, garbage collectors, drivers' license examiners, pothole fixers, highway planners, missile launchers, and lawmakers who compose our government."[55]

We also have few ways to condemn political or social failures, except to label them a breakdown of love. The language of private relations and family values consequently leads not only to a contraction but also to a deformation of the public realm. When family relations become "our only model for defining what emotionally 'real' relationships are like," we can empathize and interact only with people whom we can imagine as potential lovers or family members. The choice becomes either a personal relationship or none, a familial intimacy or complete alienation. As sociologist Robert Bellah and his collaborators argue, seeking meaning in private family values precludes the development of true community, producing instead the "lifestyle enclave." At best, this brings together only people who share similar private motivations; they construct relationships based on such personal activities as leisure and consumption. At worst, the "lifestyle enclave" leads to suspicion of people who are different and attempts to exclude them from "the family circle."[56]

Using family as a model for public life produces an unrealistic, even destructive, definition of community. With their capacity for public, impersonal discussion reduced, many people demand to share family-type feelings in inappropriate realms. Richard Sennett suggests that with the contraction of the public realm, all social facts, "no matter how impersonal in structure, are converted into matters of personality in order to have a meaning." Our "passion for fantasized intimate disclosure" makes us vulnerable to manipulation by public figures who can project a sincere or outgoing personality; what used to be considered a dignified restraint about discussing personal matters in public is now thought dishonest or "flat." Although the 1980s saw this process taken to new extremes, it is worth noting that the modern American practice of selling candidates' sincerity and family values instead of their positions on issues began during the first Gilded Age.[57]

Periodically, of course, we are disillusioned by the authenticity or the family life of public figures, but seldom do we question the very nature of our expectations. Instead, in an almost total reversal of logic, we blame the public person for betraying our expectations of love, just as we blame the family for failing to create justice and equality. The anger against bad mothers in the private sphere has a corollary in our disappointment with bad father figures in the public.

Private Life and Public Scandal: The "New Moralism" Then and Now

To their credit, most Americans have not been willing to cut the public world entirely loose from moral or ethical surveillance or to evaluate public figures on their feelings or motivations instead of on their behavior. But when people abandon hope of judging public figures by stringent political ethics, periodic personal exposés become the main weapon for controlling their ambitions and actions. In the 1880s and 1890s, the removal of moral intensity from public relations and its concentration on private ones made family relations a tempting target for public disclosure. As public standards and political vocabulary faded, debate by scandal and exposé became the rule.

The preacher Henry Ward Beecher was one of the first to discover the threat that hangs over those who encourage a concentration of public debate on private values. To demonstrate Beecher's hypocrisy in denouncing her "free love" movement, social reformer Victoria Woodhull leaked to the newspapers his alleged affair with one of his parishioners; the resultant scandal was at least as widely debated as the Jim Bakker affair in the 1980s and the Clarence Thomas hearings in 1991. American politics has been wracked by periodic scandals and moral crusades for 200 years, but they were especially virulent in the late nineteenth century, when private morals were first elevated above public virtues in mainstream ideology. Their reemergence in the last decade has similar origins, following the decline of 1960s and early 1970s social and political debate.[58]

It is in this context that we must place America's "New Moralism." Recently, we have seen a series of celebrated scandals over issues that were once considered part of private life. Public figures have been dethroned by revelations about their personal relationships; private nonentities have become public figures by making such revelations. Politicians who courted our votes by touting their home lives rather than their ideas now complain that their families are being invaded by the press, even though their campaign managers regularly leak information to the press about their opponents' personal lives. The confusion has reached the point that some enterprising "sinners" have even offered to reform their private lives in return for public office: The late Senator John Tower promised to quit drinking if confirmed as Secretary of Defense; William Bennett declared he would stop smoking if given a chance to run the nation's health agency. Perhaps Gary Hart's campaign staff should have hinted that if he was put in the Oval Office, he could be kept out of a lot of bedrooms.

There has been much debate over how to evaluate the new scrutiny of public figures' personal lives. Does it represent a breakdown of the double standard that once allowed the wealthy in general and men in particular to run roughshod over the lives of others, exploiting and discarding women with impunity? Does it signal a growing concern about the public consequences of private acts, a more stringent insistence on ethical behavior? Or have we become, as political analyst Harrison Rainie charges, a "culture of hackers," breaking into people's personal lives and reprogramming their reputations? Is this a new McCarthyism, resting on pillory by innuendo? Are the women who recount their sexual misuse in the popular press exposing male hypocrisy, or are they a new kind of gold digger? Are we forging new definitions of public accountability or destroying important distinctions between people's private peccadilloes and their public contributions?[59]

Speaking as a historian, I would have to answer "all of the above." On the one hand, we should beware of romanticizing older divisions between public and private life. Too often, Enlightenment thinkers established "civilized" limits to public debates by defining social inequities as subordinate private matters. Early republican politics, for example, rested on the neat assumption that extermination of Native Americans and enslavement of blacks were prepolitical issues, almost domestic matters. Southerners declared that it was as "impertinent" to criticize slavery as to tell a white man how to treat his wife and children. Native Americans were often referred to as children, protected by the "Great White Father" in Washington. Women's claims for justice were dismissed as family spats.

Some of the "private" scandals we see today represent a challenge to such inequities. Power, money, and sex are bound up in our society in very unsavory ways. To leave these connections unexamined is to ignore the hidden mechanisms reproducing injustice in a nominally democratic society. Isn't it important to know how a public figure uses power at home, how likely his or her judgment is to be warped by personal appetites? Should the compulsive, cold-blooded womanizing of President Kennedy really have gone unreported, especially since some of it apparently linked him to prominent figures in organized crime? Is it totally irrelevant that the Reagans apparently did not find it as easy to "just say no" as their public policies assumed it would be for the poor?

Clearly, many private issues have a political component, while public issues spill over into private life. That is what makes it so problematic, as I will show in chapter 6, to make hard-and-fast generalizations about family privacy and state intervention. Private family relations take place against a background of rules set by public authorities; public inequities of gender, race, or class get transferred into private relations; and family norms affect the ability of individuals to exercise public rights. There is, for example, much more public tolerance of violence within the family than there is of violence among strangers—and this toleration can deprive women or children of their civil rights, or even of life itself.

Too often, however, the scrutiny of private life threatens to swamp all other issues. Precisely because sex and power are bound so tightly in American society, which is a *social* problem, almost all public figures are vulnerable to at least the appearance of sexual impropriety, so that the personal attacks become frighteningly arbitrary. Distinctions fade between appearance and reality, between single transgressions and patterns of deceit. The lines between victim and perpetrator also blur. When Jessica Hahn and Donna Rice pose for men's magazines or for skintight jeans ads and women institute million-dollar paternity suits over one-night stands, it obscures the legitimate reasons for exposing cases of male sexual coercion or irresponsibility: Most sexually abused women have such low self-esteem that they cannot promote themselves so assiduously; most unwed mothers get no support payments from the fathers of their children.

Preoccupation with personal morality and sex reveals above all that, like our predecessors in the first Gilded Age, we lack a clear set of public ethics and political standards of behavior. We focus on private vices because we cannot agree on the definition of a public vice. The confirmation hearings for John Tower generated far more discussion about his drinking and womanizing than about his attitudes toward peace and war or his apparent conflicts of interest in the military-industrial complex. In the Oliver North case, his evasion of constitutional checks and balances was totally overshadowed by the suspicion that one of his improper expenditures was for silk stockings for his secretary, Fawn Hall. When committee members discovered he had only bought tights for his daughter, they were almost completely routed. In the Clarence Thomas hearings, the real debate came over Anita Hill's testimony, not over his qualifications, his oath that he had never discussed *Roe* v. *Wade*, or his misrepresentation of his sister's welfare experience.

In one sense, then, the new moralism about sex and family represents the bankruptcy of our political life. Public policy failures take second place to family irregularities; a political issue such as the status of women is reduced to courtroom brawls over palimony; rampant social ills such as childhood poverty receive far less attention than tales about prominent men who videotape young girls in sex acts.

The answer to the new moralism, however, is not the old hypocrisy. In the 1860s and again in the 1960s, people suggested alternative definitions of the public good that included the personal issues facing women, minorities, working people, and the poor. Toward the end of each period, though, the old narrow definition of the public splintered, but no new political institutions, values, or processes were developed to reconnect its fragments. Instead, dominant opinion ceased to claim that any overarching standards for public life could be agreed on. Questions of morality were displaced onto the private sphere.

The conflation of public morality with private values leads to inevitable oscillations between a repressive, divisive moralism and, in reaction, an extreme, even perverse, "tolerance" of all private behavior, whatever its social consequences. Most of us, unhappy with either extreme, grasp our family values even more tightly, as the one anchor that can protect us from being swept away by the tides of repression and permissiveness. But an anchor does not work in the open ocean. The same factors that erode public life and political standards tend, in the long run, to set personal life and family values adrift. While the antisocial tendencies of Gilded Age privatism were not immediately apparent within the family circle, the collapse of public life in that period paved the way for many recurrent strains in twentieth-century families.

The Fragility of the Private Family

Without the ballast provided by the public sphere, the family began its long slide toward subjectivism, feeding the very individualism that family morality was supposed to counter. It is not that the spread of individualism threatens to destroy the traditional privacy and intensity of family life, as is sometimes claimed; as we have seen, familial privacy and intensity were in many ways *created* by the spread of individualism. But it is certainly true that individualism constantly undermines the very family life that it originally fostered.

When obligation and reciprocity were banished from public life and confined to the nuclear family, their continued existence became very problematic, especially once the same-sex networks and community associations that formerly defused the tensions of family life began to disintegrate. The effective adult, at work and in public, is independent, individualistic, rational, and calculative. The effective family member, by contrast, shares, cooperates, sacrifices, and acts nonrationally. The character traits that keep families together are associated in all other arenas of life with immaturity or nonrationality; family interdependence is now the only thing that stands in the way of "self-actualization." At the same time, the family becomes overburdened with social expectations as well as psychological and moral ones. If *the* family would just do its job, we wouldn't need welfare, school reform, or prisons. And if *my* family would just do its job, I would be perfectly happy. The obvious next step, of course, is that if I am *not* perfectly happy, it's my family's fault.

Figuring out whether a family is doing its job, however, becomes progressively more difficult when external moral and political reference points for judging the quality of love or parenting disappear. "The world of intimate feeling," remarks Richard Sennett, "loses any boundaries"—and therefore loses any core. Where is the center of infinity? As education professor Joseph Featherstone argues: "A vision of things that has no room for the inner life is bankrupt, but a psychology without social analysis or politics is both powerless and very lonely."[60]

The triumph of private family values discourages us from meeting our emotional needs through mutual aid associations, political and social action groups, or other forms of public life that used to be as important in people's identity as love or family. So we must rely on love. If we fail to attain love, or even if we do attain it and still feel incomplete, we blame our parents for not having helped us outgrow such neediness—as though it is only "the child within" who could be needy. We may postpone confronting the shallowness of our inner life by finding one special person to love us or for us to love, yet when the love disappears, and our needs, inevitably, do not, we feel betrayed. We seek revenge, or at least contractual relief, demanding public compensation for the failure of private life to meet our social needs. Many palimony battles and bitter divorce brawls, for example, seem to be over social needs that right now can be expressed only in personal terms. They are disputes over what people owe each other after love is gone, what altruism is "worth" in our society if it does not earn you love.

These private feuds over family-type relations and obligations fascinate us, at least in part, because we have such a truncated sense of larger social obligations and commitments. At a recent dinner party, I asked a group of men and women if they didn't find some of these palimony demands and damage suits distastefully greedy. They unanimously responded that since the movie stars and entrepreneurs being sued had such inflated incomes, why blame anyone for trying to cut off a piece of the cake? Taking sides in divorce battles or sexual charges and countercharges seems to be a distorted way of registering our disgust with economic, social, or gender trends that we have no other way of debating.

The "turn toward home," then, in both the first and the second Gilded Age, not only impoverished public life but also made private relations more problematic than ever. Consequently, as historian Eli Zaretsky has pointed out, "a certain kind of alienated public life and a certain kind of alienated private life have expanded together."[61] In the next chapter, I demonstrate the intimate connection between the growth of family privacy as a moral ideal and the expansion of the interventionist, bureaucratic state.

6

A Man's Home Is His Castle:
The Family and Outside Intervention

IN 1988, Angela Carder, twenty-six weeks pregnant, lay near death from a cancer that had been in remission when she planned her pregnancy but had since flared up. The hospital, fearing legal liability if it made no effort to save the fetus, asked for a judicial ruling on whether to subject her to a caesarean operation that would shorten her life. Despite the fact that her family and doctors believed she would not want the operation, and that she later told doctors "I don't want it," the court ruled that the government's "interest in protecting the potentiality of human life" outweighed Carder's personal interests, especially since her death was imminent anyway. Two hours after the operation, the baby was dead; two days later, after regaining consciousness long enough to cry over her baby and the operation she did not want, so was Carder.[1]

Feminists and liberals expressed outrage at this "invasion of personal privacy and bodily integrity." Similarly, when two "right-to-life" activists petitioned the courts to name them the legal guardians of comatose and pregnant Nancy Klein, in order to prevent her husband from authorizing an abortion that physicians estimated would improve her chances of recovery, liberals attacked this as an arrogant attempt of outsiders to interfere in the intimacy of the marital relationship.[2]

Yet when liberals and feminists have urged governmental intervention in child abuse cases, federal funding for battered women's shelters, and prosecution of husbands for marital rape, it is conservatives who have taken up the defense of personal privacy and marital intimacy. Charging that liberal definitions of child abuse are so broad that they deny families their fundamental rights of discipline and self-regulation, for example, a commentator in the conservative magazine *The Family in America* declared: "It is naïve to think that the state can regulate human sentiment and dangerous to even try; privacy rights would never survive such intense scrutiny."[3]

Since the 1870s and 1880s, privacy has become such a cherished value that it now has attained the status of a basic right and become a major rallying cry in political disputes. Despite widely divergent positions on the respective rights and prerogatives of individuals, families, and government, almost all activists and politicians claim at some point to be defending a right to privacy against intolerable and unprecedented "outside" intervention. Yet the truth is that none of them supports personal privacy or family autonomy under all conditions.

Conservatives who endorse the Bush administration's Gag Rule, which prohibits physicians in federally funded family planning clinics from even mentioning abortion as an option, tend to be outraged that courts and federal agencies have "hamstrung" teachers and principals in the public schools by prohibiting corporal punishment. Liberals alarmed about the denial of free speech in family planning clinics and the lack of civil liberties for pregnant women accused of alcohol or drug abuse have been far less concerned about the privacy rights of men accused of child abuse or rape.[4]

In 1967, conservatives successfully advocated expansion of welfare workers' power to remove children from their families when the mothers were unmarried, on grounds that lack of marriage constituted, in and of itself, a "poor environment" for children. Liberals opposed giving professionals such discretionary powers, but by the mid-1970s, when such removals were more likely to be for suspicion of child abuse than for immorality, it was conservatives who began arguing for restrictions on state workers' rights to remove children from their families. Right-wing congressmen who had opposed the Child Abuse Prevention and Treatment Act of 1973 as an unwarranted federal intrusion into family privacy embraced the same act in 1983 as a way of preventing parents of catastrophically deformed babies from refusing surgery to prolong their children's lives.[5]

Women's advocates were quick to point out the ways that the 1991 Supreme Court ruling upholding the Gag Rule violated the rights of both medical professionals and their clients to consider a full range of options, yet few have opposed the widespread policy in women's shelters of refusing to house residents who persist in spanking their children. (While such rules were instituted to cut across the escalating pattern of violence in some abusive families, they are applied equally to people who consider spanking a normal part of discipline and do not have a history of letting it degenerate into battering.) Many liberals oppose locking pregnant women up to prevent them from using drugs that might result in brain damage for their babies, but some look with equanimity on the prospect of authorizing the state to license parents or remove children from homes that show a significant "probability" of harm. Most liberals do not believe that the right to privacy entitles a landlord to refuse to rent his downstairs apartment to someone of a different race, creed, marital status, or sexual orientation.[6]

Economic libertarians have been quick to claim the high ground in this contested terrain, pointing out that they oppose "nanny"-type rules limiting either the right to abortion or the right to associate with whomever one pleases. But their endorsement of private economic rights often means that high-priced lawyers end up establishing extensive state controls over families or individuals through private custody, palimony, or child-support suits. Their refusal to sanction limits on the use of private resources can lead, as we shall see, to tremendous invasions of privacy by creditors, advertisers, and employers. Libertarians also are historically inconsistent: Their traditional position was that the growth of manufacturing corporations and large banks was a form of outside intervention that threatened individual liberties as much as did the expansion of the state; early libertarians supported legislation and government action against the accumulation of inordinate economic power in private hands.[7]

Clearly, the privacy issue means different things to different people or even to the same people at different times. In many cases, the real question is which unit should be accorded privacy and autonomy, the family or the individual. In others, the question is whether people agree with the values of those doing the outside intervention. But there is a widespread consensus among the disputants that such outside intervention is new, in contrast to the old days when "a man's home was his castle." While most liberals and feminists disagree with the conservative value judgments expressed in the 1986 report of the White House Working Group on the Family, they have tended to accept its analysis that the historical trend has been erosion of family sovereignty by an expanding state. In the report's words, the family has "lost...much of its authority to courts and rule-writers,...

to public officials at all levels." The state has deprived American families of "the autonomy that was once theirs."[8]

Some analysts take the view that "the family is being defined out of existence" by the modern state.[9] Others hold that traditional privacy rights are now being extended to wives and children. But most share the assumption that the traditional family of male breadwinner, female homemaker, and dependent child predated the state, losing its former autonomy only as the state centralized its institutions and extended its reach into formerly private arenas of life. The problem with these analyses is that their shared assumption is wrong.

Families have never been exempt from public intervention, including that of the state. Indeed, the private, autonomous family of mythical tradition was, paradoxically, largely a creation of judicial activism in the nineteenth century and state regulation in the twentieth. Since then, different state policies and agencies have had contradictory effects on families, while different families and family members have received varying degrees of state intervention or privacy protection. The historical relationship between families, government, and individual liberty is far more intricate than is suggested by generalizations about the state "usurping" formerly private family prerogatives.

Privacy and Autonomy in Traditional American Families

Family "autonomy" was not a value either for traditional Native American societies or for the European settlers who confronted them, although the limits on family privacy came from different sources in each case. Europeans were disappointed to find that Native American families had no private right to sell the land they lived on or worked and astonished to discover that "every man, woman, or child in Indian communities is allowed to enter any one's lodge, and even that of the chief of the nation, and eat when they are hungry." Despite this lack of privacy in property rights, public authority was far from absolute in Native American groups, since leaders had no way of coercing followers: Colonists remarked contemptuously that "the power of their chiefs is an empty sound." European explorers also were scandalized to find that Indian women had "the command of their own Bodies and may dispose of their Persons as they think fit; they being at liberty to do what they please."[10]

Colonial Americans held almost antithetical notions of where private rights began and public authority ended. They gave political leaders the power of life and death over each subject and put women's bodies under the control of fathers or husbands, but they respected the property rights of private landowners and defended them against trespass by the lower classes.

Nevertheless, colonial views on privacy and family autonomy were far removed from the notion that "a man's home is his castle." In the seventeenth and eighteenth centuries, city officials, social superiors, and prying neighbors regularly entered homes and told people whom to associate with, what to wear, and what to teach their children; families who did not comply were punished or forcibly separated.

Slave families, of course, had no rights at all; slaves were a "species of property." Indentured servants and paupers also were denied parental rights and family autonomy. Since child custody was considered a male property right and children a form of chattel, women and men without property lacked a legal basis for asserting parental rights. Yet even propertied families were subject to extensive regulation. The Puritans, for example, gave masters of apprentices equal responsibilities and rights with parents in educating and disciplining the young. They also appointed special officials to oversee *both* parties. In 1745, the Massachusetts Assembly ordered that any child older than six who did not know the alphabet was to be removed to another family.[11]

Church courts, civic leaders, and neighbors enforced a legislatively sanctioned household order that took precedence over the autonomy of any particular family. Authorities might intervene if they found the household head too severe or not strict enough. In Virginia, for example, both a master and his servant were ordered dunked in the local pond, she for being insubordinate and he for failing to restrain her. Conversely, the magistrates of Essex County fined one man forty shillings when neighbors reported that he had referred to his wife as his servant, despite the fact that she denied any dissatisfaction with his treatment. In each of these cases, no one in the family *requested* aid; the intervention was initiated by outside forces.[12]

During the Revolutionary era as well, Americans expected to be scrutinized and called to account by neighbors, church authorities, and local officials. Historian Nancy Cott's study of divorce records reveals that in the late eighteenth century, people nonchalantly entered what modern Americans would consider the most intimate, secluded arenas of their neighbors' lives.

In 1773, for example, Mary Angel and Abigail Galloway testified in an adultery case that they had caught sight through an open window of a man they knew "in the Act of Copulation" with a woman not his wife. By their own report, they matter-of-factly walked into the house "and after observing them some time...asked him if he was not Ashamed to act so when he had a Wife at home." When John Backus and Chloe Gleason sneaked away from their companions one evening in 1784 and were subsequently caught in bed together, the company told them to "get up or be puled [sic] out of bed." The pair obediently got dressed, and John "agreed to treat said Company for his misconduct." The reach of neighbors, church courts, and local authorities into what was only later to be defined as "private life" continued into the first decades of the nineteenth century.[13]

During the Jacksonian period, white families gained considerable freedom from this kind of outside interference, but legal and economic trends ushered in a whole new set of processes for defining and controlling family life. What has changed since the early nineteenth century is not the extent of public regulation of family life but the formality of that regulation.

Until the first decades of the nineteenth century, the boundaries between private and public life were permeable and fluid. Interventions into family life, although pervasive, were informal and decentralized, originating from a wide range of groups and individuals. During the early 1800s, the line between family business and community affairs began to be drawn more sharply. This did not exempt families from outside intervention and public regulation, but it did change the source of intervention and the means of regulation. Over the last 180 years, the agencies through which public intervention into private life is conducted have become increasingly formalized, specialized, and centralized.

The Formalization of Outside Intervention

Most people associate formal intervention into families only with the expansion of the federal government. But this assumption misses two important points. First, the federal government is not the sole source of state intervention. Courts at all levels, police and military bodies, administrative practices, and local legislative actions also are part of the state apparatus, and these actively shaped family life from the earliest days of our nation. Second, the power of private institutions multiplied during the course of the nineteenth century, and they had developed highly centralized bureaucracies well before being taken over by the government at the end of the nineteenth century. Such private institutions were often far more intrusive into family privacy than federal agencies have ever been.[14]

Far from depriving families of prior autonomy, the federal government created family privacy even as it expanded its own reach. Many of the same state interventions that strengthened formal governmental authority created new areas of family autonomy and privacy that had never existed in the earlier period of informal intervention and weak government. As Eli Zaretsky points out: "The schematic model of the state replacing the family obscures the sense in which government intervention…was accompanied by an increasingly sharp delineation of the 'normal' family as a private and autonomous (i.e., self-supporting) institution."[15]

In fact, private institutions and courts in the late nineteenth century, and federal agencies in the twentieth, took a norm of family autonomy and privacy formerly present in only a *minority* of Americans and worked to spread it among the rest of the population—even if that meant violating the sovereignty of families that did not hold such norms. "Unwilling to accept the diversity of family life," writes a recent historian of family law, proponents of privacy and domesticity "turned to coercion to induce family conformity."[16]

Family Privacy Before the Civil War

During the antebellum period, state regulation of families was primarily conducted through courts and local legislatures. In this era, the two main goals of social policy were to free the nuclear family from its former entanglements with kin and neighbors and to concentrate previously diffused economic and social responsibilities for children within the nuclear family. Courts invalidated colonial laws establishing minimum ages at marriage and requiring parental consent or public announcement of marriage banns. Legislators lowered marriage fees and authorized increasing numbers of officials to perform marriages. These actions made it easier to form a nuclear family without consulting kin or community.[17]

Other rulings tightened obligations within the nuclear family and loosened them elsewhere. Antebellum courts rejected the tradition that a parent's duty to support his or her offspring was merely a natural obligation without legal enforcement mechanisms. They increased parental liability for minor children (and for unmarried daughters even beyond the age of majority) and gave creditors the right to sue parents for goods supplied to a child. At the same time, judges limited the "familylike" rights and responsibilities of people outside the nuclear family, abrogating reciprocal duties that had once existed beyond the self-reliant family. Individuals who voluntarily supplied goods or shelter to nonrelatives, for example, could not recover expenses from poor-law officials, as in earlier times. Most states eliminated the right of a master to discipline his apprentices or enforce residence in the master's home, as well as the responsibility of a master to educate his apprentices.[18]

Antebellum courts and legislators took as their model the new domestic family of the Northern middle class, a minority form in the population, and proceeded to privilege it, modify it, and disseminate it as widely as possible. They legalized new norms about proper family relations, including the conception of childhood as a separate, protected stage of life and the notion of female responsibility for domestic affairs. They restructured the rights and duties of men and women in middle-class families by instituting new custody criteria, inheritance rules, breach-of-promise regulations, and parental responsibilities. Women gained new contract rights as wives and mothers, including expanded inheritance and divorce possibilities, but these rights identified them more completely by their domestic roles. Married women's property acts merely protected property that women brought with them into marriage, not what they earned during marriage. Women could win a divorce only if they could prove that they embodied domestic virtues; their custody rights were expanded only insofar as they became primarily identified as nurturers and men as breadwinners. As legal historian Michael Grossberg argues, there was a symbiotic relationship between the evolution of nineteenth-century gender roles, especially the doctrine of separate spheres, and the development of "judicial hegemony over domestic relations."[19]

Yet the more courts and officials institutionalized a new ideal of childhood and parental responsibility, the more inclined they were to *literally* institutionalize people and functions that did not fit their nuclear family models. If a family failed to create personal privacy, economic independence, and "proper" gender roles, institutions were encouraged to take over the job.

It was during the early nineteenth century that governments and institutions gained authority to act *in loco parentis*—literally in place of parents. Establishment of the domestic family as the legal norm paved the way for the breakup of undomesticated families. Thus Lydia Maria Child, whose writings helped to establish the ideal of the private, sanctified domestic family, found no contradiction between romanticizing middle-class families and remarking in 1843 that it was a shame more of New York City's "squalid little wretches" were not orphans.[20]

In many cases, supporters of the domestic family got around this inconvenient state of affairs by creating orphans. Authorities gained new statutory powers to remove poor children from their families and bind them out to employers. Ironically, while voluntary apprentices could use new laws about family primacy to limit the authority of masters, involuntary apprentices lost their older family-type rights. By the 1840s, historian Maxwell Bloomfield reports, the apprentice system had ceased to supplement the family in training and socializing children from all walks of life and had become "a device for the recruitment and exploitation of young paupers."[21]

Family Privacy and the Laissez-Faire State

After the Civil War, even as the government and courts struck down older regulations governing economic development, trade, and con-tractual agreements, they multiplied the restraints and regulations on families, especially regarding women. Nineteenth-century Victorians, unlike many of their modern counterparts, were keenly aware that the family relations and sexual division of labor they favored were ar-tificial creations. They therefore devoted considerable energy and re-sources to shoring them up and shaping them into acceptable forms. The Social Darwinist William Graham Sumner, for example, opposed the traditional conviction that the state had the right to regulate cor-porations or the responsibility to relieve want but advocated decisive state intervention to defend "the property of men and the honor of women." In Sumner's view, both male property and female honor were constantly threatened by "the vices and passions of human na-ture" and therefore had to be protected by the state.[22]

In the late nineteenth century, most states reestablished waiting periods for marriage, raised the age of consent, and passed laws against interracial unions. Reversing republican practice, judges increasingly refused to accept the validity of common-law marriages. Between 1872 and 1900, the courts ruled that women were not entitled to the rights of "citizens" and even questioned whether they qualified as "persons" when it came to the applicability of constitutional rights. Although work reforms were rejected for men because they violated individual contract rights, almost every state passed protective legislation limiting women's hours and regulating their wages. These were upheld by the Supreme Court from 1876 on and culminated in national legislation during the Progressive period.[23]

Courts in the 1880s began to suspend the civil liberties of minors and create new categories of deviant behavior that could be penalized even if no crime had been committed. The Illinois Supreme Court, for example, overturned earlier decisions forbidding the involuntary commitment of youngsters to institutions without due process. It upheld the legality of one act that allowed the indefinite institutionalization of any girl who begged or received alms while selling goods or who consorted with "vicious persons." Such action could be initiated by any "responsible" resident, regardless of the parents' wishes.[24]

It was also during the laissez-faire era that courts and lawmakers reversed their antebellum tendency to sanction marital choice in reproductive behavior. In the 1870s and 1880s, abortion and contraception were criminalized. Laissez-faire hostility to "federal meddling" did not impede passage of a broad national obscenity law in 1873, banning circulation of all birth-control and abortion information or devices through the national mails.[25]

Eugenics was a natural outgrowth of Social Darwinists' concerns about the "fitness of the race," and like the trend toward treating women as a collective class in protective legislation, it steadily undermined their opposition to a national social policy and administrative apparatus. The eugenics crusade from 1885 to 1920 began with local restrictions on marriage, such as "mental capacity" tests, and eventually helped reconcile many laissez-faire supporters to more ambitious state action. Consequently, as historian Michael Katz wryly remarks, "aside from public education, sterilization was the only state-sponsored social improvement in which America led the world."[26]

In addition to these state-sponsored family regulations, a second source of family intervention during the laissez-faire period was the growth of private charities and moral reform societies. Many discussions of state intervention and family autonomy ignore the fact that private institutions and volunteers are often more high-handed than are public agencies and employees, because they are subject to less oversight and fewer constitutional restraints. Such was certainly the case with late-nineteenth-century volunteerism: Interventions into families by private reformers asserting middle-class, Christian values were far more aggressive than any actions taken by the state in our century. It was moralistic volunteer agencies, terrified that "unworthy" families might receive aid, who first set up the bureaucratic regulations and intrusive inquiries that would later come to be associated with the federal government.[27]

In the 1870s and 1880s, an odd but temporarily compatible coalition of nativists, humanitarians, antifeminist moral crusaders, women's activists, and "law and order" proponents took over older charities and formed new groups, such as The Society for the Prevention of Cruelty to Children. These groups, although privately run, could call on the police for enforcement and often received public funds. Almost invariably, they combined an exaggerated reverence for middle-class family ideals with a contemptuous, punitive attitude toward the real-life families of immigrants and the poor. Stephen Humphreys Gurteen, one of the most prominent of these reformers, declared in 1882 that the most important word in the English language was "the sacred, the holy word Home," but he opposed financial aid to poor mothers because lower-class women, unlike middle-class ones, *ought* to work; besides, he added, they were such unfit mothers that their children would do better in day nurseries than at home. The new privacy that courts accorded middle-class families in the nineteenth century was matched by the new arrogance with which such middle-class reformers intruded into or even tore apart poor families who did not live up to their ideals. To create the "true home," one charity leader explained in 1888, it was often necessary to "break up the unworthy family."[28]

In cities such as New York and Boston, "child savers" collected poor children and sent them out to work on Midwest farms. In some cases, the children were actually auctioned off to farmers. Reformers did not bother to investigate conditions in these homes, even though many farm families were obviously seeking cheap labor. When reformers did concern themselves with the exploitation of child labor, historian Linda Gordon notes, their criticisms were invariably directed against parents rather than employers.[29]

The subjugation of families to public authority did not stem from a socialist or collectivist agenda but from an attempt to build individualistic definitions of private responsibility. Institutions fostered a form of personal responsibility that was especially geared to a competitive and structurally unequal economic order. Schools, for example, as Michael Katz comments, taught children "that helping your friends is cheating." Reformatories used state power to enforce individual adjustment to the kinds of wage work considered appropriate to class, race, and gender roles. One reformatory official explained in 1890: "We aim to teach 'cooking' and 'waiting on tables' to the colored boys....If, after we do this, they still refuse to work, then they can never blame the State for their downfall."[30]

Progressive Reform: Family Preservation and State Expansion in the Early Twentieth Century

Progressive reformers shared the commitment of volunteer charity leaders to social control, economic individualism, private property, and domestic moralism, but they advocated very different methods of achieving these ends.[31] The efforts of Progressive reformers to expand state regulatory powers, have government take over the functions of private institutions, and construct a federal welfare system were associated with opposition to earlier strategies of family breakup.

In the short run, between 1895 and 1905, the combined actions of new Progressive reformers and older private charity workers actually expanded the incidence of family breakup. Between 1900 and 1904, the percentage of children in public institutions doubled. However, it was the Progressive proponents of expanded government, not the laissez-faire believers in privatism, who led the movement for family preservation, and they triumphed relatively quickly. By 1909, when the first White House Conference on Children was held, nearly everyone agreed that even a bad family could be made better than the best institution.[32]

Since in both periods the family that reformers favored existed in only a minority of the population, the alternative to destroying other kinds of families was to help them achieve the middle-class, Protestant norm. The family preservation movement aimed to extend middle-class female domesticity and prolonged childhood to the working class. It was closely associated, accordingly, not only with legislation against child labor and attempts to limit the work-force participation of mothers, but also with social welfare measures designed to help families establish a modicum of privacy and domesticity. This commitment to the nuclear family and to female domesticity provided the first wedge for the expansion of state welfare agencies and federal regulation of the market—"state building for mothers and babies," as political theorist Theda Skocpol puts it.[33]

Expanded protective legislation put the government in the business of regulating the hours and tasks that companies could assign to women, in order to make sure that reproduction remained women's primary role. Mothers' Pensions were adopted to reduce the number of widows who had to send their children to orphanages in order to ensure them food and shelter. "Motherhood, in a sense, became a civic function." Child-labor legislation and compulsory schooling aimed to root out "precocious" behaviors among children, restrict them to the home, and strengthen the adult male breadwinner role.[34]

Progressive reforms reduced the number of institutionalized children, enabled working-class children to attend school, and improved housing and sanitation to the point that domestic life became possible, for the first time, for many immigrant and poor city dwellers. Yet governmental action to keep families together was intimately connected to an expansion of the tools for monitoring, regulating, and fine-tuning their home life. For example, Judge Ben Lindsay, a noted architect of Progressivism, argued that the only way to avoid breaking families up was to develop as fully as possible the power of government to protect and supervise parents.[35]

Progressives multiplied the means available to courts and state workers for imposing middle-class norms on nonconforming families even while they instituted important humanitarian reforms and protections for women and youth. The juvenile court system is a good example. The first juvenile court was established in Illinois in 1899; by 1917, all but three states had adopted the institution. Despite its altruistic goal of treating young offenders more leniently and individually than "hardened criminals," the juvenile court system created a new rationale and instrument for intervention into families. Behaviors that were not illegal but that offended middle-class sensibilities—hanging out on street corners or at dance halls, gambling, engaging in sexual activity, resisting the authority of teachers or welfare workers, showing "carelessness about the rights of others," even exhibiting "lack of ambition to become something worthy"—became evidence of delinquency. Youths could be consigned to institutions for these sins without any of the normal constitutional protections of due process, even when their own parents objected. Social workers even developed a "predelinquent" category: "Children from poor family backgrounds were often treated for what they *might* do rather than for any wrong they had committed." Yet courts held that since the intent of such legislation was the child's "salvation," not his or her punishment, state actions against delinquents or their families were not subject to the same constitutional limits as were criminal proceedings.[36]

The most common offenses that brought boys before authorities were those that threatened social order; the most frequent charges against girls were violations of gender order, usually designated "sex offenses." Indeterminate sentences and probation further increased the power of government agents to enforce both social and gender conformity. "Vulgar language," card playing, "improper" sexual behavior, or "lack of cooperation" could tack years onto the sentence of someone in a reformatory and might even cause the reinstitutionalization of a person who had been released.[37]

Progressives advocated collective solutions to social problems and created an unprecedented expansion of the national government. But the fundamental analysis and aims of Progressivism reflected commitment to the economic individualism, sexual morality, and domestic family values of the Protestant, native-born, nineteenth-century middle class. Like their predecessors, Progressive reformers believed, as one put it, that the "privacy of the home" in any specific case must yield to the "stronger duty" of establishing a particular kind of middle-class family privacy, especially "the necessary division between home and workplace."[38]

Progressives feared that the failure of immigrant and poor families to privatize the nuclear family was a threat to individual property rights and the wage system. To remove that threat, reformers abolished local, informal institutions and agencies that had formerly been used by working-class families to exercise a degree of cooperative self-regulation. Their advocacy of government aid to the poor stemmed partly from a desire to discourage social cooperation and economic pooling beyond the family. It was not merely humanitarian sympathy, for example, that motivated Progressive housing reform.

As a University of Chicago professor explained in 1902: "A communistic habitation forces the members of a family to conform insensibly to communistic modes of thought." Commissioner of Labor Charles Neill declared in 1905: "There must be a separate house, and as far as possible, separate rooms, so that at an early period of life the idea of rights to property, the right to things, to privacy, may be instilled."[39]

Convinced that "home, above all things, means privacy," reformers advocated state action not only to regulate slum lords but also to end the "promiscuous" socializing of the lower classes in urban tenements and streets. They grew hysterical about the dangers of boarding and lodging, once respectable middle-class practices, and referred to the "street habit" as if it were a dangerous addiction, much like crack cocaine. To root out this addiction, Progressives promulgated new zoning laws and building codes prohibiting working-class families from sharing quarters. Welfare agencies spent as much time and resources establishing habits of privacy among their "clients" as they did providing material assistance; they withheld aid to families who clung to older habits of sociability and economic pooling. Such antagonism to sharing has been a persistent aspect of American welfare laws: As late as the 1970s, food stamps were automatically denied to any poor family or individual who did the sensible thing and shared cooking facilities with others.[40]

Mothers' Pensions, similarly, were made contingent on a woman's display of middle-class norms about privacy and domesticity. A recipient had to be "a proper person, physically, mentally and morally fit to bring up her children." She could not take in male boarders, work away from home more than three days of the week, or live in a morally questionable neighborhood. Investigators interviewed neighbors and entered each woman's home to find out whether she used liquor or tobacco (evidence of an "unfit" mother), kept her house clean, and attended church. A woman also "might be forced to prosecute relatives who had refused to provide her with aid."[41]

Mothers' Pensions were a substitute for other kinds of state action, such as subsidized child-care centers and across-the-board relief to needy families, that might undermine the principles of individual responsibility and male breadwinning. They were promoted as protecting the "good innocent child" from association with "undesirable children" and were predicated on the assumption that a "normal," "intact" family would not need financial assistance. The Progressive approach to social welfare was "a program for private parental responsibility and for community enforcement where parents failed." No other major industrial nation, comments historian Mark Leff, combined such concern for "worthy widows and fatherless children with such resistance to providing assistance to able-bodied poor or unemployed adult men, regardless of how many children they had to support."[42]

Progressive reform, then, expanded the role of the federal government in reinforcing both economic privatism and female domesticity. What linked these two goals was the family wage system. Federally supervised arbitration tried to ensure that men could win wage increases that were sufficient to support a family; child labor laws and public schools extended the length of childhood in the working class; the incipient welfare system aimed to relieve single mothers of the need to work full-time; and protective legislation prevented wives and mothers from being forced to accept overtime or shift work.

The family wage system, however, did not always operate as proponents desired. Many men continued to earn less than they needed to support a family. Mothers' Pensions were inadequate to live on, and racial prejudice excluded black, Native American, and Mexican-American women from benefits. Yet protective legislation kept such women from high-paying jobs, and child-care programs were available only a few hours a day. The result for many families was that the system did not so much subsidize domesticity as enforce low-paid, part-time, irregular work for women in marginal labor markets.[43]

The New Deal and the Family

New Deal welfare legislation expanded government's responsibility for creating jobs and supplementing wages while it continued to support the norm of private nuclear families with breadwinner husbands and homemaker wives. The Social Security Act of 1935, for example, enlarged the commitment of the state to helping families who could not care for dependents, but made access to aid contingent on family status. In 1939, the act specifically redefined the recipient as the worker and "his" family. Most women received benefits only through their husbands—and many discovered later that if the relationship lasted less than twenty years, they ended up with no benefits at all. The act also failed to cover a third of all married women workers and

more than three-fifths of black workers, male and female. It discriminated against the married working women it did cover because they
received the same amount as did nonworking wives, even though
they had to pay social security taxes on their income. Federal
minimum-wage legislation did not include agricultural work or domestic labor, and much New Deal legislation reinforced differential
wages for women.[44]

The New Deal state, like its Progressive and laissez-faire predecessors, related to men as if they were all independent wage earners in
the market and to women as if they were all dependent caregivers in
the family. Rejecting citizen entitlements, such as universal medical
insurance, New Dealers preferred measures such as workman's compensation, which was tied to previous participation and remuneration in the labor market. Such wage-based welfare measures perpetuated discrimination against women (and minorities), who tended to
have more difficulty persisting in the work force and ascending a job
ladder that gave them wages high enough to exist on the fraction of
their salary provided by unemployment compensation.

The result, political scientist Barbara Nelson points out, is that the
American state developed two channels of assistance—one for men,
linked to their role as breadwinners, and one for women, linked to
their roles as wives and mothers. (Blacks and other minorities, often
excluded from both, had to win social assistance through civil rights
struggles.) The first channel "was male, judicial, public, and routinized in origin." Welfare distributed through this system was conceptualized as an earned right. Although the amount of aid varied according to wages and length of time in the work force, the schedules
were standardized, and once eligibility was established there were no
controls exerted over how the recipient behaved or spent the money.
The second channel "was female, administrative, private, and non-
routinized." Assistance was seen as bestowed rather than earned,
caseworkers had much more discretion about the amounts and kinds
of assistance granted, and the state was able to intervene much more
pervasively in recipients' lives.[45]

The Irony of State Intervention

Until the early 1960s, state policy continued to be unambiguously
aimed at protection of a family package very much like that advocated by antistate, profamily conservatives today: paternal breadwin-

ning; maternal domesticity; prolonged childhood; repression of female sexuality; and an equation of family privacy with free enterprise, Americanism, and patriotism. This family pattern, remarks historian Linda Gordon, "is not 'traditional,' as is often claimed today, but was new when child protection originated. Indeed, child protection was part of the efforts to enforce this arrangement."[46]

To impose this model on working-class and immigrant populations, moral reformers at the turn of the century elaborated the system of judicial discretion and professional elitism that their intellectual descendants now blame for the demise of family autonomy. New "experts" tried to invest middle-class childrearing values with scientific weight. Profamily activists enthusiastically eliminated legal and administrative restrictions on court officials and social workers, empowering them to make arbitrary judgments as to whether a youth was "predelinquent," a family was "decent," or a widow was "morally fit" to receive a pension that enabled her to keep her children at home. Indeterminate sentences in reformatories further augmented the power of "rule writers" to discipline individuals whose ideas about family life and gender roles departed from Protestant middle-class norms.

It is ironic that conservative moralists helped to create the very institutions and bureaucracies that they now experience as a threat. The subsequent course of state intervention and legal action into family life has not always gone according to the original plan, as was only to be expected in a pluralist political system. Once the state adopted a position on "proper" family relations, the door inevitably opened to political action by those with alternative definitions of propriety; "experts" who got hands-on experience with immigrant and working-class families sometimes had to modify their preconceptions about what was proper for such populations; individuals who saw the state propagating and subsidizing one type of household were sure to demand that their living arrangements be defined as family, too, so that they could receive the same subsidies. After some groups pressured the state to make abortion illegal, to prohibit certain types of employment for women, to give tax credits for homeownership, and to deny relief to families who shared cooking facilities, others countered with demands for antidiscrimination laws in employment, child-care credits for two-income families, and mandated parental leave for working parents.

But liberals inclined to feel gleeful about this irony often underestimate how much of the original conservative dynamic remains in state policies. For example, even though the New Deal of the 1930s and the Great Society initiatives of the 1960s greatly expanded government's commitment to guaranteeing families a minimum standard of living, they maintained a simultaneous dedication to the private profit system and the notion of female domesticity. Anxiety to preserve the wage system produced the doctrine that families receiving assistance ought to remain enough below the poverty level that they would not be tempted to rely on state aid a minute longer than absolutely necessary; likewise, conditions were often attached to that aid in order to regulate the supply of cheap labor for business. Attachment to the male breadwinner ideal led to sexual stereotyping of women and to the assumption that families would not need help if they had not failed in some way. Since family failure has to be established before help is forthcoming, even today, state intervention is consistently late as well as heavily judgmental. Once approved, it is nearly always inadequate.[47]

Liberals also tend to overestimate the benevolence or neutrality of government professionals. Considerable research, however, links the notorious inefficiency of state spending in America to the tendency of professionals to "medicalize" problems, making them a matter of individual ignorance or family pathology that only "experts" can resolve. This means that federal funding often creates new career paths for professionals rather than gives poor families the resources to help themselves. Thus in the 1920s, more money went to maternal education programs than to provision of comprehensive health services, while in the 1960s, a significant percentage of the growth in welfare spending went not to fund jobs or housing but to pay new "family experts" to provide family services. Political theorist Jean Bethke Elshtain argues that a similar process has removed child abuse from its socioeconomic context and reconstructed it solely as a therapeutic problem. Historian William Graebner suggests that the growth of "democratic social engineering" from the 1920s to the present has preserved economic inequality and conservative social control.[48]

Recent State Policies: Does the Government Support Monarchy or Democracy in Modern Families?

Important realignments in state policy began in the late 1960s, emanating from several different sources and leading to an expansion of intervention into families in some areas and a contraction in others.

In 1962, physician C. Henry Kempe and colleagues publicized "the battered-child syndrome," which led to increased support for intervention into abusive families. By the end of the 1960s, women's organizations had brought the issues of incest and spousal rape under public scrutiny, winning new laws against marital rape and stricter enforcement of domestic violence ordinances. One way to look at this trend is to see it as a withdrawal of traditional state guarantees of male household authority and a reversal of antebellum laws increasing the dependence of children on the nuclear family. On the whole, though, the state's stepped-up enforcement of social norms against violence within the family should be seen as a restriction of parental autonomy.[49]

The late 1960s also saw the construction of new limits on state control over families. Growing mistrust of the good intentions and judgment of state agents produced numerous checks on the discretionary powers of the state. Cases of youngsters kept in institutions for years because they had been arbitrarily labeled "incorrigible" led to the 1967 Supreme Court ruling that juveniles facing institutionalization were entitled to many criminal protections afforded adults, such as the right to legal counsel and the opportunity to confront witnesses against them. Legal suits were brought against the "midnight raids" on welfare families in the 1960s, when government agents converged on the homes of women welfare recipients to check their beds and closets for evidence of a male presence. (Discovery of a man's suit in a woman's closet was enough to disqualify her.) In 1968, the Supreme Court ruled it illegal to deny welfare benefits to children merely because of the presence of a man in the household.[50]

By the 1970s, there were also movements to expand the rights of unmarried couples and gays and lesbians, reducing the state's power to define normalcy. In recent years, federal agencies and courts have further curtailed much of government's former authority to differentially reward a particular kind of family and legislate against others. There has been a general tendency to give families decision-making powers once denied them: the right to choose birth control, for example, or, under some circumstances, abortion. Many laws regulating the sexual practices of married couples, and eventually of other consenting adults, have also been repealed or ruled unconstitutional. This trend is far less clear cut than many people believe, however. In 1986, the Supreme Court upheld the constitutionality of a Georgia law prohibiting several sexual acts, even between consenting adults in the privacy of their bedroom. The original case was brought when

police arrested a homosexual for practicing sodomy in his own bedroom. Another man was later convicted and sentenced to jail for having oral sex with his wife.[51]

Courts tended in the 1970s and early 1980s "to emphasize the
separateness and autonomy of family members" and to restrict the
ability of parents or husbands to coerce other family members. Yet
some parental rights were strengthened, as in the new obstacles to
terminating parental rights in foster-care placements and the
Supreme Court ruling that Amish families have the right to withdraw
their children from school after the eighth grade, even if the children
object. Recent legislative and judicial acts have revived the inclination of the state to treat the family as a solid unit rather than as a collection of separate individuals. The courts have yet to rule on the
rash of recent legislative actions designed to hold parents responsible
for juvenile crime and truancy. They have, however, upheld welfare
policies requiring that support payments to one child be considered
as income of the rest of the child's co-residential family, thus reducing the eligibility of half-siblings for food stamps.[52]

The original Supreme Court abortion decision did not rule out restrictions on minors' rights to obtain an abortion without parental
consent, and such restrictions have mounted over the past ten years.
The court did uphold a woman's right to decide on an abortion without her husband's assent, but the decision was based more on respect
for her physician's authority than on personal female choice.[53]

As Superior Court Judge Phyllis Beck has pointed out, most modern laws and acts uphold the family's "integrity" and "privacy," but
when there are divisions within the family, some laws side with the
children against the parents and some with the parents against the
children, while others try to specify the respective rights and privileges of spouses. One of the most striking trends in the relation of
state and family during the past twenty years has been the emergence
of bitter public struggles around these issues, with all parties trying
to draw the courts and legislatures in on their side. In this process,
the state's role in mediating familylike disputes between unmarried
couples, as well as in regulating internal family life, has expanded.
Although the state is less likely to hold children responsible for parents' support, it has gained new powers to enforce parental support
of children. Ironically, although legislators and courts cannot make a
married couple finance their child's college education, they can make
a divorced parent do so.[54]

The contradictions in state policies are well illustrated in several recent court cases. On the one hand, the state's ability to remove children from their family has greatly expanded over the past three decades, swelling the number of children in foster care and the length of time they spend there. Yet it has simultaneously become more difficult to terminate parental rights completely; and while courts consider the "best interests" of the child in custody disputes between parents, they do not accept this as a standard in disputes between parents and foster families. In February 1991, an American Civil Liberties Union (ACLU) class-action suit on behalf of the District of Columbia's 2,200 foster children revealed that "temporary" placements had continued for years, with caseworkers blithely assuming that children would someday be reunited with their parents, even when they had not seen one another in all that time. The document recounted the story of Kevin, then eleven, who had been in "temporary" foster care all his life: While hospitalized at age eight for suicidal tendencies, he climbed into a trash can and asked to be thrown out. Or take the case of Sarah, abandoned by her mother shortly after birth and raised for five years by foster parents who wished to adopt her but were not allowed to do so because that would terminate the "natural" family bond. In 1989, the child's mother showed up and demanded custody. Sarah was considered too young for her preferences to be admissible in court, and she was turned over to the stranger who was her "natural" mother. It took the foster parents two years to win even visitation rights.[55]

Even though the right of state agents to intervene in families has expanded, recent court rulings have absolved them of the legal obligation to do so effectively. In March 1984, for example, Joshua DeShaney was hospitalized in critical condition after being severely beaten by his natural father. Wisconsin child-abuse workers had been recording evidence of the child's physical abuse since January of 1982 but had taken no action other than writing down the incidents—until the day a county official called Joshua's mother, divorced and living in Wyoming, to inform her that her son was undergoing brain surgery. Joshua survived but suffered extensive brain damage. His mother sued the county workers, alleging gross negligence that amounted to a violation of the boy's Fourteenth Amendment rights to due process. In 1989, in a six-to-three opinion, the Supreme Court ruled that the state has no constitutional duty "to protect an individual against private violence."[56]

There are intense debates about the ultimate effects of these various state policies and legal rulings. Clearly, right-wing hysteria to the contrary, the modern state still extends substantial privileges to nuclear families and upholds broad parental authority rights. It is also clear, however, that a man's claim to absolute rule in his household is no longer accepted: The castle is not supposed to have a torture chamber.[57]

Aside from these very broad generalizations, the impact of state policies on family privacy and individual autonomy is difficult to assess. Take, for example, the issue of whether state policies have favored women or men. Some observers argue that the state has undermined parental, especially paternal, authority, deferring to feminist demands to treat everyone as equal. Others claim that the state "institutionalized the power of men over women even as it helped to free women from the confines of the nuclear family." It replaced private patriarchy with "judicial" patriarchy, shored up parental authority with new techniques of therapeutic manipulation, and supplanted women's historical areas of expertise.[58]

Allan Carlson of the Rockford Institute asserts that social security replaced private family and gender responsibilities with a "socialized" system, subverting traditional intergenerational bonds, male-headed households, and full-time mothering. But political economist Nancy Folbre contends that this state takeover of intergenerational redistribution has worked to reestablish traditional gender inequalities and private family responsibilities now that male household heads can no longer impose such roles on women. Under the social security system, "men who minimize their own expenditures on children...are rewarded not only with their own tax contributions, but also by the unpaid [female] labor embodied in the younger generation whose wages are the actual source of Social Security funds." These men "may not live in traditional patriarchal households. But they enjoy a traditional patriarchal privilege." Similarly, their ex-wives are stuck with the traditional female obligation of raising their children without adequate social support.[59]

The twentieth-century tendency of courts to grant custody of children to mothers is another area in which observers disagree about the impact of state intervention on men's and women's autonomy. Organizations such as Parents Opposed to Punitive Support Payments claim that the development of mother custody rights was the result of agitation by "radical feminists." At least one radical feminist, however, argues that women were not given custody rights until children ceased to be an economic asset and began to be an economic burden: She sees easier divorce laws and the decline of father

custody rights as a way of maintaining women's reproductive obligations to the state once childrearing was no longer in the economic
interests of male household heads.[60]

How can we assess these arguments? Clearly, the state's limitation
of men's absolute power in the family does not necessarily "liberate"
women, but even "judicial patriarchy" unquestionably benefits many
abused woman and children. The impersonal power of bureaucrats
may well be preferable to the intensely personal violence that we see
in families where women and children are beaten, burned with
cigarettes, scalded with boiling water, or actually set on fire—to use
just a few examples culled from recent news reports. Women, moreover, have often been able to tilt the bureaucratic apparatus toward
their own ends. As for subversion of parental authority, women's letters to the new agencies of the Progressive state reveal considerable
relief in having "outside experts" to turn to instead of judgmental
family members. And despite resentment of professionals' rules and
regulations, Joseph Featherstone points out, "most working-class
families would prefer to be 'invaded' by a pediatrician more often."[61]

Family Autonomy, Privacy, and the State

In traditional American rhetoric, it has often been held that "Family
and State wax and wane inversely to each other," and that powerful
states seek to strip "the family of as many of its natural functions and
authorities as possible."[62] As we have seen, however, neither the family nor the state is unitary, and relations between them are far more
complicated than this. In the final analysis, the entire notion of the
state undermining some primordial family privacy is a myth, because
the nuclear family has never existed as an autonomous, private unit
except where it was the synthetic creation of outside forces. The
strong nuclear family is in large measure a creation of the strong
state.

Despite constant friction and periodic boundary disputes, strong
states have historically aligned themselves with private nuclear families against extended-kin networks, community associations, and
local rulers. The classic Greek distinction between *oikos* (household)
and *polis* (political government) emerged in large part to restrict the
claims of *genos,* or clan. Western notions of privacy and family autonomy developed as a corollary to the new claims of an expanding

state over the public sphere; both family privacy and individual autonomy were increasingly guaranteed by the state. But, of course, the
state expected the private family to be more tractable than were
the older public institutions it eclipsed; the more private the family,
the more dependent it was on the state.[63]

Trying to adopt a consistent position on whether state intervention is good or bad for privacy may be like demanding that scientists
choose whether light consists of waves or particles, when it consists
of both. As we have seen, the state created family privacy in America
even as it asserted new authority over family relations. Conversely,
some of the main expansions of state power have come from those
most eager to preserve the autonomy of the private family. Princeton
sociologist Robert Wuthnow argues, for example, that attempts by
many churches to protect family "integrity" have led to political battles that expanded rather than restricted the power of the state.
Philosopher Alasdair MacIntyre points to the mutual reinforcement
between privacy and bureaucracy: In our desire to pursue private
ends, we turn public obligations and responsibilities over to bureaucrats, producing what he calls "bureaucratic individualism."[64]

The state, moreover, is far from the largest source of outside intervention into the family in today's society. Indeed, government deregulation during the past two decades has allowed private companies
unprecedented scope to invade the privacy of families and individuals. Data-sellers market lists of families who have filed worker's compensation claims or medical malpractice suits; some vendors sell the
names of people who have been arrested, even if they were acquitted
or the charges dropped; others keep track of renters who have ever
gone to court with their landlords. Such information, of course, can
be used to blackball prospective renters, employees, or patients. The
1978 Right to Financial Privacy Act severely restricted the federal
government's right to examine bank-account records and credit reports, but it exempted private employers, state agencies, creditors,
and even solicitation firms.[65]

Business policies, from forced overtime to transfers and layoffs,
from working hours to health benefits, regulate family life far more
extensively than does the state. In this context, Featherstone remarks, "An anti-statist position, pure and simple, is a tacit endorsement of rule by the giant corporations." In the absence of federal
parental leave and child-care policies, a recent article in the *Harvard
Business Review* has pointed out, "our national [family] policy is in
the hands of front-line supervisors."[66]

Yet another complexity is introduced when we recall that struggles for personal privacy have often had paradoxical results, creating unprecedented public intrusions into formerly secret areas of life. Women's rights activist Alida Brill argues that we have made many matters "everybody's business" in order to win support for making them "nobody's business." The Nancy Cruzan case springs to mind, where the three-year effort of her parents to remove her feeding tube, after she had spent eight years in a coma, resulted in a media blitz about the family's entire life, obliged the family to make their way through daily pickets outside the hospital, and ended with protesters forcing their way onto the hospital floor to demand that the hospital not carry out the court's final ruling. Attempts by gays to prevent the state from dictating their private lives have prompted them to "come out" publicly about the very sexuality they desire to be a private prerogative; a militant minority of the gay movement believes that one way to protect homosexual autonomy from state interference is to engage in the public "outing" of prominent gays who have kept their sexuality "in the closet."[67]

Ironically, some of the most dramatic intrusions of courts and state agencies into family privacy derive from our refusal to accept a legitimate sphere of government regulation and oversight. Almost everyone is appalled by the adversarial frenzy that seems to surround family relations today; the thicket of bureaucratic regulations, time-consuming checklists, abstruse legal procedures, and conflicting lines of command through which family conflicts are negotiated sometimes suggests that we are being choked by the growth of the state. Yet Michael Grossberg points out that such judicial interventions were often designed to "deflect state activism": "Judicial dominance of domestic relations grew out of…opposition to national jurisdiction over the family." Much of the earliest legislation establishing minors' rights, complicated appeals procedures, and the like derived from familial challenges to state authority.[68]

Contrary to the popular identification of high-handed judges with governmental violations of family autonomy, the courts came to have so much power because of our historical resistance to state regulation. Since Americans have been reluctant to codify public power or give broad authority to state agencies, we have tended to let adversarial court cases institute state policy, only on an ad hoc, case by case, piecemeal basis. This not only makes state regulation of families less consistent than elsewhere, and much more complicated, but also means that people who can afford the best lawyers have the most input into establishing or overturning the precedents that shape family policy.[69]

Harvard law professor Mary Ann Glendon points out that Europeans, more willing to accept state administrative bodies, resort to the courts far less than do Americans to work out issues of marriage, divorce, child custody, child support, and abortion. In America, though, given our denial that the state has authority to regulate private relations or obligations, few people agree to arbitration. In this context, the doctrine of "best interests of the child," instead of increasing public regulation of family life, seems to encourage private custody disputes. It can be used to control both children and parents or to let a parent completely off the hook:

> Justice Richard Neely tells how he once represented a married man who had fallen in love, first with motorcycles and then with a woman who shared his fondness for motocycles. Even though this king of the road had told Neely that custody of his two children was the last thing he wanted out of his divorce, Neely suggested to him that if he indicated to his wife that he was willing to fight for custody all the way to the state supreme court, the divorce could probably be settled fairly cheaply. The wife, who was unwilling to take any chance, however small, on losing her children, settled on the husband's terms.[70]

Outraged by such perversions of justice but denying the validity of national regulation, Americans simultaneously assert more extreme rights of individual choice than those found in any other modern democracy and demand a uniformity of behavior and opinion on some questions—from the sanctity of the flag to the issue of maternal drinking during pregnancy—that seems equally extreme to every other democracy. The impact on family autonomy and personal privacy is highly inconsistent. If twentieth-century America has accorded far less extensive power or legitimacy to government regulation and public oversight than any European nation, it has also had, historian Michael Woodiwiss argues, the "most thorough oversight of personal behavior in the Western industrial world."[71]

7

Bra-Burners and Family Bashers:

Feminism, Working Women, Consumerism, and the Family

A LARGE part of the ambivalence surrounding modern family relations is connected to a sense that our lives are increasingly dominated by the schedules, needs, and seductions of the marketplace. Both at work and at home, the pace of life seems too fast and the demands on us too numerous. Single people complain that they have no leisure to find and develop relationships; couples scramble to schedule time together between work responsibilities and exercise classes. Barbara Dafoe Whitehead of the Institute for American Values argues that parents' job responsibilities are constantly colliding with their family ones. It is lack of time, she says, that makes parents fear they are losing "a struggle for the hearts and minds of their own children...to an aggressive and insidious consumer culture."[1]

For 90 percent of the people expressing and reading these ideas, parent means mother. In recent years, we have seen what journalist Susan Faludi calls an "undeclared war against American women," accusing them of destroying families, neglecting children, and poisoning intimate relationships.[2] The problem supposedly began when women embraced feminist values, which led them to abandon the family ethic of care that once provided a refuge from competitive pressures. It encouraged women to adopt self-seeking, materialistic lifestyles they would otherwise have shunned.

Christopher Lasch, an eloquent critic of modern consumer culture, puts the moderate case against feminism in these terms: it is "not that economic self-sufficiency for women is an unworthy goal," he concedes, but that its realization, under existing economic conditions, would undermine equally important values associated with the family.... Feminists have not answered the argument that day care provides no substitute for the family...that indifference to the needs of the young has become one of the distinguishing characteristics of a society that lives for the moment.[3]

The right wing is more vitriolic. According to psychologist Edward Hoffman, the eight years after 1966 saw a permissive "values upheaval" that replaced "pro-child and pro-family attitudes...with a cluster of social values that may aptly be called Personal Liberation Ideology." The epicenter of this earthquake was feminism's insistence on careers and its devaluation of motherhood. Feminists adopted a conscious "strategy" of tearing down the "social and moral order" favoring family ties, in order to install a value system based solely on individual fulfillment in the workplace and leading inevitably to child neglect.[4]

Although the right wing has made little headway in getting Americans to accept its *program* for women, it has had considerable success in promulgating its *analysis* of women's role in initiating contemporary family dilemmas. Few women are fully self-confident in the choices they have made over the past two decades. They wonder whether they should be doing more to counter the materialism of the marketplace rather than making their own way in it; they agonize over whether gains in personal independence have been bought at the cost of stable interpersonal relationships. Consequently, more and more women describe themselves as "postfeminist." In one recent poll, 76 percent of women reported that they paid little or no attention to the women's movement.[5]

This is hardly the "backlash" that some have claimed. In the poll mentioned above, 94 percent of the women declared that the women's movement had helped them become more independent, and 82 percent said that it was still helping women improve their lives; 77 percent believed that it had made life better in general, not just for women. Only 35 percent judged that the women's movement was antifamily. Nevertheless, many women have accepted a rewriting of history that attributes most changes in women's roles and family forms to the influence of "nontraditional values" promulgated by feminism.

Prior to Betty Friedan's 1963 bestseller, *The Feminine Mystique,* according to a recent account that echoes the historical sense if not the value judgment of almost every student I have ever asked to draw a time line of modern life, "the largest proportion of middle-class women on this continent were living in peace in what they considered to be a normal, traditional, worthwhile lifestyle." Life, as one right-wing author puts it, "has never been the same since." Demoralized by feminists' "constant disparagement of mother's work," thousands of women walked away from their relationships and threw themselves into careers. The acquisitive, competitive values women adopted when they forsook domesticity led them to become "clones" of men. Even many former feminists now say that the movement "went too far."[6]

The Curious History of Mother's Day

The extent to which the right-wing analysis has permeated our understanding of women's changing roles is illustrated in the ritual lamentations we hear each year about the "debasement of Mother's Day." Most people believe that Mother's Day was originally a time for an intensely personal celebration of women's private roles and nuclear family relationships. In "the old days," we brought mom breakfast in bed to acknowledge all the meals she had made for us. We picked her a bouquet of fresh flowers to symbolize her personal, unpaid services to her family. "Traditional" Mother's Day images, whether on the front of greeting cards or in the back of our minds, are always set in the kitchen or at a child's bedside, emphasizing mother's devotion to her own family and ignoring her broader kin networks, social ties, and political concerns.

But as domestic work has been devalued and formerly private arenas of life drawn into the market, the story goes, the personal element in this celebration has been lost. Mother's Day has become just another occasion for making money—the busiest day of the year for American restaurants and telephone companies, the best single week of the year for florists. So every May, between the ads for "all-you-can-eat" Mother's Day buffets, we hear a chorus of pleas for Americans to rediscover "the true meaning of Mother's Day."

Last year, for example, my son carried home from school (along with three dinner coupons from local fast-food restaurants) a handout urging children to think of some "homemade" gift or service to express their appreciation for their mothers' "special" love. It was a nice sentiment, and I was delighted to receive the fantasy book my child pulled from his personal library and wrapped in a hand-drawn heart—but the historian in me was a little bemused. The fact is that Mother's Day originated to celebrate the organized activities of women *outside* the home. It became trivialized and commercialized only after it became confined to "special" nuclear family relations.

The people who inspired Mother's Day had quite a different idea about what made mothers special. They believed that motherhood was a *political* force. They wished to celebrate mothers' social roles as community organizers, honoring women who acted on behalf of the entire future generation rather than simply putting their own children first.

The first proposal of a day for mothers came from Anna Reeves Jarvis, who in 1858 organized Mothers' Work Days in West Virginia to improve sanitation in the Appalachian Mountains. During the Civil War, her group provided medical services for soldiers and civilians on both sides of the conflict. After the war, Jarvis led a campaign to get the former combatants to lay aside their animosities and forge new social and political alliances.[7]

The other nineteenth-century precursor of Mother's Day began in Boston in 1872, when poet and philanthropist Julia Ward Howe proposed an annual Mothers' Day for Peace, to be held every June 2:

> Arise then, women of this day!…Say firmly: "Our husbands shall not come to us, reeking with carnage….Our sons shall not be taken from us to unlearn all that we have been able to teach them of charity, mercy and patience. We women of one country will be too tender of those of another country to allow our sons to be trained to injure theirs."[8]

Howe's Mothers' Day was celebrated widely in Massachusetts, Pennsylvania, and other Eastern states until the turn of the century.

Most of these ceremonies and proposals, significantly, were couched in the plural, not the singular, mode: Mothers' Day was originally a vehicle for organized social and political action by all mothers, not for celebrating the private services of one's own particular mother.

When Anna Reeves Jarvis died in 1905, her daughter, also named Anna Jarvis, began a letter-writing campaign to have a special day set aside for mothers. But by this period, there was already considerable pressure to sever the personal meaning of motherhood from its earlier political associations. The mobilization of women as community organizers was the last thing on the minds of the prominent merchants, racist politicians, and antisuffragist activists who, sometimes to Jarvis's dismay, quickly jumped on the bandwagon.[9]

In fact, the adoption of Mother's Day by the 63rd Congress on May 8, 1914 represented a reversal of everything the nineteenth-century mothers' days had stood for. The speeches proclaiming Mother's Day in 1914 linked it to celebration of home life and privacy; they repudiated women's social role beyond the household. One antisuffragist leader inverted the original intent entirely when she used the new Mother's Day as an occasion to ask rhetorically: If a woman becomes "a mother to the Municipality, who is going to mother us?" Politicians found that the day provided as many opportunities for self-promotion as did the Fourth of July. Merchants hung testimonials to their own mothers above the wares they hoped to convince customers to buy for other mothers. A day that had once been linked to controversial causes was reduced to an occasion for platitudes and sales pitches.[10]

Its bond with social reform movements broken, Mother's Day immediately drifted into the orbit of the marketing industry. The younger Jarvis had proposed that inexpensive carnations be worn to honor one's mother. Outraged when the flowers began to sell for a dollar apiece, she attacked the florists as "profiteers" and began a campaign to protect Mother's Day from such exploitation. In 1923, she managed to get a political and commercial celebration of Mother's Day cancelled in New York (on grounds, ironically, of infringement of copyright), but this was her last victory. Jarvis spent the rest of her life trying to regain control of the day, becoming more and more paranoid about those who "would undermine [Mother's Day] with their greed." She was eventually committed to a sanitarium, where she died in 1948.[11]

The history of Mother's Day is a microcosm of the simultaneous sentimentalization and commercialization of private life over the past one hundred years and of the ways in which the market has penetrated every aspect of family relations. What paved the way for this transformation was not the women's rights movement, nor the growing entry of women into the paid labor force, but the metamorphosis of domestic roles in the Gilded Age.

For all its repressiveness, the early-nineteenth-century definition of woman's sphere had given her moral responsibility beyond the household, a duty that shaded easily into social activism. Women

who participated in antislavery agitation, temperance, and welfare reform saw this work as essentially maternal in nature. Thus the earliest proponents of honoring motherhood were people allied with
such social reform movements. Toward the end of the nineteenth
century, however, a major change occurred in the role and image of
women.

The privatization of family values during the Gilded Age, described in chapter 5, meant that the roles of wife and mother lost
their transcendent moral and political significance. As historian
Paula Fass notes, by the early twentieth century the middle-class
family had become much more emotionally expressive for its members but at the same time "more and more separated from other social institutions and freed of direct responsibility to them." The
growth of family privacy, historian Barbara Laslett argues, reduced
"the sources of social support and satisfaction" for women's domestic
roles. As older political, social, and religious functions of the home
were eroded, a woman increasingly labored only for the personal
comfort of her husband and children. A focus on individual fulfillment in the home meant for many women more companionship
with their husbands, but it divested motherhood of any larger social
and political meaning.[12]

This ideological transformation of domesticity was connected to
changes in the organization and technology of production, in both
the home and the economy. These changes laid the groundwork for
the increasing entry of women into paid employment during the
twentieth century, a phenomenon largely independent of either the
suffrage movement of the early 1900s or the women's liberation
movement of the late 1960s. Indeed, the revival of feminism in the
1960s was more response than impetus to women's integration into
the labor force.

Certainly, feminism changed the terms on which women understood their work and confronted its conditions; conversely, women's
growing economic clout encouraged them to demand equality with
men both on and off the job, including the opportunity to seek fulfillment outside the family. For many women, new work opportunities *broadened* their commitment to others. To the extent that some
women, like some men, came to define self-fulfillment in terms of
materialism, immediate gratification, and "me-first" individualism,
the source of such values lay in mainstream economic and cultural
trends, not in feminism or any other dissident movement of the
1960s or 1970s.

In this chapter, I first trace the evolution of women's paid employment since the end of the nineteenth century, demonstrating that it accompanied the maturation of industrial capitalism and occurred independently of the organized women's movement. Next, I turn to a discussion of materialism and consumerism, which *do* appear increasingly androgynous in our modern culture. What links these topics is the contention that although both women's employment and the spread of consumerism derive from the expansion of mature industrial capitalism, their effects are not necessarily the same. Most of the family problems associated with women's entry into the work force stem from the *inadequate* and *incomplete* integration of women into productive work: their low wages and stressful working conditions; the failure of employers and government to adjust work patterns to new demographic realities; and the refusal of many men to share childraising and domestic work. Consumerism, however, contains inherent impediments to family and community solidarities. But consumerism was not spread by the liberation movements of women, gays or lesbians, or any other sector advocating nontraditional families or values: It emanated from the traditional assumptions and dynamics of American individualism when these were attached to the growing hegemony of business in organizing modern work, leisure, and even fantasy life. Feminism has generally *opposed* consumerism; the popular association of women's equality with an individualistic, materialistic ethic occurred after the decline of organized feminism and the co-optation of "liberated" rhetoric by the mass media and marketing industry.

Women and Work in the Nineteenth Century: The Temporary Removal of Married Women from Market Production

The first point to make about the growing participation of women in the work force during the twentieth century is that their nineteenth-century separation from productive work was itself a new—and, it turns out, transitory—state of affairs. The factory system established a more rigid division of labor and location than had previously existed between household production and production for the market. Middle-class families adapted to this division by putting men on the market side of the line and women and children on the household one, while working-class families assigned only married women to the household side, sending men, unmarried women, and youngsters out of the household into paid work. The result was a decline in the number of women, especially married ones, who produced goods and services for circulation beyond the household. Colonial wives had been referred to as "yoke-mates" or "meet-helps"; nineteenth-century wives became "dependents." Female workers ceased to be called "ladies" and were referred to as "girls," reflecting their increasing youth and single status.[13]

By 1870, women comprised only 16 percent of the labor force, and as late as 1900 a mere 5 percent to 9 percent of married women worked for wages. These figures underestimate the real contributions wives made to household income: Much paid work, such as taking in boarders or selling homemade items, was unreported; census calculations of the labor force did not then count, as they now do, persons who worked fifteen hours or more a week as unpaid laborers in a family business. But the fact remains that there was a period of more than fifty years when female labor-force participation (except for black women) was exceedingly low. And even though every decade after 1880 saw an increase in women's representation in the labor force, the reentry of married women into the mainstream of production did not occur until several decades into the twentieth century.[14]

When married white women did work at the turn of the century, they tended to do so when their children were very young, withdrawing from paid labor as soon as their sons and daughters were old enough to take jobs outside the home. This pattern was reversed during the middle years of the twentieth century: Married white women tended to work only before childbearing or after their children were in school. Not until the 1970s did a large proportion of working mothers again go out to work while their children were very young, only by this time there were many more working mothers than in the early 1900s and they tended to stay in the labor market permanently.[15] How did these transformations come about?

1900 to the Second World War: Steady Growth in Married Women's Employment

As demographer Andrew Cherlin argues, the increase in the proportion of married women who work outside the home has been a long-term consequence of maturing industrial capitalism, originating in rising real wages, shifts in the demand for labor, greater education for women, and better control over childbearing. It is an international, not just an American, phenomenon and has taken place in countries with a wide variety of cultural attitudes toward women. This suggests, of course, that structural and demographic changes associated with industrialization rather than "value upheavals" have been the prime impetus for this trend. Many of these structural and demographic innovations were evident in America as early as the 1920s, and there was already a large rise in employment of single women in the early 1900s. Economist Claudia Goldin suggests that the real question is not so much why married women, including mothers, joined the labor force during the twentieth century as why they joined it so slowly prior to the 1950s.[16]

By the early 1900s, the diffusion of household technology, the mass production of food and clothes, and the decline of home-based industry were advanced enough so that daughters were relieved of many household duties, and even married women should have been free to take on work outside the home at a much higher rate than they did. Fertility rates, moreover, had been falling steadily. The average number of children born to a woman who survived to menopause fell from 4.24 in 1880 to 3.56 in 1900 and to 3.17 by 1920.[17]

At the same time, demand for female labor grew rapidly after 1900, as the clerical and sales industries burgeoned. Employers in these sectors hired women both because of a general need for new labor and because women's lack of prior paid work experience, along with their gender, made it easier to pay them less and expand or contract their employment more easily. Women's family roles were, in fact, a form of training for many of the new jobs, which required tact, skill at pleasing people, and a certain degree of submissiveness.

Yet from 1880 to 1930, while single women entered the work force in growing numbers, married women still held back. This was partly because they were less well educated than were younger women and partly because there were serious barriers to their entry in the way work was organized and hiring conducted. Until the 1930s, the usual work week was five and a half to six days, too long to permit a married woman to complete her household tasks, even with the help of labor-saving devices. Many firms also flatly refused to hire married women. At the same time, the consumer economy that accompanied the triumph of mass production in the early 1900s may have temporarily increased some aspects of married women's work at home.

Mass production involved a *decrease* in the provision of some goods and services from outside the home: Door-to-door peddlers, for example, were replaced by centralized shopping districts. Consumption was an "expandable" job, moreover, and women who hesitated to seek full-time paid employment could easily maintain full-time housewifery by simply increasing their expectations of domestic productivity. The 1920s saw a significant increase in the amount of time wives devoted not just to shopping but also to laundering and house cleaning, despite the fact that the most arduous aspects of these tasks were eliminated in the same period.[18]

Still, there is considerable evidence that by the 1920s, participation of married women in paid work had become much more acceptable. By 1930, almost 20 percent of clerical workers were married women. In addition, consumerism had produced a new cultural rationale for the employment of married women: an ideology stressing the importance of the home as a center of consumption and encouraging aspirations toward a higher standard of living.[19] As one working wife of the 1920s expressed the new attitudes:

> No, I don't lose out with my neighbors because I work; some of them have jobs and those who don't envy us who do....We have an electric washing machine, electric iron, and vacuum sweeper....The two boys want to go to college, and I want them to. I graduated from high school myself, but I feel if I can't give my boys a little more all my work will have been useless.[20]

The Depression and the Second World War affected women's proclivities for work in contradictory ways. During the 1930s, many more married women sought employment, as their husbands were laid off or took wage cuts. Yet even while married women increased their employment from 29 percent to 35.5 percent of the female labor force, public acceptance of such employment plummeted. Federal laws and business policies discouraged the hiring of married women and mandated that they be first fired in cutbacks; twenty-six states passed laws prohibiting their employment. Despite such discrimination, the proportion of married women who worked for pay increased to more than 15 percent; however, women lost the foothold they had gained in the professions during the 1920s and were increasingly relegated to lower-status and lower-paid jobs. Rather than taking men's jobs, as opponents feared, women were primarily recruited into sex-segregated work during the course of the Depression.[21]

The effect of the Depression was to decrease the "taste" of married women for paid work. The Depression temporarily expanded the value and amount of women's household work, reducing the relative returns of full-time employment, not to mention the time available for it. Concurrently, the cultural prejudices against married working women and the undesirable nature of their jobs made work seem an act of desperation rather than a free choice. Many women who began their families in the 1940s and 1950s associated their mothers' employment during the 1930s with economic hardship and family failure. They looked forward to establishing a different pattern in their own marriages.[22]

A major reason that married women failed to develop a strong commitment to the labor force prior to the Second World War was the powerful role of sexual stereotypes in pay and promotion from 1900 to 1940. Indeed, the creation of a segregated women's sector of the economy (as opposed to segregated jobs within the same workplace) occurred during this time. One economist calculates that the contribution of outright wage discrimination to the long-standing difference in male and female earnings increased from 20 percent in 1900 to 55 percent in 1940. This was largely due to management policies that tried to bind male employees to the firm through pay raises and promotions not directly linked to productivity but excluded women as a group from advancement, however productive they may have been. Consequently, few women earned enough to give them any options other than marriage; most working women remained dependent on men for "treats," favors, and access to the increasingly commercialized world of leisure and entertainment.[23]

The Second World War brought a major shift in women's work. Between 1940 and 1945, the female labor force increased by more than 50 percent: Three-fourths of the new female workers were married, and a majority were mothers of school-age children. Government spearheaded a large and rapid shift in attitudes toward the employment of married women and mothers. The state also financed child care for mothers working in defense industries. At their peak, these centers served 1.5 million children, more than were in all other kinds of day care combined as late as 1974. The war eliminated many barriers to the employment of wives, mothers, and older women. It also gave thousands of women who had already been working their first experience of occupational mobility and the rewards of challenging, well-paid work.[24]

In the long run, the Second World War seems to have increased women's taste for work, even though in the immediate aftermath a combination of factors led married women to temporarily pull back from full-time work or at least to downgrade its centrality in their lives. Following the war, women were laid off from manufacturing jobs in droves, despite polls showing that most wished to continue working. The proportion of women in the labor force fell from 36.5 percent in 1944 to 30.8 percent in 1947.

Most women workers did not lose their jobs permanently but were simply downgraded to "women's work," such as clerical and service jobs. By the end of 1947, female employment had begun to climb again. As early as 1950, moreover, 21 percent of all married white women, and 23 percent of all urban married white women, were in the labor force. Married women accounted for more than half the total female labor force.[25]

However, it took a while for women to regain the positive image of work that they had begun to absorb during the war. There was an almost universal reimposition of sexual segregation and pay differentials by companies after the war. Working women were also the target of vehement attacks by academics, professionals, and politicians. Such setbacks interacted with pent-up desires of both women and men to start a family, producing an idealization of family life that may have slowed down and certainly concealed the steady rise in the number of married women workers.[26]

The 1950s—A Turning Point in Women's Work

At first glance, the 1950s represented a reassertion of female domesticity. But single women's employment rose rapidly, and the postwar baby boom merely created a backlog of supply-and-demand pressures that unleashed an explosion of employment among married women as the decade progressed. As large numbers of men remained in the military and new consumer industries mushroomed, demand for women workers outstripped the supply, leading to a rise in real wages in women's jobs and a relaxation of barriers to women's work. By the end of the decade, 40 percent of all women over the age of sixteen held a job. Growing numbers of these women stated that they were working for self-esteem and personal fulfillment as well as for economic needs.[27]

Rising real wages in women's industries increased the costs of staying home and provided new incentives for married women to work. The rapid disappearance of small farms and other family businesses led to the elimination of remaining pockets of female household production, while the diffusion of new appliances finally overwhelmed the ability of make-work and heightened domestic expectations to preserve housewifery, in the absence of young children, as a full-time job. Increasing numbers of married women in the 1950s had time on their hands—a relatively new experience.[28]

Ironically, the young women who chose early marriage, domesticity, and increased fertility in the postwar years, departing from their own mothers' tendency to prolong education or work before marriage, contributed both to the growing demand for married women in the labor market and eventually to its supply. A tremendous expansion of women's jobs in clerical work, teaching, nursing, and retail sales occurred after the war. Yet the postwar marriage boom, on top of the Depression fertility drop, decreased the supply of single women to fill these vacancies. Consequently, employers changed their hiring practices to accommodate married women. Government policy encouraged the expansion of married women's employment, not because government was dominated by liberals or feminists, but out of desire to foster industrial expansion—as well as a cold war fear that the Russians would win educational and technological superiority if Americans did not use their "womanpower" more effectively. The GI Bill also fostered employment of wives by offering men incentives to stay in school but paying family allowances so low that wives needed to work in order to supplement them. Married women comprised the majority of the growth in the female work force throughout the 1950s, and between 1940 and 1960 there was a 400 percent increase in the number of working mothers; by 1960, women with children under the age of eighteen accounted for nearly one-third of all women workers.[29]

The women who first initiated these changes in work patterns were older married women with grown children who had accumulated premarital job experience as young singles in the 1920s or 1930s. But the demographic strategies of their daughters, especially early fertility and closer spacing of children, also increased the supply of married women workers. By the 1950s, the average age of a woman at the time of her last birth was only thirty; most women had

their youngest child in school by the time they were in their late thirties, and they therefore had opportunities to take jobs at that time.[30]

The increasing integration of women's work-force participation
with marriage, then, preceded the growth of feminism, as did the
shortening of the period of life in which women made a full-time
commitment to motherhood. Women's behavior, as both wives and
workers, changed *prior* to the rise in feminism. Even after the revival
of the women's rights movement in the mid-1960s, most of the
women who pioneered new marital, fertility, and work patterns were
not in revolt against mainstream culture. Steven McLaughlin and his
fellow researchers conclude that "for the most part, women modified
their attitudes toward work, family, marriage, childrearing, and other
aspects of the life course only *after* they had already established patterns of behavior markedly different from those of previous generations of women."[31]

Women's Work in the 1960s and 1970s

In the 1960s and 1970s, a variety of new circumstances and motives
impelled even more married women, and unprecedented numbers of
mothers, to enter the labor force. Demographers have minor disagreements over what these motives were but agree that, initially at
least, they were largely independent of the reemergence of organized
feminism.

Many of the new women workers were from age and income
groups that already had established long histories of participation in
paid labor: women over forty; women in lower-income households;
young, childless married women of all educational levels; and black
women in general. Lower-middle-class married women with a high
school education had not adopted the high-fertility strategies of the
1950s, so they were available earlier than were women from other income groups to take jobs in expanding sectors of the economy. Thus
"a large proportion of the increase in the women's work force between 1960 and 1980" is explained by the existence of historically
precedented motivations and long-range trends, many of which became obvious in the 1970s because their accumulated impact was so
great. In every decade since 1880, after all, there had been an increase in women's paid work; no group of women who chose to work
in any of those decades ever permanently returned to the home. Be-

tween 1940 and 1950, there was a 29 percent growth in the number of women in the labor force. In the 1960s, the number of women at work grew by 39 percent. The 41 percent growth rate in the 1970s, accordingly, did not come out of the blue, but the absolute increases had become highly visible by then.[32]

For a minority of women workers, though, both the behavior and the motivations were qualitatively new. Demographer Richard Easterlin suggests that the relative affluence of the 1950s stimulated an increase in fertility among middle-class Americans. However, children born during the late 1940s and early 1950s faced a contradiction: They aspired to a high standard of living but their numbers created an oversupply of competitors for well-paying jobs. The clash between this cohort's high expectations and the reality of a tight labor market caused many couples to postpone marriage and childbearing in the 1970s or to send wives to work.[33]

Historian Susan Householder Van Horn argues that the same kind of factors were present as early as the 1960s for some middle-class wives and mothers. Their entry into the work force was an attempt to maintain the relative status of the middle class in a period where, in all but the highest professional and management jobs, wage increases for white-collar salaried workers did not rise as fast as did wage increases for blue-collar workers. Although their absolute pay remained greater, middle-class families may have had a sense that they were losing the relative advantage they had learned to expect in the 1950s; they therefore adopted new work strategies not so much to "keep up with the Joneses" as to stay ahead of the O'Malleys.[34]

The unprecedented entry of upper-middle-class wives into work during the 1960s, however, cannot be explained by economic need or even by relative deprivation. It reversed the earlier inverse correlation between a husband's income and the likelihood that his wife would work. By the late 1960s, for the first time, college-educated wives were *more* likely than high-school graduates to contribute financially to their families. Although the pioneers of married women's employment in the 1950s and early 1960s had been lower-middle-class or working-class women with high school educations, it was largely these upper-middle-class, college-educated women who initiated "the ideological revolution" of the 1960s, including the demand for gender equality and the idea that work was an important component of life satisfaction for women. For these women, Van Horn argues, "the prime motivation lay in the declining attractions of the home."[35]

Working Women and the Revival of a Women's Rights Movement

In the nineteenth century, it was not merely beliefs about women's nature that had kept housewives close to home. Even in the middle class, household chores and food preparation were far too time consuming and complicated to be turned over entirely to hired help, and in the working class the value of a woman's household labor generally outweighed her potential wage earnings.[36]

By 1900, the relative value of home work and paid work had begun to be reversed. Between 1900 and 1940, the economic necessity for full-time home work further declined: Fewer children were born, products for use in the home were increasingly purchased from outside sources, and income-producing home work almost disappeared. But the sentimentalization of motherhood continued unabated. The result, historian Glenna Matthews argues, was an increase in make-work and a further trivialization of domesticity. By the 1950s, as we have seen, housewives were supposed to find their moral meaning, political significance, and societal worth in clean laundry collars, new curtains, and creative cookery.[37]

This trivialization paved the way for feminism among the same middle-class educated women who had led the postwar family boom. In 1957, a Smith College survey of its graduates found that the homemakers who responded "resented the wide disparity between the idealized image society held of them as housewives and mothers and the realities of their daily routines." A study of younger women who graduated from college between 1945 and 1955 revealed that the full-time housewives in the sample suffered from lower self-esteem, more fears about aging, and greater insecurity about their childraising skills than did the employed women. Friedan, in her 1963 bestseller, did not *cause* homemakers' self-doubt and discontent; she merely put together the Smith College Survey data to generalize about "the feminine mystique" that enveloped these women's lives and left them so unsure of their own identity.[38]

It was not the campus activists of the 1960s but their mothers who initiated the women's movement. As some of these women went back to work or school or found themselves divorced after years of homemaking, they rediscovered the muted protests of women workers in the 1930s and 1940s and made connections with the small generation of women's rights proponents who had survived the 1950s.[39]

My own mother is a good example of the kind of woman who recognized herself in Friedan's book. She attended college in the late
1930s, married, and then worked in the war industry for a while. It
was satisfying work, but she and her fellow workers were fired as
soon as the first shipload of veterans came home. She found a new
job when my father went back to school on the GI Bill but quit when
she became pregnant. As a housewife in the 1950s and early 1960s
she spent every summer, full-time, with her children. Only during
the school year did she try her hand at other projects: supervising
the building of a new home, redecorating, writing, painting a little,
and being active in community affairs.

Gradually, she found something that seemed particularly fulfilling:
writing a novel. In later life, she admitted that many days she could
hardly wait to get her family out the door so she could get back to her
book. But we children certainly never suspected this, and neither did
her husband, since she made sure to put everything away and start
dinner before he got home. Like many 1950s men, my father didn't
like his wife to have projects that distracted her attention from him.
At the same time, again like many 1950s fathers, he wanted something different for his daughters: They should go to college, and even
though their marriage was to be expected, his girls were "too smart"
to spend their whole lives "darning socks and cooking dinner."

By the 1960s, with one child in high school and another leaving
for college, my mother began to think about going back to school
herself. Struggling with her own fears, the social prejudices against
women, and a rocky marriage no longer held together "for the sake
of the kids," she read *The Feminine Mystique*. I can still remember her
excited letters and phone calls about the book. Indignantly, she recounted what she had learned: how merchandisers had purposely
added extra steps to cake mix instructions to make wives feel more
needed in the kitchen, how advertisers manipulated women's insecurities and used sex to sell new products.

Personally, I was bored stiff. So were my many other friends who
received similar phone calls from their mothers. To us, it was yet another example of the older generation's foibles, absolutely irrelevant
to our lives: We were studying for tests, worrying about dates, con-
templating the decline of the sexual double standard with mixed
curiosity and dismay, and gradually expanding our interest in intellectual ideas and international events. The dilemmas of either housewives or working women were miles away.

The reemergence of a women's rights movement occurred some

time between the publication of *The Feminine Mystique* in 1963 and the founding convention of the National Organization for Women in 1966. It was strengthened in the late 1960s by young college women who were outraged at their treatment by men with whom they worked in the civil rights and antiwar movements or who were shocked to bump into a glass ceiling in their education after having been encouraged to aim for excellence. On August 26, 1970, the first mass women's march in America since the suffrage struggle brought more than 50,000 women, ten times more than had been expected, to Central Park in New York. In the 1970s, the movement was further fueled when college-educated young women entering the job market had their "consciousness raised" by the gap between the skills they brought and the way they were treated on the job. Poor black women brought yet another dimension to the movement when they established the National Welfare Rights Organization. A feminist current also developed within the traditional labor movement, leading to formation of the Coalition for Labor Union Women in 1974.[40]

The revival of feminism changed the ways women analyzed and confronted their experiences at both work and home, but it is important to reiterate that married women's work entry was well under way before there was a significant rise in feminist values and consciousness. Naturally, however, there were mutual influences and feedback effects between women's employment, feminism, and marital norms. As more and more married women worked, single women came to expect that they would eventually return to work after marriage. They might therefore postpone marriage and childbearing to complete their education or establish themselves in the work world. As women gained experience and self-confidence, they won benefits that made work more attractive and rewarding; with longer work experience and greater educational equalization, they became freer to leave an unhappy marriage; and as divorce became more of a possibility, women tended to hedge their bets by insisting on the right to work. Although very few researchers believe that women's employment has been a direct cause of the rising divorce rate, most agree that women's new employment options have made it easier for couples to separate if they are dissatisfied for other reasons. In turn, the fragility of marriage has joined economic pressures, income incentives, educational preparation, and dissatisfaction with domestic isolation as one of the reasons that modern women choose to work.[41]

The issue of divorce is a good example of how changes in behavior preceded changes in attitudes. The postwar rise in divorce, aside from a sharp but temporary surge in 1946, began in the early 1960s. The sources of this increase are hotly debated, but the first cracks in the 1950s marital facade were not made primarily by feminists. Perhaps the most significant component of the early increase in divorce was the rising rate among 1950s parents whose children had left home. Author Barbara Ehrenreich suggests that it was men rather than women who began the "flight from commitment" in the 1950s and 1960s and that it was women's growing recognition of their vulnerability that eventually led many toward feminism.[42]

Be that as it may, feminist views on divorce were not the trigger for its increase, because new attitudes did not arise until marital behaviors had already changed substantially. In 1945 and 1966, national polls asked adults if they thought that the divorce laws in their states were too strict or not strict enough. In both years, the most frequent response was "not strict enough," and the proportion expressing this opinion was nearly identical. Not until after 1968 did the percentage declaring that divorce should be made easier begin to rise. This change in attitude seems to have been a result of experience rather than ideology. A long-term study of women in the 1960s and 1970s found that a woman's attitude toward divorce did not affect the likelihood of her getting a divorce in the future, but women who had gone through a divorce tended to be more approving of divorce in general.[43]

This pattern even applied to women whose ideology specifically condemned divorce. In the 1970s, Anita Bryant, a national spokeswoman for traditional marital and sexual values, gained widespread publicity for her drive to repeal gay rights legislation in Florida. By 1980, divorced and sidelined by her own movement, she confided to an interviewer that she could see "some valid reasons why militant feminists are doing what they are doing....I guess I can better understand the gays' and the feminists' anger and frustration."[44]

Perhaps nothing better sums up the extent to which women's work patterns and values have changed in the twentieth century than the dramatic influx of mothers of young children into the work force. This is what links female employment to feminism and "family collapse" for most conservative commentators. Only women who put their own selfish aspirations above duty to their children, they reason, would curtail their maternal responsibilities so drastically. And since there is nothing in traditional values to foster such behavior, it must have come from the women's liberation movement.

But even the dramatic rise in maternal employment seems to have preceded feminist values. "On the threshold of adulthood in the late 1960s and early 1970s, baby-boom women imagined they would lead lives very similar to those their mothers had led." In 1969, a majority of college women expected to quit work when their first child was born and not return until the youngest was grown. As late as 1970, 78 percent of married women under age forty-five said that it was better for wives to be homemakers and husbands to do the breadwinning. It was largely economics rather than feminism that led these women to violate their own expectations and eventually to reorder their values: For many, Van Horn argues, "work begun as an opportunity soon became an economic necessity as cohort effects intensified and the economy changed." Inflation in the 1970s made two incomes especially essential for families who wished to buy a house, so that mothers of young children had the strongest incentives to work.[45]

Certainly, the role of rising aspirations is relevant here. In the early 1970s, people's perceptions of a family's required minimum income rose faster than did real economic growth. These perceptions may have been fanned by the consumerism and materialism discussed below, but they also turned out to be remarkably prescient: By the mid-1970s, the inflation rate exceeded the average income gain for Americans, and by the end of the 1970s, as we shall see in chapter 11, two wages were necessary for families to maintain any continued improvement in real income.[46]

One might argue that such improvement was not a true need, that people were sacrificing the quality of family life in their endless pursuit of a higher standard of living. If so, there is no evidence that such motives derived from the feminist movement or any other dissident element in American culture. Instead, they were built into the consumer culture that grew logically and naturally out of rearrangements in capitalist production in the early twentieth century.

Feminism developed hand in hand with women's employment and the rising divorce rate; the interactions between these phenomena are complex and multistranded, and a lot of personal pain has been associated with adjustment to these changes. I will argue later that most of the pain is caused not by the equality women have won but by the inequalities they have failed to uproot.[47] For now, I will consider one particular myth—that it is feminism or careerism, or some insidious combination of the two, that is responsible for the rise in materialism and the decline in commitment in America. Feminists certainly support the right of women to work full-time, whether or not they have children, as well as a woman's right to leave an unsatisfactory marriage. Yet the growth of a materialist consumer mentality that values things above relationships should not be confused either with the increase in women's employment or with the rise of feminism.

Consumerism and Materialism in American Life

In chapter 9, I show that it is a mistake to equate expansion of maternal employment with a decline in commitment to family life or a deterioration in the well-being of children. I am not denying that many Americans, male and female, do place pursuit of material gain above cultivation of intergenerational obligations and social, familial, or personal commitments. But I suggest that an acquisitive, consumerist outlook is an *alternative* response than is feminism to the dynamics of democratic capitalism in the twentieth century.

Consumerism and materialism affect working adults and nonworking ones, both sexes and all ages, people who endorse new roles for women and people who oppose them. But unlike feminism, consumerism and materialism are not movements for social change. They take no critical stance toward mainstream culture; indeed, they proceed from the routine operations of advanced industrial capitalism. They are as American as apple pie.[48]

Certainly, modern consumerism seems to violate traditional American values about the work ethic, self-restraint, and participation in voluntary associations. But it is important to realize that these earlier values arose in the initial period of capital accumulation; they began to erode from the moment that mass production became dominant within the private enterprise system and a national market took the place of separate, localized markets that had left large areas of production and exchange ungoverned by the principles of profit maximization.

The Origins of Consumerism—1900 to the 1960s

By the late nineteenth century, political economists realized that the ethic of hard work and self-restraint that had helped to industrialize

America had serious drawbacks now that most industries had the capacity for mass production. If everyone deferred gratification, who would buy the new products? Between 1870 and 1900, the volume of advertising multiplied more than tenfold. Giant department stores were built to showcase new consumer items for urban residents, while rural residents were exposed to the delights and temptations of mail-order catalogs. The word *consumption* increasingly lost its earlier connotations of destroying, wasting, or using up, and came instead to refer in a positive way to the satisfying of human needs and desires.[49]

Historians may debate the periodization of consumer culture, but they agree that by the 1920s a new ethos was widespread. As a newspaper in Muncie, Indiana, editorialized: "The American citizen's first importance to his country is no longer that of citizen but that of consumer." Merchandisers explicitly aimed to sell products by promoting ever-increasing desires for "a better way of life." Soap manufacturers were advised to sell not just cleansing products but "afternoons of leisure"; advertisers tried to wrap each product "in the tissue of a dream."[50]

Since women were thought to buy more than three-fourths of all personal commodities, much of the consumer campaign was aimed at them. Many books, such as *Selling Mrs. Consumer,* laid out the various ways in which women might be brought to embrace the concept of "creative waste." Women's consumer role was somewhat more morally ambiguous than the almost religious veneration accorded to entrepreneurs and salesmen in the 1920s, but the vices involved in consumerism were socially acceptable enough so that theft by women was increasingly accounted a disease—kleptomania—instead of a crime; and the virtues of consumption were lofty enough to justify a little contamination by the market. As "purchasing agent for the home," the housewife was told, she had the chance to create a space where each member of her family could find personal fulfillment.[51]

Consumerism highlighted women in another way as well. By the early 1920s, advertisers had discovered that they could also "profit by skilful [sic] appeals to sex sentiment in men." Marketing specialists soon found that "pretty little girls" as well as attractive women appealed to this sentiment; there was the added bonus that little girls, unlike women in that period, could be shown in various states of undress.[52]

The prominence of women in consumerism coincided with the

depoliticization of their drive for autonomy and the eclipse of an activist women's political culture. The older generation of activists was outraged by the self-indulgence promulgated by mass culture in the 1920s and the way it substituted for social purpose in women's lives.[53]

The real takeoff of consumer culture, though, like the expansion of married women's employment, began during the 1950s. Advertising increased by 400 percent between 1945 and 1960, a growth rate faster than that of the GNP. As motivational researcher Ernest Dichter explained advertising's aim: "We are now confronted with the problem of permitting the average American to feel moral...even when he is taking two vacations a year and buying a second or third car. One of the basic problems of prosperity, then, is to demonstrate that the hedonistic approach to life is a moral, not an immoral one."[54]

It was the marketing strategists of the 1950s, not the "permissive" child-care ideologues or political subversives of the 1960s, who first attempted to bypass parental authority and "pander" to American youth. As one marketing consultant pointed out: "An advertiser who touches a responsive chord in youth can generally count on the parent to succumb finally to purchasing the product." In 1958, *Life* magazine ran an article entitled "Kids: Built-In Recession Cure." American four-year-olds, marveled the author, represent "a backlog of business orders that will take two decades to fulfill."[55]

In the 1950s, "patriotism, freedom, and consumption became interchangeable ideas, continually reinforced through the magic of television." This equation has imparted a materialistic cast to American ideology ever since. In 1985, for example, one of the survivors of the Iran hostage crisis told the *New York Times* how his experience made him "appreciate my freedom, the things we take for granted": In America, "we can watch television, change channels. We have choices." After the fall of the Berlin Wall, news reports repeatedly illustrated the freedoms being sought by East Germans by showing the overflowing counters of West German shops.[56]

Although the 1950s introduced new levels of hedonism and materialism into American culture, the decade "contained" the radical implications of these values by attaching them to family togetherness. By the 1970s, such values were more often turned *against* family togetherness, but this potential was certainly there from the beginning, as anyone who has ever watched "The Bob Cummings Show" (1955–59) would have noticed. Cummings played a swinging bachelor whose career as a photographer allowed him to caress his "girls" as he positioned them for shots. His job also gave him the opportunity to "play the field," sometimes juggling two or three dates in one evening. His promiscuity was not officially admitted because he never took the "girls" home to bed in the house he shared with his widowed sister and her teenage boy, but it was leeringly implied in every episode.

During the 1960s, characters like Cummings managed to dump their chaperons. The tight links between patriotism, consumerism, sexual titillation, and eventual encasement in the family were weakened. The first blows against family sentimentality were struck by people who had no connections with student radicals or women's liberationists but who accepted the traditional double standard entirely. *Playboy* magazine, for example, featured in its first issue an article entitled "Miss Gold-Digger of 1953." Most of its articles and ads were devoted to the idea that since women were only out to catch a man, men needed to learn how to get as much sex from them as possible without getting trapped. *Playboy* invited men to take over areas of domestic and personal consumption formerly managed by females: food, clothes, wine, and body scents. Men didn't need a "purchasing agent for the home" anymore; all they needed was a nubile partner for the bedroom.[57]

Weighing in on the women's side, Helen Gurley Brown's 1962 bestseller, *Sex and the Single Girl,* revealed attitudes that would have been equally antithetical to feminists but certainly broke with gender stereotypes. Brown counseled women not to limit their gold-digging to marriage, which "is insurance for the *worst* years of your life. During your best years you don't need a husband. You do need a man of course every step of the way, and they are often cheaper emotionally and a lot more fun by the bunch." She advised flirting with mechanics and butchers to get good service and gave hints about how to extract the presents and treats that "are part of the spoils of being single." As for married men, the single woman should "use" them "in a perfectly nice way just as they use you."[58]

By 1965, Madison Avenue had picked up on this greater openness about what was actually traditional sexual commerce and launched a "creative revolution" involving the sexualization of hitherto sacrosanct objects and ideas. In one ad, for instance, the Statue of Liberty suggestively modeled a new zipper. Few people charged the makers of such ads with unpatriotic disrespect: They were selling private enterprise, after all, not registering a political protest.[59]

Dissident groups used the same irreverence for diametrically opposed political and economic purposes. They attacked 1950s family and sexual morality for tolerating racism and foreign interventionism. The student counterculture—a different group, for the most part, from the politicos—mocked consumer conformity and advocated a more open sexuality. Women's activists criticized the gender inequalities in the ideal family, the countercultural alternatives, *and* the political dissident movement. All these forces helped loosen the strings that had made a package deal out of the cult of youthfulness, the expansion of sexuality, the equation of patriotism with consumerism, and the continued sentimentalization of family life as the final culmination of the search for personal self-fulfillment.

In this sense, the counterculture, the student movement, and feminism, although they originally developed as a critique of consumer culture, contributed to its evolution away from "family values." But most of the individualistic excesses attributed to these movements actually stemmed from the advertising industry, which appropriated the imagery of rebellion for entirely different ends, and from exaggerated press reports: Woodstock, for example, was a one-time "happening," while the antiwar movement routinely mobilized much larger crowds in peaceful, legal, cooperative, far more sober political demonstrations; the infamous "bra burning" never actually occurred.

Consumerism, the Mass Media, and the Family Since the 1960s

In the 1970s, the continuing influx of women into the labor market, along with the entry of younger workers who had been influenced by the counterculture or the antiwar movement, led business to seek new marketing techniques. American advertisers were asking themselves, according to the *New York Times,* "How Do You Talk to a Working Woman?" Their answer was to use the language of liberation to focus attention on personal and *purchasable* ways of breaking older restrictions.[60]

A recent historian of American television points out that "it was largely as a marketing device that the turbulence of the middle to late 1960s and the adversarial spirit of the generation coming of age during this period found their way into the genres of television entertainment." The fashion industry translated the 1960s revolt into a series of ready-to-wear "statements" about "individual" identity. Ads such as

"You've Come a Long Way, Baby" reduced women's demands for equality into the right to smoke and wear sexy clothes. It was *Playgirl* magazine (established in 1973), not radical feminists or lesbians, who interpreted the protest against the sexual double standard as leading to an equal-opportunity right to leer at the naked opposite sex.[61]

By the 1970s, the baby-boom generation had separated pursuit of the American Dream from its former tight connection with family formation. Their spending became "less home centered," for example, and oriented more toward personal recreation. As historian Elaine Tyler May remarks, however, "the moral distance between the baby boomers and their parents is a matter of some debate. The baby boomers continued to pursue the quest for meaning through intimacy that had been at the heart of the containment ethos, but they gave up on containment."[62]

For significant numbers of this generation and the one after it, the quest for meaning, especially after the decline of organized feminism and other social movements, tended increasingly toward individualistic and materialistic goals. Many of the young women interviewed in the 1980s by sociologist Ruth Sidel, for example, had adopted the egalitarian goals of feminism without its emphasis on transforming social values, and they simply modified the American Dream to include achievement by women. Their vision of equality was that they would be able to move freely into an affluent world envisioned "straight out of 'Dallas', 'Dynasty', or 'L.A. Law.'"[63]

But the world view imparted by such television shows did not derive from the nontraditional or antifamily values of liberal writers and producers, as conservatives claim. Advertising departments in the mass media refer to the content of their various productions as the "wrapper" for the real product, the ads themselves.[64] Once we understand that the primary driving force behind most editorial or programming decisions is what attracts advertisers, we can see why the eclipse of traditional family themes in the media during the 1970s and 1980s was pioneered by the same forces that first marketed such themes in the 1950s.

The 1950s family, supposedly the peak of tradition, was in many ways simply the "wrapper" for an extension of commodity production to new areas of life, an extension that paved the way for the commercialization of love and sex so often blamed on the 1960s. The "wholesome" television serials that some people confuse in memory with actual 1950s life were early attempts to harness mass entertainment to sales of goods. With only three to five channels for viewers to choose from, a show that hoped to be competitive had to attract approximately 30 percent of all viewers. Consequently, advertisers favored shows that presented "universal themes" embodied in homogenized families without serious divisions of interest by age, gender, income, or ethnic group. The hope was that everyone could identify with these families and hence with the mass-produced appliances that were always shown in conjunction with the mass-produced sentiments: Ozzie and Harriet, for example, had some of their most heartwarming talks in front of the Hotpoint kitchen appliances that the show was supposed to help sell.[65]

Once the market for such big-ticket family items began to slow, the next growth area had to be the individual: a Hotpoint range for the family, but "A Sony of My Owny." Radio pioneered "micromarketing," but television soon got into the act, partitioning the mythical family of the 1950s into as many different varieties and subsets as possible. The modern media has not become antifamily, it has simply become more sophisticated in targeting distinct audience segments—preteens, yuppies, buppies, swinging singles, alienated youth, seniors, and working parents—and wooing their dollars by emphasizing the differences that require separate images and their own products.[66]

The Impact of Consumerism on Personal Life

Consumerism constitutes the major source of materialistic individualism in American life, creating powerful pressures against long-term family commitments and social solidarities. Of course, the hegemony of consumerism should not be overdrawn. Historians and pollsters are continually surprised by the persistence of alternative values in modern consumer culture. There are even sources of shared meaning and social action in some of the expanded expectations fanned by consumerism. Audiences, furthermore, are not passive, and they may extract different meanings from ads and cultural products than are intended by their producers.[67]

Nevertheless, advertisers powerfully reinforce a world view in which every thing or person we encounter is evaluated by its ability to satisfy needs or improve self-images that are constantly in flux. Philosopher Lawrence Cahoone argues that we live "in thrall to a material world" that we manipulate with increasing ease but cannot understand as a unified whole; Christopher Lasch suggests that many people are enslaved "by fantasies" even more than by things.[68]

Fantasies are not the best basis on which to construct family relationships and personal ties. Western individualism has always fed daydreams about escaping external constraints and family obligations, but prior to the era of mass consumption, most people had no doubt that the real world imposed limits on self-aggrandizement. They knew that the only sure source of self-identity and security lay in relationships with others. Consumer society has increasingly broken down our sense that we depend on others, that we have to live with tradeoffs or accept a package deal in order to maintain social networks.

"The sky's the limit." "Go for the gusto." "Why settle for anything less than the best?" Consumer culture insists that we can pick and choose from the "free market" of goods, emotions, images, relationships: If we are "smart shoppers" we can "have it all" and still "stand out from the crowd." Revlon alone offers women more than 150 different shades of lipstick, but saleswomen at cosmetic counters tell prospective buyers that the way to customize the "perfect look for *you*" is by layering two or three different colors at the same time. "The only limit is your imagination." The cumulative result of these messages is that many people have learned to experience liberation "not as the freedom to choose one course of action over another but as the freedom to choose everything at once." We have begun to believe that we can shop around not only for things but also for commitments, that we can play mix and match even with our personal identities and most intimate relations. Simultaneously, we experience a blurring of the distinction between illusion and reality, people and goods, image and identity, self and surroundings.[69]

The flip side of the urge to have it all is the fear of settling for too little. Something *more* real might come along; or what we thought was permanent might dissolve at any moment. The modern urge to transcend constraints—of nature, other people, or even of our own human limitations—is itself a sort of compulsion. "Struggling to liberate ourselves from time, space, and culture, we are too busy to be satisfied." Economist David Levine claims that market society has created "a social hierarchy of neediness," in which people define their worth by the number of needs they seek to fill. A recent article in *USA Today* reports that the "perfect day," spent on pursuits recommended by time management experts, is forty-two hours long! Some individuals turn even leisure into a form of relentless work as they strive to avoid "missing out" on opportunities. Others are terrified by the possibility of "premature" commitment: The sense that all choice is good and more choice is better is a profoundly destabilizing one for interpersonal relationships.[70]

It is important not to exaggerate this trait. Most people whose relationships break up, for example, are not pursuing individual "liberation" or hedonism. One major study of divorced fathers found that they deeply desired "sustained, meaningful relationships" rather than "superficial encounters." The difficulty of building such relationships today is as much a product of the unrealistic private family ideals I described in chapters 3 and 5 as it is of purely selfish individualism. Many people's "self-absorption" results not from desire for instant gratification but from a desperate attempt to reconstruct their inner selves to cope with new life experiences and changing roles.[71]

Still, the more people deny the social basis of their identity, the more easily seduced they are by consumerism's promise that one can become anything one wishes. And the more we see our identity as a personal achievement that can be constructed or made over with the aid of commodities, self-help books, or new social skills, the more we value but the less we are able to define the one good that becomes scarce in a consumer society: sincerity. As targets of too many competing claims from advertisers and as perceptive observers of our own self-presentation, we are acutely aware of our vulnerability to delusion and our capacity to delude. Thus we are haunted by doubt about our authenticity, our "true feelings," our very existence apart from the "dazzling array of images" with which we have surrounded ourselves.[72]

This self-preoccupation is what numerous observers have called narcissism, and its consequences for family life and personal commitments are profound. While narcissism may lead to hedonistic behavior, in a more fundamental way it stems, as Lasch argues, "not so much [from] self-indulgence as self-doubt." Distrusting their capacity for authentic feeling but enamored of their ability to manipulate sensation, narcissists alternate between feelings of worthlessness and grandiose fantasies of self-importance. They seek self-sufficiency in order to avoid the conflicts, tradeoffs, and disappointment of personal commitments, yet their sense of self is so unstable that they rely on experts, audiences, consumer purchases, or love relationships to confirm their existence. They vacillate between an abject dependence on relationships, mind-altering substances, or outside approval and a blanket repudiation of all neediness as an "addiction."[73]

The search for newness that drives consumer society combines with our lack of public values to both heighten our dependence on love and undermine our ability to sustain it. The yearning to receive validation from new things and people, along with the expectation that all needs can be filled if we just shop in the right place, creates individuals who are both "in love with love" and unable to prevent themselves from "outgrowing" any particular love. Our dependence on love leads us to demand the constant renewal of romance, gift exchange, and self-revelation. But as soon as we can take someone's gifts for granted, or their novelty wears off, the love is at risk. Boredom, argues sociologist Richard Sennett, is the logical consequence of relationships constructed according to the cult of private intimacy; infidelity and planned obsolescence are consumer society's answer to boredom: "When two people are out of revelations,...all too often the relationship comes to an end."[74]

Consumerism, the Work Ethic, and the Family

The problem of consumerism is sometimes posed as a collapse of the work ethic, often by the same people who blame women's adoption of the work ethic for ruining family life. However, a work ethic does not necessarily provide an alternative to the consumer ethic; frequently both stem from the same sources and have the same effects. Almost everyone knows the workaholic father who is as totally unavailable to his children as any man who abandoned his family to pursue a hedonistic life.

Sociologist Robert Bellah and associates point out that "an emphasis on hard work and self-support can go hand in hand with an isolating preoccupation with the self....The problem is not so much the presence or absence of a 'work ethic' as the meaning of work and the ways it links, or fails to link, individuals to one another." The private family values generally thought of as traditional have a built-in tendency to degenerate into me-first individualism because they ignore the fact that "work is a moral relationship between people," a relationship that can support family life only if it extends beyond any particular family and forges bonds throughout the community as a whole.[75]

The way work is organized and rewarded in America today exacerbates consumerism and individual alienation by eating away at family time, neighborhood cohesion, and public solidarities. Most individuals still attempt to carve out space for personal commitments, family ties, and even social obligations, but they must do so in *opposition* to both job culture and consumer culture. To blame their frequent setbacks or defeats on "abandonment of traditional family roles" is ahistorical and unfair. Nowhere is this more evident than in the tremendous changes that have occurred in sex, reproduction, aging, and the life course—the subjects of the following chapter.

8

"First Comes Love, Then Comes Marriage, Then Comes Mary with a Baby Carriage":

Marriage, Sex, and Reproduction

IN 1963, I worked for a time at a mental hospital in Washington state. Although the psychiatrist and psychologist in charge were men, 90 percent of the rest of the staff, from the lowest-paid attendant counselors to the more highly trained occupational therapists and researchers, were women. Despite our different pasts and trajectories—some of us going on to college, some likely to work at the hospital for life; some young and unmarried, others older women with children in school—we exchanged confidences that now seem rare among people of such different racial, class, and age backgrounds. What bridged the gap between us was our sense that we all shared, or would share, a common life course—a predictable pattern in which women fell in love, got married, had sex, and bore children. Sometimes, granted, they had sex first, but they eventually married; if they did not, any children that resulted were adopted into a family that had proceeded in the accepted manner. Marriage, after all, was central to everyone's establishment of adult status and identity, and since we were women, marriage and childrearing would occupy the bulk of our active adult lives.

Jeri,* the physical therapist, married since 1951, had three children. She had gone "all the way" with her future husband while in college, a fact he often threw up to her when they argued over whether she could bring friends home from work. Sue, who dropped out of high school in 1952 to get married, had a similar sexual and marital history,

*I have changed the names of these women for obvious reasons.

though her fights with her husband were usually triggered by his infidelities. Sherry and Gwen had had sex with a couple of other men before their marriages in the late 1950s, but they would never admit this to their husbands. Camilla had been a virgin at marriage in 1961, and she now regretted it. Carol and Willie Lee did not expect to be virgins when they married and claimed they would never put up with Jeri's husband's attitudes, but they did think I was too "young and innocent" to hang out with Annette, the "wild" one in the bunch. Still single at twenty-four, she had a tendency to develop huge crushes on men who stood out from the crowd in any way, from hospital administrators to the lead singer in the band at the local bar. If the only way she could spend some time with them was in a one-night stand, so be it. Annette was hardly permissive, however. She joined the older women in condemning the counselor who had gotten pregnant a few years earlier, put her baby up for adoption, and come back "pretending nothing had happened."

In 1983, I went to a twenty-year reunion of people who had worked in our ward. Many of the older women still worked there, although half were divorced and one had died. Of the younger ones, almost a quarter remained unmarried, two with children out of wedlock; another quarter had been divorced at least once. Annette, after admitting to herself that she had never been sexually attracted to men anyway, had finally settled down in a monogamous, long-term relationship: She and an older divorced woman had been together for eleven years. Willie Lee's husband had had a vasectomy in his previous marriage, so they were trying to adopt a baby.

The breakdown of the expectations of these women was not exceptional, nor was it caused by willful abandonment of traditional family roles and values. None of the women I spoke with was quite sure how she got where she was today. Yet even those who had experienced the most pain in their transitions saw no way of going back to older patterns, either for themselves or for their children.

The breakdown of the tight links and orderly progression we had once assumed to exist between marriage, sex, reproduction, and childrearing provides compelling evidence for those who contend that a "revolution" has occurred in family life. Marriage, for example, is no longer the major transition into adulthood. The average age for marriage has risen by six years since 1950. More than three-quarters of today's eighteen- to twenty-four-year-old men and women have never married, and the majority of young adults today leave their parental homes and establish themselves in jobs well before marriage. Marriage also is less likely to last until death. About 50 percent of first marriages, and 60 percent of second ones, can be expected to end in divorce. In 1988, sixteen out of every thousand children under age eighteen saw their parents divorce, down from nineteen in 1980, but still twice as many as in 1963. As a result of both the rising age for marriage and the frequency of divorce, men and women spend, on average, more than half their lives unmarried.[1]

Men and women also live more of their lives alone. Despite recent increases in the number of grown children who live with one or both of their parents, the number of single-person households has risen dramatically. Almost four times as many Americans between the ages of thirty-five and forty-four live alone today as did so in 1970.[2]

Childrearing is no longer as tightly linked to marriage as in the past. Approximately three-quarters of a million unmarried couples in America are raising children together. In 1990, a quarter of all new births were out of wedlock; in half of them, there was no identified father. Since parenthood has ceased to inhibit divorce the way it did as late as 1970, more than half of American children will live in a single-parent household for some period during their childhood.[3]

Sex is far more likely to occur outside of marriage than at any time during recent history. By the mid-1980s, 75 percent of American women were sexually active before marriage. There are 2.9 million cohabiting couples in America today, an increase of 80 percent since 1980. People also are initiating sex at an earlier age. The percentage of women aged fifteen to nineteen who had had sexual intercourse at least once increased by one-third between 1971 and 1979.[4]

The separation of sex, marriage, and childrearing is most dramatically demonstrated in the new legal and social definitions of family that have emerged over the past two decades. Many states and cities have adopted "domestic partner" laws, allowing unmarried heterosexual or homosexual couples certain privileges that used to be accorded only to traditional married couples. In 1989, New York's highest court ruled that the surviving member of a gay couple held the same legal rights to the apartment they had shared as would a surviving wife or husband—the relationship had been exclusive, long-lasting, committed, self-sacrificing, and public enough to qualify as a family.[5]

There are more than two million gay mothers and fathers in America. Although most of their children come from earlier heterosexual relationships, up to 10,000 lesbians have borne children through sperm donations or other such procedures, and many gay and lesbian couples have won the right to adopt children.[6]

Compared to the first sixty years of the twentieth century, then, there is now an increasing diversity of family types in America. The male-breadwinner family no longer provides the central experience for the vast majority of children, but it has not been replaced by any new modal category: Most Americans move in and out of a variety of family types over the course of their lives—families headed by a divorced parent, couples raising children out of wedlock, two-earner families, same-sex couples, families with no spouse in the labor force, blended families, and empty-nest families.[7]

Something Old ...

Throughout most of this book, I have emphasized that many recent innovations in family behaviors have deep roots in our past, and many so-called traditional norms never really existed. It would be easy, from one perspective, to organize this chapter along the same lines. None of these changes, taken by itself, is unprecedented or qualitatively new. While comparisons between 1960 and 1990 show enormous discontinuities in patterns of marriage, sex, and reproduction, 1960 represented the end year of a very deviant decade.

Today's diversity of family forms, rates of premarital pregnancy, productive labor of wives, and prevalence of blended families, for example, would all look much more familiar to colonial Americans than would 1950s patterns. The age of marriage today is no higher than it was in the 1870s, and the proportion of never-married people is *lower* than it was at the turn of the century. Although fertility has decreased overall, the actual rate of childlessness is lower today than it was at the turn of the century; a growing proportion of women have at least one child during their lifetime. Many statistics purporting to show the eclipse of traditional families in recent years fail to take into account our longer life spans and lower mortality rates. As one author asks: "Are an eighty-year-old husband and wife really to be counted as 'nontraditional' just because they've lived long enough to see all their children leave home?" Even though marriages today are more likely to be interrupted by divorce than in former times, they are much less likely to be interrupted by death, so that about the same number of children spend their youth in single-parent households today as at the turn of the century, and far fewer live with neither parent.[8]

The 1960s generation did not invent premarital and out-of-wedlock sex. Indeed, the straitlaced sexual morality of nineteenth-century Anglo-American societies, partly revived in the 1950s, seems to have been a historical and cultural aberration. Anthropologist George Murdock examined cultural rules concerning sexual behavior in 250 societies and found that only 3 shared our "generalized sex taboo" on sexual behavior of any type outside marriage. Nor is there evidence that homosexual or lesbian activity is more frequent now than it was in the past; the claim that increased toleration of such activity portends reproductive doom does not mesh with the fact that two-thirds of the historical societies for which evidence is available have condoned homosexual relations.[9]

America's Founding Fathers were not always married: In Concord, Massachusetts, a bastion of Puritan tradition, one-third of all children born during the twenty years prior to the American Revolution were conceived out of wedlock; during the 1780s and 1790s, one-third of the brides in rural New England were pregnant at marriage. A study of illegitimacy in North Carolina found that out-of-wedlock birth rates for white women were approximately the same in 1850 as in 1970, though the pattern was more indicative of class exploitation than it is today: The fathers tended to be well-off heads of intact families, while the mothers lived in poor, female-headed households.[10]

In nineteenth-century America, the "age of consent" for girls in many states was as low as nine or ten, which rather makes a mockery of the term. What one author calls "the myth of an abstinent past" stems in part from lower fecundity and higher fetal mortality in previous times, making early sexual activity less likely to end up in pregnancy or birth. The proportion of fecund fifteen-year-old girls in America increased by 31 percent between 1940 and 1968 alone. In 1870, only 13 percent of European girls were fully fecund at age 17.5, compared to 94 percent of American girls the same age today.[11]

It is also estimated that there was one abortion for every five live births during the 1850s, and perhaps as many as one for every three in 1870. Although abortion and birth control were criminalized in the 1880s, and the age of consent for girls was raised, the triumph of the "purity" movement was short-lived. America experienced a sexual revolution in the 1920s that was every bit as scandalous to contemporaries as that of the past few decades.[12]

Even the 1950s were hardly asexual. My modern students, who accept premarital sex between affectionate partners quite matter-of-factly, are profoundly shocked when they read about panty raids and the groups of college boys who sometimes roamed through a campus chanting, "We want girls! We want sex!" Much of the modern sexual revolution, indeed, consists merely of a decline in the double standard, with girls adopting sexual behaviors that were pioneered much earlier by boys. This has led to a remarkable *decrease* in at least one form of extramarital sexual activity: Prostitution is far less widespread than it was in the nineteenth century, when New York City contained one prostitute for every sixty-four men and the mayor of Savannah estimated his city to have one for every thirty-nine men.[13]

And Something New ...

I do not, however, want to make a case that nothing has changed. Taken together, the rearrangements in marriage, childrearing, intergenerational relations and responsibilities, sexuality, and reproduction have been tremendous, far-reaching, and unprecedented. For many cultural conservatives, the framework that best describes and explains these changes is summed up in the words *permissiveness* and *self-indulgence*. For cultural liberals, less pejorative terms reflect an equally linear view of change: New family patterns are the result of pluralism, increased tolerance, and the growth of informed choice. I will argue that neither the notion of "permissiveness" nor that of "enlightenment" captures the complexity and breadth of the demographic and attitudinal changes we have experienced. To assess the opportunities and problems posed by these changes, we must accurately describe the full range of the new social and demographic territory through which modern men, women, and children are required to make their way.

The Changing Role of Marriage and Childrearing in the Life Course

Perhaps the most visible rearrangement of family terrain is that both marriage and childrearing occupy a smaller proportion of adults' lives than they did at any time in American history. They define less of a person's social identity, exert less influence on people's life-course decisions, and are less universal, exclusive, and predictable than ever before. (The one seeming exception to the declining salience of marriage—that divorce is now a stronger predictor of poverty for women and children than any other factor—is true only in the short run. Even in the short run, the causative role of divorce and illegitimacy in poverty has been greatly overstated, as I will discuss in chapter 11.)

A white woman can now expect, on the average, to spend only 43 percent of her life in marriage, while a black woman can expect marriage to occupy only 22 percent of her life. Marriage has ceased to be the main impetus into or out of other statuses, and it increasingly coexists for women, as it has long done for men, with several other roles. The orderly progression from student to single jobholder to wife to mother to married older worker that prevailed from the 1920s to the 1960s, for example, is now gone. Modern women take on these functions in different orders or occupy all of them at once. In 1967, half of all women in their thirties were married mothers who remained at home full-time; by 1982, only a quarter of all women in their thirties could be found specializing in this way.[14]

Despite the high value that Americans continue to attach to marriage and family, there is a new tolerance for alternative life courses. In 1957, 80 percent of Americans polled said that people who chose not to marry were "sick," "neurotic," and "immoral." By 1977, only 25 percent of those polled held such views. In 1962, the overwhelming majority of mothers believed that "almost everyone should have children if they can"; by 1985, only a minority agreed. Most women still want children but feel less pressure to get married first. A national survey conducted in 1989 found that 36 percent of the single women polled had seriously considered raising a child on their own.[15]

Parenthood, like marriage, is a less salient, central, and long-lasting part of life than it used to be. Parents are having fewer children than they had in most decades of American history and are spacing them somewhat closer. At the beginning of this century, most women saw their last child married when they were fifty-six and then lived, on average, only ten or fifteen years longer. Today, despite the "boomerang" child phenomenon, the average woman has forty years to live after her children leave home. A couple who stays together after their kids depart faces more than a third of a century with no other company in the household besides each other, compared to the short time of child-free years experienced by couples in previous centuries. Men, who are more likely to let their contact with children lapse after a divorce, live an even greater proportion of their lives today without involvement in childrearing. In 1960, men aged twenty to forty-nine spent an average of 12.3 years in families with children under age eighteen; by 1990, that had fallen to 7 years.[16]

This decline in the centrality of marriage and parenthood for adults has been building for 150 years, with only a partial and temporary interruption during the 1950s. Changes in the life course of American youth, less linear, appear especially dramatic because the first sixty years of the twentieth century saw an *increase* in the centrality of family formation for young people and in the predictability of patterns of schooling, work, marriage, and parenthood.

Changes in the Roles and Experiences of Youth

Until the end of the nineteenth century, the major transitions of youth—leaving home, finding a job, exiting school, getting married, and setting up an independent household—all occurred at more variable ages and in more random order than they have during most of this century. There was nothing random about gender behavior, of course. Gender determined more of an individual's options and constraints than in the twentieth century, but those options and constraints varied tremendously between classes and occupational groups.[17]

In the early twentieth century, youthful transitions for both genders became much more predictable in their order and concentrated in time, as well as more prevalent throughout the population. With the abolition of child labor and the prolongation of schooling, a dramatic shift in the flow of intergenerational resources occurred and a new life cycle was established: Almost all children gained a protracted period of freedom from productive responsibilities and then moved quite rapidly from school to work to leaving home to getting married and establishing a separate family.[18]

This "institutionalization" of youth as a separate stage of life seems to have been a transitory stage. It helped create a youthful independence that has recently allowed individuals of both sexes to discard the normative sequences without returning to older dependencies and subordinations. Entry into work, school, sexual activity, independent residence, and parenthood are much more variable today than they were during the first two-thirds of this century. It appears that youth are returning to a diversity and randomness of life-course transitions more characteristic of earlier periods yet are combining this with a new convergence of behaviors between men and women and a reduction of family responsibilities. Young people increasingly move in and out of their parents' homes, other living arrangements, jobs, education, and marriage at different times and in a bewildering combination of orders. At age twenty-nine, nearly 40 percent of American men have not yet settled in to a stable long-term job.[19]

Between 1965 and 1975, the proportion of young people living alone more than doubled. Most of this increase occurred because of a rise in their disposable income, so the fall in real incomes after 1973, discussed in chapter 11, soon reversed this trend. By the 1980s, growing numbers of young people were choosing to live at home with their parents. In 1990, more than half of eighteen- to twenty-four-year-olds were living with their parents, well above the 42 percent living at home in 1960 but far less than the figures for 1975. One in nine young adults aged twenty-five to thirty-four was also living in a parent's home, an increase of more than 25 percent since 1960.[20]

Interestingly, however, most of this increase occurred among families with higher-than-average incomes, and substantial anecdotal evidence suggests that youths who remained home longer, as well as their "boomerang" siblings who returned home, did not accept greater obligation within the family in237 exchange for parental subsidization. While such youths could not support full adult establishments, historian John Modell argues, they could still take advantage of a wide variety of opportunities for enlarging their independent economic roles as both workers and consumers. Perhaps they were more likely to spend money on cars and stereos because they had less hope of ever saving up enough for a house. The trend shows up at younger ages as well: By the end of the 1980s, three out of four high school seniors were working an average of eighteen hours a week, but only 11 percent of them saved all or most of their earnings for college or other long-range goals.[21]

In recent years, then, youths have had more leeway in terms of personal consumption but less opportunity to acquire the "big ticket" items usually associated with family formation and adult independence. The resulting confusion between adult and youth prerogatives has reinforced the homogenizing effect of television on children's and adult's knowledge, as well as the outright role reversal in new technologies, such as computers, where most of us are out-paced by our children. Perhaps this is why so many recent movies and television series (*Big* and *Like Father, Like Son*) have experi-mented with the notion of switching a child's mind into an adult's body or vice versa, while others (*Home Alone,* and "Doogie Howser, M.D.") have portrayed youths as far more competent than most of the adults around them.[22]

Of course, most such productions are aimed at a white audience. There are similar ambiguities in youth and adult roles among African Americans, but they take different forms. A major concern for par-ents of white youths, for example, is whether the jobs their children take in fast-food outlets and concession stands retain any of the val-ues traditionally associated with work; a major concern of black par-ents is whether their children will find any jobs at all. After high school, it is interesting to note, young African Americans receive less material aid from their families and contribute more income *to* their families than do white youth. This youthful sacrifice confounds racist stereotypes about the decline of parental authority in the black community, but it severely disadvantages black youth in terms of their educational prospects.[23]

The Graying of America

Another major reshaping of the demographic terrain is the aging of the population. The median age in America today is slightly over thirty-two, approximately twice the median age of the population at the time of the American Revolution. In the past two decades, with fertility rates at near-record lows, the population aged sixty-five and above has grown twice as fast as the general population. Today, there are thirty million Americans sixty-five or older, representing 13 per-cent of the population. More than six and a half million of them re-quire long-term care. By 2030, elder Americans will represent almost 21 percent of the population, and the number of aged persons requir-ing long-term care is expected to rise even more quickly. If current rates of disability persist, for example, the number of elderly requir-ing institutional care will more than triple in the next forty years.[24]

One of the cheap shots directed at modern families is the charge that they have abandoned their commitment to the old, fobbing them off on government or private nursing homes. In fact, however, care of the elderly was never a major function for most families in the past, since so few people lived to an advanced age. In 1900, the proportion of the population aged sixty-five or over was only 4 percent, and though elders had more children than today to share the burden of their support, their poverty rates were the highest in the nation.[25]

If the total years families devote to childrearing have declined over the past half century, the total years they devote to elder care have increased significantly. Eighty percent of the long-term care that the elderly require is provided by family members, and more than twice as many impaired elderly are cared for at home as in institutions. Contrary to the bleak view presented in the mass media, two recent local studies of death patterns found that 30 percent of elderly Americans died at home and 45 percent were transferred to the hospital shortly before dying, while only 25 percent died in a nursing home. Ninety percent of those who died, in whatever location, saw family and friends within the last three days of life.[26] But there are high costs to families associated with these relatively comforting facts.

When Judy Stanley's* mother became incapacitated in 1949, Judy was forty years old. She kept her mother at home until her death five years later. Even though Judy's two children were old enough not to suffer unduly from the drain on their mother's time, they were five exhausting years that strained Judy's marital relationship and left her determined never to "be a burden" to her own children. But when Judy developed Alzheimer's in 1977, her physical health was excellent; she is still alive at this writing. Her daughters managed to keep Judy in her own home for six years, by juggling their schedules and hiring part-time help. Then the younger daughter, Barbara, moved her mother in with her, despite the fact that she had two preschool children to deal with as well. It was three years before Judy's paranoia made her so difficult to deal with and her forgetfulness made her so dangerous to herself that Barbara committed her to a nursing home. "After all that work," says Barbara bitterly, discussing how she and her sister organize their personal lives and job schedules to make sure their mother gets a visit every day, "we became just another statistic for the people who claim baby boomers are too selfish to do their family duty."

Barbara is part of the "sandwich generation," the unprecedented number of families and individuals who have elders and children de-

*Not her real name.

pendent on them *at the same time*. More than a quarter of caregivers to the elderly are in this situation.[27]

Elder care takes a tremendous toll on families. Twenty-two percent of caregivers have not had a vacation away from their responsibilities for a year or more. Marital relations fray; aging caregivers find that their own health suffers; and the children of "sandwich generation" caregivers get reduced time and attention. Corporations report that elder-care problems are at least as great a cause of absenteeism and employee stress as are child-care ones. And the financial burden is stunning. The average bed in a nursing home costs $30,000 a year; special medical bills can triple or quadruple this. Private insurance plans pay less than 2 percent of nursing home expenses, and Medicare covers a maximum of one hundred days of acute services in a rehabilitative center.[28]

More than half the total nursing-home bill in America is paid by patients and their families out of their pockets. When their pockets run dry, Medicaid steps in, but the fact that it does so only after all other resources are exhausted creates painful dilemmas. While Peter Ferrara of the Cato Institute argues that government should not tax us to pay the bills of someone with $50,000 in assets, elders are understandably dismayed at the idea of losing a lifetime's savings in less than a year: Those bumper stickers announcing "We're spending our children's inheritance" begin to sound a lot less selfish. However, patients who spend down to the required limit sometimes find that they have lost their ability to pay rent or other expenses if they do get well enough to move home![29]

The Technological Revolution in Reproduction: Separation of Sex from Procreation

Another major, and probably irreversible, shift in the contours of family life is the revolution in contraceptive and reproductive technology that permits an almost total dissociation of the sex act from the act of procreation. Human beings have always attempted to separate sex and procreation: Every known society has some form of birth control and some arenas of sexual activity that are not expected to produce children. But there has always been a tether, sometimes longer, sometimes shorter, that prevented one from getting too far from the other. As late as 1960, virtually all contraceptive practice was coitus-related. Today, the spread of oral contraceptives, in-trauterine devices (IUDs), female sterilization, and vasectomies allow prevention of pregnancy to take place without any temporal relation-ship to actual sexual intercourse.

Conversely, new methods of in vitro fertilization, artificial insemi-nation, sperm banks, and ovum transfers increasingly allow child-birth to occur with very little relation to actual intercourse or biolog-ical rhythms. "You can't fool Mother Nature," snaps columnist Midge Decter about proposals to include homosexual households in the definition of family; but as it turns out, you can. Scientists have even discovered how to allow menopausal women to bear children. While this last feat fails to exhilarate most older women whom I know, it does suggest that alternatives to traditional biological constraints are likely to become more widespread, not less.[30]

The Changing Role of Sexuality in Society

Perhaps the most dramatic, and certainly the most emotionally loaded, reconfiguration of the family terrain has occurred in the realm of sexual behavior and expression. The "sexual revolution" did not occur as suddenly as most people think: In fact, there have been two sexual "revolutions" in the twentieth century, and their roots go back to demographic and economic changes in the nineteenth cen-tury. Even when put in historical perspective, however, the transfor-mations in sexuality seem profound.

In early America, reproductive and productive activity took place in the same settings, and both were subject to extensive community supervision. Many sexual norms and rules were directly linked to regulation of household work and social hierarchies, which meant that the notion of a purely private sexual life or personal sexual iden-tity was unthinkable. Such regulation, we should note, was perfectly compatible with a wide range of sexual expressiveness and an under-standing that people's sexual urges extended beyond the procreative act. In one Puritan adultery case, for example, the wife admitted that she had taken a lover but justified her behavior because her husband spent so much time hunting and fishing that he had neglected his conjugal duties. The court sentenced not only the woman and her lover to sit in the stocks, but also her husband, since he had clearly driven her to it.[31]

As the family ceased to be the site of labor regulation, intimate personal relationships became much more sharply distinguished from economic and political ones. They became less subject to supervision by social superiors and community institutions; it was even possible to imagine that intimate affiliations and feelings could be detached from social roles, productive assignments, and authority relations. People's initial reaction to these increased opportunities for personal sexual choice, at least among the middle class whose economic success depended on impulse control and careful planning, was to substitute self-regulation for community regulation.

The widespread nineteenth-century hysteria about masturbation, or "self-pollution," highlighted a strong connection in people's minds between sexual control and the requirements of democratic capitalism. Doctors and purity reformers preached against masturbation in the same phrases that economists used about the work ethic. "Reserve is the great secret of power everywhere." "Careless waste," it was said, in either sexual energy or finances, was the greatest danger of the age. Neither time, money, nor semen should be wasted: "The fancies, once turned in this direction, wear a channel, down which dash the thoughts, gathering force like a river as they move away from the fountain-head." In the second half of the century, early concerns about masturbation gave way to general attempts to "desexualize" all arenas of society—people began to refer to the "white meat" and "dark meat" of poultry in order to avoid naming body parts, such as thighs and breasts. Fears of unregulated sexuality merged with new concerns about loss of social control over immigrants and workers to produce a shift from self-control to outright repression.[32]

The separation of sexuality from both productive and reproductive relations, however, went on apace, even in the middle class. By 1900, white middle-class women had reduced their fertility rates by more than 50 percent. Urban centers provided havens for sexual subcultures such as those of prostitutes or early networks based on homoerotic ties. The Victorian moral order was "in crisis" well before 1900.[33]

The First Sexual Revolution and Its Impact

In the early 1900s, a series of economic, political, and cultural factors further weakened the institutions and ideologies reinforcing sexual restraint. Economic and educational innovations allowed youthful peer groups in high schools, colleges, work settings, and urban boarding houses to take over a large part of the socialization process from parents and to establish new areas of heterosexual interaction. The expansion of commercial recreation gave people movie houses, dance halls, and amusement parks to congregate in, away from the view of family and neighbors. Heightened urbanization and the experience of the First World War brought more individuals into contact with alternative sexual mores. The growth of a consumer economy meant that demands for personal fulfillment were no longer necessarily in conflict with economic priorities. Sex came to be seen as a new cement for marriage rather than as a threat to its stability.[34]

By the 1920s, a radical reorientation of popular culture and courtship had occurred in America, making sexual expressiveness "normative" for young heterosexuals and introducing a generation gap at least as wide as that of the 1960s or 1970s. At the end of the nineteenth century, writes historian Ellen Rothman, middle-class courtship had been "more carefully supervised and more formal than at any time since the Revolution." Thirty years later, that courtship structure was almost completely dismantled. It was replaced by the dating system, which moved courtship out of the home and into the public world, replacing family surveillance with peer supervision in an increasingly age-specific youth culture.[35]

Couples in 1900 had gotten to know each other on the front porch of their parents' home. By the 1920s they went out on dates—perhaps to participate in the "petting parties" that were a national craze, perhaps to take advantage of the nonfamilial privacy afforded when the boy had a car. Youths, no longer dependent on introductions by friends or family, met at school or work or picked each other up at dance halls, restaurants, and cabarets.

While the increase in youthful premarital coitus was not as dramatic as that in the 1960s, there was a pronounced eroticization of noncoital relations and a greatly liberalized definition of what kinds of physical interactions were permissible between unmarried persons of the opposite sex. And, in some groups at least, premarital sex became more common, too: A 1938 study of 777 married women found that only 26 percent of those born between 1890 and 1900 had lost their virginity before marriage, but two-thirds of those born after 1910 had done so. One sign of the new sexual freedom was that a young man was increasingly likely to have his first sexual encounter with a girlfriend rather than with a prostitute; among men born between 1900 and 1909, sex with prostitutes declined by over 50 percent. Once married, couples were able to explore their sexuality further, as new sex manuals expanded their knowledge of techniques and they gained greater access to birth control.[36]

Sexuality not only entered the public sphere during the 1920s but also became a major source of identity and self-discovery. Freudianism reached America just in time to validate and accelerate this process, which was very much a new cultural construction. The ancient Greeks had interpreted dreams about sex as being *really* about political power and economic fortune; Americans, by contrast, enthusiastically adopted Freud's view that dreams about almost everything were really about sex. Advertisers found in sexuality a common denominator that they thought could reach a mass audience; doctors and sociologists considered it the wellspring of human growth and the main explanation of health or disease.[37]

The impact of this sexualization of interpersonal relations was complex. In some ways, it was clearly liberating. The partial replacement of gender by sex as a mode of self-definition fostered a new "companionate" ideal of marriage, in which both men and women reached higher levels of sexual and emotional compatibility. Emphasis on the sex act as the logical, indeed inevitable, outcome of sensual interaction allowed women and men to explore techniques of giving and receiving pleasure. But there were also new constraints inherent in this elevation of sexuality to center stage.

People's interpretation of physical contact became extraordinarily "privatized and sexualized," so that all types of touching, kissing, and holding were seen as sexual foreplay rather than accepted as ordinary means of communication that carried different meanings in different contexts. This sexualization of touching invested adult-child interactions with some tension. It could lead to qualms about touching, as in doctors' strict instructions never to let a child climb into the parents' bed; it is also possible, though, that the association of touching with sexual release paved the way for an erosion of old inhibitions about engaging in sex with children.[38]

The new focus on the sex act as the culmination of intimacy undermined an earlier tolerance for a continuum of sensual and erotic relations. It is not that homosexuality was acceptable before; but now a wider range of behavior opened a person up to being branded as a homosexual. The passionate female bonds discussed in chapter 3 were stigmatized and labeled perverse. The romantic friendships that had existed among many unmarried men in the nineteenth century were no longer compatible with heterosexual identity; old frontier habits of sharing beds or "rolling up together around campfires to keep each other warm" were ruled out of bounds. Increasingly, either genital sex between men or careful physical and emotional distancing "crowded out more sublimated erotic relations" and replaced more nuanced male friendships.[39]

The institution of dating delivered youth from much parental control, but also "shifted power from women to men." In the older courtship system, a young man was invited to come "calling" at the girl's home; the initiative lay with the girl and her family. Etiquette books were firm: It was as improper for a male of the early 1900s to suggest that he would like an invitation to call as it was for a girl of the 1950s to hint that she would like to be asked out. A date, by contrast, was an invitation into the public world, involving consumption of goods and services in the market. It was therefore initiated by men, who were more familiar with that world and had the economic resources to operate within it. A date often represented the only way that a girl could gain access to the new world of public consumption, but the question immediately arose of what she owed in return for the money that was spent on her. While the dating system may have helped lessen prostitution, it also heightened the element of sexual commerce in everyday heterosexual interactions among peers. Many of the elaborate dating codes that emerged between the 1920s and 1960s represented the effort of women to reshape the system to limit male prerogatives within it.[40]

Rising standards of intimacy and sexual compatibility gave women a new kind of influence over men, and new arenas of communication with them, but the dependence of marriage on sexual attractiveness and excitement gave both men and the mass media more influence over standards of beauty. Women began to try to live up to new expectations promulgated by movies, advertisers, and marriage experts. Acknowledgment of female sexuality also meant its incorporation into a competitive, consumerist model of behavior; it coincided with the dissolution of the organized women's movement that had emerged in the late nineteenth century. Psychology professor Howard Gadlin suggests that the move to liberalize and equalize *sex* tended to substitute for a more substantive equalization of *gender*.[41]

The Second Sexual Revolution

The sexual liberalism established in the 1920s continued to gain ground during the next three decades, albeit at a slower pace and with some countervailing trends. During the 1950s, the ongoing sex-ualization of dating and marriage was combined with a campaign against "abnormal" sex: homosexuality, lesbianism, or even attempts by heterosexual women to assert their own sexual desires against un-realistic definitions of "normal" female sexual response. All but two states dropped their bans on contraceptive information or devices. At the same time, though, restrictions on "obscene literature" and abor-tions mounted. It is estimated that 250,000 to a million women a year sought illegal abortions, and that these were responsible for 40 percent of all maternal deaths.[42]

The 1960s saw a dramatic acceleration of sexual liberalization and a reversal of most opposing trends of the 1950s. The first component of this sexual revolution was the growth of a singles culture, predat-ing the rise of political and cultural protest, that accepted sexual ac-tivity between unmarried men and women. A second stage was reached when women began to demand that this singles culture be readjusted to meet their needs. A third came in the 1970s, as a gay movement questioned the exclusive definition of sexual freedom in terms of heterosexuality.

Many different social forces and demographic changes contributed to these developments: the rising age for marriage; educational con-vergence of men and women; women's growing autonomy; invention of birth-control methods that were independent of coitus (first the oral contraceptive pill, introduced in 1960, then the IUD); the sheer rise in the absolute number of singles as the baby-boom generation reached sexual maturity; and revulsion of a politically active genera-tion against what they saw as the hypocrisy of their elders. The pro-cess was both advanced and redirected by attempts of American manufacturers to tap into these demographic, social, and political changes.[43]

Not all the forces worked toward the same ends. Political radicals tended to be contemptuous of the way that advertisers and the mass media romanticized sex and attached it to commodities; feminists felt that too many political radicals were pushing a kind of "libera-tion" that denied women the right to say no; gays and lesbians argued that the feminist movement was too oriented toward the im-pulses of heterosexual women. It is often forgotten that the second sexual revolution not only fought for abortion rights and against re-strictions on the behavior of consenting adults, but also demanded the restriction and criminalization of nonconsenting sex, as in cam-paigns against rape and sexual harassment.

Nonetheless, the cumulative result was an increase in the acceptability, prevalence, and early initiation of sexual activity. In the 1970s, there was a huge surge in the proportion of single girls having had coitus and a comparable shift in attitudes accepting of this behavior. According to one survey, three-fifths of males aged fifteen to nineteen and 53 percent of females the same age had experienced sexual intercourse as of 1988. The median age of first sexual intercourse for female teens was sixteen. Twenty-two percent of boys and 7 percent of girls, another survey found, had lost their virginity by age thirteen.[44]

Even more disconcerting for many has been the unprecedented openness, even exhibitionism, about sexuality. This has gone far beyond the "coming out" of gays and lesbians during the 1970s or the refusal of young heterosexual couples to keep their sexual activity secret from their parents. Today, talk-show guests parade the most intimate details of their sex lives before audiences; neighbors videotape a couple having sex in an apartment where the blinds have been left open; and reporters research the minutiae of public figures' sexual behavior and preferences. A 1987 study by Planned Parenthood estimated that 65,000 sexual references were broadcast on prime-time television each year—and that was before the debut of shows such as Fox's "Studs," in which three women date the same two men and then compare notes in front of a live audience. (One young woman described her date as having "buns to die for.")[45]

The high point of the sexual revolution may have come in the 1970s. Polls have registered a sharp drop in approval of promiscuity since then, and since 1979 there has been a slight decline in the percentage of never-married females aged seventeen or younger who have had sexual intercourse. (While this seems to contradict the fact that starting in 1986, there was a rise in the number of teens aged fifteen to seventeen who gave birth, the increase is probably linked to the declining availability of abortion, or similar factors, rather than to greater sexual activity.) Since 1979, there has also been a decline in the proportion of males who had intercourse before their fifteenth birthday. For older individuals, disillusionment with the amount of "liberation" connected to sexual promiscuity has combined with fear of AIDS and the natural slowing down of an aging baby-boom generation to produce a new caution about sexuality in America.[46]

However, caution should not be confused with sexual conservatism. "The sexual revolution is over because it was won," remarks Cheryl Russell, a researcher for American Demographics magazine.

Neither the prevalence nor the cultural acceptance of sex outside marriage is likely to be reversed, despite widespread distaste for the obsessive and indiscriminate sexuality with which we are bombarded by the media. Relatively early commencement of sexual intercourse is also probably here to stay, as is a general acceptance of gay and lesbian activity. The double standard has waned, and youthful peer groups seem less concerned to enforce the "dating game" of male pursuit and female "holding out."[47]

Assessing the Impact of the Second Sexual Revolution

Extreme claims come easily to those who seek to assess the extent and consequences of recent trends in sexual behavior. Cultural conservatives, for example, greatly exaggerate the amount of sexual activity that goes on in modern America. One recent book has compared the escalation of the "sex revolution" to the "drug revolution." In fact, there is a lot more sex on television than there is in the bedroom. Most premarital sex among teens occurs with only one partner, and on the average, youths who report themselves as "sexually experienced" have spent six of the last twelve months without any sexual partner. Four out of five adults surveyed by the National Opinion Research Center in 1988 reported that they were monogamous during the prior year. Only 1.5 percent of the married couples reported having an affair in the previous year. A 1991 survey found that the average adult has had seven sex partners since age eighteen but only one in the past year. Married people had sex an average of sixty-seven times during the year, while divorced and never-married singles had it fifty-five times.[48]

Cultural liberals, on the other hand, tend to exaggerate the decline of the double standard and the degree of enlightenment reached by most sexually active individuals. Actually, the most striking aspect of the sexual revolution is its unevenness. As research sociologist Lillian Rubin points out, women still get "wildly mixed" messages about acceptable sexual behavior, preventing them from being clear about what they really want or need in a relationship. A 1991 survey of sixth- through ninth-grade students in Rhode Island found that a majority believed a woman was "asking" to be raped if she went out at night in a "seductive" outfit; 80 percent thought a man had a right to force a woman to have sex if he were married to her. There has been no clear progression from "ignorance to wisdom," even when it comes to the facts of life. When the Kinsey Institute recently gave people a quiz on fundamental facts of biology and sexual behavior, the majority flunked: Fifty-five percent answered more than half the questions incorrectly.[49]

Contrary to predictions that sexual liberalization would defuse the tensions associated with sex, allowing it to become a normal, non-problematic area of life, our acceptance of sex has not become more matter-of-fact. American culture invests sex with much more emotional freight and conflicting messages than do most other developed nations. We allow more sex and violence on afternoon television than do most European countries, but we are less forthright than they about nudity, sex education, and birth control. We also are far more apt to have periodic bouts of hysteria about whether high school literature classes can read novels with four-letter words. Perhaps Americans are so much more preoccupied by sex than are Europeans precisely because they are still much more likely to consider it dirty.[50]

British psychiatrist John Ashton suggests that Americans fantasize about sex more than do other national groups at the same time as they treat it less realistically. Studies of U.S. teenagers' fantasies, for example, reveal an obsession with every detail of seduction and foreplay but a complete failure to consider the practical matters of avoiding pregnancy or exposure to disease. Male teenagers fear that prior discussion of preventive measures will botch the seduction; females think it will spoil the romance or their reputation or both.[51]

To understand this unevenness, we need to go beyond analyses that stress the role of feminism, 1960s student radicals, or the gay and lesbian movement in charting modern sexual boundaries. While the feminist and gay movements had considerable influence in expanding the notion that a person should have the right to choose (or refuse) sex, ultimately the most powerful and visible models of sexual "liberation" have been provided by advertisers and the mass media. As two recent historians of American sexuality point out, the revolutionary hopes of feminists and gay liberationists "never materialized." Instead, "the consumerist values that had already made sex a marketable commodity" were increasingly applied to female and gay sexuality as well as to traditional gender roles and marriage, for purposes dictated by a multibillion-dollar sex industry, not the aims of personal liberation or social transformation.[52]

By the early 1980s, sexually permissive attitudes had entirely lost their initial association with political radicalism or liberalism. In 1984, more than 60 percent of people aged twenty-three to thirty-eight approved of casual sex, as compared to only 28 percent of those over thirty-eight, yet more of the younger generation than their elders were willing to support a U.S. war either to "stop the spread of communism" or to "protect our economic interests." Books advocating extremely conservative gender roles had begun to give explicit instructions to women on how to get and keep a man by varying their sexual techniques.[53]

Several theorists have suggested that the convergence of sexual permissiveness with political conservatism is no accident. Herbert Marcuse, for example, characterizes the twentieth-century eroticization of society as a "repressive desublimation" that fosters depoliticization and facilitates elite social control. Michel Foucault argues that modern sexuality emerged out of a medical discourse that regulated human behavior through classification, surveillance, seduction, and control.[54]

Such sweeping critiques of the sexual revolution are as one-sided as are blanket endorsements of the "new pluralism." Changes in family, sex, and reproductive behavior have had mixed effects. Few people who lived through the anxiety and pain of 1950s sexual repression would advocate reversing sexual liberalization. Even though sexual freedom has made marriage less automatic and less permanent, it has also eased the misery of many marriages, relieved paralyzing guilt feelings, and permitted self-acceptance for people whose sexuality or temperament is not suited to marriage. Yet it is clear that the sexual revolution has problematized some areas of life that were once thought safe from the misuse of sexuality; its effects on the experience of childhood seem particularly troublesome. Historian Lawrence Birken suggests that the sexualization of childhood, for all its dangers, may be related to an extension of personhood to youngsters that has made us more aware of their mistreatment. The fact remains, however, that important boundaries between childhood sensuality and adult sexuality seem to have been blurred.[55]

New reproductive technologies are similarly complex in their effects. They have brought joy to many infertile couples and set back the "biological clock" that worries so many women in their thirties. But this technology has also confronted women with agonizing choices, tempted them into costly experiments with low success rates, created the dilemmas of genetic counseling and surrogate motherhood, and led to custody disputes over fertilized ova. Many women complain that there has been an objectification of the birth process: Women's own voices have been drowned out by the high-tech babble of scientists who talk of "bombing" women's ovaries with fertility drugs, "harvesting" ova, "screening" the fetus, and finding "nubile young wombs," not to mention the excited jabber of venture capitalists who have discovered that working in this market is "easier than selling soap."[56]

Such problems stem from a combination of factors: cultural lag, where old values prevent people from coping realistically and responsibly with changing behavior; rejection of sexual hypocrisy without acceptance of an alternative ethic; and, in many cases, economic and social conditions that distort and deform the liberating possibilities of new options, turning them into new fetters. America's teenage pregnancy patterns reveal these factors in operation.

Teenage Mothers and the Sexual Revolution

Judging from the number of op-ed pieces about children having children, one would think that teen pregnancy reached unprecedented proportions in the 1980s. The first thing to note about the so-called "epidemic" of teen parenthood is that it is far past its peak. The highest rate of teenage childbearing in twentieth-century America was in 1957, when more than 97 out of every 1,000 women aged fifteen to nineteen gave birth. Today, only half as many teenagers bear children. Although birth rates among the youngest teens, aged ten through fourteen, have increased in the past two decades, this is a very small phenomenon: Only 2 percent of all births to teenagers occur to girls under fifteen.[57]

The real source of most people's concern lies in two rather different facts. First, America has a dramatically higher incidence of teen pregnancy than does any other contemporary industrial democracy. From 1980 to 1989, according to a recent United Nations report, both the birth *and* the abortion rates of U.S. teens were twice those of other countries in the developed world. Second, an increasing proportion of teen births occur out of wedlock. In 1960, 15.4 percent of all teen births were to unmarried mothers; by 1970, that proportion had doubled; and by 1986, it had doubled again, with the result that a majority of all teen births today are to unmarried mothers.[58]

There are some serious problems associated with very early sexual activity, especially with early pregnancy. Teenagers have a higher level of sexually transmitted diseases than do other groups of the population. Teenagers who give birth are more likely to have children with a variety of physical, emotional, or cognitive deficits, while those who have abortions are more likely to have traumatic experiences with the abortion. Teen mothers who marry are three times more likely to be separated or divorced within fifteen years than are women who postpone childbearing; married or single, teen mothers attain lower educational levels and earn lower wages than do older mothers.[59]

But are these problems, as the Rockford Institute claims, an outcome of the "New Freedom" established by the sexual revolution of the 1960s? Is teen pregnancy a result of "liberated" women embracing "hedonism" and demanding sexual satisfaction?[60] The evidence suggests quite a different interpretation. It is important to note that most problems with teen sex occur among very young teens. There is a considerable difference between the ability of a fourteen-year-old and an eighteen-year-old to handle sex. Among the teens most likely to become sexually active at a very young age and most likely to impregnate a partner or to become pregnant, what strikes the observer most forcefully is not their "liberation" but their inhibition and ignorance about sexuality, their tenacious double standard, and their limited horizons in general.

Most sexually active young teens are startlingly unaware of their own sexual responses and biological processes. One of the major contributors to high teen-pregnancy rates is the denial of youngsters, to themselves and to others, that they *are* sexually active. Girls in particular are likely to feel that it's okay to be "swept away," but that "nice girls" don't plan for sex. One girl explained her reasons for not using a contraceptive: "If I did, then I'd have sex more. It would be too easy." Teens whose parents are frank with them about their bodies and sexual drives, by contrast, are more likely than are others to postpone initial coitus until age sixteen or later.[61]

For many male teens who impregnate their partners, sex is something you "get away with" or "put over" on someone rather than an act that flows naturally from an intimate relationship. Girls who become sexually active at an early age, far from being feminist in outlook, tend to have exceptionally strong dependency needs. They are more often motivated by a desire to please their partners than by a search for their own sexual satisfaction, and frequently they seem to receive very little pleasure from the sex act itself. Girls who have pos-

itive attitudes toward education and clear goals for their future are
less likely to start sex at a very early age and less liable to become
pregnant once they become sexually active.[62]

But it is not merely cultural lag at work here. In general, teen
pregnancy rates seem to be related to poor life prospects. In 1981,
only 3 percent to 5 percent of all teens who had good academic skills
and lived above the poverty line were mothers, as compared to 20
percent of poor teens with below-average academic skills. These
rates were the same for whites, Hispanics, and blacks, but black teen
mothers were much less likely to be married, a fact that is more related to the employment and earnings crisis among young black men
than to major differences in values about marriage.[63]

Teenagers with the fewest options, not the most, are those likely to
get pregnant. Teen pregnancy, in or out of wedlock, is more frequently associated with old economic, gender, and racial inequalities
than with the "New Freedom" that has allowed some women to
choose unwed motherhood as a positive alternative for both themselves and their children.[64]

Finding Our Way Through the New Reproductive Terrain

We will not solve any of the problems associated with the new family
terrain by fantasizing that we can return to some "land before time"
where these demographic, cultural, and technological configurations
do not exist. Much of the new family topography is permanent. It is
the result of a major realignment of subterranean forces, much like
plate tectonics and continental drift. Women will never again spend
the bulk of their lives at home. Sex and reproduction are no longer
part of the same land mass, and no amount of pushing and shoving
can force them into a single continent again.

This is not to say that we should simply ignore the problems
raised by shifting realities. Many problems, however, are not inherent
in the changes themselves but in the choices that have been made
about where to draw new boundaries or how to respond to the transformations. The dilemmas of reproductive technology, for example,
might be quite different if women were more involved in setting priorities for research or if venture capitalists were less involved. Too
often, people waste time bemoaning the changes instead of debating
the choices they pose.

Take the example of America's aging population. Many commentators claim that the crisis of rising health costs in America is a direct, inevitable result of the aging of our population; newspapers are full of dire tales about how the elderly are monopolizing our medical resources. This leads to a zero-sum approach in which we blame the deterioration in the well-being of America's children on the gains that elders have made, instead of recognizing the stake that each generation has in the well-being of other generations.[65]

The population of Denmark is already more elderly than the U.S. population will be in 2015. Although it has a generous care network for elders, Denmark spends only half as much of its GNP on health care as does the United States, and it has actually reduced the share spent on medical care over the past decade. As health finance researcher Thomas Getzen points out, the American health-care crisis "is a result of political and professional choices, rather than the outcome of objective trends in demography, morbidity, technology or other relentless forces beyond our control." Getzen's comment on how to develop an effective approach to modern health-care dilemmas applies equally well to modern family dilemmas: "We must first halt the search for someone else to blame—the poor, the old, the disabled, the drug abuser, the bureaucrat—" and turn our attention toward constructing a system that provides us with better choices.[66]

Or consider modern marital trends. Accessible, low-cost divorce has been an important reform for people trapped in abusive or destructive relationships. Yet the living standards of women and children tend to drop sharply after divorce and bitter custody disputes leave tremendous scars on all concerned, most especially on the children who may have to take sides. The majority of women who gain custody of children receive inadequate child support payments, while the children often lose contact with their fathers entirely. Law professor Mary Ann Glendon argues that most of our divorce laws are "no responsibility" rather than "no fault."[67]

But these ill effects of divorce are not inevitable and do not prevail in many other societies. As I shall show in the next chapter, in the absence of serious financial loss or bitter custody disputes between parents, divorce does not necessarily have disastrous results. Attempting to solve the financial and emotional inequities of divorce by making it harder or reintroducing adversarial proceedings would only exacerbate the conflict that is associated with the *worst* outcomes for children. It would also do little to improve the situation of women: Most recent research shows, contrary to some well-publicized studies during the 1980s, that no-fault divorce has *not* left women worse off overall than has adversarial divorce; it has simply failed to mitigate the economic losses that women have *always* experienced after divorce. There is no point in forcing bad marriages to continue, but there is no reason we cannot establish more equitable "exit rules" for marriage, parenting, or other social, economic, and personal commitments. Just because a relationship changes does not mean that its obligations end, a point that can be applied to corporate relocations as well as to familial ones.[68]

Putting Our Family Maps in Perspective

Ancient Chinese maps of the world put China at the center and the "barbarian" world at the periphery; modern American maps place North America in the middle and cut Asia in half. Similarly, many "maps" of modern family patterns accentuate one or another feature at the cost of distorting the total panorama of reproductive and marital change.

One of the worst things about distorted maps is that when people reach dead ends, they are falsely blamed for "losing their way." Policymakers assume that if people would just avoid the one exaggerated feature on their particular ideological map, all would be well: If couples would stay together, if mothers would stay home, if women would have babies only when they were safely married, if parents would revive older childraising values—then we wouldn't face the problems we do today.

Chapter 9 examines how such myths lead to unwarranted parent bashing. Both contemporary studies and historical experience show that children are resilient enough to adapt to many different innovations in family patterns: When they cannot adapt, this is caused more often by the economic and social context in which those innovations take place than by their parents' "wrong turns" away from traditional family patterns.

9

Toxic Parents, Supermoms, and
Absent Fathers:

Putting Parenting in Perspective

MERICAN parents get it coming and going. Pictures of kidnapped children stare out from supermarket bags. Newspapers detail lurid stories of pornography rings, satanist cults, and day-care workers engaging in ritual sexual abuse of children. "No town is safe—no child is safe—from the sick, sadistic monsters and killers who roam our country at random," declares the anguished father of one murdered boy. "It can be anybody," warn the television ads. "You can never tell." Never leave your child with someone you don't thoroughly know and trust, we are told; the only safe place is home.[1]

Yet on closer examination, home is an even scarier place. Ninety-nine percent of kidnappers and the large majority of physical and sexual abusers of children are their parents. More youngsters run away from unhappy homes each year than are kidnapped. The well-publicized (and greatly exaggerated) poisonings of children on Halloween generally turn out to have been perpetrated by family members. And we are constantly reminded of the psychological injuries that we inflict on our children by every addition to the various support groups for "adult children" of alcoholics, divorced parents, or other "dysfunctional families."[2]

Best-selling author John Bradshaw claims that "the major source of human misery" is the "neglected, wounded child" inside each of us. A flourishing business in self-help books, tapes, seminars, and group therapy has grown up around the idea that all our adult woes stem from the various ways that parents blighted our childhoods.

Two specialists in the "at risk" industry have gone so far as to assert that *96 percent of the population* comes from dysfunctional families.[3]

While such commentators trace every personal and social problem in modern America back to parental failure, they differ over exactly what it is that parents do to produce such calamities. Columnist John Rosemond argued in the aftermath of the Central Park jogger rape that the "wilding" teens were "nothing more than overindulged, undersupervised, undisciplined, out-of-control brats. Society hasn't failed them; their parents have." Cultural critic Christopher Lasch indicts white suburban parents for the same sins Rosemond attributes to black urban parents: They have abandoned parental authority by fostering inappropriate democracy and generational equality in the family, failing to instill guilt, discipline, or a sense of limits in their children.[4]

But psychotherapist Susan Forward suggests that a much larger problem lies in the "toxic parents" who poison their children with "guilt and inadequacy" by criticizing or punishing them too harshly. Many authorities argue that highly aggressive, violent children are more likely to come from punitive, authoritarian families, especially abusive ones, rather than from permissive ones.[5]

Some authors claim that we have introduced our children to adult responsibilities too early, depriving them of childhood, others that we have prolonged their childhood and adolescence to the point that young people have totally unrealistic expectations of life. Articles on the "superbaby" hype of the 1970s criticized parents' compulsive overinvestment in their children, while other analysts bemoaned the "erosion of the bond between parent and child."[6]

Mothers have tended to receive the lion's share of blame. As one psychiatrist notes, mothers have "been variously accused of causing epilepsy, colitis, asthma,...rheumatoid arthritis, ulcers, anorexia nervosa, manic-depressive illness, juvenile delinquency, and drug addiction in their children." However, fathers do not escape unscathed: Overbearing, pushy fathers are blamed for one set of emotional disabilities, uninvolved or ineffectual ones for another.[7]

We are surrounded by constant reminders of how complex the parenting task is and how consequential our every act as a mother or father. "Have you hugged your kid today?" reads the bumper sticker on the car in front of me on the way to work, reminding me that I not only shoved him out the door too quickly but also may have put the wrong snack in his backpack. "Do you know where your children are?" demands the ad before the nightly news, making me wonder what he's doing upstairs while I engage in such a self-indulgent activity as watching television. Books, articles, and risk-reduction entrepreneurs offer us conflicting advice on how to negotiate the fine line between overprotecting our children on one side and neglecting them on the other, building their self-esteem while introducing them to realistic criticism, loving them without smothering them, fostering independence without pushing them too fast.

Most parents believe that we have fallen off this tightrope on *both* sides, so we scramble for handholds to get back on course. We devour snippets of information in the mass media about correlations that researchers have found between certain family characteristics and various outcomes for children. Unfortunately, superficial reporting often implies that correlations are the same as causes and averages are goals we ought to aim for, a confusion that only feeds our guilt. If our family fails to duplicate a "good" correlation or happens to meet one of the "bad" ones, we are "at risk." Never mind that sometimes the increased risk merely means a rise from a 2 percent chance of a bad outcome to a 4 percent chance—that's twice the risk, after all; never mind that even a strong correlation seldom demonstrates a causal relationship; and never mind that there isn't even agreement, as we shall see, on what a "bad outcome" is—it's all grist for the guilt mill.

If you stayed too long in the Jacuzzi or took a couple of drinks during pregnancy, your baby is "at risk" for learning disabilities. If you failed to bond with your infant in the critical early months or even minutes, your child is "at risk" for insecure attachment. If you put your boy in a certain kind of day care at a particular age, he is "at risk"; if you don't put your girl in the same kind of day care at the same age, *she is* "at risk." If you are divorced, your kids are "at risk." If you and your spouse stayed together for the sake of the kids and couldn't hide the tension, then they are still "at risk." And if your own behavior hasn't put your kids at risk, their future is threatened by the parents who *have* ruined their kids, causing the rise in crime and the disintegration of our schools.

To some extent, of course, *all* our children are "at risk," because we are fallible human beings in a society that expects us singlehandedly, or at most two-parently, to counter all the economic ups and downs, social pressures, personal choices, and competing demands of a highly unequal, consumption-oriented culture dominated by deteriorating working conditions, interest-group politics, and self-serving advertisements for everything from toothpaste to moral values. We are expected to teach our children to sort through the claims of rival authorities without rejecting authority, to pursue self-reliance without abandoning commitment, and to resist the seductions of consumerism while preparing for jobs that will allow them to provide a better life for their own children.

It's a daunting proposition, and from conversations that I have had with my students, the reason many young people are reluctant to have children has less to do with their alleged self-preoccupation than with their terror that they will mess things up. As a historian, I suspect that the truly dysfunctional thing about American parenting is that it is made out to be such a frighteningly pivotal, private, and exclusive job.

Even those of us who know better get caught up in this obsessiveness about parental responsibility for every aspect of a child's development and behavior. Despite years of studying the many varieties of healthy family life and parenting styles, I realized how unrealistic, not to mention exhausting, were modern American myths about good parenting only when I spent some time with Hawaiian-Filipino friends on the island of Lanai. My child was still in diapers, and I greatly appreciated the fact that nearly every community function, from weddings to baptisms to New Year's Eve parties, was open to children. I could sit and socialize and keep an eye on my toddler, and I assumed that was what all the other parents were doing. Soon, however, I noticed that I was the only person jumping up to change a diaper, pick my son up when he fell, wipe his nose, dry his eyes, or ply him with goodies. Belatedly, I realized why: The other parents were *not* keeping an eye on their kids. Instead, each adult kept an eye on the *floor* around his or her chair. Any child who moved into that section of the floor and needed disciplining, feeding, comforting, or changing was promptly accommodated; no parent felt compelled to check that his or her *own* child was being similarly cared for.

I will argue later that the rest of American culture should adopt standards of childrearing that do not confine responsibility to parents, and I will show that many modern discussions of maternal employment, day care, divorce, and single parenthood are distorted by the myth that parents can or should be solely responsible for how their children grow. First, though, I want to put some of our assumptions about normal or traditional childrearing into historical perspective.

What Is a Normal Family and Childhood?

The historical and cross-cultural record reveals an astonishing variety of family forms and childrearing arrangements. Few societies in the past, it turns out, have shared our insistence on the unique role of the nuclear family, especially the mother, in raising healthy children. In traditional Chinese families, the patrilineal extended family had far more say over childrearing than did the nuclear unit. In parts of southern China, however, and in many kinship societies, women have lived together and raised their children apart from their husbands for significant periods of time. While modern Americans tend to think that a girl needs an especially close relationship to her mother and a boy to his father, other societies create well-adjusted children in different ways. Among the Cheyenne, a girl is expected to have strained, even hostile, relations with her mother and to go to her aunt for comfort and guidance. In the Trobriand Islands, a man has much closer relations with his sister's sons than with his own; his biological sons are counted as part of his wife's family, not his own.[8]

The Zinacantecos of southern Mexico lack a word differentiating parents and children from other social groupings; instead, they identify the basic unit of social and personal responsibility as a "house." In medieval Europe and colonial America, as well as in many contemporary West African societies, fosterage, child exchange, and adoption have been as central to childrearing as have actual blood ties. In preindustrial Europe, "contracts of brotherhood" and other arrangements linked domestic groups into "tacit communities" of both extended families and nonkin. In the Caribbean, "close and imperishable bonds are formed through the act of 'raising' children, irrespective of genetic ties." These coparenting relationships "are just as strong as 'real' kinship ties." Shared responsibilities are forged through godparenting and through the concept of "shipmates," a powerful link conceptualized as stemming from the experience of being bound together in slavery.[9]

Failure to understand that these family forms are as meaningful to the people who live in them as our own families are to us leads to tragic misunderstandings. In West Africa, fostering a child out is a way of building social trust and providing the child with new resources and educational experience; the natal family does not relinquish its claim or commitment to the child. But when West Africans engage in this practice in England, they often find that English cou-

ples sue for permanent custody and English judges consider them to
have abandoned their children.[10]

If it is hard to find a "natural" parent-child relationship in this variety of family arrangements, it is also difficult to make pat historical
judgments about what kind of family is best for children. Talcott Parsons and other sociologists of the 1950s claimed that the small, intense nuclear family was best suited to childraising in modern industrial society, and the Moynihan Report of the 1960s argued that lack
of a tight nuclear family with a strong father figure created weak egos
among black Americans. But Richard Sennett found in nineteenth-
century Chicago that it was the small nuclear families of the white
middle class who were least able to operate successfully in the industrial economy and most likely to produce weak egos. Historian
Tamara Hareven suggests that "the family type best equipped to
interact with the complexities of modern life" is one "enmeshed
with extended kin and closely integrated with the community."
On the other hand, historian Linda Gordon points out that in late
nineteenth-century America, the support offered by kin networks
was much less than commonly assumed, while extended families
often exerted brutal repression over women and youth.[11]

For some commentators, "the history of childhood is a nightmare
from which we have only recently begun to awaken." They point to
the whippings administered even to young kings and nobles in medieval Europe or to the childhood of King Louis XIII of France, who
was encouraged to run his little hand up the dresses of women in the
court and to fondle his own genitals in public. In the absence of reliable birth control, they show, both infanticide and abandonment
were common until recent times.[12]

Indeed, abandonment was so widely practiced that the main argument of some prominent early Christian theologians against a man's
recourse to prostitutes was the possibility that he might thereby un-
knowingly commit incest with his own abandoned child. The sentimentalization of motherhood and childhood discussed in chapter 3
did not immediately reverse these practices. Jean-Jacques Rousseau,
whose idealization of domesticity we have already encountered, put
all five of his own infants in a foundling hospital.[13]

As usual, however, history does not lend itself to value-laden, uni-
lineal generalizations. Certainly, previous ages had sometimes shock-
ingly different values about what was "good" for children, as in the
instruction of King Henry IV of England to his son's governess "to
whip him every time that he is obstinate or mischievous," because "I

know it from experience" that "there is nothing in the world which will be better for him than that." Colonial Americans also sanctioned the beating and whipping of children as a legitimate form of punishment. Yet historian John Demos argues that there was no pattern of systematic, severe, and escalating abuse such as we see in so many modern child-battering cases. Other historians have pointed out that despite different ways of showing it, people in earlier times clearly loved their children and did their best by them according to their own lights.[14]

Colonial Americans believed it important to inspire fear in their children. The clergyman Cotton Mather, for example, described taking his young daughter into his study and explaining that when he died, which might be very soon, she must remember all he had taught her about combating "the sinful and woeful conditions of her nature." After the eighteenth century, by contrast, there was a growing desire to protect children from fear, but parents attempted to instill *guilt* in its place. One of Louisa May Alcott's vignettes about how to deal with a recalcitrant child involved having the naughty boy hit the *grownup* with a ruler: As this was fiction, the child was immediately overcome with "a passion of love, and shame, and penitence." Some parents claimed to accomplish the same results in real life. The minister Francis Wayland, for example, described how he avoided using physical punishment by isolating his stubborn fifteen-month-old child for thirty-one hours (going into the room periodically to see if he would do as bidden), until the boy not only submitted but also "repeatedly kissed me." In fact, reported the delighted father, he would now kiss anyone he was asked to, "so full of love was he to all the family." Historian Jan Lewis, however, argues that such childrearing practices produced not love but obsequiousness.[15]

Toward the end of the nineteenth century, there developed what historian Viviana Zeliger calls a "sacralization" of childhood in America. This helped spur the abolition of child labor and made it unacceptable to value children for their economic contributions to the family. While most modern Americans find older calculative attitudes toward children's economic worth repulsive, it is by no means clear that "altruistic" parenting produces better childhood experiences. As historian E. P. Thompson comments: "Feeling may be *more,* rather than less, tender or intense *because* relations are 'economic' and critical to mutual survival." The fact that children have less to offer the middle-class family in modern America and that there are fewer economic reinforcements of parent-child interactions means there are few supports to shore up the bonds of "love."[16]

The degree of instrumental or affective feeling that seems to prevail in a family predicts very little about actual relationships. Louise
Tilley has demonstrated through careful individual histories that
family strategies based on economic calculation and even child-
sacrificing work patterns could be extremely loving *or* extremely
brutal; conversely, families who value love and altruism often experience bitter disillusion and violence. There are also class and cultural
components to childrearing values that lead easily to misunderstand-
ing. Working-class and peasant families, for example, have historically tended to disguise individual, personal feelings in "tough talk,"
partly in order to ensure that family ties do not threaten larger social
solidarities; middle-class families have tended to wrap material interests and status considerations in an individualized, voluntaristic, and
sentimental language. To assume that one familial language reveals
more "pure" or "admirable" sentiments toward children is very
naïve.[17]

If parental, class, and cultural ideas about childrearing have varied
enormously over time, so have the pronouncements of "experts"
about what parents must and must not do. In the eighteenth and
early nineteenth centuries, it was thought that children should be
taught academic subjects at a very early age; in 1830, a substantial
portion of children under the age of four were enrolled in school. By
the mid-nineteenth century, however, expert consensus held that
early schooling caused children to burn out or even become stupid
in later years.[18]

In the early twentieth century, experts counseled parents against
"fussing" over infants or picking them up when they cried, and advocated rigid feeding and sleeping schedules. "The rule that parents
should not play with the baby may seem hard," cautioned one government pamphlet, "but it is without doubt a safe one." During the
same period, however, many teens and preteens, such as urban news-
boys and peddlers, were granted a freedom from supervision that
makes many modern latchkey children look positively cosseted.[19]

By the 1940s and 1950s, a more flexible, affectionate approach to
babies was in vogue, although this was also the period when breast-
feeding was judged inferior to "scientific" artificial feeding. Permissive attitudes toward babies, moreover, coexisted with far tighter
reins on adolescents. While some authors offer 1950s mothering as a
model for good parenting, arguing that since the 1960s, women's
search for fulfillment outside the family has loosened family ties and

created insecure, narcissistic personalities, others suggest that narcissism is rooted in the 1950s family model itself, which "isolates mothers from adult companionship, denies their needs for meaningful work, and enforces their exclusive responsibility for child rearing."[20]

Changes in childrearing values and parental behaviors are seldom a result of people suddenly becoming nicer or meaner, smarter or more irresponsible. They reflect realignments in the way families articulate with larger social, economic, and political institutions, as well as changes in environmental demands on adults and children. Clearly, the demographic and occupational shifts described in the last two chapters have significantly altered the experience both of parenting and of growing up, requiring adjustments from parents and children.

The tremendous variety of workable childrearing patterns in history suggests that, with a little effort, we should be able to forge effective new institutions and values. Instead, however, many commentators seek out every scrap of evidence they can find to "prove" that all innovations are bad. Since the changes in gender roles and economic patterns that have transformed childrearing are unlikely to be reversed, such blanket condemnations of nontraditional practices are unproductive, to put it mildly. By heaping more and more guilt on individual families, they make childrearing even *more* difficult than it already is in today's changing society.

Maternal Employment and Childrearing

Some of the most widespread concerns about contemporary parenting revolve around the unprecedented expansion in maternal employment and child care outside a family setting. Recall that it is the location, not the existence, of maternal work and nonmaternal child care that is new: Throughout most of human history, mothers have devoted more time to other duties than to child care and have delegated substantial portions of childrearing to others.[21] But there *are* new conflicts between women's work and family responsibilities today, since they take place in mutually exclusive locations and times. Work, school, and medical care in America are still organized around the 1950s myth that every household has a full-time mother at home, available to chauffeur children to doctor and dentist appointments in the middle of the day, pick up elementary school children on early dismissal days, and stay home when a child has the flu.

Consequently, many parents—especially mothers, who are still expected to take prime childrearing responsibility—are intensely ambivalent about the tradeoffs between work and parenting. Such ambivalence is fed by a stream of often-contradictory research and wild speculation about the effects of maternal employment on children. For example, the conservative Rockford Institute on the Family, which deplores the employment of mothers, sends out monthly updates of research purporting to demonstrate that maternal employment causes every ill from head colds to temper tantrums to social decay. Rockford Institute researcher Bryce Christensen points out ominously that child homicide rates are higher in countries with high levels of maternal employment than in countries with low levels.[22]

It is true that children in day-care centers get more colds and infections than do home-care children. But they also build up immunities that home-care children entering school lack, so that later on they get sick *less* often. As for the implication that female employment leads to child murder, this is nonsense. Although child homicide rates *are* higher in countries where more women work for pay, they are not higher *among* the women who work. Indeed, there is evidence that "full-time housewives are more likely than working mothers to use violence against their children." But such correlations, on either side of the argument, prove absolutely nothing about causes anyway; they likely derive from some other characteristics of modern industrialism and gender roles. It *is* interesting, though, that the lowest levels of child homicide in countries where women work outside the home are found in societies that have generous social welfare spending and higher proportions of women in college or professional occupations—an argument for more, not less, effort to improve women's work equality with men.[23]

A National Academy of Sciences panel has found that in most spheres there are no substantial differences between children of employed mothers and those of nonemployed mothers. For children from lower socioeconomic backgrounds, and for girls in general, maternal employment correlates with higher intelligence test scores for preschoolers and fifth-graders and higher achievement test scores for high schoolers. Sons of middle-class employed mothers, on the average, turn in somewhat lower academic performances than do sons of middle-class at-home mothers. On the other hand, sons of working mothers appear to have more respect for women than do other boys and are more likely to see men as warm and expressive. Most of these differences, moreover, are fairly minor, and the averages hide substantial variation among individual families.[24]

Many studies of maternal employment are suspect because they exclude the effects of *paternal* employment on children, the interactions between working fathers and working mothers, the quality of child care, and other significant variables. One study of working women, for example, found that the sons of employed mothers tended to have less secure attachments not to their mothers but to their fathers. This may indicate that the only reason male breadwinner families have seemed more functional for boys is that nonworking women have spent so much time compensating for paternal absence or neglect. In this case, it is surely as logical to do something about the father's work and parenting patterns as to insist that his wife stay home to make up for his weaknesses. One project, for example, initially supported the supposed ill effects of maternal employment on four-year-old boys, but when researchers studied families with fathers who were active in childrearing, the IQ deficits for boys with employed mothers disappeared.[25]

Several studies show that it is a woman's degree of satisfaction with *either* the housewife role or paid work, and the continuity of her work experience when she does work, that best correlates with positive outcomes in her children. Mothers whose work is complex and challenging tend to create more enriching environments for their children than do mothers whose work is boring—a finding completely counter to accusations that career women are distracted by their jobs or claims that women who have to work should find jobs that do not compete with their commitment to mothering. Maternal employment has negative effects when a woman's working conditions are demeaning, her husband's attitude hostile, or her child-care arrangements inadequate, says pediatrician Mary Howell, but "otherwise, maternal employment seems to offer many advantages to family relations and for the lives of children."[26]

The Impact of Day Care

The greatest controversy around maternal employment is associated with the fact that a majority of women with babies under one year of age are now working outside the home, often leaving their infants in day care. In 1986, the noted psychologist Jay Belsky expressed some reservations about placing children in day care for more than twenty hours a week during their first year of life, suggesting that this posed a "risk factor" for "insecure attachment" to mothers. A recent study in Dallas, Texas, found that the children of mothers who returned to work during their child's first year scored more poorly than did other children in social and academic functioning. But other studies do not replicate the Texas finding, even for mothers who return to work very shortly after birth. And Belsky himself has strongly objected to conservative attempts to turn his tentative cautions into a full-scale indictment of early day care. In Sweden, Belsky notes, where women have more well-resourced child-care centers to choose from after their six months of paid parental leave are up, studies find no such negative effects of maternal return to employment before the child's first birthday.[27]

Of course it is important for a child to form secure attachments with adults. Continuity of care during the first eighteen months of life seem to be especially consequential in establishing the trusting relations that facilitate future social and emotional growth. Yet there is no reason that such continuity cannot be established by a combination of parental attention and stable day care. Indeed, some studies show that, in many contexts, bonding with other caregivers is a better predictor of healthy development than attachment to mother.[28]

One authority estimates that maternal employment during a child's infancy increases the risk of "insecure attachment" between women and children by 15 percent but has no effect on the rate of "avoidant attachment," which is considered the most serious kind of attachment disruption. Insecure attachment, researchers hypothesize, occurs when a child believes that while his mother wants to behave sensitively toward him, she often does not know how. Given children's sensitivity to parental ambivalence, it could be that the increased risk of insecure attachment with working mothers tells us more about the guilt women feel than it does about the way they actually behave. Or it could mean that some women's work situations prevent them from getting to know their child's patterns as well as they otherwise might. But psychologists are now discovering that their very measures of attachment and predictions of its effects may be hopelessly biased toward one kind of family setting.[29]

Because many children of at-home mothers show distress in the presence of a stranger, cry when their mothers leave the room, and seek contact with their mothers when they come back, for example, researchers have tended to assume that this is a measure of attachment—and therefore "good." Both Native American and white women in colonial America, of course, would have considered this behavior disturbingly abnormal. Without a historical or cross-cultural perspective, however, researchers concluded that because children of working mothers did *not* cry or interact with a returning parent as often, they were less attached than were "normal" children. But recent studies demonstrate that "stranger anxiety" is a matter more of temperament than of anything else, while the other behaviors depend on whether babies have *experience* with their mothers leaving and coming back. Day-care children are less likely to cry and seek contact because they are more likely to take such separations in stride.[30]

Generalizations about negative results of day care in America are extremely suspect, since the United States, unlike Europe, has almost no national legislation establishing a miminum quality of care. Most studies thus average together both high-quality and low-quality child-care situations. If the jury is still out on full-time day care for very young infants, though, there is simply no evidence that adequate day care has baleful effects on children over a year old. Although researchers consistently report that children in day care are less compliant with their parents and more assertive with their peers, day-care children do as well or better than their at-home counterparts in the areas of sociability, social competence, problem solving, achievement, language skills, empathy, and self-confidence.[31]

Some observers believe that day care's apparent influence on assertiveness/aggression and noncompliance is a negative outcome. An alternative interpretation is advanced by psychology researcher Alison Clarke-Stewart. In her view, noncompliance may merely show "that children who have been in day care…think for themselves and that they want their own way." One study found that preschoolers who had been in day care were likely to condemn moral transgressions, such as hitting or stealing, much more strongly than social ones, such as failing to put one's toys away, while children just starting preschool thought both were equally bad. Obviously, children who make such distinctions take more energy to control, but there is no reason to believe that they end up being worse persons. It would be tempting to say that they might end up being better persons were it not for the fact that all these early differences seem to fade very rapidly anyway.[32]

At any rate, day care is obviously here to stay, so a more useful research question might be what kind of child care tends to yield the best results. The fact is, as Edward Zigler of Yale University's child development program puts it, "we have learned enough to know how to deliver good quality care to children of every age."[33]

Despite fears of conservatives that attempts to subsidize or monitor child care would create "the one great nanny of us all," most child development specialists agree that we need to find creative ways to finance and regulate child care. Belsky points out, for example, that high-quality day care tends to emerge when providers receive material and emotional supervision and assistance from community agencies. Zigler proposes that families be allowed to dip into their social security accounts while their children are young, so that they can choose either to forego the earnings of one spouse or to place their children in quality child care. For those who choose the latter, he advocates development of child-care centers organized around the schools and available for children from age three.[34]

Latchkey Kids

In the absence of programs such as Zigler proposes, many children are unsupervised after school until their parents return from work, and almost every employer notices the surge in personal calls between 3:30 P.M. and 5:00 P.M. as worried parents check in. For many children, being home alone after school is not an ideal situation. A recent study of eighth-graders in Los Angeles and San Diego, conducted by the American Academy of Pediatrics, generated many headlines and much soul-searching in parents when it reported that latchkey kids were twice as likely as were kids under supervision to try marijuana at least once, to smoke cigarettes, and to drink alcohol—regardless of whether they came from one- or two-parent families or what kind of grades they received at school. Some much scantier evidence suggests that latchkey children tend to be more anxious and run a higher risk of delinquency. These findings obviously raise serious concerns about leaving even older children at home alone after school. Yet a North Carolina study found that teachers rated latchkey children as better adjusted socially than were children in either home care or child-care centers, while studies in Philadelphia and the South showed latchkey children performing equally well with others in school. Researchers also have noted posi-

tive effects of self-care on children's sense of self-discipline and responsibility.[35]

Perhaps the key to incorporating these studies in personal decision making is to take a balanced perspective. The safety, effectiveness, and impact of latchkey arrangements depends on the location
of the home, the characteristics of the neighborhood, and the resources available to the child, as well as the child's emotional and
chronological ages. Even in the California study, the increased risk of
substance abuse should be put in perspective: More than three-
quarters of the latchkey eighth-graders had never tried marijuana
and did not use alcohol; only 13 percent had ever smoked more than
a pack of cigarettes. The tendency to engage in these behaviors depended on the youngsters' previous risk-taking inclinations and the
kinds of friends they associated with. Averages and correlations cannot substitute for parental judgment on this question, and parents
who take all these factors into account have no reason to live in
guilt—even if their child does end up trying marijuana. A fifteen-
year study of San Francisco children reported in the May 1990 issue
of *American Psychologist* found that even adolescents who experiment casually with drugs are not necessarily on the road to ruin. In
fact, "those who tried illegal drugs in small amounts during adolescence tended to be healthier and better adjusted" than were either
complete abstainers or frequent users.[36]

Divorce and Single Parenthood

Another major concern about modern family life is the impact on
children of divorce and residence in single-parent homes. Psychologists Judith Wallerstein and Sandra Blakeslee touched a tender nerve
in America with their 1989 study claiming that almost half the children of divorced parents experience long-term pain, worry, and insecurity that adversely affect their love and work relationships. A spate
of other studies showing that children from divorced and single-
parent homes score lower on self-esteem and tend to be more "at
risk" in school unleashed a response that was immediate, heartfelt,
and occasionally a tad extreme. One author, claiming that divorce is
transmitted much like the "cycle of violence" postulated by child-
abuse authors, has argued that as the "background divorce pressure"
has risen, it raises the question of whether the spiraling divorce syn-

drome "threatens societal viability—or even the persistence of human life itself." Even more moderate voices have begun to talk about legislation discouraging divorce.[37]

Divorce creates many stresses for children: loss of income (even in single-father families); changes in residence, neighborhood, friends, and schools; and unhappy, distracted, or angry parents. Again, however, there are several problems with the hard-and-fast generalizations that some have drawn, especially their implied message that if you are a single parent you have inevitably handicapped your child and if you are considering divorce you had better reconsider, no matter how unhappy your marriage. Wallerstein's study, for example, did not compare the children of divorced couples with those of nondivorced ones to determine whether some of their worries and adjustment problems might have stemmed from other factors, such as work pressures, general social insecurities, or community fragmentation. Nor was her long-term follow-up of divorced families based on a random sample: It was drawn from families already experiencing difficulty and referred to the divorce clinic for short-term therapy. "Only a third of the sample was deemed to possess 'adequate psychological functioning' *prior* to the divorce."[38]

More representative samples of children from divorced and intact families have found less dramatic differences in school achievement and psychological well-being. Children from intact families in which their parents fought constantly were no better off than the children of divorced parents, and sometimes they experienced worse problems. One large sample of American children did find some consistent negative traits in children of divorced parents, but "the proportion of variation…that could be attributed to marital dissolution was generally quite small, never amounting to more than 3%." Often, the adverse effects observed in children were there *prior* to the divorce. In other cases, they derived from a hostile family environment rather than from parent absence per se.[39]

One point to remember is that even in two-parent families, paternal absence has often been the norm. One study, for example, found that employed fathers living with their children shared, on the average, only two hours of activity with them per week. The astonishing popularity of poet Robert Bly's work on men suggests that thousands of men from two-parent families feel as damaged by the inaccessibility of their fathers as do the children of divorce. When two researchers controlled for paternal inaccessibility, they found that the sons of relatively uninvolved fathers in intact homes had the same kind of academic deficits as did boys in mother-only families. Therapist Deborah Luepnitz even suggests that "fathers' *emotional* absence may be more difficult to contend with than their physical absence, since, like all ambiguous losses, it cannot be easily acknowledged and grieved."[40]

Many studies that have found negative effects of divorce on children have not adequately controlled for other variables, such as economic loss, conflict, and biased reporting. Researchers who managed to disentangle the effects of divorce itself from the effects of a change in physical location, for example, found that dislocation was much more likely to interfere with school completion than parental separation. A reanalysis of earlier research claiming that single-parent families caused delinquency found that levels of parental crime and family conflict were better predictors of delinquency than was family form. In Washington state, the Department of Social and Health Services found that the broadest, most consistent predictors of school failure, substance abuse, delinquency, and adolescent pregnancy were poverty and having parents, whether still married or not, who had not graduated from high school. Another study concluded that "the negative effects on achievement of living in a one-parent family are almost entirely mediated by other variables, particularly by income" but also by effective time use on the part of mother and child.[41]

An increased risk for certain behaviors, even in the short run, does not necessarily mean all or even most of the children involved will have those outcomes. A Netherlands project showed that while 47 percent of children from mother-headed families were less successful than their match from two-parent families, 24 percent were just as successful, and 29 percent were *more* successful.[42]

Some of the ill effects of divorce and residence in single-parent families, furthermore, may result from self-fulfilling prophecies. One review of literature on single-parent families found that the only situations in which children of one-parent families suffered losses of self-esteem were those in which the families were stigmatized. Teachers shown a videotape of a child engaging in a variety of actions consistently rate the child much more negatively on a wide range of dimensions when they are told that he or she comes from a divorced family than when they believe the child to come from an intact home.[43]

Given that single parenthood is likely here to stay, a more productive research issue might be to move away from broad generalizations and identify which aspects of single-parent families produce negative outcomes and which are associated with positive outcomes. Adults in single-parent families tend to spend less time supervising homework or interacting with teachers, behaviors that have negative effects on school performance, but they also spend more time talking with their children than adults in two-parent families, a behavior that has positive effects on school achievement. Single parents are less likely to pressure their children into social conformity and more likely to praise good grades than are two-parent families, behaviors that tend to produce higher academic performance. Here they have an advantage over many two-parent families. But single parents are more likely to get upset and angry when their children receive bad grades, a response that is associated with a further decline in grades. Single parents also are more apt to relinquish parental decision-making prerogatives too early, but this problem is almost entirely eliminated when another adult joins the household, whether that adult is a relative, a lover, or a friend. Being made aware of these variables is more likely to help single parents cope than being sweepingly labeled "at risk."[44]

In the real world, there are tradeoffs in all decisions. Children's initial response to divorce is often negative, although they do adjust if the parents do not continue battling afterward. But women, despite initial pain and income loss, tend almost immediately to feel that they benefit from divorce. A 1982 survey found that even one year after a divorce, a majority of women said they were happier and had more self-respect than they had in their marriages. The proportion rises with every passing year. Researchers at the University of North Carolina report that women are more likely to have a drinking problem *prior* to a divorce or separation than after it, and that divorce reduces the risk of alcohol dependence among women who were problem drinkers before. What are the tradeoffs, even for the child, between short-term disruptions and long-term maternal misery? Is it worse to end up an adult child of divorced parents or an adult child of an alcoholic?[45]

Of course it's a strain for one parent to raise a child. It's hard enough for two parents to do so, and many factors in our society make single parenthood especially traumatic—poverty, parental conflict, lack of time, social prejudice, and the absence of a strong social safety net. Still, it is important to remember that most children recover in the long run, and in the short run there is much that can be done to mitigate the problems. Educational researcher James Coleman, for example, has shown that the higher risk of children from single-parent families for dropping out of school disappears where there are supportive community, educational, and religious networks beyond the family. Anthropologist Colleen Johnson and sociologist Judith Stacey have both commented on the ways in which some creative people have even turned divorce itself into a "resource rather than a rupture," extending their social networks by incorporating former in-laws and new spouses of former husbands or wives into their child-care arrangements, holiday celebrations, borrowing and lending patterns, and problem solving.[46]

The Myth of Parental Omnipotence

I am not trying to play Pollyanna. American youth have serious problems, and many parental behaviors or choices exacerbate those problems. Single-parent families are not simply "growth experiences"; latchkey children are often frightened and lonely; divorce is not merely a hiccup in anyone's life; the difficulties of working parents are very real and fall with special severity on working mothers. Despite the evidence that we can help our children rise above these difficulties, most parents who do not fit the ideal norm are painfully aware of the times when they fail to help. Other parents may feel self-righteous because they have never even exposed their children to such risks.

But neither self-congratulation nor self-castigation is in order. Both responses assume that parents have primary control over how their children turn out, when in fact there are many factors affecting children that have nothing to do with our own family choices, be they good or bad. Research psychologist Arlene Skolnick comments that "the myth of the vulnerable child" exaggerates both "the power of the parent and the passivity of the child." In fact, parents seldom have "make-or-break" control over the child's growth.[47]

Parenting is both easier and harder than many researchers and self-styled family experts admit: easier because, as we will see, children are resilient enough to survive many of our mistakes, and even to benefit from them; harder because some forces affecting children are simply too complicated for parents to control. Recent research demonstrates, for example, that neither one particular family type nor one particular classroom style guarantees school success. It is the "fit" between student background, classroom style, and particular

teacher that counts: "Children from *any* type of home can be relatively advantaged in some classrooms and relatively disadvantaged in
others."[48]

At home, children's temperamental differences interact with
parental idiosyncrasies in equally complex ways. Research on siblings suggests that they are raised in completely different environments within the same family. Parents relate differently to different
children, children react differently to similar treatment, and when we
throw in all the complications of sibling interactions as well, it is
very difficult to isolate what parents did or did not do that deserves
praise or blame.[49]

People's adjustment and achievement are also greatly affected by
factors beyond the family's direct control. Class background severely
limits the options of many parents and gives tremendous advantages
to others. Lower-class parents are especially ill-served by an overemphasis on parental responsibility for children's outcomes, since research shows that the social dynamics of poverty and low status give
them less influence over their children in relation to peer groups
than parents in other classes. Low-income parents must use what influence they do have to prepare their children for work that is likely
to stifle initiative and produce a degrading combination of boredom
and insecurity. Blaming parents in this situation for failing to
"broaden their child's horizon" is like calling people shortsighted because they cannot see through the mountains that surround them.[50]

For both high- and low-income workers, conditions of work often
are as influential on mental and physical health as are family background and childhood experiences. Psychotherapist Douglas LaBier
has argued that much of the anxiety, rage, depression, and substance
abuse found in neurotic patients does not stem from childhood dis-
turbances or basic personality flaws but from problems on the job.
Upheavals at work, in fact, can be even more traumatic than is marital dissolution. One study in Sweden concluded that "the psychoso-
cial situation at work appears to have a greater impact on psychological well-being than do family situations." A recent American poll
found that 27 percent of workers cited their job as the single greatest
stress factor in their life, ahead of either divorce or death. Perhaps we
need a support group for "infantalized adults of toxic employers."[51]

If nonfamilial influences can cause trauma, they can also heal it.
Support from coworkers is an important contributor to mental and
physical health; responsible jobs can build self-esteem; and supportive communities can overcome the effect of "truly awful homes." For

those with an adequate store of educational, economic, or social resources, there are many ways to compensate for deficiencies as parents: the summer camp that sparks an intellectual or leisure interest
parents had never been able to tap; the baby-sitter who teaches a skill
the child resisted learning from mom; the extra attention given by a
teacher because "he's from a good family, so there's no reason he can't
do better." At the top of the social scale, a recent study of upper-class
mothers points out, such institutions as boarding schools, private tu-
tors, and nannies routinely counteract serious weaknesses in the parent or child. "Upper-class students, including those who are admittedly poor students, are simply not allowed to fail academically or
personally. This gives them striking advantages over children of
other classes."[52]

There are limits to what parents can do to counter the effects of
class position, economic pressures, working conditions, and the all-
pervasive television. But the fact that parental power is limited makes
parenting easier in some ways, too. As it turns out, time and individual initiative heal many of the wounds of childhood. A W. T. Grant
Foundation study of aging found that many early life experiences,
even seemingly devastating problems in childhood, had virtually no
influence on well-being at age sixty-five.[53]

I am not saying that we should disregard the impact of our actions
on our children, putting blind faith in time, luck, class advantages,
or a child's natural resiliency. There are measurably different consequences of various parental behaviors and family patterns. But in
many cases, researchers simply do not know what they're measuring
or what significance the differences they are finding will have. Psychologist Lois Hoffman points out that "traits that seem maladaptive
at one age may develop into strengths as the child matures, or the
converse pattern may emerge."[54]

There is one study I keep on a wall in my bedroom to comfort me
when I have seen too many news releases claiming that conditions I
either cannot or will not create are essential to my child's adjustment.
It is a long-term study of individuals who were first tracked from infancy to adolescence. Researchers then predicted which youths were
likely to lead successful, happy lives and which would turn into
troubled adults. When they revisited the subjects at age thirty, they
were shocked to find that their predictions were wrong in *two-thirds*
of the cases—a record worse than if they had just made random
guesses. However, there was a pattern to the researchers' errors: They
had consistently overestimated both the damaging effects of early

family stresses and the positive effects of having a smooth, success-ful, nonchallenging childhood and adolescence. They had failed to anticipate that depth, complexity, problem-solving abilities, and ma-turity might derive from painful experiences rather than easy suc-cesses. Boys and girls who had been happy and popular as athletes or beauties in high school were especially likely to have their later growth forestalled: Their seeming "adjustment" as youths gave them no incentive for ongoing innovation and struggle.[55]

And then, of course, there are the late bloomers who confound the expectations of parents and experts alike: Albert Einstein could not read until he was seven; Beethoven's music teacher said he was "hopeless" as a composer; Edison's teacher labeled him unable to learn; Winston Churchill failed the sixth grade; Helen Keller seemed "irredeemable"; and Louis Armstrong was a neglected and aban-doned child who learned to play music at the New Orleans Colored Waifs Home for Boys.[56]

There are, in other words, many roads to success, each with its own rough sections. There are also plenty of wrong turnings to take, as well as several "right" places to end up. The idea that there is one single blueprint for parents to follow, one family form that always produces well-adjusted children, or one "normal" set of family ar-rangements and interactions is not true now and never has been. The evidence suggests that as long as we respond to the uncertainties with common sense, flexibility, and affection, most of us can be, in therapist Donald Winnicott's words, "good enough" parents.[57] We may be only muddling through, but we are not dysfunctional. We can afford to be "at risk" in a few areas of our lives and can even manage to turn those risks into personal and social growth.

When the Risks Become Overwhelming

Of course, there are always some families who are *not* "good enough." And there are many more who might be "good enough" in some settings but are exposed to so many risks at once that they or their children are extremely likely to fail. In recent years, we have seen a rise in the number of what one book calls "families in perpet-ual crisis."[58]

The most horrific examples of truly dysfunctional families are the ones in which there is wife battering, severe-injury child abuse, or incest. An estimated 1,200 children die each year from such abuse or neglect; those who survive are often damaged for life. The experience of physical abuse as a child, for example, increases the risk of chronic aggressive behavior patterns by almost 300 percent.[59]

Occasionally, the problem with such families is one of individual pathology, as in the Joel Steinberg case and other well-publicized instances of family brutality or neglect with no obvious socioeconomic component. More commonly, dysfunctional families are trapped in a feedback situation, where parental inadequacies are not countered or softened by other influences but rather exacerbated by the social environment and the family's lack of resources.

Although the causes of abuse and neglect are complex, and cases may be found in all income levels and ethnic groups, the "myth of classlessness" does not help us to understand this phenomenon. It is true that there is significant class and racial bias in the reporting of abuse and neglect, but it is not true that these are distributed randomly across the population. Neglect is the type of child maltreatment most strongly correlated with poverty, incest the least; but economic stress, material deprivation, social isolation, and educational deficits, such as unrealistic expectations of children's capacities—all closely associated with poverty—substantially increase the chances that maltreatment will occur.[60]

Sometimes, the only way to stop the cycle is to remove the children, abandoning any illusion that the "natural" family is always best. We must recognize that nonkin or distant kin may be more responsible than parents, that even institutionalization may be preferable to the kind of abuse some children experience. Child psychiatrist Michael Rutter argues that even children who have lived in severely deprived or abusive situations for six or seven years can make surprising progress if they are moved into new environments. One study showed an increase of thirty points in IQ scores of orphaned children who were moved from a poor institution to a better one.[61]

In many cases, though, intervention or prevention *can* help the family. Home visitors programs, lay counseling, and parent education classes seem to be especially effective. Head Start programs have been shown to increase school attendance rates among the poor, raise self-esteem, decrease the need for remedial classes, and reduce juvenile delinquency rates. Recent reanalysis of fatalistic "cycle of violence" theories reveals that two-thirds to three-fourths of those who were abused in childhood do *not* abuse their own children, offering hope that we can identify those factors that break the cycle and help more individuals to do so. Finally, research on severely "at risk" children who succeed demonstrates that the intervention of just one caring person from outside the nuclear family, not necessarily a relative, can put a child on the path to success.[62]

If even such dysfunctional, multiple-risk families and individuals can be helped, there is little reason for the rest of us to despair. But there is very good reason for us to be concerned, for our society devotes very few resources to such aid. Just as most business ventures could never get off the ground were it not for public investment in the social overhead capital that subsidizes their transportation and communication, parents need an infrastructure of education, health services, and social support networks to supplement the personal dedication and private resources they invest in childrearing. Yet America spends proportionately less on such social investment in children than does almost any other major industrial country. As one Chinese immigrant to America commented to me, the helping resources in America are devoted only to picking people up (or disposing of them) after they have fallen off the cliff, whereas elsewhere such resources are used to prevent people from getting too near the edge.[63]

American families need more access to "social capital" if parental investments in children are to pay off. The debate over whether one parent can raise a child alone, for example, diverts attention from the fact that good childrearing has always required *more* than two parents. If there is any pattern to be found in the variety of families that have succeeded and failed over the course of history, it is that children do best in societies where childrearing is considered too important to be left entirely to parents. In modern America as well, a growing body of research demonstrates that the crucial difference between functional and dysfunctional families lies not in the form of the family but in the quality of support networks outside the family, including the presence of nonkin in those networks.[64]

As long as we conceive of parenting only in terms of responsibility to our "own" kids, we put both them and ourselves at risk. The notion that parental love and dedication should be the exclusive source of children's material well-being and emotional health creates a very fragile security, even with the most well intentioned parents in the world. It means that any child is only one death, one divorce, one blood test away from having nothing.

If recent trends and research are not enough to demonstrate the danger of overemphasizing parents' exclusive responsibility for their own children, it might be worth listening to the views of people with far older and quite different family traditions. When Jesuit missionaries from France first encountered the Montagnais-Naskapi Indians of North America in the sixteenth century, they were impressed by the lack of poverty, theft, greed, and violence but horrified by the childrearing methods and the egalitarian relations between husband and wife. The Jesuits set out to introduce "civilized" family norms to the New World. They tried to persuade Naskapi men to impose stricter sexual monogamy on the women of the group and to moderate their "excessive love" for children by punishing them more harshly. One missionary spent an entire winter in a Montagnais lodge, recording in his journal both his efforts to impart these principles and the unsatisfactory responses of the Indians.

At one point, having been rebuffed on several occasions, the missionary obviously thought he had found an unanswerable argument for his side. If you do not impose tighter controls on women, he explained to one Naskapi man, you will never know for sure which of the children your wife bears actually belong to you. The man's reply was telling: "Thou hast no sense," said the Naskapi. "You French people love only your own children; but we love all the children of our tribe."[65]

That may be the best single childrearing tip Americans have ever been offered. Unless we learn to care for "all the children of the tribe," then no family, whatever its form, can be secure.

10

Pregnant Girls, Wilding Boys,
Crack Babies, and the Underclass:
The Myth of Black Family Collapse

AS we saw in the last chapter, the pervasive anxiety about childraising in America often shades into parent bashing. Among all classes and ethnic groups, charges have been leveled against "toxic parents," absent fathers, and selfish mothers for putting children "at risk." But the most powerful visions of parental failure, at-risk youth, and family collapse in the past few years have been tinted black. "Wilding" gangs; crazed cocaine addicts; macho men lacking the slightest shred of decency toward women and children: these images so pervaded the mass media that in 1989, Charles Stuart of Boston believed he could get away with murdering his pregnant wife by blaming a black mugger. His ploy almost succeeded: Public pressure to catch the criminal reached near-hysteria and police swarmed over black sections of town, strip-searching men and boys on street corners, until they settled on an ex-convict who fit the category. Stuart committed suicide when authorities finally began to act on the well-known criminological fact that 90 percent of crimes involve people of the same race and the most likely suspect in a murder is generally the victim's spouse.

The image of black family collapse, like Stuart's choice of a murder scapegoat, feeds on racist stereotypes and media distortions, ignoring the diversity of African-American family life.[1] Yet it also draws on some real, and very disturbing, trends affecting a section of black America. The most striking of these is a social and economic polarization in which poor African Americans have lost ground, both relatively and absolutely, for the past twenty years. Conditions in the inner cities provide obvious examples of deterioriation, but in many other areas progress has also stagnated or even been reversed since the late 1960s.

It is possible, of course, to find impressive exceptions, and in comparison to forty or fifty years ago, there have been undeniable gains. The percentage of blacks living in poverty fell from 92 percent in 1939 to 30 percent in 1974. (The figures for whites dropped from 65 percent to 9 percent, though, in the same period.) In 1960, employed black men averaged 49 percent of what employed white men made; that had increased to 64 percent by 1980. By 1984, employed black women earned 97 percent as much as did employed white women (even though they worked more hours a week to reach this wage parity and their gains still left them earning only 78 percent as much as black men and 53 percent as much as white men). The educational gap between blacks and whites also narrowed substantially between the 1950s and the 1980s.[2]

Forty years ago, African Americans in many areas of the country could not attend the same schools as did whites, drink from the same fountains, eat at the same restaurants, or ride at the front of public buses. Today, formal segregation has ended. The number of elected black officials increased more than fivefold between 1970 and 1987, from 1,479 to 6,384. In 1990, there were 316 black mayors in America, compared to 48 in 1973. For the first time, blacks other than athletes, from Bill Cosby to Colin Powell, won the respect of millions of white and black Americans alike.[3]

But these improvements coexisted with many more negative continuities and some ominous new trends. In 1990, hiring audits in Washington, D.C., and Chicago found that among black and white job seekers whose qualifications and even personalities were carefully matched, blacks were discriminated against in 20 percent of the cases. Young black men applying for entry-level jobs were rejected three times more often than were their white peers. Discriminatory treatment of black children remains widespread, both in the resources their schools receive and in the attitudes of teachers. Blacks, regardless of income, receive less intensive and high-tech medical treatment for their diseases than do whites.[4]

In 1989, the *Atlanta Journal/Constitution* traced home-loan applications received by the nation's banks between 1983 and 1988 and found that rejection rates were much higher for blacks than for whites, even when such variables as neighborhood wealth, vacancy rates, and personal income were taken into account. In many areas, rejection rates for *high-income blacks* were higher than for *low-income whites*. An Asian or Hispanic who finished only the third grade or who earns less than $2,500 a year has a higher chance of living in an integrated neighborhood than does a black person who has a Ph.D. or earns more than $50,000. College-educated black men now make 75 percent as much as their white counterparts when employed, but their unemployment rate is four times higher. And even though the average income of two-earner, college-educated African-American households is now 93 percent that of similar white families, white households typically have *ten times* as much wealth as black ones with comparable income. Meanwhile, the divisive use of racial images in political sloganeering has increasingly undermined the new, and in many cases still precarious, acceptance of civil rights.[5]

Furthermore, for all sectors of the black population except college graduates, gains have stagnated or reversed since the mid-1970s. The continued improvement in the position of college graduates affects a relatively small proportion of the African-American population: Indeed, the percentage of black students going on to college from high school dropped from 34 percent in 1976 to 26 percent in 1985. The poverty rate for black household heads who graduated from high school but did not attend college climbed from 18.7 percent in 1978 to 27.8 percent in 1987. The number of African Americans who are desperately poor—with incomes 50 percent *below* the poverty line— has increased by 69 percent since 1978, and the number of blacks living in areas of the city where almost all their neighbors are also poor has increased by about 20 percent.[6]

This magnification and concentration of poverty is associated with dramatic social and familial changes. Life expectancy for black Americans has now declined for four years in a row, an unprecedented trend in a modern industrial nation. The infant mortality rate for black babies is twice as high as for whites, and it has not improved for the past ten years. Forty-five percent of black children live in poverty for several years of their childhood. The homicide rate for black teens soared by 51 percent between 1984 and 1988, reversing the situation in 1984, when white teens were more likely than black ones to die an accidental or violent death. A majority of black children are born out of wedlock today, compared to three out of ten in 1970. Black women have higher divorce rates and lower remarriage rates than do whites, so that black children in one-parent homes remain in them for much longer periods of time than do white children.[7]

Blaming the Black Family

For many commentators, the last two aforementioned facts explain all the rest. Robert Rector of the Heritage Foundation, writing in the *Wall Street Journal,* asserts that "the primary cause of black poverty" is neither economic nor racial inequality but "disintegration of the family." Columnist Georgie Ann Geyer claims that today's racial predicament "is not any longer...a story of 'rights'; it is a story of 61.2 percent of black births today being 'out of wedlock.'"[8]

It is not only conservatives but also liberals who blame African-American economic and social distress on "disintegration of the black family." Indeed, *New Republic* writer Morton Kondracke has declared that "it is universally accepted that black poverty is heavily the result of family breakdown."[9]

Journalist Ken Auletta's *The Underclass* (1982) first popularized the concept that black poverty is linked to a degraded inner-city sub-culture locked into self-defeating personal and familial behaviors. The argument became increasingly stark over the 1980s: Black poverty exists because black men are irresponsible, black women are immoral, and black children run wild. Lyndon Johnson's son-in-law, Senator Charles Robb, claims that in LBJ's time, "racism, the tradi-tional enemy from without," was the problem; today, "it's time to shift the primary focus...to self-defeating patterns of behavior, the new enemy within." What African Americans need, according to what is often called "the new consensus," is not government pro-grams but a good dose of sexual restraint, marital commitment, and parental discipline.[10]

This "new consensus" about black families and poverty is hardly original. In almost every decade, for 200 years, someone has "discov-ered" that the black family is falling apart. After the American Revo-lution, politicians argued that the loose morals of blacks made them poor candidates for citizenship. In 1844, Secretary of State John Cal-houn announced that free northern blacks were rushing headlong into "vice," "pauperism," and insanity because they lacked natural family virtues and could not survive without slaveholders' paternalism. In the 1870s, former senator Robert Toombs declared that "the negro know[s no more] about the obligations of the marriage relation...than the parish bull or village heifer." In the 1890s, historian Philip Bruce argued that black children were being born into "moral degeneracy" because emancipation had removed the constraints slaveowners had wisely imposed on black immorality.[11]

While nineteenth-century whites had bemoaned how quickly the restraints of slavery dissipated, 1920s reformers depicted black families as "vicious" and "depraved" because of the *persistence* of slave traditions. In the 1930s, sociologist E. Franklin Frazier theorized that slavery and migration had destroyed any natural order in the black family, leaving a vacuum that blacks had not yet learned to fill. Welfare workers in the 1950s warned of a threat to social order posed by the "immorality" of black mothers. In 1964, Daniel Moynihan described black families as a "tangle of pathology." In 1986, Bill Moyers said they were "vanishing."[12]

The truth is that black people in America know far more about white families than white people know about black families. Many blacks, after all, have lived and worked inside white households, while whites usually have learned about black families from mass-media reports that focus on atypical, sensational, and distorted incidents. Yet while most blacks have maintained a dignified silence about what they saw and heard in white families, many white commentators haven't hesitated to sound off about black family matters of which they know next to nothing. As it turns out, most of their "common knowledge" concerning the history of black families is simply false, and many of the modern "facts" they cite are half-truths that seriously hamper responsible discussion of the dilemmas facing African Americans today.

As an example of a widespread myth, consider the so-called "explosion" of childbearing among single black women. Birth rates of unmarried black women have actually *fallen* by 13 percent since 1970 (compared to an increase of 27 percent among unmarried white women). But since birth rates of married black women have dropped by 38 percent, the *proportion* of black children being raised by unmarried mothers has grown. As we shall see, putting these facts together with data on economic and residential trends affecting young African Americans leads to quite a different interpretation of problems in the black community, including those of single-parent families, from that offered by the "new consensus."[13] For now, though, I will review some of the historical myths about African-American family life.

African-American Families in U.S. History

For an institution that has been deteriorating for 200 years, the black family has taken a remarkably long time to curl up and die. To be sure, many black families have differed from the white middle-class ideal, because their *circumstances* were different, but these differences have often been exaggerated, and where they have prevailed they have frequently been sources of strength rather than weakness.

The experience of black families has been qualitatively different from that of whites, or even other minorities, all along the line, creating distinct family and gender traditions. Slavery was far harsher and more extensive than any other form of indentured labor, and coerced labor of blacks continued in the South right up into the late twentieth century. It was especially widespread during the 1920s and 1940s, but incidents were found as late as the 1970s. No other group in America has been subjected to the systematic violence that was perpetrated against blacks, especially the concerted attacks on those who were economically or socially successful. Lynchings and race riots were only the tip of the iceberg: Millions of African Americans have lived their lives in subjection to various forms of white violence.[14]

More than other minorities, blacks encountered periodic increases in discrimination and segregation, first as democratic politicians tried to justify the continuation of slavery, then as blacks were pushed not *up* but *off* the job ladder by successive waves of immigrants. After a brief period of progress for free blacks following the American Revolution, racism escalated in the early nineteenth century and again after the end of radical Reconstruction. Jim Crow laws were introduced in the 1890s and established in the nation's capital in 1914.[15]

No other minority got so few payoffs for sending its children to school, and no other immigrants ran into such a low job ceiling that college graduates had to become Pullman porters. No other minority was saddled with such unfavorable demographics during early migration, inherited such a deteriorating stock of housing, or was so completely excluded from industrial work during the main heyday of its expansion. And no other minority experienced the extreme "hypersegregation" faced by blacks until the present.[16] All of these circumstances greatly affected African-American family life.

Slave families, of course, were under constant pressure. One study of marriages between slaves in Tennessee, Louisiana, and Mississippi found that from 1864 to 1866, almost one-third were broken up by the masters. Historian Herbert Gutman estimates that prior to the Civil War, only one in six or seven was so dissolved. But all slaves lived with the threat of such dissolution. Masters could control who married whom and who stayed married, and they did not confine their sexual exploitation of female slaves to single women.[17]

Most modern Americans know the first verse of the lullaby that slave nurses crooned to their white charges: "Hush a bye, don't you cry, go to sleepy, little baby. When you wake, you shall have all the pretty little horses. Blacks and bays, dapples and greys, a coach and six-a little horses." But not many parents sing their children the second verse, which vividly sums up the anguish slave women felt about their own babies: "Hush a bye, don't you cry, go to sleepy, little baby. Way down yonder in the meadow, lies a poor little lambie; bees and butterflies pecking out its eyes, poor little thing cried, 'Mammy.'"

Under such conditions, slaves had to improvise new family relations, as well as draw on African traditions of child fosterage and extended lineage ties. They developed courtship norms and marriage rituals that differed from those of free Americans. Grandmothers played a more central role in childrearing than they did in most white families, and slaves built "a generalized kinship system in which all adults looked after all children."[18]

Still, most slaves lived in two-parent families that lasted until the death of one spouse, and historian Eugene Genovese argues that what some white observers have interpreted as a debilitating matriarchy was in fact merely a rather close "approximation to a healthy sexual equality." When fathers were parted from the children, their names were preserved in the family line, while kinship ties on both sides were strengthened by careful attention to retaining grandparents, aunts, uncles, and cousins in family stories, rituals, and names. The centrality of family in slave traditions can be seen in the case of the descendants of a slave and an Irish servant who, nearly one hundred years after the marriage, supported a suit for freedom by listing relationships with more than one hundred kinfolk and recounting extraordinarily detailed stories passed down over the years. They recalled the wedding service, the priest's name, and the servant girl's response when the governor of Maryland attempted to dissuade her from marrying the slave: "She rather go to bed to Charles than his lordship."[19]

In the antebellum North as well, African-American families were subject to outside compulsions. In Philadelphia, for example, growing discrimination after the 1830s caused a decline in wealth and skill levels for blacks between 1838 and 1847, foreshadowing a trend that would spread to other cities after the Civil War. One in five adult blacks in Philadelphia had to live as a servant in a white household because of the unavailability of other work. There was a steady decline in the viability of two-parent households among the poorest sections of the black population in these years: By mid-century, one-third of the poorest half of the black community lived in female-headed households. In Boston, similarly, unskilled and semiskilled black workers were displaced by Irish ones in the mid-nineteenth century. The resultant poverty made separate nuclear families difficult to maintain, and a large proportion of blacks lived in multiple-family dwellings, often with nonrelatives in the household.[20]

After the Civil War, African Americans went to tremendous lengths to track down kin, reunite families, and resist destabilizing family conditions, such as gang labor. Their efforts enraged former slaveowners, who had once labeled black mothers as lacking in maternal sentiments but now accused them of "female loaferism" when they attempted to stay home with their infants. Unreconstructed southerners tried to force black mothers to work full-time in the fields. They passed "apprentice" laws to limit parental rights and keep black children in bondage. Northern "liberators" also disrupted black families when they shanghaied black men to work for the army. In response to these pressures, many blacks turned to sharecropping as a way of keeping their families together. Others moved to the cities or made their way North, taking their families along or sending for them as soon as possible.[21]

Despite these unique difficulties, the tremendous commitment of African Americans to family ties meant that the history of black family life was never as different from that of whites as some observers have claimed. Throughout the nineteenth century, most black Americans lived in two-parent households. Herbert Gutman demonstrates that between 1855 and 1880, 70 percent to 90 percent of black households contained two parents, and at least 70 percent were nuclear. From Ohio to Pennsylvania to Virginia, local studies confirm that the most common family form among blacks was the two-parent nuclear family.[22]

But we should not overstate the resemblance of black families to what has become the white, middle-class ideal. Between 1880 and 1900, the number of households comprising separate nuclear families seems to have declined among urban blacks in both the North and the South. Historian Elizabeth Pleck estimates that about 25 percent of African-American households in northern cities and 34 percent of those in southern cities were female-headed in the late nineteenth century, although contrary to historical myth, female-headed families were associated with urban poverty, unemployment, and underemployment rather than with the heritage of slavery or migration. The major source of difference between black and white households was increasing numbers of augmented households or subfamilies—a marked rise in the coresidence of black nuclear families with relatives or other individuals. By 1905 in New York City, 1 out of 7.9 black households included a subfamily, compared to 1 in 22.9 for Jews and 1 in 11.2 for Italians, while female-headed households represented 17 percent of the black total and 7 percent for both Jews and Italians. In New York, the proportion of nonaugmented nuclear families among black households had dropped to 49 percent by 1905; in Richmond it had fallen to 40 percent by 1900.[23]

Clearly, the viability of a household dependent on a single male breadwinner diminished for many African Americans during the latter part of the nineteenth century, as job opportunities "narrowed both relatively and absolutely" for northern and southern blacks. In Buffalo, New York, African Americans were driven out of skilled occupations between 1855 and 1905 and were hit harder than other groups by the depressions of the 1870s and 1890s. In Birmingham, Alabama, blacks "were constantly pushed out of various occupations toward the bottom of the occupational hierarchy." Throughout the South, "traditional black artisanal skills, which had reached a high point in the late eighteenth century and were maintained throughout the antebellum period by free Negroes, were liquidated in the last decades of the nineteenth century."[24]

The exclusion of African Americans from skilled trades and factory work led to poverty and unemployment that made it necessary for many families to pool their resources and for others to split up, as members went different directions in search of work or security. The dangerous jobs black men had to take and the unsanitary living conditions of urban slums, most of which lacked plumbing and sewage systems, produced high mortality, increasing the rate of marital dissolution caused by death. Both dire necessity and cultural traditions led to different gender norms as well as to alternative household arrangements among African-American families: Married black women were five times more likely to work for wages than were married white women.[25]

The Strengths of Black Families

But these alternative family forms and gender roles were hardly "pathological" or "disorganized." They were part of a rich extended kin and community life. In nineteenth-century Washington, D.C., for example, black working people supported more than one hundred associations, while poor alley residents developed vibrant and cohesive community networks. Studies of many cities in the nineteenth and twentieth centuries reveal that African-American families maintained tighter and more supportive kin ties than did other urban families, taking care of elders, paupers, and orphans within family networks rather than institutionalizing them as frequently as other groups did.[26]

Blacks who migrated to northern cities in the early twentieth century may have faced harsher housing and job segregation than did any other ethnic group in America, but they creatively used kinship ties, churches, and political organizations to build high levels of solidarity and mutual protection. They also maintained a strong commitment to work and education. In the 1920s, blacks had lower unemployment rates than did whites and kept their children in school much longer than did most immigrant groups. Almost twice as many black children as Italian ones attended school, for example. From 1900 to 1950, marriage rates were higher for black women than for white ones, and black men were just as likely to marry as were white men.[27]

While African-American households were more likely than white ones to contain nonfamily members, they generally contained two parents. In 1925, five out of six black children under the age of six were living with both parents, even if there were also boarders or other relatives in the household. Until the 1960s, 75 percent of black households with a child under the age of eighteen included both a husband and a wife. Death rather than divorce was the primary cause of the higher rate of marital dissolution among blacks prior to the 1950s.[28]

Even the growing differences among black and white families in the postwar era have often been sources of strength rather than failure, as black families adapted to changing economic and political circumstances. In the 1950s and 1960s, for example, researchers in many regions of the country demonstrated that alternative family forms in black communities were flexible, effective ways of pooling resources and building community while coping with long-term poverty and growing unemployment rates among men. The centrality of women in these extended-kinship networks helped compensate for the increasingly precarious employment situation of black men, whose relative marginalization was produced by white discrimination, not by black matriarchy. The emphasis on matrilateral ties in such families left plenty of room for men to play active roles as fathers, husbands, stepfathers, grandfathers, or uncles. Single-parent households were not cut off from extended networks of male and female kin during the 1960s.[29]

These historical strengths, clinical psychologists have recently begun to realize, should not be forgotten in dealing with black families today. Instead of berating them for failing to conform to an idealized white model, educators and therapists should build on the special traditions of African-American family adaptations and variations—role flexibility (including the fact that black men, in spite of "macho" images and language, are *more* likely to share housework than are their white counterparts); extended-kin networks, including effective fostering traditions; parallel institutions, such as black newspapers, churches, and professional organizations; bicultural experiences, languages, and values; racial solidarities; and a tradition of pooling economic resources.[30]

There is nothing in the rich history of African-American family and kinship, in other words, to mandate the outcomes that so many commentators blame either on black family traditions or on the lack of such traditions. Many of the family variations practiced by black Americans have produced healthy individuals with a strong group consciousness, allowing them to cope with widespread violence, discrimination, and poverty, and in many cases to rise above these.[31]

Furthermore, between 1890 and 1950, the *similarities* between white and black families were actually more striking than the differences. Although blacks had higher incidences of household extension, and, to a lesser extent, of female-headed families, the differences were not dramatic in the first half of the twentieth century. The general trends in marriage, fertility, and divorce moved in similar directions up to the 1950s and in some cases pointed toward convergence. It was only during the 1950s that black and white families began to diverge in qualitatively new ways, with the biggest differences appearing in the 1970s and 1980s. This divergence was not a legacy of slavery, migration, or the social welfare programs of the 1960s: It was a response to the paradoxes and discontinuities of the African-American experience in the postwar period.

The Postwar Experience of African-American Families

The changing economic and political configuration of postwar America created a paradoxical situation for African Americans. The Second World War opened better-paying blue-collar jobs to blacks, sparking fresh migration to urban centers and offering significant economic mobility to those who could find work in the booming industries of the cities, especially the ones unionized in the 1930s and 1940s. The mass mobilization of black Americans and their allies in the 1950s and 1960s also produced many inroads against traditional legal and political inequalities, while 1960s antipoverty programs provided new job opportunities for young African Americans. Dynamic leaders, such as Martin Luther King, Jr., and Malcolm X, inspired positive self-definitions and rich debates over strategy.

Yet as early as the mid-1950s, the displacement of blacks from southern agriculture began to outstrip the job openings in other areas of the economy, leading to steadily rising unemployment even in periods when employed blacks made relative wage gains. Even during the height of black social and legal progress, unemployment and economic polarization increased, and poverty remained severe. It was also during the postwar period that the modern ghetto emerged; not until 1950 did the typical African American live in a census tract with a black majority.[32]

The immediate effects of ghetto creation were not all inimical: A black business class emerged there, and working-class youth could see real possibilities for economic mobility. Within a relatively short period, however, political, economic, and social trends combined to slam shut the fifteen-year "window of opportunity" opened by the postwar boom, the civil rights movement, and the "war on poverty."

At the same time, the leadership of the black struggle was decimated by assassinations.

Contrary to the contentions of those who hold up the 1950s as their model or condemn civil rights and antipoverty legislation as useless, the biggest absolute gains for blacks were made in the economic booms of the 1940s and the 1960s, and the largest improvements in relative earnings occurred during the Great Society initiatives from the mid-1960s to the early 1970s. "For both sexes," write the authors of the most comprehensive recent study of African Americans, the 1940s and the 1960s "accounted for nearly all the relative gain of the 45 years. After 1970, blacks' relative economic position improved only slowly, and since 1980 it has deteriorated." Thus the decline in black teenage employment that provided a somber counterpoint to economic gains between 1950 and 1970 was concentrated in the period *before* the antipoverty programs of the 1960s; virtually all of it resulted from mechanization of southern agriculture. "In the north, where welfare benefits were higher and welfare participation grew much faster than in the south, black youth employment did *not* drop" until job competition and urban decline accelerated in the 1970s.[33]

The economic and political gains of the postwar period allowed many poorly educated black Americans to find blue-collar jobs in which they could work up to a level of security and seniority that permitted them to establish families, buy homes, and contemplate sending their children to school for longer periods. This, contrary to myth, is the traditional route to mobility for *all* social and ethnic groups in American history, especially migrants to the cities: *First* they achieved income security; *then* they invested in education. For the first time in American history, some blacks were offered the same route to success, and they took advantage of it, during the short time it was available, in percentages at least as high as those for any other group.[34]

Yet even during the period of their greatest opportunity, blacks faced more severe obstacles than did other low-income Americans and migrants to the cities. Continuing job discrimination created black unemployment rates twice those of whites; the late entry of blacks into unionized industries meant they had less seniority and were more vulnerable to the periodic layoffs that plagued such industries; and racist housing policies and lending practices made it difficult for blacks to buy homes in areas that would rise in value. None of the postwar gains changed the historic concentration of black Americans in the lowest rungs of every job, income, and educational category, which made them least likely to have reserves to help them through hard times.[35]

The hard times hit in the 1970s, as government cutbacks and the economic restructuring of America fell with special force on the blue-collar occupations and urban regions that had seemed only a few years earlier to offer the best opportunities for black self-improvement. Deindustrialization of northeastern and midwestern cities in the 1970s drastically accelerated the problem of rising unemployment that had plagued African-American communities even at the height of the postwar boom. Industries such as steel and auto, where blacks had made the biggest postwar gains, were especially affected. Between 1979 and 1984, half the black workers in durable-goods manufacturing in the Great Lakes region lost their jobs.[36]

The proportion of black men who found employment fell from 80 percent in 1930 to 56 percent in 1983, while the gap in employment rates between blacks and whites, rising steadily since 1955, increased especially sharply in the 1970s. Since 1973, even the gains that employed black men made during the 1960s have largely been reversed. The average real income of young black men fell by almost 50 percent between 1973 and 1986. The biggest losers were unskilled or uneducated black men who could once by dint of hard work and strenuous exertion make an adequate income to support a family: The "bottom fell out" of the market for poorly educated labor in the cities; by 1986, the average black high school dropout earned 61 percent less than he had in 1973.[37]

Since the 1970s, the demoralizing effects of growing poverty and unemployment have been magnified by "hyperghettoization." Ironically, some authors argue, the victories of the civil rights movement have combined with cutbacks in antipoverty programs and economic deterioration of industrial urban centers to exacerbate destruction of the old integrity of inner-city neighborhoods. People who had made gains in the 1940s and 1960s were finally able to move out to areas of more desirable housing, but no new jobs or social mobility programs opened up for those who were left. Simultaneously, white professionals, financial specialists, and well-paid workers in high-technology industries moved back into some urban conclaves, stimulating "gentrification" programs that further decreased the supply of affordable housing in the cities.[38]

Increasing isolation of low-income blacks from middle-class blacks has been a trend characterizing the period since 1970; however, this factor should not be misunderstood as the primary cause of deterioration in the ghetto. Most of the concentration of poverty in the inner cities is a result of job and income loss there, not the mobility of moderate-income blacks. The spatial mismatch between inner-city residents and the jobs available in urban areas has left growing numbers of workers permanently marginalized and discouraged, no longer even counted in the unemployment statistics. Detroit, for example, has lost half of its jobs to deindustrialization and a third of its population to "white flight"; today the inner city is in a crisis far worse than that which sparked the riot of 1967.[39]

In both the 1970s and 1980s, the effects of deindustrialization and urban decay were magnified by city governments that consciously put low-income housing, prisons, homeless shelters, methadone clinics, battered women's shelters, and drug treatment centers in the same already destitute neighborhoods, in order to avoid the "not in my back yard" protests of more organized and prosperous communities. The resultant concentration of poverty and social problems has led to an isolation of poor blacks unprecedented even in the most racist periods of American history.[40]

These circumstances simply foreclose the possibility of individual economic mobility for inner-city residents, aside from the occasional athlete, rap singer, or especially disciplined drug dealer. Inner-city homeowners face plummeting house values; nonhomeowning families can barely afford housing rentals, much less job training, child care, or savings; only 18 percent of the jobless have access to cars. As sociologist William Julius Wilson points out, neighborhoods that lack networks of employed acquaintances to pass on job tips and personal recommendations, offer mutual assistance, or provide a population and revenue base for schools, shops, churches, and recreational centers cannot support stable social ties, resist the influx of drugs, or offer positive economic and educational options to their inhabitants. Many residents scrape by only through welfare or crime; others turn to drug or alcohol abuse. Still more live in constant fear that they or their families will be victims of crime or will surrender to the chemicals that offer temporary transcendence of the filth, poverty, pain, and despair around them.[41]

Black Families and the "Underclass"

It is among these poorest groups of inner-city blacks that the most visible and wrenching changes in social and family life have taken place. As any observer might expect, chronic, persistent poverty does not breed stable interpersonal relations, high marriage rates, or middle-class family values. Single mothers, crack-addicted babies, and neglected children are found in growing proportions in the central cities. The level of violence there has clearly escalated, as recent homicide statistics attest. Between 1983 and 1987, there was a 600 percent increase in cocaine-related emergency-room visits in urban hospitals.[42]

But to blame the problems in such neighborhoods, as so many articles in the popular press have done, on a "socially alien" culture, dysfunctional families, or an underclass of "have-nots drifting further apart from the basic values of the haves" is very dubious. We know, for instance, that families whose members are police officers or who serve in the military have much higher rates of divorce, family violence, and substance abuse than do other families, but we seldom accuse them of constituting an "underclass" with a dysfunctional culture; more reasonably, we relate these problems to work stresses and other situational or structural issues.[43]

There is considerable debate among researchers about whether to use the term *underclass* in describing the admittedly special problems of the inner cities. Some find it a useful term for summarizing the new acceleration of poverty and social stress in certain neighborhoods and the resultant concentration of individuals and families with severe problems. Others argue that the term confuses the individual traits that many poor people acquire over the years with the cause of their poverty and that it lumps too many disparate people together. Among the persistently poor urban black population, after all, only one in eight persons lives in a household headed by a never-married black woman. Three-fifths, by contrast, have one or more of the characteristics usually associated with the "deserving poor": They are elderly, seriously disabled, or employed for a substantial portion of the year.[44]

At its best, the concept of the underclass remains imprecise: Estimates on its size range from 3 percent to 38 percent of the urban poor. At its worst, the notion perpetuates the myth that inner-city blacks are solely or primarily responsible for drug use and crime. In fact, however, a study published in the New England Journal of Medicine found that rates of substance abuse are slightly higher for white women than for nonwhite women, even though the latter are ten times as likely as white women to be reported for such abuse. Seventy to eighty percent of illicit drug consumption goes on *outside* the ghettos; the typical crack addict, according to a survey reported by the *Oakland Tribune,* is a middle-class white male in his forties. Similarly, while FBI reports show that the proportion of blacks arrested for aggravated assault in 1987 was three times greater than was the proportion of whites, the National Crime Survey, which interviews *victims,* found that the proportion of blacks and whites committing aggravated assault was virtually the same. The discrepancy, of course, lies in different arrest and reporting rates.[45]

Discussing the problems of poor African Americans in terms of values obscures many urgent issues confronting policymakers. For example, a recent study of three different ethnic neighborhoods in Brooklyn, New York, all relatively poor, found few differences in premarital sexual activity and responsibility between blacks and whites. A much higher proportion of white men married their partners on discovery of pregnancy, but most black fathers provided some degree of support for their children: Their lower marriage rates and total amount of maintenance were not a consequence of different family values, reports researcher Mercer Sullivan, "but rather of blocked access to decent jobs." Indeed, in one national study, poor African-American, officially absent fathers actually had *more* contact with their children and gave them more informal support than did white, middle-class absent fathers. Similarly, black women overwhelmingly report a preference for raising children in a two-parent family. I will discuss below some of the reasons that preference does not always translate into behavior; for now my point is simply that the description of the ghetto as an alien nation, with totally different family values from mainstream America, is a gross exaggeration.[46]

Among some individuals, it is true, concentrated poverty, long-term despair, and urban decay do breed special attitudes and norms, many of which cannot by any stretch of the imagination be called healthy or effective adaptations. The African American sociologist Elijah Anderson has described the growth of a subculture in the ghetto where some young men boast of their sexual conquests, sneer at conventional family life, and find a sense of manhood in impregnating women but escaping marriage. There seems to be a sense among some inner-city youth that life is cheap; many drug dealers have abandoned older inhibitions about ensnaring friends, lovers, and children into addiction; thugs prey on the old and weak of their own community; and the crack epidemic has in some instances deprived mothers of the capacity to care for their youngsters. Although the evidence is clear that the majority of inner-city residents do not sanction this behavior, the presence of a significant minority with these characteristics is profoundly shocking to most Americans, black or white.[47]

Yet even these extreme examples of antisocial behavior and values are not the cause but the result of long-term experience with defeat and brutalization. Black children start life with the same enthusiasm and social trust as any other children; in the inner cities, however, these are steadily eroded. Ronald Ferguson of Harvard has shown how black boys who scored in the ninetieth percentile on the Iowa Achievement Tests in third grade have dropped into the twenty-fourth percentile by the seventh grade. Low achievement and preda-tory behavior are learned through years of poverty and social neglect. They reflect a realistic, if grim, assessment of how little society values the lives of poor African Americans and a fierce attempt to find some sources of self-esteem and power. As Anderson points out, many of the young boys he studied were far more ambivalent about "the game" than they admitted to their peer group; they wanted to "do right" by the women they courted. Because their poor economic prospects made it so difficult to follow through on good intentions, however, they increasingly made a virtue out of necessity. The longer they stayed with the peer groups that were their only source of men-toring, the more committed they became to the idea that "putting one over" on a woman was a sign of strength, shrewdness, or power.[48]

It is difficult for people who have not experienced long-term poverty, racism, social contempt, police brutality, and political ne-glect to fathom the kind of deprivation that structures people's strug-gle for psychic survival and self-esteem in America's inner cities. Consider the description by one ghetto child of how he and his sister tortured a bird to death after their baby sister, who had the syndrome diagnosed as "failure to thrive," finally died:

> When our baby die we start to sit by the window. We just sit an' sit all wrapped up quiet in old shirts an' watch the pigeons. That pigeon she fly so fast, move so fast. She move nice. A real pretty flyer.
>
> She open her mouth and take in the wind. We just spread out crumbs, me and my brother. And we wait. Sit and wait. There under the window sill.
>
> She don't even see us til we slam down the window. And she break.

She look with one eye. She don't die right away. We dip her in, over and over, in the water pot we boils on the hot plate.

We wanna see how it be to die slow like our baby die.[49]

The consequences of behaviors and attitudes such as these are chilling, but so are the consequences of *not* rejecting mainstream values when people have no way of living up to them: self-contempt, depression, even insanity and suicide. In fact, embracing dominant values has sometimes had *negative* effects in the context of the pressures on African Americans. Historian Elizabeth Pleck argues that in nineteenth-century northern cities, adoption of mainstream values by blacks often promoted marital dissolution, for racial discrimination against black men made such values unrealistic guides to family life and caused strain in marriages. Today, similarly, the black men most likely to leave their families when faced with unemployment or income loss are those who subscribe most firmly to the idea of a self-reliant male breadwinner. Middle-class blacks who believe in a color-blind meritocracy experience tremendous stress when they encounter setbacks; some studies show that blacks who let themselves off the hook by admitting the obstacles posed by racism are better able to maintain work and educational commitment in the face of reverses than those who believe in the ethic of individual achievement.[50]

While the "new consensus" claims that weak family ties and values create black poverty, an equal number of examples can be adduced to show that black family ties are so *strong* that they often hamper individual economic mobility. Anthropologist Carol Stack describes the case of an older inner-city couple who inherited $1,500. Originally, they planned to make a down payment on a house. Unfortunately, some relatives needed money to attend a funeral; another would have faced eviction without help; still another needed a little bit to keep her phone. Within six weeks the money was gone—spent not on booze or drugs or fancy clothes but on family obligations, in what turns out to be a very typical dynamic underlying the "lack of deferred gratification" or "planning for the future" that some observers attribute to ghetto residents. African Americans who *do* attain upward mobility, often by resisting such demands, have higher rates of guilt and depression than stable or downwardly mobile blacks, in large part because of their sense that they have failed in their obligations to kin and community.[51]

Black Family "Pathology" Revisited

To the extent that family forms and values among some African Americans do differ from the white middle-class norm, whether by being "too weak" or "too strong," this still does not explain the prevalence of poverty in the black population. Undeniably, the rising proportion of black children being raised in desperately poor one-parent families is a serious threat to the economic status, educational possibilities, and psychological well-being of large sectors of the black community. But this consequence of sustained and concentrated urban poverty should not be confused with its "primary cause." Much growth in black female-headed family poverty is merely a "reshuffling" of economic distress, according to Harvard researcher Mary Jo Bane. Two out of every three poor blacks living in single-parent families were poor *before* their families split up. Additionally, the poverty of female-headed families is due more to job structure than to family structure. Black women have an unemployment rate two and a half times that of white women or men; 43 percent of black women below the poverty line are involuntary part-time workers.[52]

The rising proportion of single-mother families among blacks results from both the declining birth rate of married black women and a drop in marriage and remarriage rates. Both these phenomena should be connected more to the deteriorating economic and social position of lower-income black men, denied job prospects by hyper-segregation and deindustrialization, than to any element of black "culture." As economists William Darity and Samuel Myers argue, "the statistical driving force behind the increase in black female-headed families appears to be the decline in the supply of black males." University of Chicago researcher William Julius Wilson estimates that for every one hundred black women aged twenty to twenty-four in 1980, there were only forty-five employed black men of the same age. Northeastern University economist Andrew Sum calculates that nearly half the decline in marriage rates among high school dropouts since 1973 can be attributed to the drop in their earnings power. Recent income losses and decreases in job security have led even some higher-income men and women to "hedge their bets" by postponing or foregoing marriage, but these trends remain much more common among the poor.[53]

Injunctions to cultivate stronger family values ring hollow in the economic void surrounding America's poor and working-class blacks. Providing jobs would be much more useful. Researchers at the University of Chicago, for example, found that employed black men in the inner city were over two and a half times more likely to marry the mother of their child than were unemployed men; the higher a woman's earnings potential the more likely she was to marry.[54]

It is true that some of the increase in divorce and decline in marriage represents an element of choice as well. Women choose single motherhood partly because the general expansion of their options since the 1960s makes it more possible for them to forego marriage or leave an unhappy relationship, partly because black women have a strong tradition of economic independence and collective childrearing that makes them less dependent on men than are many white women, and partly because the black community has always valued children, in or out of wedlock, more than has mainstream white culture. There is good reason to believe that these are healthy, not pathological, qualities. But even if we should or could convince black men and women to have a child only when they can marry and to stay in unhappy marriages under all circumstances, it would not significantly reduce the incidence of poverty.

Economists David Ellwood and David Wise calculate that family type can explain "at most only two points" in the fourteen-point widening of the employment gap between young blacks and whites from 1969 to 1979. "Even if family structures and income for blacks were identical to those of whites, the overall employment rate for black teenagers living at home would rise only from 21 to 27 percent." (The white employment rate, by contrast, is 48 percent.) If black family structures had been the same in 1984 as in 1973, the proportion of black children living in poverty would have fallen from 41 percent to 38 percent instead of rising to 43 percent—hardly enough of a difference to win a war on poverty.[55]

Black men face such frequent bouts of unemployment that the *long-term* poverty rates of black children who live continuously with both parents over a decade are as high as those of white children who spend the decade in a mother-only family. As Barbara Ehrenreich points out, the median incomes of black men are so far behind the national median that the ideal family form for most African Americans would be one based on polyandry, not monogamy: It takes *three* black men, making the median income for blacks, "to clear the median U.S. family income, which is $26,433. If our hypothetical Black family is to enter the middle-class mainstream, which means home ownership, it will need at least $36,595 or four Black men."[56]

The majority of the difference in black and white unemployment and poverty rates comes from higher rates for African Americans within the *same* family types. Even though female-headed families are more likely than two-parent ones to be among the poorest of the poor, maintaining a two-parent household is no guarantee that blacks will escape from this group. The 69 percent increase in the number of blacks living at a level below *half* the poverty line since 1978 has occurred among both black married-couple and female-headed families.[57]

In fact, the single event most often associated with a black child's transition out of poverty is an increase in the work hours of individuals in the household *other* than a mother or father. This should remind us that "traditional" nuclear families based on a male breadwinner are often not the most adaptive form for a people facing pervasive discrimination and unemployment.[58]

Is the Future Black?

Black Americans are at the cutting edge of a number of changes in our society—some negative, some positive. Far from being the "last of the migrants," they are the first of the postindustrial discards. They have borne the brunt of the restructuring of the American economy and the two-decades–long war against working people's living standards and employment security. Even though African Americans have taken the highest proportion of casualties, they are merely the frontline troops. All low-income and working-class Americans, of every ethnic group, are involved in this battle; few are likely to escape unscathed, whatever their family traditions or values.

Thus, for example, despite the idea that Asians form a "model minority" with strong family values, a similar polarization is occurring within the Asian community. There is a growing class of inner-city Chinese, Vietnamese, and Laotians, whose desperation has spawned gangs, violence, and alienation from kin. Likewise, a tradition of valuing male-headed families has not prevented Hispanic groups from experiencing the fastest-growing poverty rates in recent American history: Most of the growth in Hispanic poverty is due to the worsening position of married-couple families, whose poverty rate grew by more than 50 percent between 1978 and 1987. Native Americans often stay on reservations because of their commitment to cultural traditions and extended-family ties, yet almost 50 percent of reservation Indians live below the poverty line, and their economic deprivation produces some of the same demoralization seen among migrants to the city. In the next chapter, I will show that the black experience, far from being "alien," is an exaggerated, intensified, and particularly painful expression of economic and cultural contradictions that have now begun to face many other Americans as well, including whites.[59]

The fact that blacks have been hit hardest by the reconstitution of American economics and politics in the past two decades accounts for their leadership in some negative indicators—persistent poverty, job displacement, infant mortality, and reverses in life expectancy. But many African Americans have also managed to pull positive lessons out of their hardships. African-American working women, for example, have made the largest income gains relative to men of any ethnic group, producing new options for women both inside and outside of marriage. Many black women are models of strength, courage, and independence. It is black high school seniors, similarly, not whites, who have spearheaded the steady decline in drug use in the schools during the past five years. And black husbands have gone much further than their white counterparts in increasing their share of housework and child-care duties.[60] These examples suggest that there are sources of solidarity and strength even in the experience of extreme adversity—and growing numbers of white working-class Americans may have to seek those sources in the next decade.

11

•••

The Crisis Reconsidered

THE period from the late 1970s until the early 1990s was one of sharp economic setbacks in a series of regions and industries, followed by economic and cultural "recoveries" that excluded many Americans and left even the "winners" feeling anxious and dissatisfied. Per capita income rose; new jobs were created; women and minorities moved into new careers; political rivals abroad turned to America for leadership; the gross national product grew; new technologies spawned consumer booms in personal computers, videocassette recorders, and microwave ovens; and Americans near retirement age were better off financially than ever before. Yet more people fell deeper into poverty; children's life prospects worsened by several measurements; and even those who managed to maintain or improve their living standards felt more pressed for time and more precarious in their achievements than they remembered feeling in the past. While Chinese students built replicas of the Statue of Liberty, Americans thinking about their own society were more likely to raise images of Wall Street speculators, declining educational achievement, negative political campaigns, widespread personal immorality, senseless violence, and cultural fragmentation.

The obvious question was, "If America is so rich, why aren't we happy?" And the answer that made sense to many was, "because of the collapse of the family." This explanation also seemed to answer two related questions: "If America is so rich, why are there more poor people than there were in the 1960s? Why do our young people seem so desperate and so angry?" The "crisis of the family" became the key to explaining the paradox of poverty amid plenty, alienation in the midst of abundance.

According to many commentators, "the root cause" of the problems Americans face as the twentieth century draws to a close is an "epidemic of family breakdown." Samuel Sava, head of the National Association of Elementary School Principals, blames the decline of American education on a "parenting deficit." "It's not better teachers, texts, or curricula that our children need most...we will never see lasting school reform until we see parent reform." Divorce and unwed motherhood are said to be the major causes of poverty and inequality in contemporary America. In his State of the Union address for 1992, President Bush claimed that the crisis of the cities results from "the dissolution of the family." Kate O'Beirne of the Heritage Foundation asserts that people of all political persuasions are coming to understand that America's troubles stem from the collapse of "family stability and the work ethic."[1]

"Why launch new school reforms when...the real key to educational performance is whether a child comes from a two-parent family? Why experiment with new anti-poverty programs when...the most important indicator of poverty is whether there are two parents at home?" Instead, strengthened family ties and values are put forward as the primary solution to America's economic difficulties and cultural malaise. "It sounds too simple to be true, but the statistics seem to bear it out: Marriage is the ticket out of poverty." And the key to a lasting marriage is family commitment, the only sure answer to the increasing individualism and fragmentation of American society.[2]

It's a powerful argument, because so many of our most tragic family problems revolve around children, whom we might expect to be better protected by caring parents. One in five American children— almost one in two black American children—lives in poverty; the proportions are even higher among children under the age of six, who comprise the fastest-growing poverty group in America. Fewer than half of all high school seniors read at levels considered adequate to follow even moderately complex directions. After decreases in crime rates between 1980 and 1985, crime is on the rise again, with younger persons and more savage violence involved. More than two million cases of child abuse are reported to child-protection agencies each year; while some of these reports are false or unprovable, there is evidence that actual cases of abuse far exceed the reports. Seven million children live with an alcoholic parent; almost 1.2 million children run away from home each year; and suicide is the leading cause of death among American teenagers. The number of youths living in abject poverty—below half the poverty line—has increased, but even youths from more stable economic backgrounds exhibit many of the same symptoms seen among the very poor: alienation, cynicism, depression, hopelessness, lack of connection to others.[3]

The question, however, is how many of these problems are caused primarily by changes in family forms and values, or could be solved by attempts to "revive the traditional family." The answer is surprisingly few. Historically, Americans have tended to discover a crisis in family structure and standards whenever they are in the midst of major changes in socioeconomic structure and standards. Today's family crisis follows a major economic and political restructuring going on since the late 1960s: the eclipse of traditional employment centers, destruction of formerly high-paid union jobs, expansion of the female and minority work force, and the mounting dilemmas of welfare capitalism. America has seen a major shift in the organization of work and its rewards: Family values, forms, and strategies that once coordinated personal life with older relations of production and distribution are now out of sync with economic and political trends. In past crises, as in this one, such imbalances caused pain and disruption in families, and families or individuals reacted to the changes in ways that sometimes made things worse, but neither then nor now could the larger crisis have been averted if only families had "tried harder."

Earlier family crises, unlike today's, took place in periods when the expansion of productivity and growth of democratic political institutions provided a basis for long-term optimism about social trends, in spite of short-term dislocations. If we once had long-range optimism in the midst of short-range hardship, today we have long-term despair in the midst of short-term benefits. This makes it tempting to focus on something small enough to seem manageable: If we cannot strengthen America's political and economic infrastructure, maybe we can at least shore up our families. But focusing attention on family arrangements diverts us from the research, programs, and hard choices necessary to bring families back into balance with economic and political realities. Under current circumstances, strengthening traditional family structures and values is going to be an uphill struggle; and to the extent that such strengthening does not change the economic and social context of modern family life, it is unlikely to solve the problems that continually lead people to engage in personal behavior that goes *against* many of their family values.

Blaming the Family: A Gross Oversimplification

Certainly, several of the problems Americans face in the 1990s exhibit themselves in family dysfunction; many families engage in behaviors that trigger or exacerbate economic and social distress for their individual members. However, blaming our ills on family breakdown oversimplifies the issue and ultimately leads to a scapegoating mentality that is unfair and unhelpful.

Consider the issue of single-parent families and poverty. It is true that poverty is disproportionately concentrated in single-parent families, especially female-headed ones, but the bulk of poverty in America is not caused by family type. Approximately 48 percent of all poor families are female-headed, but female-headship does not account for 48 percent of poverty, as superficial interpretations often claim. Conversely, while 36 percent of female-headed families are poor, female-headed families are not synonymous with poor families. Much growth in poor female-headed families "represents a reshuffling of poor people into different household types rather than a change in poverty caused by household changes."[4]

Economists Christine Ross, Sheldon Danziger, and Eugene Smolensky studied poverty rates from the 1940s to the 1980s, then applied the 1980 poverty rates for each group studied to the 1940 demographic composition of the population. Their figures showed that if *no* changes had occurred in the age, race, and gender of household heads since 1940, the poverty rate in 1980 would have been 23 percent lower than it actually was.[5]

But this still leaves 77 percent of poverty that is not associated with familial transformations. It also overstates the effect of change in family arrangements in two ways. First, it includes race and age factors that are not caused by family dissolution. Second, it assumes that people who moved into female-headed families in the 1970s were basically the same as those who were married. In fact, however, marital dissolution and illegitimacy occur disproportionately among sectors of the population who are more vulnerable to poverty *anyway*; I will discuss below how the position of these groups has deteriorated in the past two decades.

A 1991 Census Bureau study found that the average family who falls into poverty after the father leaves was *already* in economic distress before his departure, often because the father had recently lost his job. The University of Michigan Panel Study of Income Dynamics, which has followed a representative sample of 5,000 families since 1968, found that only one-seventh of childhood transitions into long-term poverty were associated with family dissolution, while more than half were linked to changes in labor market participation or remuneration.[6]

Furthermore, ironically, the discovery of single-parent poverty in the 1980s actually coincided with a growth in two-parent poverty. A majority of the increase in family poverty since 1979 has occurred in families with both spouses present, with only 38 percent concentrated in single-parent families; the percentage of the poor living in female-headed families has declined since 1978. Today, approximately 40 percent of America's poor children live in two-parent homes, and 52 percent of total years of childhood poverty occur while the children are in two-parent rather than one-parent homes. If previous recessions are any guide, the proportion of two-parent families in poverty is likely to rise when we get the final figures for the recession that began in 1991.[7]

Certainly, single-parent families are more likely to be poor than are two-parent families and much more likely to remain poor during periods of economic recovery, but a closer analysis suggests that this fact itself needs explaining. It is not an inevitable fact of nature. America, for example, has not only the highest total child poverty rate among eight industrialized Western democracies recently studied, but also the highest poverty rate among children in single-parent families, with the sole exception of Australia. A cross-national comparison of poverty rates within similar household types reveals that "different family structures play at best a small part in the higher absolute poverty of American children."[8]

The superior position of female-headed families in modern Europe is primarily a result of more generous state policies toward families with children, but even in societies where the state does not step in, there is no necessary reason that female-headed families be poor. In kinship-based foraging societies of the past, for instance, women and children were entitled to resources simply by being members of the group. They were not forced to rely for their living on maintaining a particular relationship with a man.[9]

Even in modern America, the divergence between single-parent and two-parent families has not always been as wide as it became during the 1970s and 1980s. In the 1940s and 1950s, the poverty gap between single-parent and two-parent families was much smaller, and prior to 1969, the increase in the number of female-headed families was accompanied by a *decline* in the proportion of such families that lived in poverty. It thus makes more sense to blame family-related poverty on larger economic and political factors that have widened the gap between one- and two-parent families than to blame it on divorce or illegitimacy per se. One such factor is the inflation that now makes it difficult to support a family even on the wages of a man. Modern two-parent families have avoided poverty only to the extent that they, too, have broken with traditional family arrangements. Without the work of wives, the entire bottom 60 percent of the U.S. population would have had real income losses between 1979 and 1986, and 80 percent of married-couple families with children would have suffered such declines. More than one-third of all two-parent families today would be poor if both parents did not work.[10]

Another factor is discriminatory wages paid to women. Female workers in America earn about 70 percent of what male workers earn. While this is a gain over the 60 percent rate in the 1960s and 1970s, America's wage gap remains one of the largest in the advanced capitalist world. The average woman worker's earnings peak at $22,000 per year somewhere between the ages of forty and forty-four. Almost half of women's improvement relative to men, moreover, has been due to falling real wages for men.[11]

Still another piece of the puzzle can be found in the distribution of social welfare (transfer) payments, which have, contrary to popular impression, increasingly penalized single-parent families. "Transfers took a greater percentage of all two-parent families out of poverty in 1984 than in 1967," report researchers Sheldon Danziger and Peter Gottschalk, "but a smaller percentage of female-headed families." Since 1984, transfer payments have had smaller antipoverty effects for *both* kinds of families. Indeed, several studies estimate that at least one-third, and up to half, of the increase in poverty among all families with children during the 1980s was caused by the declining antipoverty impact of government programs. The increase in the poverty rate for persons in single-parent families since 1979 is entirely attributable to changes in taxes and government benefits rather than to demographics.[12]

Thus the concentration of poverty in single-parent families during the past two decades was as much a result of gender discrimination, inflation, and government policy as of divorce or illegitimacy, while the increase in single parenthood itself was more often a *result* of economic slide than its cause. Income insecurity, job disruption, and economic reverses are three of the biggest predictors for family stress and disruption. And during the past two decades, income insecurity, job disruption, and economic reverses were precisely what most affected ever-increasing numbers of young people, those in the time of life when many marital and childbearing decisions are made.

The Deteriorating Position of Young Families

Single-parent families are most likely to be found in the age and educational groups that, independently of family status, have suffered the most from recent economic changes. According to Northeastern University economist Andrew Sum, "the relative income position of the nation's youngest families has deteriorated...sharply and continuously" since 1967. Regardless of their structure, families with adults in their twenties were much more likely to be poor in the 1980s than in the two previous decades. In 1963, 60 percent of men aged twenty to twenty-four earned enough to keep a family of three out of poverty; by 1984, only 42 percent could do so.[13]

An insight into the economic stress experienced by young families can be gained by noting that between 1929 and 1932, during the Great Depression, per capita income fell by 27 percent; between 1973 and 1986, the median income of families headed by a person under age thirty fell by almost exactly the same amount. The drop took longer than in the Depression, and it was masked by a general rise in per capita income during the period, but that by no means negates the magnitude of the losses suffered by young Americans. In fact, it may simply have made the decline harder to understand, and therefore more demoralizing.[14]

Within the younger population, the lion's share of this loss was borne by those least able to afford it: those with limited educational attainment and prospects. Since 1967, the increased demand for college graduates has been largely at the expense of high school graduates and dropouts. Real wages for college-educated workers have risen, albeit unevenly, but only 25 percent of the work force have college degrees. Between 1979 and 1987, the real wages of high school graduates declined by 18 percent; today, the real wages of a young

male high school graduate are lower than those earned by a comparable worker in 1963. Accordingly, the poverty rate for young
married-couple families with children doubled between 1973 and
1988.[15]

Single parenthood and family dissolution, then, are not the primary cause of the deterioration in living standards among young
families or the rise in poverty among children. In many cases, they
are a result of that deterioration. The rise in divorce and unwed
motherhood is a complex phenomenon, part of which is certainly at
women's initiative and much of which occurs at all income levels.
But we should not underestimate the connection of changes in marriage and out-of-wedlock childbearing to setbacks in male economic
achievement. Regardless of race or educational attainment, young
men aged twenty to twenty-four with earnings above the poverty
threshold for a family of three are three to four times more likely to
marry than men of the same age with below-poverty earnings. Almost half the decline in marriage rates for young male high school
dropouts, and virtually the entire decline for young black high
school dropouts, is tied directly to their earnings losses.[16]

The main way out of poverty, furthermore, for women as well as
for men, remains work, not marriage. In Washington state, for example, a detailed longitudinal study of 2,000 households receiving public assistance found that only 11 percent of the women who left public assistance did so because they got married, while 54 percent left
because of improvements in the labor market. Similarly, although developing and enforcing adequate child-support payments would certainly enhance the economic status of many women and children, it
would not lift out of poverty the many children whose noncustodial
parents are themselves poor.[17]

Modern Families and the Collapse of the "American Dream"

The family arrangements we sometimes mistakenly think of as traditional became standard for a majority of Americans, and a realistic
goal for others, only in the postwar era. The gender roles and intergenerational relations that emerged in this period were shaped by the
unusual economic and political alignments described in chapter 2.
Poverty in the 1950s was higher than it is today and did not drop
sharply until the antipoverty initiatives of the 1960s, but unlike the

1970s and 1980s, the poverty rates were headed down rather than up, so that perseverance rather than innovation seemed the route to success. Private life was far from idyllic for either poor or affluent families, but a sense of optimism and expanding choice was fostered by the sustained growth in real income and by the effectiveness of government programs supporting upward economic and residential mobility.

Life might not be perfect right now, people could reason, but it would get better; and improvement would take place within the culturally approved family form. Between 1949 and 1973, the average man passing from age twenty-five to thirty-five saw his real wages rise by about 110 percent. Job pressures and rewards slowed down after age forty, but men could still expect to see their earnings rise by 30 percent between the ages of forty and fifty, while the homes that a majority of such men had bought in their early years of marriage continued to rise in value.[18]

This impressive rise in real income during the 1950s and 1960s, fed by America's privileged international economic position, allowed the United States to look with relative equanimity on a rather high degree of economic inequality. In 1963, the bottom 90 percent of families had only 36 percent of total wealth, while the bottom 60 percent had less than 10 percent. Inequality at the bottom was not much less than that of 1983, when the bottom 90 percent of families had just 32.1 percent of total wealth, but so long as the total pie—of both income and wealth—was growing larger and larger, people's share of wealth was not their urgent concern. And during the 1950s and 1960s, economic growth did not increase inequality, even if it did little to wipe it out. America thus saw no sharp struggles over the redistribution of wealth, even during the antipoverty programs of the 1960s. People assumed that each generation would live better than had its parents, and even if the rich got larger portions, economic growth and government policies eventually trickled down to everyone.[19]

Since 1973, however, quite a different economic and political climate has prevailed. By 1988, "the average hourly earnings of private, nonsupervisory workers were lower than in any other year since 1966, after adjusting for inflation." There has been a growing mismatch between occupation and schooling for large sectors of the young adult population. Half the new jobs created in the 1980s paid a wage lower than the poverty figure for a family of four. Today, only 18 percent of the nonagricultural labor force is unionized, half the percentage of the 1950s. The fastest-growing sector of the economy has been service work, which is only 5 percent unionized (down from 15 percent in 1970); the fastest-growing part of this sector (indeed of the whole economy) is part-time work.[20]

The number of involuntary part-time workers grew by 121 percent between 1970 and 1990, according to the Bureau of Labor Statistics. The hourly wages of such workers are just 60 percent of those of full-time workers. Only 22 percent of part-timers are covered by employer-sponsored health insurance, compared to 78 percent of full-time workers. Between July 1990 and July 1991, one in five Americans experienced a cut in take-home pay, a reduction in overtime, or an increase in their medical insurance premiums.[21]

This decline in job prospects, real wages, and benefits is not just a temporary phenomenon that was caused by an oversupply of baby-boom workers or will be solved automatically by renewed economic growth. The smaller, post–baby-boom generation has now entered the job market, but rather than finding themselves in a sellers' market, they have found that their real incomes are even lower than those of their predecessors. "Employment projections now suggest that by the year 2000 American workers may need more education to qualify for jobs that will pay less." Although unemployment rates fell during the second half of the 1980s and the number of millionaires mushroomed, economic growth was based largely on financial speculation at the top and multiplication of low-wage jobs at the bottom. The "recoveries" of the 1980s did little to raise living standards all along the line. Instead, rising averages obscured polarizing incomes. In 1987, after five years of recovery from the 1982 recession, inequality was greater than at the height of that recession and much greater than it was in 1973. The poverty rate was higher than it had been a decade earlier, and the poorest 20 percent of the population were living on incomes that were lower than they were in 1979.[22]

One consequence of all this is that it became more difficult for the current generation to achieve the house in the suburbs that was an integral part of the postwar American dream. The proportion of a young family's income required to pay the principal and interest on a median-priced home increased from approximately 16 percent in the 1950s and 1960s to 28 percent in 1983. When this statistic is put in terms of the traditional male breadwinner, the change becomes even more stark. In the 1950s and 1960s, it took 15 percent to 18 percent of the average thirty-year-old man's income to pay the principal and interest on a median-priced home. By 1973, it took 20 percent of his income, and by 1983, it took more than 40 percent. A college educa-tion lowers this percentage, but college tuition now requires 40 per-cent of family income, up from 29 percent in 1970.[23]

Wage stagnation has changed the life course of men immensely. Where young men in the previous period had seen their earnings double as they passed from twenty-five to thirty-five, men who were twenty-five in 1973 saw their income grow by only 16 percent in the next ten years, while older men passing from age forty to fifty saw their real earnings decline by 14 percent. Researchers at Dartmouth College and Hofstra University project that only 35 percent of the men who will be twenty-five to thirty-four in the year 2000 have a chance of attaining a better job than their fathers had.[24]

Women's lives have also changed, though in more complicated ways. The average real wages of women, unlike those of men, rose modestly over the past two decades. Even though the bottom 75 per-cent of male workers saw their real wages fall between 1979 and 1985, only the bottom 25 percent of female workers were in the same boat. Wives' contribution to household income seems to have given them more say in family affairs; their growth in real wages has also made it easier for women to leave an unsatisfactory relationship, though not without economic hardship. But women's relative eco-nomic improvement is neither a feminist victory nor an attack on men. Women have by no means reached parity with men at work, and they are *not* replacing men on the job. Almost 50 percent of women work in occupations that are more than 80 percent female; 71 percent of men still work in jobs that are more than 80 percent male. Most decreases in sex segregation have been caused by men entering traditionally female jobs (as telephone operators and flight attendants, for example) rather than vice versa. Women remain much more likely than men to be forced into involuntary part-time labor: Moonlighting, or holding multiple jobs, increased by 500 per-cent for women between 1970 and 1989, as compared to a 20 per-cent increase for men.[25]

Philosopher Alan Wolfe points out that the "moral life cycle" of most families in postwar America was based on the assumption of a common upward trajectory, tightly connected to family status. Youths who deferred to adults would progress through the system to a higher status in middle age, gaining a single-family home that would provide them with security in their old age; community soli-darity was achieved through the fact that most of one's neighbors were experiencing the same rites of passage, so that young families could share child care and school activities while older couples could expect to be self-sufficient; gender roles were based less on any well thought out principles than on the simple fact that both husband and wife made gains from marriage they could not make outside it. But this mode of organizing family, community, and gender was based on wage, work, and housing conditions that ceased to prevail in the 1970s.[26] And it turns out that the values associated with these roles could not be sustained when the economic incentives behind them ceased to operate.

Economic Polarization, Personal Readjustment, and the Unraveling of the Social Safety Net

The immediate effects of the past two decades' decline in real incomes were less catastrophic statistically than they were personally. Throughout the 1980s, many economic indicators remained good. Despite the decline in men's real wages, for example, the real income of most families remained fairly stable, and per capita income within families actually grew by 11 percent. The reason economic decline did not always show up in economic averages was that young Americans preserved many trappings of the postwar *economic* dream by sacrificing many aspects of the postwar *family* dream. Increasingly, young people postponed marriage and decreased their fertility. By the mid-1980s, more than two-thirds of all young wives were working, compared to less than half as late as 1973. By 1989, 79.3 percent of all homebuyers came from two-income households.[27]

As birth rates fell and women's labor participation soared, per capita income rose even though per-worker income stagnated or declined. In the poorest two-fifths of American families, the gain in women's income was less than the decline in men's earnings, so that family income fell. For families in the middle two-fifths, women's increases in earnings were enough to slightly outweigh the decline in real wages for men, so that these families made modest economic improvement, at the cost of greater hours spent at work. But in the wealthiest 20 percent of families, both male and female earnings increased significantly; these households accounted for 80 percent of the increase in family income between 1979 and 1987. Throughout the population, moreover, two-earner families with zero to two children pulled ahead of both single-parent families and two-parent families with larger numbers of children. Since small, two-earner families had become the majority type, the American economic dream seemed alive and well to many; it was the American family dream that seemed to be in trouble.[28]

The family adjustments required to sustain the American economic dream put many Americans in a personal bind and exposed the limits of postwar social solidarities. Families who chose to postpone childbearing or hold down family size were ambivalent about their decision; they did not necessarily feel that they were acting out some "New Freedom" or delivering themselves from old constraints. Two-earner couples with children were glad to be able to buy a bigger house and some of the new consumer items designed for the convenience of busy families; yet maintaining their living standards produced the greatest time crunch in precisely the period of their lives when they could have used extra time away from work. Family, school, and community relations were harder to maintain, as more family members worked longer hours to keep living standards rising at a more modest pace than two decades earlier.

Resentments grew between members of different occupational and educational cohorts as well as between alternative kinds of families. During the 1970s, many young college graduates slid down the job ladder, but they managed to maintain themselves on a relatively high rung by bumping less educated workers "into still lower jobs or out of the labor force altogether."[29]

Two-earner families yearned to simplify their lives yet felt they were caught on a treadmill from which neither parent could afford to step off; they criticized themselves for being too attached to their living standards, yet they also blamed poverty and declining productivity on people who didn't have the same family work ethic as themselves. One-earner families or two-earner families with more children resented their relative impoverishment compared to those who had seemingly abandoned older family values: "It is difficult enough to keep up with the Joneses under normal circumstances but when both of them are working it becomes virtually impossible."[30]

Two-parent families were horrified by the rise of single motherhood among the poorest of the poor, but the stress of "balancing" paid work, housework, child care, and the rising cost of living created new risks of dissolution in their own conjugal relations. Researchers estimate that the pressures of maintaining a two-earner family added roughly three weeks of full-time work to the paid and unpaid labor of each parent in a two-income family with two children. This increase caused both parents to feel burdened. Men felt that they had made a lot of accommodations to new gender roles, and so they had in comparison to their previous behavior. At the same time, the failure of men's increase in household labor to keep pace with women's increase in paid labor caused women to feel indignant when men congratulated themselves on the new burdens they had shouldered: One study found that the presence of men in a household, at least as late as 1981, created about eight hours of additional work for women per week—almost three weeks of unpaid work per year itself; a more recent study found that men had increased their share of housework, but even so, women with children still had less free time when they were married than when they were not. A female "rational egoist" might have been forgiven for wondering whether marriage was more trouble than it was worth; so, however, might a male, especially in light of the rise in living standards available to a divorced noncustodial father willing to use the law, or lack of it, to his own advantage.[31]

Debates over personal costs and benefits became moot for many Americans in the late 1970s and the 1980s. It was only the upper half of the population that could afford to consider the "downscaling" and "reorientation of priorities" that provided so many movie and magazine themes in the late 1980s; many families could not afford to balance "extra" income against "extra" time. As of 1987, more than 40 percent of all working wives were married to men earning less than $20,000 a year. And the majority of American families, as we have seen, could not have bought a house or sent their children to college without curtailing fertility and sending wives to work.[32]

Changes in economic behaviors during the 1970s and 1980s were complemented by important shifts in community relations and political functioning. Between 1981 and 1991, politicians shifted the tax burden from income to more regressive payroll taxes, cut back on politically vulnerable services, and postponed seemingly less pressing long-term investments in productive capacity or renewal of social capital such as housing and public transportation.

As unemployment rose in the 1970s and 1980s, the proportion of jobless Americans covered by unemployment insurance declined. When unemployment insurance was enacted in 1935, almost all the jobless qualified. By 1990, only four in ten of those officially classified as unemployed—people actively seeking work—received benefits. The number of Americans without either private or public health-insurance coverage rose from 30.9 million in 1980 to 37.1

million in 1987. Between 1970 and 1991, the purchasing power of the typical AFDC benefit decreased by 42 percent, primarily as a result of state and federal funding cuts.[33]

While other countries faced similar economic reverses, they cushioned the impact with social services and support for jobs and education programs. Among other industrial nations, the United States has the fewest tax and transfer policies to create income security. In addition, public and private spending on preschool, primary, and secondary education in America is lower than that in most of the industrialized world.[34]

The combination of falling incomes, deteriorating social capital, and cutbacks in public support programs has created a housing crisis that can no longer be obscured by the ability of two-earner middle-income buyers to maintain housing demand. In 1973, 23.4 percent of people under age twenty-five owned a home; by 1988, this had fallen to 15.5 percent. But affordable rentals were no more easy to come by. By 1987, more than a third of all American households were "shelter poor"—unable to buy enough food, clothes, and other necessities after paying for their housing. As of 1991, somewhere between 600,000 and 3 million people were homeless. Yet federal support for low-income housing dropped from $32.2 billion in 1978 to $9.8 billion in 1988.[35]

The effects of these changes on families have been dramatic. Today, one in eight American children is hungry. Twenty-six percent of pregnant women have no insurance coverage in the early months of their pregnancy; 15 percent have not managed to obtain it by the time of delivery. Between eight and eleven million children in America are completely uninsured, and large numbers go without needed medical and dental care. Economic loss creates other risks for families as well. One study in Wisconsin found that cases of child abuse increased by an average of 123 percent in counties where the unemployment rate had risen by 3.1 percent or more; counties in which unemployment declined had reduced reports of abuse. Outside the family, the United States has seen a sharp increase in child labor law violations over the past ten years; they more than doubled between 1983 and 1989.[36]

As economic and social safety nets have unraveled, not only have more people fallen into the ranks of the poor, but they have fallen further down. In 1989, twelve million Americans—almost 40 percent of the poor—had incomes less than *half* the amount designated as poverty-level by the federal government. For a family of four, this means trying to make do on $6,300 or less per year; for a family of three, it means receiving less than $5,000 a year. The number of these "hyperpoor" Americans has increased by nearly 45 percent since 1979. Although 60 percent of hyperpoor families are female-headed, 40 percent are not, and they defy most stereotypes in other ways—61 percent of them are white, and 62 percent of them live outside the central cities.[37]

In the cities, however, such poverty is made especially over-whelming, both by decay of the urban infrastructure and by the "de-institutionalization" of the mentally ill during the past three decades. On top of these stresses has come the influx of crack cocaine, which greatly escalates the deterioration of the physical community, multi-plies the dangers facing youth, and boosts the violent crime rate. The fundamental connection between the growing impoverishment of large sectors of America and these mounting problems is clear. As former Surgeon General C. Everett Koop has remarked: "When I look back on my years in office, the things I banged my head against were all poverty."[38]

The Values Issue in Modern Families: Erosion of the American Conscience

Not all the problems in American family life are caused by economic deprivation. Levels of callousness, anger, and selfishness in America are higher than can be explained by poverty alone; self-centeredness, lack of empathy, and violence are not a necessary concomitant of want, as evidenced in the instances of solidarity and cooperation during the Great Depression and in poor areas that do support a vi-able community life. Liberals are unconvincing when they blame crime and violence solely on unemployment: Being poor does not force a man to rape and stab a woman after robbing her. Conserva-tives are equally unconvincing, though, when they suggest that the problem lies in the failure of parents to inculcate "middle-class val-ues" or in the corruption of such values by "street culture," drugs, rap music, or whatever their current bogeyman.

Much hysteria about the "underclass" and the spread of "alien" values is what psychologists call projection. Instead of facing dis-turbing tendencies in ourselves, we attribute them to something or someone external—drug dealers, unwed mothers, inner-city teens, or satanist cults. But blaming the "underclass" for drugs, violence, sexual exploitation, materialism, or self-indulgence lets the "over-class" off the hook. It also ignores the amoral, privatistic retreat from social engagement that has been a hallmark of middle-class response to recent social dilemmas.

The values of Americans, for good or for ill, cut across race and class. Most poor and unemployed people desire to "make it" in middle-class society in much the same way that better-off Americans do.[39] The erosion of civic duty, declining appeal of deferred gratification, and growth of cynicism in America are not something unique to the poor, to minorities, or to people who reject "tradition." They are built in to the mainstream culture's response to recent socioeconomic trends. Our youngsters don't have to look to any so-called underclass in order to learn that deferred gratification is for suckers. That lesson is driven home by Wall Street speculators, HUD bandits, corporate raiders, and S&L criminals. Any preteen knows that an American has a better chance of winning a fortune by committing a crime or some truly sleazy act, then selling the media rights to the story, than by working hard at a menial job.

The exact analogs of the Crips and Bloods, with their Gucci T-shirts and Nike Air shoes, are the "Masters of the Universe" described by Tom Wolfe in his *Bonfire of the Vanities*. But cultural critic Mike Davis also directs our attention to disturbing parallels between the territorial clannishness of youth gangs and that of middle-class homeowners' associations. The homeowners do not normally initiate violence, of course, remaining defensively behind their "armed response" security signs, yet they fight their own bitter turf battles and exhibit the same kind of calculative self-interest in their "not in my back yard" movements. What both groups have in common is their seeming inability to recognize the humanity of those who don't belong to their own "gang" or "lifestyle enclave." Lacking this larger sense of community and connection, "kids of all classes and colours are grasping at 'undeferred gratification'—even if they pave the way to assured self-destruction."[40]

The pressures against commitment exerted by traditional American individualism and consumerism were greatly magnified in the 1970s and 1980s by the ways in which socioeconomic and political changes exacerbated inequality and removed most of the rewards that used to be associated, however imperfectly, with hard work, thrift, and planning. Although most Americans worked harder and harder during the 1980s only to stay in one place or even fall behind, some Americans did very well indeed. Between 1979 and 1986, 82 percent of all income growth went to the top one-fifth of the population. Measured in constant dollars, the top 5 percent of households increased their after-tax income by 60 percent between 1977 and 1988, and the top 1 percent increased their income by 122 percent. The failure of tax rates to keep up with this growth cost the treasury $75 billion in revenue.[41]

In both 1986 and 1987, by contrast, the poorest two-fifths of American families, black *and* white, received a smaller share of national family income—just over 15 percent—than had been recorded since 1947, when the Census Bureau first began collecting this data. By 1990, the total income of the richest one percent of Americans, after taxes, was just about the same as the total income shared by the poorest 40 percent; the income of the richest 5 percent of American families today is roughly the same as that of the entire bottom 60 percent. Wealth is even more unequally distributed: The top 1 percent of families owns 42 percent of the net wealth of U.S. families, including 60 percent of all corporate stock and 80 percent of all family-owned trusts.[42]

Some of this growth in inequality was due to the increased prevalence of two-income families among the top 20 percent of the population where real wages continued to rise. But even among the privileged, benefits went disproportionately to the very top, and they had far more to do with interest, dividends, tax shelters, and capital gains than with work. Most of the new wealth did not come from studying hard, saving diligently, inventing a better mousetrap, or working longer hours. Rather, it represented a shuffling of paper assets and the acquisition of "instant wealth" when fluctuating rates of return in financial markets made certain investments suddenly pay off. Many of the new fortunes in the 1970s and 1980s were made by athletes and entertainers; others were won by people who essentially played the lottery, taking what economist Lester Thurow calls "the random walk" through the stock market—though a few improved their odds by insider trading.[43]

The inflationary 1970s and speculative 1980s confounded older assumptions that financial gains depend on increases in real wealth, productivity, and jobs. As business writer Peter Drucker notes, "the 'real' economy of goods and services and the 'symbolic' economy of money, credit and capital are no longer bound tightly to each other." Wealth no longer seems to have much connection with producing anything at all.[44]

Even in the more lowly realm of salaries, inequality has only the most tenuous relation to how hard one works or what real wealth one produces. The Founding Fathers of America thought there should be enough inequality of condition to give people incentives to work, but not enough to demoralize them. By 1980, the amount of inequality thought necessary to provide incentives was already much higher than is tolerated by most of our economic rivals: The average chief executive officer (CEO) of a Fortune 500 company earned 38 times as much as the average school teacher and 42 times as much as the average factory worker. (In Japan, the average CEO's pay is only 17 times as high as that of the average worker.) But by 1988, the average chief executive of a large American company earned 72 times as much as a teacher and 93 times as much as a factory worker! In 1990, the highest-paid CEO, at United Airlines, earned 1,272 times the starting pay of a flight attendant. Meanwhile, the number of people who worked full-time year round but still remained poor increased by nearly 57 percent between 1978 and 1987. In 1990, the chairman of Time-Warner took home more than $78 million, an amount that could keep the average secretary or clerk on the payroll for more than 1,500 years. Yet the following year, 600 of *Time*'s employees were told they would be "let go."[45]

Politicians, meanwhile, have assiduously avoided such issues. When they attack one another, it is always over personal scandals or accusations. When they "take the high road," it is by issuing meaningless reassurances that America is "still number one." As novelist Eric Ambler once commented, in a sick civilization "political prestige is the reward not of the shrewdest diagnostician but of the man with the best bedside manner."[46]

Cynicism and Self-centeredness: Not Just a Family Affair

The increased visibility of economic and social inequities, and the refusal of politicians to address them, cannot help but breed cynicism and self-interested behavior. People who attribute contemporary economic and social predicaments to deterioration of family values cite the reluctance of poorer Americans to make a long-term commitment to "working their way up" through low-wage, low-status jobs. They also shake their heads at the tendency of the baby-boom generation to borrow money or decrease savings in order to maintain living standards. Much hand-wringing has been done, for example, about the well-known 1986 *Time* magazine survey which found that baby boomers were far less willing than their parents had been to "make sacrifices" for the future. Less often mentioned is the fact that the economic and political trends of the past two decades have decreased the possibility of working one's way up the job ladder and the rationality of making "sacrifices" for the future. Many of the low-status, blue-collar jobs that once offered a modicum of economic mobility disappeared in the economic restructuring since 1973; housing inflation has risen much faster than interest rates on savings, making it seem almost silly to scrimp and save for a home; people who bought "beyond their means" in the 1970s were rewarded when the housing market took off in the early 1980s.

But the widespread impression that Americans were on a "spending spree" in the 1980s is not borne out by the facts. It is true that household debt grew rapidly in relation to household income from the mid-1970s through the early 1990s, but for families in the lower 80 percent of the income distribution, most borrowing went to meet real increases in living costs, especially for housing, rather than for a surge of consumer spending. It was only those in the top 20 percent who appear to have borrowed for financial speculation and expanded consumption. And, even here, some of this behavior stemmed from insecurity rather than from flat-out greed. Corporate consolidation greatly decreased the number of management jobs available in the past fifteen years, while the combination of housing inflation and prolonged stagnation meant that even families in the upper half of the income distribution could "still feel that they are not living as well as their parents did."[47]

The real binge consumers, of course, were the corporations that engaged in trillions of dollars' worth of buyouts, simultaneously reducing their spending on research, development, and capital equipment, and the government, which tripled the national debt in ten years, even while it cut subsidies to education and other forms of social capital. If modern American families have sometimes placed personal consumption above their children's welfare, very few have such distorted "values" as does the national government: The burden of the federal debt had reached more than 180 percent of the GNP by the end of 1989, but federal spending on children in that year amounted to 1.1 percent of the GNP.[48]

Certainly, the willingness to tolerate such inequities indicates a certain insensitivity, to say the least, toward notions of fairness and social justice. That insensitivity shows up in personal relations, including decreasing willingness to make sacrifices for children or parents. But the "flight from commitment" is even more pervasive *beyond* the family than within it. James Coleman points out that the "destruction of social capital" available to youth has been greater in the community than in the family, despite the rise in single parenthood. People's family commitments remain exceptionally strong in comparison to their social, economic, and political commitments. While 97 percent of Americans consistently say that family life and family time are among their top priorities, two-thirds of the respondents to an in-depth national poll published in 1991 reported that they never give any time to community activities; more than two-thirds could not even name their congressional representative. Almost all Americans say they believe in a parent's obligations to a child, but 62 percent of high school seniors said they did not think a company going out of business had any moral obligation to repay its debts. Three decades of polls have found no decline in people's faith in family, but cynicism about political and economic elites has grown steadily since 1966.[49]

Such cynicism is derived less from people's family experiences and beliefs than from their economic and political experiences. Public figures who lie, steal, or ruin other people's lives often make more money from lectures and memoirs than if their wrongdoings had never been exposed. If the lack of "exit rules" in marriage allows fathers to run away from obligations they contracted, what about the lack of exit rules in the economy? American industries have closed thousands of factories, exported entire operations abroad, and moved from region to region seeking tax advantages; they have held towns and states for ransom, threatening to move unless given tax breaks that effectively cripple local government.

In Tarrytown, New York, for example, GM's successful campaign to cut its taxes by more than $1 million a year forced the public schools to lay off workers, eliminate new orders for library books and school supplies, and postpone repair of school buildings. At the end of 1991, GM announced it would close twenty-one plants, laying off 74,000 workers, but declined to reveal which plants until it saw what concessions various groups of workers would offer. Many companies have adopted an "accordian" staffing policy, hiring far more workers than they need in order to meet an immediate demand, then firing them just as quickly. Blue-collar workers in America receive, on average, just a single week's notice before losing their jobs—only two days when there is no union behind them. More and more white-collar workers and middle-management employees are coming back from vacation to find their jobs cut.[50]

Another source of cynicism and social alienation lies in a growing perception that Leona Helmsley was right: "Only little people pay taxes." The percentage of federal tax receipts from corporate income tax revenues dropped from 32.1 percent in 1952 to 12.5 percent in 1980 to 6.2 percent in 1983. When payroll taxes are counted along with the more progressive income tax, the "true" marginal tax rate for a couple making $14,000 a year is now 30 percent, higher than the 28 percent rate for a couple making $326,000 a year. Even after the tax reform of 1986, the percentage of income paid in taxes by the richest 1 percent of the population will be 20 percent lower in 1992 than it was in 1977.[51]

The past two decades also eroded our sense of social solidarity. Layoffs in one region or industry opened up new windows of opportunity in others. Two-tiered union contracts increasingly pitted retirement benefits against wage gains, new workers against old, temporary workers against full-timers. Volatile interest rates and housing booms meant that families with similar houses on the same block had payments ranging from $200 to $1,000 a month. One family could put in a Jacuzzi, but another could barely afford to go to the movies at the end of the month. The perception of arbitrary injustice that accompanies such contrasts was heightened during the 1980s because the price of big-ticket discretionary items "fell precipitously compared with the cost of other consumer expenditures," allowing those who already had a housing advantage to buy better cars, stereos, and computers.[52]

A central enemy is hard to discern in all this. Instead, the dominant feeling becomes "Why them?" or "Why not me?" As families with children have fallen further and further behind single-person households and smaller families, they resent the "selfishness" of the two-income small families who seem to bid up the price of housing and are the favored targets of manufacturers, advertisers, and television programmers. Two-income families who postponed childbearing, in turn, resist paying higher taxes to help families who failed to wait. Modern welfare is another divisive issue: It penalizes recipients for working, though in no state does the welfare check bring a family above the poverty level; inadequate as it is, though, welfare does provide recipients with medical protections and housing benefits not available to the working poor.[53] All these factors, added to the growing gap between rich and poor, have sown envy and discord among neighbors, workers, and community members.

America needs more than a revival of obligation within the family. As business writer Bob Kuttner has commented, it "desperately needs an *economy* based upon notions of mutual obligation and reciprocity." People should be able to expect "that our home, our church, our kid's school, our bank, and the place where we live will stay put."[54] Without such commitments in the economy and polity, family life will remain precarious no matter how many family values we try to inculcate. When there is so little trust and commitment outside the family, it is hard to maintain them *inside* the family. Old family strategies and values no longer seem to fit the new rules of the game.

It's not that the old rules of the game were fair. But the past two decades have stripped away the illusion of fairness, as well as much hope of winning by the old rules, without leading to construction of any new rules. The result is that some people break the old rules even as they espouse the values behind them, others throw all values into question, and still others try desperately to get their own families and loved ones to play by rules that have no general support in larger institutions or the popular press. Consequently, people feel embattled, if not embittered, and, above all, very much alone.

Only the family, it seems, stands between individuals and the total irresponsibility of the workplace, the market, the political arena, and the mass media. But the family is less and less able to "just say no" to the pressures that emanate from all these sources or even to cushion their impact on its members. It is no wonder, then, that many people experience recent cultural trends as a crisis of parental authority and family obligations. It is no wonder they hope for a renewal of family values that would soften these social stresses. But very few people can sustain values at a personal level when they are continually contradicted at work, at the store, in the government, and on television. To call their failure to do so a family crisis is much like calling pneumonia a breathing crisis. Certainly, pneumonia affects people's ability to breathe easily, but telling them to start breathing properly again, or even instructing them in breathing techniques, is not going to cure the disease.

The crisis of the family in late-twentieth-century America is in many ways a larger crisis of *social* reproduction: a major upheaval in the way we produce, reproduce, and distribute goods, services, power, economic rewards, and social roles, including those of class and gender. The collapse of social interdependence and community obligation in America challenges us to rethink our attitudes toward the periods of dependence that characterize the life of every human being, young or old, in or out of a family.

To handle social obligations and interdependency in the twenty-first century, we must abandon any illusion that we can or should revive some largely mythical traditional family. We need to invent new family traditions and find ways of reviving older community ones, not wallow in nostalgia for the past or heap contempt on people whose family values do not live up to ours. There are good grounds for hope that we can develop such new traditions, but only if we discard simplistic solutions based on romanticization of the past.

In fact, given recent changes in the occupation and income structure, work force, political climate, and cultural milieu, some traditional family arrangements are part of the problem, not part of the solution. The privatism that relies on nuclear, biological bonds to ensure the well-being of children, for example, is an *obstacle* to solving the problem of childhood poverty now that demographic and economic changes have redistributed income away from families that have children or other dependents. In the 1950s, when almost 70 percent of the adult population had children in school, we could rely on people's private parental interests to keep the education system going. In that period, parents' private interests added up to a majority, creating a prochild bloc in spite of our failure to develop a coherent social policy for children. Today, only 28 percent of the adult population has children in school. Maintaining the tradition of private responsibility for children's issues ensures that education will be a minority interest and encourages desperate parents to attack their problems ever more individualistically, sometimes by abandoning the public schools entirely.

Along the same lines, recent research on stepfamilies suggests that many of their predicaments stem from the fact that traditional negative stereotypes and prejudices about "broken" families still prevail among teachers, psychologists, and the general public, while no new values, guidelines, or support systems have evolved to nourish the strengths that many stepfamilies do exhibit. This is a truly astounding example of burying our collective head in the sand of traditional expectations, given that nearly half of all recent marriages are remarriages, approximately 40 percent of these involve children, and most of the conflicts in stepfamilies result from inappropriate application of traditional parent-child values in new circumstances.[55]

An extreme example of a traditional cluster of values that is part of the problem rather than the solution is found in cases of incest and other forms of child sexual abuse. The sexual abuse of children is overwhelmingly a family affair, reproducing very old-fashioned gender and power relations. Ninety-two percent of the victims of child sexual abuse are girls; 97 percent of the abusers are male. Incest tends to occur in families with strong patterns of paternal dominance and authoritarianism, along with values reinforcing the submission of women and children. Incestuous fathers often complain about loose sexual mores in the wider culture. In both anorexia and incest, a noted psychologist has recently argued, "we find the reduction of the whole girl or woman to her parts....The anorectic feels that she is nothing but her thighs and buttocks; the sexual abuser also sees the girl as little more than that. Both anorexia and incest are supported by a social system that makes use of female fragmentation in many ways." Feminist researcher Judith Herman even suggests that overt incest is "only the furthest point on a continuum—an exaggeration of patriarchal family norms, but not a departure from them."[56]

In any case, incest and sexual abuse reveal the pathological side to an overly privatistic approach to the family. The abusive family typically has a "rigid boundary between the family and the outside world" and a strong belief that a man's power within his family is not subject to outside surveillance or checks. Incestuous fathers and stepfathers "tend to be socially isolated and to have an intrafamily orientation."[57]

Wife and child battering provide other examples of how traditional values can go wrong. John Demos cites studies showing that abusive families are marked by "constant competition over who will be taken care of." This suggests that abuse is sometimes an *extension* of demands for privacy, intimacy, and individual fulfillment through the family. Battering often occurs in the most private parts of the house; it tends to be triggered by very traditional demands for domestic services from the man and perpetuated by passive rather than assertive responses by the woman.[58]

Men who institute violence against women tend to hold "old-fashioned" views of male prerogatives. Indeed, the traditional male function of "protecting" women contains seeds of violence *against* women—sometimes "for her own good"; sometimes out of the frustration of not being able to extend expected protections; sometimes out of rage at a woman's unwillingness to accept "protection" in a particular instance. Female child batterers, while violating traditional

norms of maternal patience and compassion, tend to hold very traditional values about the centrality of motherhood in women's identity:
These values often lead them to bear children they do not truly want
or to harbor unrealistic expectations of the fulfillment they will find
in their children—expectations that lead to frustration and fury
when they are not met.[59]

Like incest, rape lies along a continuum, on one end of which is
the "normal" toleration of male sexual aggression and the traditional
assumption of female responsibility for establishing sexual limits.
Unlike incest, rape is distributed on many points along that continuum, with marital and date rape often unreported and seldom
treated very severely. No identifiable pathology or unique value system separates the rapist from the respectable married man next door.
But a recent study of college men who raped and a control group
who did not found some intriguing differences that contradict many
stereotypes about the strengths of traditional families. The families of
the rapists were far more likely than those of the nonrapists to contain wives who were full-time homemakers. The fathers were typically successful career men who disappointed their children by their
physical and emotional distance. Rapists were more likely to feel
hostile toward these distant fathers than toward their mothers, but
when they did express negative feelings about their mothers these
tended to revolve around fear that the mother hindered them from
achieving a separate masculine identity—a common enough problem in traditional families that make women exclusively responsible
for childrearing and emotional bonding. Cross-cultural research suggests that such sex identity conflicts, and the male violence that
often results from them, occur much more frequently in societies
that impose a strictly gendered division of labor in childrearing and
production than in societies where there is more egalitarian sharing
of responsibility between men and women.[60]

In other instances, traditional family values may work very well as
long as other aspects of life are going as expected, but be too rigid to
allow people to cope effectively with stress. Economic reverses seem
to have the worst effects, for example, in families who subscribe to
traditional conjugal and gender ideologies. Ironically, the authority
of fathers who lose their jobs deteriorates most sharply in families
where their previous behavior had been coercive or authoritarian.[61]

Many family conflicts associated with the increased involvement
of wives in the workplace stem less from adoption of new behaviors
and new values than from refusal to adjust traditional expectations

to new realities. The failure of employers or government to offer assistance with parental leaves, child care, and flexible hours means that employed mothers work the equivalent of two full-time jobs and employed fathers the equivalent of a job and a half. Still, sociologist Arlie Hochschild's investigation of two-earner families found that couples were happier and marriages more stable when men did more housework and child care; the most serious marital strains arose from a "stalled revolution" where changes in women's roles were not matched by changes in men's.[62]

The most severe setbacks after divorce, similarly, are experienced by women who had lived prior to their divorce as full-time homemakers in "traditional" families. Children suffer most from divorce in settings where the dominance of private family values stigmatizes "nontraditional" families and prevents parental loss from being compensated for by extrafamilial social support networks in the wider community.[63] It is those wider networks, not just nuclear family ties, that stand in urgent need of reconstitution. Nostalgia for traditional families, and myths about their strengths, prevent us from drawing useful lessons from the past and making effective innovations for our families' future.

Epilogue

Inventing a New Tradition

I ARGUED in the last chapter that the so-called "crisis of the family" is a subset of a much larger crisis of social obligation that requires us to look beyond private family relations and rebuild larger social ties. Some people are very pessimistic about the possibility of extending social reciprocities and interdependencies beyond the family. Sociobiologists argue that altruism is genetically determined, and therefore quite limited, directed toward those with whom we share the most genes. From a different political stance, Freudian theorists, such as Christopher Lasch, argue that our instinctual drives are essentially antisocial and that we need to rely on the family to counter them.[1]

These approaches greatly underestimate the human potential for cooperation. The latest research on human evolution suggests that the most critical human adaptation was a tremendous enlargement of the capacity to share with others. Investigation of ancient hunting-and-gathering societies is gradually replacing the stereotype of primitive warriors with a picture of peaceful, egalitarian, cooperative cultures. I have already discussed the traditions of gift giving and reciprocity in precapitalist societies and noted the persistence of cooperation and community-building in early American history.[2]

Even today, despite pressures fostering competitive individualism, people are deeply dissatisfied with the lack of community and larger purpose in their lives. Americans "ache to do the right thing," claim the two pollsters who have documented the most stunning examples of cynicism in 1990s America; political researchers now believe that outrage rather than apathy best describes people's attitudes toward the political system. A journalist friend of mine reports that people are desperate to get past the nightly barrage of random violence and disconnected tragedies on the news to find something, however small, that they can do; when her television station suggests a number to call or a concrete act to take, the response is overwhelming. The major barrier to social involvement is not people's commitment to a purely individualistic way of life but their feeling of helplessness, the fear that they are the only people who feel this way, and their pessimism about the cravings of human nature.[3]

Such pessimism, either about human nature or about the possibility of constructing social institutions that bring out our best rather than our worst qualities, is understandable but tragically unnecessary. Human beings are social animals. This explains why, in a system with so many pressures by special interests and so little accountability to the public, individuals who join the elite get corrupted, over and over again, whatever their original intentions. But it also means that collective decision making (as opposed to periodic poll answering) *does* broaden people's minds and deepen their social values, a fact almost every jury panel discovers, while individual dissent that touches a shared framework can inspire others to act responsibly for social change.

When I was in college, two of my professors were fond of quoting the results of an experiment conducted by Stanley Milgram, in which individuals who had been told that they were participating in a learning demonstration were directed to administer an electric shock to the ostensible "subject" for every incorrect answer they were given. Placed in a room alone with the white-coated expert "in charge" of the "learning experiment," who kept instructing them to increase the voltage, 62.5 percent of the people put into this position administered shocks they had reason to believe were in the lethal range—even when they could hear their unseen "subjects" supposedly crying in pain. The lesson my professors drew was that Americans lacked independent moral standards and the courage to say no.

Much less publicity was given to a later variant of this experiment, when two confederates of the experimenter worked along with the subjects in administering the supposed shocks. When these two challenged the experiment, 90 percent of the subjects refused to follow the authority figure's instructions to increase the voltage. To me, this suggests that the example of just a few individuals can inspire others to tap into their own resources of compassion and courage.

Along similar lines, Urie Bronfenbrenner, Alan Wolfe, and other researchers show that human beings are capable of both nuanced decision making and extensive cooperation when they are not paralyzed
by authoritarian hierarchies, conflicting cues, or impersonal structures that diffuse individual responsibility, or when they are involved
in decision-making processes that involve *constructing* preferences
rather than merely registering them. Social history also demonstrates
that people are capable of changing their minds and working
through deeply held prejudices to collaborate with people they formerly scorned.[4]

But if people get involved in social change, is their compassion and
effort merely an exercise in futility, as has been claimed so often during the past twenty years? Are the problems families face so big, so
overwhelming, that nothing will do much good? Not at all. In fact,
there are plenty of programs that work. Head Start is one impressive
example, even though it continually has to scrape for funding. The
Eisenhower Foundation recently identified several community-based
programs that have reduced school dropout rates, crime, drug use,
teen pregnancy, and family violence. Children's advocate Lisbeth
Schorr recounts the success of such programs as Homebuilders, Resource Mothers, local Prenatal and Early Infancy projects, various
school reform efforts, and federal Medicaid screening or supplemen-
tal food assistance. Project SMART—School Mediators Alternative
Resolution Team—has achieved dramatic reductions in fights among
youths at the schools in which it operates. The Children's Defense
Fund mobilizes its supporters in an extremely effective way to press
for better legislation for children. Some employers have introduced
innovative child- and elder-care policies, job sharing, flexible hours,
and parental leaves, making it much easier for employees to attend to
family needs. Other countries have instituted mandated parental
leave policies for all firms, universal health care programs, and family allowances—all without going broke. There is strong evidence
that American welfare policies could be made both more effective
and more humane.[5]

Even some of our seemingly most intractable problems can be
solved. There *are* ways of raising the IQ scores and social skills of
crack-affected babies. Children from dysfunctional families do not
have to be written off. One long-term study of men born in the late
1920s, for example, found that even those who came from chroni-
cally dependent, multiproblem, "at risk" families were not distin-
guishable from their more fortunate age mates by the time they

reached the age of forty-seven. They had grown out of their difficulties and established stable lives. But, as Schorr points out, "these men belonged to a historical cohort that entered the work force in the late 1940s, when high employment levels, a steady demand and good pay for unskilled workers, and outside support of higher education through the G.I. Bill offered escape routes unavailable to those who came of age in the next generation."[6]

For the most recent generations, such economic, political, and educational aid has been more rare, yet many high-risk children do surmount their difficulties. In one long-term study of such children in Hawaii, two factors stood out in the life histories of those who showed positive change. One was the presence of even one caring adult, often a mentor or surrogate parent from outside the family. The other was access to a "second chance"—some opportunity, such as education, vocational training, or involvement in a community group, that allowed individuals to achieve gains they had been unable to make in their early years.[7]

Today, there are approximately 350,000 poor youths between the ages of sixteen and twenty-four in the poorest neighborhoods of America's cities. With adequate economic, interpersonal, and educational help, most could probably achieve significant gains; without it, we know for sure that most will not. As the William T. Grant Foundation puts it: "They are too numerous to ignore—yet few enough that a determined society can vastly improve their life chances."[8]

Can we afford such programs? Well, we could deliver a year's worth of prenatal care, immunizations, diet supplements, Head Start programs, and housing allowances to every mother and child who needs them for less than what it cost to finance three weeks of Desert Storm. We could provide jobs for all of America's unemployed teenagers for much less than Congress voted for the S&L bailout. Redistributing just 1 percent of the income of America's richest 5 percent would lift one million people above the poverty line. A 1 percent tax on the net wealth of the richest 2 percent of American families would allow us to double federal spending on education and still have almost $20 billion left to spend somewhere else. One commission has recently suggested that it would be possible to restructure the military to transfer $125 billion a year to other uses over the next ten years. A mere 1 percent cut in military expenditures would free up enough money to fund the ABC child-care bill, double the AIDS research budget, and triple the budget for the homeless. And divert-

ing money from the military to the schools would have other benefits, since $1 billion of spending on missiles creates only 9,000 jobs,
and the same amount spent on education creates 63,000 jobs.[9]

Perhaps even more to the point, can we afford *not* to spend this
money? Each class of high school dropouts costs taxpayers $242 mil-
lion. A year of Head Start or a summer job costs $3,000 per child or
teen; a year of prison costs $20,000 per inmate. Yet America keeps a
higher proportion of its population in prison than any other country
in the world, while Head Start serves just 20 percent of eligible children. It costs $600 to provide an expectant mother with prenatal
care, but for every case of low-birth-weight babies thereby averted,
the health care system saves $14,000 to $30,000. It costs $47 for a
full set of immunizations for a child, but it costs $25,000 a year to in-
stitutionalize a child mentally or physically damaged by a pre-
ventable childhood disease.[10]

What Does This Mean for My Family?

At first glance, it may seem depressing to think of our current family
problems as part of a much larger socioeconomic crisis. But surely it
is even more depressing to think that the problem is caused by people's rotten values or irredeemable selfishness. That kind of analysis
leads people to give up in despair. When I go out to lecture on family
history, I sometimes feel that half the people I talk to are torturing
themselves trying to figure out what *they* did wrong in their families
and the other half are torturing themselves trying to figure out what
their *parents* did wrong. Seeing our family pains as part of a larger social predicament means that we can let ourselves—or our parents—
off the hook. Maybe our personal difficulties are not *all* our family's
fault; maybe our family's difficulties are not *all* our personal fault.

Most people who come to this conclusion do not use it as an ex-
cuse for complacency; instead, they find that it frees valuable time
and energy for figuring out what they can actually do to help solve
the problem. There are a lot of places to start—in the local schools,
in the programs described by Schorr, in the advocacy groups cited in
some of my notes. Wherever a person starts, he or she *will* make a
difference in the lives of others. And that person will probably find
an unexpected side benefit. For, despite all the difficulty of making

generalizations about past families, the historical evidence does suggest that families have been most successful wherever they have built meaningful, solid networks and commitments *beyond* their own boundaries. We may discover that the best thing we will ever do for our own families, however we define them, is to get involved in community or political action to help others.

Notes

Introduction

1. *Los Angeles Times*, 23 March 1992, p. A3; Janet Simons, Belva Finlay, and Alice Yang, *The Adolescent and Young Adult Fact Book* (Washington, D.C.: Children's Defense Fund, 1991); *The State of America's Children, 1991* (Washington, D.C.: Children's Defense Fund, 1991); *Kids Count Data Book* (Washington, D.C.: Center for Social Policy, 1991); *Seattle Post-Intelligencer,* 13 August 1991, p. 8A; "Children and Youths," Government Accounting Office publication PRMD-89-14, 15 June 1989; *Morning News Tribune,* 20 September 1991; *The Urban Institute Policy and Research Report,* Fall 1989, p. 18; *Washington Post National Weekly Edition,* 1–7 April 1991; Maxine Phillips, "Our Children as Victims," *Dissent* (Spring 1991): 193–94; Sylvia Porter, "Death Rate for Infants a Tragedy," *The Olympian,* 15 April 1991; Sylvia Ann Hewlett, *When the Bough Breaks: The Cost of Neglecting Our Children* (New York: Basic Books, 1991), pp. 64–65, 152; *Washington Post,* 14 May 1990, 28 October 1990, and 18 June 1991; *Washington Spectator,* 1 May 1991, p. 1; *University of California Wellness Letter,* October 1990; *Liberal Opinion Week,* 31 December 1990, p. 2; *Newsweek,* 23 July 1990, p. 48.

2. Ann Rosewater, "Child and Family Trends," in *Caring for America's Children,* ed. Frank Macchiarola and Alan Gartner (New York: Academy of

Political Science, 1989), pp. 4–19; *New York Times,* 6 July 1990, and 19 March 1991; "Backtalk," *Phi Delta Kappan* 65 (1988): 375; *Newsweek,* 9 April 1990; Associated Press (AP) wire service report, 29 September 1990; James Patterson and Peter Kim, *The Day America Told the Truth: What People Really Believe About Everything that Really Matters* (New York: Prentice Hall, 1991), pp. 7, 66; *The Olympian,* 17 October 1991; *Chicago Tribune,* 16 October 1991.

3. *Washington Spectator,* 1 May 1991, p. 3; *Christian Science Monitor,* 28 October 1991, p. 20.

4. See notes 1 and 2.

5. Laura Owen, "The Welfare of Women in Laboring Families: England, 1860–1950," *Feminist Studies* 1 (1973); Martine Segalen, *Historical Anthropology of the Family* (New York: Cambridge University Press, 1986), p. 268; Roberta Spalter-Roth, "Comparing the Living Standards of Husbands and Wives: In and Out of Marriage," *Institute for Women's Policy Research,* Washington, D.C. (n.d.); Julia Brannen and Gail Wilson, *Give and Take in Families* (London: Allen and Unwin, 1987); Mimi Abramovitz, *Regulating the Lives of Women* (Boston: South End Press, 1988); Christine Delphy, *Close to Home: A Materialist Analysis of Women's Oppression* (Amherst: University of Massachusetts Press, 1984), pp. 45–56; Claudia Goldin, *Understanding the Gender Gap: An Economic History of American Women* (New York: Oxford University Press, 1990), p. 212.

6. Viviana Zeliger, *Pricing the Priceless Child: The Changing Social Value of Children* (New York: Basic Books, 1985); Michael Katz, *In the Shadow of the Poorhouse: A Social History of Welfare in America* (New York: Basic Books, 1986), pp. 121, 126; Linda Gordon, *Heroes of Their Own Lives: The Politics and History of Family Violence, 1880–1960* (New York: Viking, 1988).

7. Eric Monkkonen, "The American State from the Bottom Up: Of Homicides and Courts," *Law and Society Review* 24 (1990): 527; Charles Lockwood, "Gangs, Crime, Smut, Violence," *New York Times,* 20 September 1990.

8. Mark Lender and James Martin, *Drinking in America: A History* (Glencoe: Free Press, 1982); W. S. Rorabaugh, *The Alcoholic Republic: An American Tradition* (New York: Oxford University Press, 1979); David Musto, "America's First Cocaine Epidemic," *Wilson Quarterly* 13 (1989); David Courtwright, Herman Joseph, and Don Des Jarlais, *Addicts Who Survived: An Oral History of Narcotic Use in America, 1923–1965* (Knoxville: University of Tennessee Press, 1989), pp. 1–2.

9. David Popenoe, *Disturbing the Nest: Family Change and Decline in Modern Societies* (New York: Aldine De Gruyter, 1989), p. 1.

Chapter 1

1. Philip Greven, *Four Generations: Population, Land, and Family in Colonial Andover, Massachusetts* (Ithaca, N.Y.: Cornell University Press, 1970); Vivian Fox and Martin Quit, *Loving, Parenting, and Dying: The Family Cycle in England and America, Past and Present* (New York: Psychohistory Press, 1980), p. 401.

2. John Demos, *A Little Commonwealth: Family Life in Plymouth Colony* (New York: Oxford University Press, 1970), p. 108; Mary Ryan, *Cradle of the Middle Class: The Family in Oneida County, New York, 1790–1865* (New York: Cambridge University Press, 1981), pp. 33, 38–39; Carroll Smith-Rosenberg, *Disorderly Conduct: Visions of Gender in Victorian America* (New York: Oxford University Press, 1985), p. 24.

3. Frederick Douglass, *My Bondage and My Freedom* (New York: Dover, 1968), p. 48.

4. David Roediger and Philip Foner, *Our Own Time: A History of American Labor and the Working Day* (London: Greenwood, 1989), p. 9; Norman Ware, *The Industrial Worker, 1840–1860* (New York: Quadrangle, 1964), p. 5; Barbara Wertheimer, *We Were There: The Story of Working Women in America* (New York: Pantheon, 1977), p. 91; Sean Wilentz, *Chants Democratic: New York City and the Rise of the Working Class, 1788–1850* (New York: Oxford University Press, 1984), p. 126.

5. Faye Dudden, *Serving Women: Household Service in Nineteenth-Century America* (Middletown, Conn.: Wesleyan University Press, 1983), p. 206; Susan Strasser, *Never Done: A History of American Housework* (New York: Pantheon, 1982); Lawrence Glasco, "The Life Cycles and Household Structure of American Ethnic Groups," in *A Heritage of Her Own: Toward a New Social History of American Women,* ed. Nancy Cott and Elizabeth Pleck (New York: Simon & Schuster, 1979), pp. 281, 285.

6. Robert Bremner et al., eds., *Children and Youth in America: A Documentary History* (Cambridge: Harvard University Press, 1970), vol. 1, p. 39; Barbara Cross, *Horace Bushnell: Minister to a Changing America* (Chicago: University of Chicago Press, 1958); Ann Douglas, *The Feminization of American Culture* (NewYork: Knopf,1977), p. 52.

7. Peter Laslett, "Characteristics of the Western Family Over Time," in *Family Life and Illicit Love in Earlier Generations,* ed. Peter Laslett (New York: Cambridge University Press, 1977); William Goode, *World Revolution and Family Patterns* (New York: Free Press, 1963); Michael Anderson, *Family Structure in Nineteenth-Century Lancashire* (Cambridge, England: Cambridge University Press, 1971); Tamara Hareven, ed., *Transitions: The Family*

and the Life Course in Historical Perspective (New York: Academic Press, 1978); Tamara Hareven, "The Dynamics of Kin in an Industrial Community," in Turning Points: Historical and Sociological Essays on the Family, ed. John Demos and S. S. Boocock (Chicago: University of Chicago Press, 1978); Linda Gordon, Heroes of Their Own Lives: The Politics and History of Family Violence, 1880–1960 (New York, Viking, 1988).

8. Helen Campbell, Prisoners of Poverty: Women Wage Workers, Their Trades and Their Lives (Westport, Conn.: Greenwood Press, 1970), p. 206.

9. Rosalyn Baxandall, Linda Gordon, and Susan Reverby, eds., America's Working Women (New York: Random House, 1976), p. 162.

10. Rose Schneiderman, All For One (New York: P. S. Eriksson, 1967); John Bodnar, "Socialization and Adaption: Immigrant Families in Scranton," in Growing Up in America: Historical Experiences, ed. Harvey Graff (Detroit: Wayne State Press, 1987), pp. 391–92; Robert and Helen Lynd, Middletown: A Study in Modern American Culture (New York: Harcourt Brace Jovanovich, 1956), p. 31; Barbara Wertheimer, We Were There: The Story of Working Women in America (New York: Pantheon, 1977), pp. 336–43; Francesco Cordasco, Jacob Riis Revisited: Poverty and the Slum in Another Era (Garden City, N.Y.: Doubleday, 1968); Campbell, Prisoners of Poverty and Women Wage-Earners (Boston: Arnoff, 1893); Lynn Weiner, From Working Girl to Working Mother: The Female Labor Force in the United States, 1829–1980 (Chapel Hill: University of North Carolina Press, 1985), p. 92.

11. For examples of the analysis of the Chicago School, see Ernest Burgess and Harvey Locke, The Family: From Institution to Companionship (New York: American Book Company, 1945); Ernest Mowrer, The Family: Its Organization and Disorganization (Chicago: University of Chicago Press, 1932); W. I. Thomas and F. Znaniecki, The Polish Peasant in Europe and America, 5 vols. (Boston: Dover Publications, 1918–20). On families in the Depression, see Steven Mintz and Susan Kellogg, Domestic Revolutions: A Social History of American Family Life (New York: Free Press, 1988), pp. 133–49, quote on p. 136.

12. Glen Elder, Jr., Children of the Great Depression: Social Change in Life Experience (Chicago: University of Chicago Press, 1974), pp. 64–82; Lillian Rubin, Worlds of Pain: Life in the Working-Class Family (New York: Basic Books, 1976), p. 23; Edward Robb Ellis, A Nation in Torment: The Great American Depression, 1929–1939 (New York: Coward McCann, 1970); Ruth Milkman, "Women's Work and the Economic Crisis," in A Heritage of Her Own: Toward a New Social History of American Women, ed. Nancy Cott and Elizabeth Pleck (New York: Simon & Schuster, 1979), pp. 507–41.

13. Rudy Ray Seward, The American Family: A Demographic History (Beverly Hills: Sage, 1978); Kenneth Winkle, The Politics of Community: Migra-

tion and Politics in Antebellum Ohio (New York: Cambridge University Press, 1988); Michael Weber, *Social Change in an Industrial Town: Patterns of Progress in Warren, Pennsylvania, from the Civil War to World War I* (University Park: Pennsylvania State University Press, 1976), pp. 138–48; Stephen Thernstrom, *Poverty and Progress* (Cambridge: Harvard University Press, 1964).

14. Thomas Bender, *Community and Social Change in America* (New Brunswick: Rutgers University Press, 1978).

15. Edward Kain, *The Myth of Family Decline: Understanding Families in a World of Rapid Social Change* (Lexington, Mass.: D. C. Heath, 1990), pp. 10, 37; Theodore Caplow, "The Sociological Myth of Family Decline," *The Tocqueville Review* 3 (1981): 366; Howard Bahr, "Changes in Family Life in Middletown, 1924–77," *Public Opinion Quarterly* 44 (1980): 51.

16. *American Demographics,* February 1990; Dennis Orthner, "The Family in Transition," in *Rebuilding the Nest: A New Commitment to the American Family,* ed. David Blankenhorn, Steven Bayme, and Jean Bethke Elshtain (Milwaukee: Family Service America, 1990), pp. 95–97; Sar Levitan and Richard Belous, *What's Happening to the American Family?* (Baltimore: Johns Hopkins University Press, 1981), p. 63.

17. Daniel Kallgren, "Women Out of Marriage: Work and Residence Patterns of Never Married American Women, 1900–1980" (Paper presented at Social Science History Association Conference, Minneapolis, Minn., October 1990), p. 8; Richard Sennett, *Families Against the City: Middle Class Homes in Industrial Chicago, 1872–1890* (Cambridge: Harvard University Press, 1984), pp. 114–15.

18. Mary Jo Bane, *Here to Stay: American Families in the Twentieth Century* (New York: Basic Books, 1976); Stephen Nock, *Sociology of the Family* (Englewood Cliffs, N.J.: Prentice Hall, 1987); Kain, *Myth of Family Decline,* pp. 71, 74–75; Joseph Veroff, Elizabeth Douvan, and Richard Kulka, *The Inner American: A Self Portrait from 1957 to 1976* (New York: Basic Books, 1981); Norval Glenn, "The Recent Trend in Marital Success in the United States," *Journal of Marriage and the Family* 53 (1991); Tracy Cabot, *Marrying Later, Marrying Smarter* (New York: McGraw-Hill, 1990); Judith Brown, *Sanctions and Sanctuary: Cultural Perspectives on the Beating of Wives* (Boulder, Colo.: Westview Press, 1991); Maxine Baca Zinn and Stanley Eitzen, *Diversity in American Families* (New York: Harper & Row, 1987).

19. Dorrian Apple Sweetser, "Broken Homes: Stable Risk, Changing Reason, Changing Forms," *Journal of Marriage and the Family* (August 1985); Lawrence Stone, "The Road to Polygamy," *New York Review of Books,* 2 March 1989, p. 13; Arlene Skolnick, *Embattled Paradise: The American Family in an Age of Uncertainty* (New York: Basic Books, 1991), p. 156.

20. Frank Furstenberg, Jr., "Good Dads–Bad Dads: Two Faces of Fatherhood," in *The Changing American Family and Public Policy*, ed. Andrew Cherlin (Washington, D.C.: Urban Institute Press, 1988); Joseph Pleck, "The Contemporary Man," in *Handbook of Counseling and Psychotherapy*, ed. Murray Scher et al. (Beverly Hills: Sage, 1987).

21. National Commission on Children, *Beyond Rhetoric: A New Agenda for Children and Families* (Washington, D.C.: GPO, 1991), p. 34; Richard Gelles and Jon Conte, "Domestic Violence and Sexual Abuse of Children," in *Contemporary Families: Looking Forward, Looking Back*, ed. Alan Booth (Minneapolis: National Council on Family Relations, 1991), p. 328.

22. Arlene Skolnick, "The American Family: The Paradox of Perfection," *The Wilson Quarterly* (Summer 1980); Barbara Laslett, "Family Membership: Past and Present," *Social Problems* 25 (1978); Theodore Caplow et al., *Middletown Families: Fifty Years of Change and Continuity* (Minneapolis: University of Minnesota Press, 1982), p. 225.

23. *The State of America's Children, 1991* (Washington, D.C.: Children's Defense Fund, 1991), pp. 55–63; *Seattle Post-Intelligencer*, 19 April 1991; National Commission on Children, *Beyond Rhetoric*, p. 32; *Washington Post National Weekly Edition*, 13–19 May 1991; James Wetzel, *American Youth: A Statistical Snapshot* (Washington, D.C.: William T. Grant Foundation, August 1989), pp. 12–14.

24. *USA Today*, 12 May 1991, p. 1A; Richard Morin, "Myth of the Drop Out Mom," *Washington Post*, 14 July 1991; Christine Reinhardt, "Trend Check," *Working Woman*, October 1991, p. 34; Howard Hayghe, "Family Members in the Work Force," *Monthly Labor Review* 113 (1990).

25. Morin, "Myth of the Drop Out Mom"; Reinhardt, "Trend Check," p. 34.

26. "Too Late for Prince Charming," *Newsweek*, 2 June 1986, p. 55; John Modell, *Into One's Own: From Youth to Adulthood in the United States, 1920–1975* (Berkeley: University of California Press, 1989), p. 249; Barbara Lovenheim, *Beating the Marriage Odds: When You Are Smart, Single, and Over 35* (New York: William Morrow, 1990), pp. 26–27; *U.S. News & World Report*, 29 January 1990, p. 50; *New York Times*, 7 June 1991.

27. William Mattox, Jr., "The Parent Trap," *Policy Review* (Winter 1991): 6, 8; Sylvia Ann Hewlett, "Running Hard Just to Keep Up," *Time* (Fall 1990), and *When the Bough Breaks: The Cost of Neglecting Our Children* (New York: Basic Books, 1991), p. 73; Richard Whitmore, "Education Decline Linked with Erosion of Family," *The Olympian*, 1 October 1991; John Robinson, "Caring for Kids," *American Demographics*, July 1989, p. 52; "Household and Family Characteristics: March 1990 and 1989," *Current*

Population Reports, series P-20, no. 447, table A-1. I am indebted to George Hough, Executive Policy Analyst, Office of Financial Management, Washington State, for finding these figures and helping me with the calculations.

28. John Robinson, "Time for Work," *American Demographics,* April 1989, p. 68, and "Time's Up," *American Demographics,* July 1989, p. 34; Trish Hall, "Time on Your Hands? You May Have More Than You Think," *New York Times,* 3 July 1991, pp. C1, C7; Gannett News Service Wire Report, 27 August 1991.

29. *New York Times,* 10 October 1989, p. A18.

30. E. J. Dionne, Jr., *Why Americans Hate Politics* (New York: Simon & Schuster, 1991), pp. 110, 115, 325; *The Olympian,* 11 October 1989; *New York Times,* 10 October 1989; *Time,* 20 November 1989; *Seattle Post-Intelligencer,* 12 October 1990; Jerold Footlick, "What Happened to the Family?" *Newsweek Special Issue,* Winter/Spring 1990, p. 18.

31. Dionne, *Why Americans Hate Politics.*

32. David Blankenhorn, "Does Grandmother Know Best?" *Family Affairs* 3 (1990): 13, 16.

Chapter 2

1. *Boston Globe,* 11 April 1989; David Blankenhorn, "Ozzie and Harriet, Alive and Well," *Washington Post,* 11 June 1989; "Ozzie and Harriet Redux," *Fortune,* 25 March 1991; Richard Morin, "Family Life Makes a Comeback: Maybe Ozzie and Harriet Had a Point," *Washington Post National Weekly Edition,* 25 November–1 December 1991.

2. William Chafe, *The American Woman: Her Changing Social, Economic, and Political Roles, 1920–1970* (New York: Oxford University Press, 1974), p. 217.

3. Joseph Mason, *History of Housing in the U.S., 1930–1980* (Houston: Gulf, 1982); Martin Mayer, *The Builders* (New York: Gulf, 1978), p. 132.

4. William Chafe, *The Unfinished Journey: America Since World War II* (New York: Oxford University Press, 1986), pp. 111–18; Stephen Mintz and Susan Kellogg, *Domestic Revolutions: A Social History of American Family Life* (New York: Free Press, 1988), pp. 182–83; Elaine Tyler May, *Homeward Bound: American Families in the Cold War Era* (New York: Basic Books, 1988), p. 165.

5. May, *Homeward Bound,* p. 167; Clifford Clark, Jr., "Ranch-House Suburbia: Ideals and Realities," in *Recasting America: Culture and Politics in the*

Age of Cold War, ed. Lary May (Chicago: University of Chicago Press, 1989), p. 188.

6. David Marc, *Comic Visions: Television Comedy and American Culture* (Boston: Unwin Hyman, 1989), p. 50; May, *Homeward Bound,* p. 28; Mintz and Kellogg, *Domestic Revolutions,* p. 180.

7. Steven D. McLaughlin et al., *The Changing Lives of American Women* (Chapel Hill: University of North Carolina Press, 1988), p. 7; Donald Brogue, *The Population of the United States* (Glencoe, Ill.: Free Press, 1959).

8. Susan Ware, *Holding Their Own: American Women in the 1930s* (Boston: Twayne, 1982); Ruth Milkman, "Women's Work and Economic Crisis: Some Lessons from the Great Depression," *Review of Radical Political Economics* 8 (1976): 84; "Marriage and Divorce," a *March of Time* film, vol. 14, no. 7, 1948.

9. Talcott Parsons and Robert Bales, *Family, Socialization, and Interaction Process* (Glencoe: Free Press, 1955); Judith E. Smith, "The Marrying Kind: Working Class Courtship and Marriage in Postwar Popular Culture" (Paper presented at American Studies Association Conference, New Orleans, October 1990), p. 3; Linda Gordon, *Heroes of Their Own Lives: The Politics and History of Family Violence, 1880–1960* (New York: Viking, 1988), p. 161.

10. May, *Homeward Bound,* p. 137; Mary Ryan, *Womanhood in America from Colonial Times to the Present* (New York: Franklin Watts, 1983), pp. 271–72; Susan Householder Van Horn, *Women, Work, and Fertility, 1900–1986* (New York: New York University Press, 1988); Landon Jones, *Great Expectations: America and the Baby Boom Generation* (New York: Ballantine, 1980), p. 34.

11. May, *Homeward Bound,* p. 11.

12. Glenna Mathews, *"Just a Housewife": The Rise and Fall of Domesticity in America* (New York: Oxford University Press, 1987); Betty Friedan, *The Feminine Mystique* (New York: Dell, 1963), p. 204.

13. Peter Biskind, *Seeing Is Believing: How Hollywood Taught Us to Stop Worrying and Love the Fifties* (New York: Pantheon, 1983), pp. 252, 255.

14. Lary May, "Movie Star Politics," in *Recasting America: Culture and Politics in the Age of Cold War,* ed. Lary May (Chicago: University of Chicago Press, 1989), p. 146; May, *Homeward Bound,* pp. 64, 140–42.

15. Clifford Clark, *The American Family Home, 1800–1960* (Chapel Hill: University of North Carolina Press, 1986), pp. 209, 216; Clifford Clark, "Ranch-House Suburbia: Ideals and Realities," in *Recasting America,* ed. Lary May, pp. 171, 182; May, *Homeward Bound,* p. 162.

16. Marc, *Comic Visions,* p. 81; May, *Homeward Bound,* p. 18.

17. Lynda Glennon and Richard Bustch, "The Family as Portrayed on Television, 1949–1978," in *Television and Behavior: Ten Years of Scientific*

Progress and Implications for the Eighties, ed. David Pearle et al. (Washington, D.C.: U.S. Department of Health and Human Services, 1982); May, *Homeward Bound,* p. 146; Ella Taylor, *Prime-Time Families: Television Culture in Postwar America* (Berkeley: University of California Press, 1989).

18. Samuel Bowles, David Gordon, and Thomas Weisskopf, *Beyond the Wasteland: A Democratic Alternative to Economic Decline* (Garden City, N.Y.: Doubleday, 1983), pp. 66–67, 74; Chafe, *Unfinished Journey,* pp. 111–18; James A. Henretta et al., *America's History,* vol. 2 (Chicago: Dorsey Press, 1987), p. 852; David Potter, *People of Plenty* (Chicago: University of Chicago Press, 1959).

19. James Patterson, *America Struggles Against Poverty, 1900–1985* (Cambridge: Harvard University Press, 1986), p. 13; Douglas Miller and Marion Nowak, *The Fifties: The Way We Really Were* (Garden City, N.Y.: Doubleday, 1977), p. 122; Michael Harrington, *The Other America: Poverty in the United States* (New York: Macmillan, 1962); *Social Security Bulletin,* July 1963, pp. 3–13; Chafe, *Unfinished Journey,* p. 143; Mark Stern, "Poverty and the Life-Cycle, 1940–1960," *Journal of Social History* 24 (1991): 538.

20. Taylor, *Prime-Time Families,* p. 40; David Marc, "The Sit-Com Sensibility," *Washington Post,* 25 June 1989; Eric Barnouw, *Tube of Plenty: The Evolution of American Television* (New York: Oxford University Press, 1975); Richard Griswold del Castillo, *La Familia: Chicano Families in the Urban Southwest, 1848 to the Present* (Notre Dame: University of Notre Dame Press, 1984), pp. 113–14; Henretta et al., *America's History,* vol. 2, p. 845.

21. Glenda Riley, *Inventing the American Woman* (Arlington Heights, Va.: Harlan Davidson, 1987), p. 240; Harrington, *Other America,* p. 53; Edward R. Murrow, "Harvest of Shame," *CBS Reports,* 25 November 1960; John Collier, "Indian Takeaway," *Nation,* 2 October 1954.

22. Herbert Shapiro, *White Violence and Black Response: From Reconstruction to Montgomery* (Amherst: University of Massachusetts Press, 1988); Michael Danielson, *The Politics of Exclusion* (New York: Columbia University Press, 1976); Miller and Nowak, *The Fifties,* pp. 199–201; *Life,* 9 November 1953, p. 151; "The Negro and the North," *Life,* 11 March 1957, p. 163.

23. Joan Ellen Trey, "Women in the World War II Economy," *Review of Radical Political Economics,* July 1972; Chafe, *American Woman,* pp. 178–79.

24. Ruth Milkman, *Gender at Work: The Dynamics of Job Segregation by Sex During World War II* (Urbana: University of Illinois Press, 1987), p. 102; Sheila Tobias and Lisa Anderson, "What Really Happened to Rosie the Riveter" *MSS Modular Publications* 9 (1973); Steven D. McLaughlin et al., *The Changing Lives of American Women* (Chapel Hill: University of North Carolina, 1988), p. 24.

25. Marynia Farnham and Ferdinand Lundberg, *Modern Woman: The Lost Sex* (New York: Harper and Brothers, 1947), p. 24; Susan Hartmann, *The Home Front and Beyond: American Women in the 1940s* (Boston: Twayne Publishers, 1982), pp. 173, 179–80; May, *Homeward Bound,* pp. 96–97.

26. Carol Warren, *Madwives: Schizophrenic Women in the 1950s* (New Brunswick: Rutgers University Press, 1987); Hartmann, *Home Front,* p. 174.

27. Miller and Nowak, *The Fifties,* pp. 164–65.

28. Mintz and Kellogg, *Domestic Revolutions,* p. 181; Barbara Ehrenreich, *The Hearts of Men: American Dreams and the Flight from Commitment* (Garden City, N.Y.: Anchor Press, 1983), pp. 14–28; Miller and Nowak, *The Fifties,* p. 154.

29. Paul Boyer, *By the Bomb's Early Light: American Thought and Culture at the Dawn of the Atomic Age* (New York: Pantheon, 1985); Roger Morris, *Richard Milhous Nixon: The Rise of an American Politician* (New York: Holt, 1990); Ellen Schrecker, *No Ivory Tower: McCarthyism and the Universities* (New York: Oxford University Press, 1986); David Caute, *The Great Fear: The Anti-Communist Purge Under Truman and Eisenhower* (New York: Simon & Schuster, 1978); Henretta et al., *America's History,* p. 867; May, *Homeward Bound,* pp. 13–14, 94–95.

30. Benita Eisler, *Private Lives: Men and Women of the Fifties* (New York: Franklin Watts, 1986), p. 341.

31. May, *Homeward Bound,* p. 91.

32. May, *Homeward Bound,* p. 109; James B. Gilbert, *A Cycle of Outrage: America's Reaction to the Juvenile Delinquent in the 1950s* (New York: Oxford University Press, 1986), pp. 3, 8, 66.

33. For a defense of the suburbs, see Scott Donaldson, *The Suburban Myth* (New York: Columbia University Press, 1969). See also John Seeley, R. Alexander Sim, and E. W. Loosely, *Crestwood Heights: A Study of Culture in Suburban Life* (New York: Basic Books, 1956), and William H. Whyte, *The Organization Man* (New York: Simon & Schuster, 1956). Though Whyte criticized the lack of individualism in the suburbs he described, his description of boring group life might sound rather comforting to many alienated modern Americans.

34. Susan Allen Toth, *Blooming: A Small-Town Girlhood* (Boston: Little, Brown, 1978), pp. 3, 4.

35. Marilyn Van Derbur Atler, "The Darkest Secret," *People,* 6 July 1991.

36. Eisler, *Private Lives,* p. 170. See also Nancy Hall, *A True Story of a Drunken Mother* (Boston: South End Press, 1990).

37. Mintz and Kellogg, *Domestic Revolutions,* p. 194; C. Henry Kempe et al., "The Battered Child Syndrome," *Journal of the American Medical Associa-*

tion (1962): 181; Elizabeth Pleck, *Domestic Tyranny: The Making of Social Policy Against Family Violence from Colonial Times to the Present* (New York: Oxford University Press, 1987), pp. 169, 182.

38. Pleck, *Domestic Tyranny,* pp. 162–63.

39. Pleck, *Domestic Tyranny,* pp. 156–57; Gordon, *Heroes of Their Own Lives,* pp. 206–22.

40. Mirra Komarovsky, *Blue-Collar Marriage* (New Haven: Vintage, 1962), p. 331.

41. Mintz and Kellogg, *Domestic Revolutions,* p. 194; May, *Homeward Bound,* p. 202.

42. Mintz and Kellogg, *Domestic Revolutions,* p. 195; Miller and Nowak, *The Fifties,* p. 174. The physician reported that most of these women had fulfilled their wifely and motherly roles for years, in seemingly irreproachable ways, but were nevertheless unfulfilled. Unable to accept the logic of his own evidence, the doctor concluded that their problems were a result of their "intense strivings for masculinity."

43. Christina Crawford, *Mommie Dearest* (New York: William Morrow, 1978), especially pp. 51–56, 82–88; Chafe, *Unfinished Journey,* p. 126; Edith Lisansky, "The Woman Alcoholic," *Annals of the American Academy of Political and Social Sciences* (1958): 315.

44. Eisler, *Private Lives,* pp. 209–10; Friedan, *The Feminine Mystique,* pp. 44, 59.

45. Mathews, *"Just a Housewife,"* pp. 219–20.

46. Ehrenreich, *The Hearts of Men.*

47. Jones, *Great Expectations,* pp. 41–49; Friedan, *Feminine Mystique,* pp. 250–51.

48. Chafe, *Unfinished Journey,* p. 144.

49. Chafe, *Unfinished Journey,* p. 125; Eisler, *Private Lives,* p. 369; Chafe, *American Woman,* p. 218; Ryan, *Womanhood in America,* p. 277; May, *Homeward Bound,* pp. 149–52; Joseph Demartini, "Change Agents and Generational Relationships: A Reevaluation of Mannheim's Problem of Generations," *Social Forces* 64 (1985).

50. Ellen Rothman, *Hands and Hearts,* pp. 304–5; May, *Homeward Bound,* pp. 117, 121, 127; Maris Vinovskis, *An "Epidemic" of Adolescent Pregnancy?: Some Historical and Policy Considerations* (New York: Oxford University Press, 1988), p. 25; Rickie Solinger, *Wake Up Little Susie: Single Pregnancy and Race in the Pre–Roe v. Wade Era* (New York: Routledge, forthcoming).

51. Rothman, *Hands and Hearts,* p. 301; Eisler, *Private Lives,* p. 199.

52. May, *Homeward Bound,* pp. 101–2, 127–28; Andrea Sanders, "Sex, Politics, and Good Taste in Nabokov's *Lolita* and Ike's America" (Paper de-

livered at "Ike's America, a conference on the Eisenhower Presidency and American Life in the 1950s," University of Kansas, Lawrence, 4–6 October 1990), pp. 11–12.

53. Beth Bailey, *From Front Porch to Back Seat: Courtship in Twentieth-Century America* (Baltimore: Johns Hopkins University Press, 1989), p. 90; Rothman, *Hands and Hearts,* pp. 304–6.

54. Paul Taylor, "Who Has Time to Be a Family?" *Washington Post National Weekly Edition,* 14–20 January 1991; David Blankenhorn, "American Family Dilemmas," in *Rebuilding the Nest: A New Commitment to the American Family,* ed. David Blankenhorn et al. (Milwaukee: Family Service America, 1990), pp. 10–12.

Chapter 3

1. George Gilder, *Naked Nomads* (New York: Times Books, 1974), p. 10. See also Gilder's *Sexual Suicide* (New York: Quadrangle, 1973).

2. "Family Policy Debated at AEI Conference," *American Family,* December 1987–January 1988, p. 24; Connaught Marshner, *Why the Family Matters: From a Business Perspective* (Washington, D.C.: Currents in Family Policy, 1985), pp. 2–8, 23; Germaine Greer, *Sex and Destiny: The Politics of Human Fertility* (New York: Harper & Row, 1984); Susan Brownmiller, *Femininity* (New York: Fawcett Columbine, 1984).

3. Allan Bloom, *The Closing of the American Mind: How Higher Education Has Failed Democracy and Impoverished the Souls of Today's Students* (New York: Simon & Schuster, 1987), pp. 86, 104–5, 115, 129.

4. For a fuller description of this family and its gender roles, see Nancy Cott, *The Bonds of Womanhood: Women's Sphere in New England, 1780–1835* (New Haven: Yale University Press, 1977); Kirk Jeffrey, "The Family as Utopian Retreat from the City," *Soundings* 55 (1972): 28; Mary Ryan, *The Empire of the Mother: American Writing About Domesticity, 1830–1860* (New York: Haworth Press, 1982); Barbara Welter, "The Cult of True Womanhood: 1820–1860," *American Quarterly* 18 (1966): 152.

5. On the gradual and comparatively late emergence of the family as a center of love, distinguished from other institutions and associations, see David Herlihy, "Family," *American Historical Review* 96 (1991). This is not the place to review the tremendous variability of gender roles in history and the way that gender differences have been socially constructed. A summary of recent research can be found in Judith Lober and Susan Farrell, eds., *The*

Social Construction of Gender (Newbury Park: Sage, 1991), and Deborah Rhode, ed., *Theoretical Perspectives on Sexual Differences* (New Haven: Yale University Press, 1990).

6. Carole Pateman, "'The Disorder of Women': Women, Love and the Sense of Justice," *Ethics* 91 (1980); Larry Blum, Marcia Homiak, Judy Housman, and Naomi Scheman, "Altruism and Women's Oppression," in *Women and Philosophy: Toward a Theory of Liberation,* ed. Carol Gould and Max Wartofsky (New York: Putnam, 1976), p. 224; Teresa Brennan and Carole Pateman, "'Mere Auxiliaries to the Commonwealth': Women and the Origins of Liberalism," *Political Studies* 27 (1979); Susan Okin, "Women and the Making of the Sentimental Family," *Philosophy and Public Affairs* 11 (1982).

7. Carol Gilligan, *In a Different Voice* (Cambridge: Harvard University Press, 1982); Mary Field Belenky, *Women's Ways of Knowing: The Development of Self, Voice, and Mind* (New York: Basic Books, 1986).

8. Marshall Sahlins, *Stone Age Economics* (Chicago: Aldine-Atherton, 1972); Ken Jordaan, "The Bushmen of Southern Africa," *Race and Class* 17 (1975): 156–59; Bronislaw Malinowski, *Argonauts of the Western Pacific* (New York: E. P. Dutton, 1961); James Axtell, *The Indian Peoples of Eastern America* (New York: Oxford University Press, 1981); Marcel Mauss, *The Gift: Forms and Functions of Exchange in Archaic Societies,* trans. Ian Cunnison (New York: Cohen and West, 1967), p. 19.

9. Dorothy Lee, *Freedom and Culture* (New York: Prentice Hall, 1959), pp. 113–14; Sahlins, *Stone Age Economics;* "Indians in the Land: A Conversation Between William Cronon and Richard White," *American Heritage* 37 (1986): 24.

10. Mauss, *The Gift;* Jan Van Baal, *Reciprocity and the Position of Women* (Assen, Netherlands: Van Gorcum, 1975), pp. 30–69.

11. For a description of the contradictions of reciprocity, see Stephanie Coontz and Peta Henderson, "Property Forms, Political Power, and Female Labour in the Origins of Class Societies," in *Women's Work, Men's Property: The Origins of Gender and Class,* ed. Coontz and Henderson (London: Verso, 1986). For an introduction to the dynamics of reciprocity and repression in medieval societies, see Marc Bloch, *Feudal Society,* trans. L. A. Manyon (Chicago: University of Chicago Press, 1974), and Emmanuel Le Roy Ladurie's study of a thirteenth-century village, *Montaillou: The Promised Land of Error* (New York: G. Braziller, 1978).

12. Edmund Morgan, *American Slavery, American Freedom: The Ordeal of Colonial Virginia* (New York: Norton, 1975), p. 384.

13. For a discussion of these aspects of capitalist thought and the ways in

which they fostered such progressive forces as the antislavery movement, see David Brion Davis, *The Problem of Slavery in the Age of Revolution* (Ithaca, N.Y.: Cornell University Press, 1966); Thomas Haskell, "Capitalism and the Origins of the Humanitarian Sensibility," pts. 1 and 2, *American Historical Review* 90 and 91 (1985): 339–61, 547–66; and Howard Temperley, "Capitalism, Slavery, and Ideology," *Past and Present* 75 (1977): 95–118.

14. John Donne, "An Anatomie of the World," in *Seventeenth-Century Verse and Prose,* ed. Helen White et al. (New York: Macmillan, 1969), p. 87.

15. Donne, "Meditation 17," in *Seventeenth-Century Verse,* p. 109; Merwyn James, *Family, Lineage, and Civil Society; A Study of Society, Politics, and Mentality in the Durham Region, 1500–1640* (Oxford, England: Clarendon Press, 1974), p. 189.

16. Daniel Defoe, *Robinson Crusoe* (New York: Holt, Rinehart & Winston, 1961).

17. Thomas Hobbes, *Leviathan* (Aylesbury Buck, England: Penguin, 1971), pp. 189, 256; C. B. Macpherson, *The Life and Times of Liberal Democracy* (New York: Oxford University Press, 1977), p. 1.

18. C. B. Macpherson, *The Political Theory of Possessive Individualism* (New York: Oxford University Press, 1962); Morton Horwitz, *The Transformation of American Law, 1780–1860* (Cambridge: Harvard University Press, 1977).

19. Ruth L. Smith and Deborah Valenze, "Mutuality and Marginality: Liberal Moral Theory and Working-Class Women in Nineteenth-Century England," *Signs* 13 (1988): 280.

20. Adam Smith, *An Inquiry into the Nature and Causes of the Wealth of Nations* (London: Clarendon Press, 1961), and *The Theory of Moral Sentiments* (New York: Clarendon Press, 1976). See also Donald Winch, *Adam Smith's Politics: An Essay in Historiographic Revision* (Cambridge, England: Cambridge University Press, 1978); Edward Cohen, "Justice and Political Economy in Commercial Society: Adam Smith's 'Science of a Legislator,'" *Journal of Politics* 51 (1989); and Garry Wills, *Inventing America: Jefferson's Declaration of Independence* (Garden City, N.Y.: Doubleday, 1978), p. 232.

21. Alison Jaggar, *Feminism and Human Nature* (Totowa, N.J.: Rowman & Allanheld, 1983), pp. 32–33; Frances Olsen, "The Family and the Market: A Study of Ideology and Legal Reform," *Harvard Law Review* 96 (1983): 1415.

22. Robert Bellah et al., *Habits of the Heart: Individualism and Commitment in American Life* (New York: Harper & Row, 1986), pp. 23, 55; Macpherson, *Possessive Individualism,* p. 263.

23. Michael Ignatieff, *The Needs of Strangers* (New York: Viking, 1985), p. 13.

24. Philippe Aries, "The Family and the City in the Old World and the New," in *Changing Images of the Family,* ed. Virginia Tufte and Barbara Myerhoff (New Haven: Yale University Press, 1979), p. 32, and Philippe Aries, *Centuries of Childhood: A Social History of Family Life* (New York: Random House, 1962); Alice Clark, *The Working Life of Women in the Seventeenth Century* (New York: A. M. Kelly, 1968); Renate Bridenthal and Claudia Koonz, *Becoming Visible: Women in European History* (Boston: Houghton Mifflin, 1977).

25. Linda Kerber, "Women and Individualism in American History," *The Massachusetts Review* (Winter 1989): 597–98; Okin, "Women and the Making of the Sentimental Family"; David Leverenz, *Manhood and the American Renaissance* (Ithaca, N.Y.: Cornell University Press, 1989), p. 86.

26. Alexis de Tocqueville, *Democracy in America,* vol. 2 (New York: Knopf, 1969), pp. 211–12; Bellah et al., *Habits of the Heart,* p. 40.

27. Lawrence Stone, *The Family, Sex, and Marriage in England, 1500–1800* (New York: Harper & Row, 1977); Randolph Trumbach, *The Rise of the Equalitarian Family* (New York: Academic Press, 1978); Eli Zaretsky, *Capitalism, The Family, and Personal Life* (New York: Perennial Library, 1986); Carl Degler, *At Odds: Women and the Family in America from the Revolution to the Present* (New York: Oxford University Press, 1980).

28. Jeffrey, "The Family as Utopian Retreat," p. 28.

29. John Berger, *G* (New York: Viking, 1972), p. 34.

30. Jaggar, *Feminism and Human Nature,* pp. 34, 175; Michael Walzer, *Obligations* (Cambridge: Harvard University Press, 1970), p. 89; Robert Westbrook, "'I Want a Girl, Just Like the Girl that Married Harry James': American Women and the Problem of Political Obligation in World War II," *American Quarterly* 42 (1990): 588, 611.

31. Mary Lowenthal Felstiner, "Family Metaphors: The Language of an Independence Revolution," *Comparative Studies in Society and History* (1983); *Ladies' Book* 1 (1840): 338.

32. Alan Dawley, *Class and Community: The Industrial Revolution in Lynn* (Cambridge: Harvard University Press, 1976), p. 34.

33. Elizabeth Drew, *Washington Journal: The Events of 1973–1974* (New York: Random House, 1975), p. 415.

34. For a comment on the ways in which modern parents tend to sacrifice their larger ideals in the name of their children, see Jason DeParle, "The Case Against Kids," *Washington Monthly,* July–August 1988.

35. Bellah et al., *Habits of the Heart,* p. 62.

36. This argument does not imply that there was a "golden age" of sexual equality before this rearrangement. It is even possible that women were worse off when they were not distinguished so sharply from men, because

they were considered *lesser* beings rather than *different* beings. I review this issue in regard to American women in chapters 3 and 4 of my previous book, *The Social Origins of Private Life: A History of American Families, 1600–1900* (London: Verso, 1988).

37. Barbara Welter, "The Cult of True Womanhood, 1820–1860," *American Quarterly* 18 (1966): 152; Virginia Sapiro, "The Gender Basis of American Social Policy," in *Women, the State, and Welfare,* ed. Linda Gordon (Madison: University of Wisconsin Press, 1990), p. 39.

38. Charles Murray, *Losing Ground: American Social Policy, 1950–1980* (New York: Basic Books, 1984), p. 65; Richard Vedder, "Shrinking Paychecks: The New Economics of Family Life," *The Family in America* 3 (1989): 5.

39. Carole Pateman, *The Sexual Contract* (Stanford: Stanford University Press, 1988); Pateman and Brennan, "'Mere Auxiliaries to the Commonwealth'"; Gerda Lerner, "The Lady and the Mill Girl: Changes in the Status of Women in the Age of Jackson," *American Studies Journal* 10 (1969); Michael Grossberg, *Governing the Hearth: Law and the Family in Nineteenth-Century America* (Chapel Hill: University of North Carolina Press, 1985); Nancy Erikson, "Muller v. Oregon Reconsidered: The Origins of a Sex-Based Doctrine of Liberty of Contract," *Labor History* (Spring 1989): 230, 232; Susan Moller Okin, *Justice, Gender, and the Family* (New York: Basic Books, 1989), p. 110.

40. Kerber, "Women and Individualism," pp. 589–90.

41. Nancy Cott, *The Bonds of Womanhood* (New Haven: Yale University Press, 1977), pp. 80–83.

42. Donald Mitchell, *Reveries of a Bachelor: Or, a Book of the Heart* (New York: A. L. Bert, 1893), p. 97.

43. Carroll Smith-Rosenberg, *Disorderly Conduct: Visions of Gender in Victorian America* (New York: Knopf, 1985), p. 108; Susan Gubar, "'This Is My Rifle, This Is My Gun': World War II and the Blitz on Women," in *Behind the Lines: Gender and the Two World Wars,* ed. Margaret Higonnet et al. (New Haven: Yale University Press, 1987).

44. Jean-Jacques Rousseau, *Emile* (New York: Harper, 1960).

45. Berger, *G,* p. 34.

46. Elizabeth Rapaport, "On the Future of Love: Rousseau and the Radical Feminists," in *Women and Philosophy,* pp. 197, 199.

47. John Gillis, "From Ritual to Romance: Toward an Alternative History of Love," in *Emotion and Social Change: Toward a New Psychohistory,* ed. Carol and Peter Stearns (New York: Holmes and Meier, 1988), p. 107.

48. Ann Barr Snitov, "Mass Market Romance: Pornography for Women Is Different," *Radical History Review,* Spring–Summer 1979, p. 146. For an-

other view on how women use romance novels to make gender differences work for them, see Janice Radway, *Reading the Romance: Women, Patriarchy, and Popular Literature* (Chapel Hill: University of North Carolina Press, 1984).

49. Barrie Thorne, "Feminist Rethinking of the Family: An Overview," in *Rethinking the Family: Some Feminist Questions,* ed. Barrie Thorne with Marilyn Yalom (New York: Longman, 1982), pp. 12–15; Arlie Hochschild, *The Managed Heart* (Berkeley: University of California Press, 1983), p. 164.

50. Marcia Millman, *Warm Hearts, Cold Cash: The Intimate Dynamics of Families and Money* (New York: Free Press, 1991), pp. 9, 11.

51. Peter Marin, "The Prejudice Against Men," *The Nation,* 8 July 1991, p. 48.

52. Deborah Luepnitz, *The Family Interpreted: Feminist Theory in Clinical Practice* (New York: Basic Books, 1988), pp. 10–11.

53. On male retreats, see "Drums, Sweat and Tears," *Newsweek,* 24 June 1991; Robert Bly, *Iron John: A Book About Men* (Reading, Mass.: Addison-Wesley, 1990); Sam Keen, *Fire in the Belly: On Being a Man* (New York: Bantam Books, 1991). On marriage and male health, see Cathleen Zickand and Ken Smith, "Marital Transitions, Poverty, and Gender Differences in Mortality," *Journal of Marriage and the Family* 53 (1991).

54. Smith-Rosenberg, *Disorderly Conduct,* pp. 35–36, 53–89; John D'Emilio and Estelle Freedman, *Intimate Matters: A History of Sexuality in America* (New York: Harper & Row, 1988), pp. 125–27; Lilian Faderman, *Surpassing the Love of Men: Romantic Friendship and Love Between Women from the Renaissance to the Present* (New York: William Morrow, 1981).

55. Jonathon Katz, ed., *Gay American History: Lesbians and Gay Men in the USA* (New York: Crowell, 1976); D'Emilio and Freedman, *Intimate Matters,* pp. 127–29; Anthony Rotundo, "Romantic Friendship: Male Intimacy and Middle-Class Youth in the Northern United States, 1800–1900," *Journal of Social History* 23 (Fall 1989).

56. Elaine Tyler May, *Great Expectations: Marriage and Divorce in Post-Victorian America* (Chicago: University of Chicago Press, 1980); Steven Mintz and Susan Kellogg, *Domestic Revolutions: A Social History of American Family Life* (New York: Free Press, 1988), p. 109.

Chapter 4

1. For more on Bush's history and that of other black pioneers, see William Loren Katz, *The Black West* (Seattle: Open Hand Publishers, 1987).

2. David Broder, "Phil Gramm's Free Enterprise," *Washington Post,* 16 February 1983; Marian Wright Edelman, *Families in Peril: An Agenda for Social Change* (Cambridge: Harvard University Press, 1987), pp. 27–28.

3. Allan Carlson, "How Uncle Sam Got in the Family's Way," *Wall Street Journal,* 20 April 1988, and "Is Social Security Pro-Family?" *Policy Studies* (Fall 1987): 49.

4. James Axtell, *The European and the Indian: Essays in the Ethnohistory of Colonial North America* (New York: Oxford University Press, 1982), pp. 292–93; William Cronon, *Changes in the Land: Indians, Colonists, and the Ecology of New England* (New York: Hill and Wang, 1983), pp. 37–53; Richard White, *Land Use, Environment, and Social Change: The Shaping of Island County, Washington* (Seattle: University of Washington Press, 1980), pp. 20–26.

5. Lorena Walsh, "Till Death Do Us Part," in *Growing Up in America: Historical Experience,* ed. Harvey Graff (Detroit: Wayne State University Press, 1987); Edmund Morgan, *The Puritan Family: Religion and Domestic Relations in Seventeenth-Century New England* (New York: Harper & Row, 1966); John Demos, *A Little Commonwealth: Family Life in Plymouth Colony* (New York: Oxford University Press, 1970); Lawrence Cremin, *American Education: The Colonial Experience, 1607–1783* (New York: Harper & Row, 1970), pp. 124–37.

6. Laurel Thatcher Ulrich, "Housewife and Gadder: Themes of Self-sufficiency and Community in Eighteenth-Century New England," in *"To Toil the Livelong Day": America's Women at Work, 1780–1980,* ed. Carol Groneman and Mary Beth Norton (Ithaca, N.Y.: Cornell University Press, 1987); James Henretta, "Families and Farms: *Mentalite* in Pre-Industrial America," *William and Mary Quarterly* 35 (1978); Rhys Isaac, *The Transformation of Virginia, 1740–1790* (Chapel Hill: University of North Carolina Press, 1982), pp. 11–138.

7. James Henretta, *The Evolution of American Society, 1700–1815* (Lexington, Mass.: Heath, 1973), p. 212; Stuart Blumin, *The Urban Threshold: Growth and Change in a Nineteenth-Century American Community* (Chicago: University of Chicago Press, 1976), p. 46; Paul Johnson, *A Shopkeeper's Millennium: Society and Revivals in Rochester, New York, 1815–1837* (New York: Hill and Wang, 1978).

8. Michael Katz, *Poverty and Policy in American History* (New York: Academic Press, 1983), p. 183.

9. S. J. Kleinberg, *The Shadow of the Mills: Working-Class Families in Pittsburgh, 1870–1907* (Pittsburgh: University of Pittsburgh Press, 1989), pp. 270–75; Herbert Gutman, *Work, Culture, and Society in Industrializing America* (New York: Knopf, 1976); John Bodnar, *Natives and Newcomers:*

Ethnicity in an American Mill Town (Pittsburgh: University of Pittsburgh Press, 1977); Margaret Byington, *Homestead: The Households of a Mill Town* (Pittsburgh: University of Pittsburgh Press, 1974), p. 16; James Borchert, *Alley Life in Washington: Family, Community, Religion, and Folklife in the City, 1850–1970* (Urbana: University of Illinois Press, 1980); Jacquelyn Dowd Hall et al., *Like a Family: The Making of a Southern Cotton Mill World* (Chapel Hill: University of North Carolina Press, 1987); David Montgomery, *The Fall of the House of Labor* (New York: Cambridge University Press, 1989); David Goldberg, *A Tale of Three Cities: Labor Organization and Protest in Paterson, Passaic, and Lawrence, 1916–1921* (New Brunswick: Rutgers University Press, 1989); Katz, *Poverty and Policy,* p. 49.

10. Richard Griswold Del Castillo, *La Familia: Chicano Families in the Urban Southwest, 1848 to the Present* (Notre Dame: University of Notre Dame Press, 1984), pp. 42–43, 118; Carol Stack, *All Our Kin: Strategies for Survival in a Black Community* (New York: Harper & Row, 1974).

11. Michael B. Katz, *In the Shadow of the Poorhouse: A Social History of Welfare in America* (New York: Basic Books, 1986), pp. 190, 240.

12. Abraham Epstein, *Insecurity: A Challenge to Americans: A Study of Social Insurance in the United States and Abroad* (New York: H. Smith and R. Hass, 1933); Katz, *Poverty and Policy,* pp. 121, 126, 244.

13. Linda Kerber, "Women and Individualism in American History," *The Massachusetts Review* (Winter 1989): 604–5.

14. Patricia Nelson Limerick, *Legacy of Conquest: The Unbroken Past of the American West* (New York: Norton, 1987), p. 82.

15. Stephen Thernstrom, *Poverty and Progress: Social Mobility in a Nineteenth-Century City* (Cambridge: Harvard University Press, 1964); Peter Knights, *The Plain People of Boston: A Study in City Growth* (New York: Oxford University Press, 1971); Lilian Schlissel, Byrd Gibbens, and Elizabeth Hampsten, *Far From Home: Families of the Westward Journey* (New York: Schocken, 1989); John Farragher and Christine Stansell, *Women and Men on the Overland Trail* (New Haven: Yale University Press, 1979).

16. John Mack Farragher, "Open-Country Community: Sugar Creek, Illinois, 1820–1850," in *The Countryside in the Age of Capitalistic Transformation,* ed. Steven Hahmond and Jonathon Prude (Chapel Hill: University of North Carolina Press, 1985), p. 245; John Mack Farragher, *Sugar Creek: Life on the Illinois Prairie* (New Haven: Yale University Press, 1986), pp. 132–33, 114; Michael Cassity, *Defending a Way of Life: An American Community in the Nineteenth Century* (Albany: State University of New York Press, 1989).

17. Steven Mintz and Susan Kellogg, *Domestic Revolutions: A Social History of American Family Life* (New York: Free Press, 1988), pp. 146–47.

18. Limerick, *Legacy of Conquest,* pp. 45–47, 82, 136; Scott and Sally Ann McNall, *Plains Families: Exploring Sociology Through Social History* (New York: St. Martin's, 1983), p. 9; Willard Cochrane, *The Development of American Agriculture: A Historical Analysis* (Minneapolis: University of Minnesota Press, 1979); "Lincoln Policy Shaped Local Forest Landscape," *Seattle Post-Intelligencer,* 20 April 1990; John Opie, *The Law of the Land: Two Hundred Years of American Farmland Policy* (Lincoln: University of Nebraska Press, 1987); Imhoff Vogeler, *The Myth of the Family Farm: Agribusiness Dominance of U.S. Agriculture* (Boulder: Westview Press, 1981).

19. William Chafe, *The Unfinished Journey: America Since World War II* (New York: Oxford University Press, 1986), pp. 113, 143; Susan Hartmann, *The Home Front and Beyond: American Women in the 1940s* (Boston: Twayne Publishers, 1982), p. 165; Michael Parenti, *Democracy for the Few* (New York: St. Martin's, 1988), pp. 82–83.

20. Dwight Lee, "Government Policy and the Distortions in Family Housing," in *The American Family and the State,* ed. Joseph Peden and Fred Glahe (San Francisco: Pacific Research Institute for Public Policy, 1986), p. 312.

21. Kenneth Jackson, *Crabgrass Frontier: The Suburbanization of the United States* (New York: Oxford University Press, 1985), pp. 196–204, 215; Chafe, *Unfinished Journey,* p. 113; Henretta et al., *America's History,* vol. 2, pp. 849–50; Alan Wolfe, *Whose Keeper?: Social Science and Moral Obligation* (Berkeley: University of California Press, 1989), p. 62.

22. James A. Henretta et al., *America's History,* vol. 2 (Chicago: Dorsey Press, 1987), p. 848; Jackson, *Crabgrass Frontier,* pp. 248–50; Neal Pierce, "New Highways Next Big Issue to Divide Nation," *The Olympian,* 28 May 1990, p. 8A.

23. Eric Monkkonen, *America Becomes Urban: The Development of U.S. Cities and Towns, 1780–1980* (Berkeley: University of California Press, 1988), p. 203; George Lipsitz, "Land of a Thousand Dances: Youth, Minorities, and the Rise of Rock and Roll," in *Recasting America: Culture and Politics in the Age of Cold War,* ed. Lary May (Chicago: University of Chicago Press, 1989), p. 269; Jackson, *Crabgrass Frontier,* pp. 190–230; Patricia Burgess Stach, "Building the Suburbs: The Social Structuring of Residential Neighborhoods in Post-War America" (Paper presented at "Ike's America, a conference on the Eisenhower Presidency and American Life in the 1950s," University of Kansas, Lawrence, 4–6 October 1990), pp. 17–18; Michael Danielson, *The Politics of Exclusion* (New York: Columbia University Press, 1976), p. 12; John Bauman, *Public Housing, Race, and Renewal: Urban Planning in Philadelphia, 1920–1974* (Philadelphia: Temple University Press, 1987); Elaine Tyler May, *Homeward Bound: American Families in the Cold*

War Era (New York: Basic Books, 1988), pp. 169–70; Charles Hoch and Robert Slayton, *New Homeless and Old: Community and the Skid Row Hotel* (Philadelphia: Temple University Press, 1989); Robert Fairbanks, *Making Better Citizens: Housing Reform and the Community Development Strategy in Cincinnati, 1890–1960* (Urbana: University of Illinois Press, 1988), p. 148 and passim.

24. Jackson, *Crabgrass Frontier,* pp. 169–170; Parenti, *Democracy for the Few,* p. 111.

25. Douglas Miller and Marion Nowak, *The Fifties: The Way We Really Were* (Garden City, N.Y.: Doubleday, 1977), pp. 142–43. Eric Monkkonen's *America Becomes Urban* warns against romanticizing early transportation or blaming too many evils on the car, but the point remains that the dominance of the car, with its attendant problems of pollution and oil dependency, was not a result of free consumer choice alone; it stemmed from government decisions to allow private cars public funding for the "social overhead capital" investments they required, while treating public transport as private investment that must pay for itself.

26. Michael Katz, *In the Shadow of the Poorhouse: A Social History of Welfare in America* (New York: Basic Books, 1986), p. 244; Marian Edelman, *Families in Peril: An Agenda for Social Change* (Cambridge: Harvard University Press, 1987), p. 90; Mimi Abramovitz, *Regulating the Lives of Women* (Boston: South End Press, 1988), pp. 325–27.

27. Katz, *Shadow of the Poorhouse,* p. 269.

28. Charles Murray, *Losing Ground: American Social Policy, 1950–1980* (New York: Basic Books, 1984), p. 228. See also George Gilder, *Wealth and Poverty* (New York: Basic Books, 1981).

29. Edelman, *Families in Peril,* p. 47; David Broder, "The Chief Myth-Maker," *Washington Post National Weekly Edition,* 27 May–2 June 1991; Fred Harris and Rogers Wilkins, *Quiet Riots: Race and Poverty in the United States* (New York: Pantheon, 1988), p. 50.

30. Robert Greenstein, "Losing Faith in 'Losing Ground,'" *The New Republic,* 25 March 1985, p. 17; Katz, *Shadow of the Poorhouse,* p. 264; Sara McLanahan et al., *Losing Ground: A Critique* (University of Wisconsin Institute for Research on Poverty, Special Report no. 38, August 1985).

31. Sheldon Danziger and Peter Gottschalk, "The Poverty of *Losing Ground,*" *Challenge,* May–June 1985, p. 33; David Ellwood and Lawrence Summers, "Is Welfare Really the Problem?" *The Public Interest* 83 (1986): 64–65; Katz, *Shadow of the Poorhouse,* p. 264.

32. William Darity and Samuel Myers, "Does Welfare Dependency Cause Female Headship?" *Journal of Marriage and the Family* (November 1984): 770, and review of Murray, *Review of Black Political Economy* 19 (1986):

172; David Ellwood and Summers, "Poverty in America: Is Welfare the Answer or the Problem?" in *Fighting Poverty: What Works and What Doesn't*, ed. Sheldon Danziger and Daniel Weinberg (Cambridge: Harvard University Press, 1986), pp. 93–94; Sanford Schram, J. Patrick Turbett, and Paul Wilken, "Child Poverty and Welfare Benefits," *American Journal of Economics and Sociology* 47 (1988): 412.

33. Michael Katz, *The Undeserving Poor: From the War on Poverty to the War on Welfare* (New York: Pantheon, 1989), p. 175.

34. Ellwood and Summers, "Poverty in America," pp. 93–94; David Ellwood and Mary Jo Bane, "The Impact of AFDC on Family Structure and Living Arrangements," *Research in Labor Economics* 7 (1986): 139; Robert Moffitt, "Incentive Effects of the U.S. Welfare System: A Review," Institute for Research on Poverty Special Report (Madison: IRP, 1990), p. 50; Edelman, *Families in Peril*, p. 71; MaryLee Allen and Karen Pittman, *Welfare and Teen Pregnancy: What Do We Know? What Do We Do?* (Washington, D.C.: Children's Defense Fund, 1986).

35. Mark Rank, "Fertility Among Women on Welfare," *American Sociological Review* 54 (April 1989): 296; Edelman, *Families in Peril*, p. 71.

36. Moffitt, "Incentive Effects," pp. 91–92. The GAO report and other studies on this subject are summarized in Frances Fox Piven and Richard A. Cloward, "The Historical Sources of the Contemporary Relief Debate," in *The Mean Season: The Attack on the Welfare State,* ed. Fred Block, Richard Cloward, Barbara Ehrenreich, and Frances Fox Piven (New York: Pantheon, 1987), pp. 58–62.

37. Sanford Schram, J. Patrick Turbett, and Paul Wilken, "Child Poverty and Welfare Benefits: A Reassessment with State Data of the Claim that American Welfare Breeds Dependence," *American Journal of Economics and Sociology* 47 (1988): 417; Sanford Schram and Paul Wilken, "It's No 'Laffer' Matter: Claims that Increasing Welfare Aid Breeds Poverty and Dependence Fails Statistical Test," *American Journal of Economics and Sociology* 48 (1989): 213–16; Edelman, *Families in Peril*, p. 69; Committee on Ways and Means, U.S. House of Representatives, "Overview of Entitlement Programs," *1990 Green Book* (Washington, D.C., June 5, 1990); Kathryn Porter, *Making Jobs Work: What the Research Says About Effective Employment Programs for AFDC Recipients* (Washington, D.C.: Center on Budget and Policy Priorities, 1990).

38. Piven and Cloward, "Historical Sources of the Contemporary Relief Debate," p. 37; Robert Goodin, "Self-reliance versus the Welfare State," *Journal of Social Policy* 14 (1985): 40–41.

39. Ellwood and Summers, "Is Welfare Really the Problem?" pp. 72, 76–77.

40. William Graebner, *The Engineering of Consent: Democracy and Authority in Twentieth-Century America* (Madison: University of Wisconsin Press, 1987); Neal Peirce, "Bureaucrats Strangle Poor Neighborhoods," *The Olympian,* 26 November 1990.

41. Paul Mattvick, "Arts and the State," *The Nation,* 1 October 1990.

42. Isabel Sawhill, "Escaping the Fiscal Trap," *The American Prospect* (Spring 1990): 21.

43. Paul Taylor, "Like Taking Money from a Baby," *Washington Post National Weekly Edition,* 4–10 March 1991, p. 14; Alfred J. Kahn and Sheila B. Kammerman, "Social Assistance: An Eight-Country Overview," *The Journal* (Winter 1983–84): 93–112, and "Income Transfers and Mother-Only Families in Eight Countries," *Social Policy* (September 1983): 448–63.

44. Jackson, *Crabgrass Frontier,* p. 224; Alan Wolfe, *The Limits of Legitimacy* (New York: Free Press, 1977).

45. *Washington Post,* 29 October 1983, 1 January 1985, and 30 July 1989.

46. Paul Leonard, Cushing Dolbeare, and Edward Lazere, *A Place to Call Home: The Crisis in Housing for the Poor* (Washington, D.C.: Center on Budget and Policy Priorities, 1989), pp. 32, 34; Low Income Housing Information Service, *Special Memorandum* (Washington, D.C., April 1988).

47. John Kenneth Galbraith, *The Affluent Society* (Boston: Houghton Mifflin, 1958); Miller and Nowak, *The Fifties,* pp. 120–21.

48. Mark Baldassare, *Trouble in Paradise: The Suburban Transformation in America* (New York: Columbia University Press, 1986), pp. 7–8, 28, 148–49; Jackson, *Crabgrass Frontier,* p. 191.

49. Jon Teaford, *City and Suburb: The Political Fragmentation of Metropolitan America, 1850–1970* (Baltimore: Johns Hopkins University Press, 1979); Danielson, *Politics of Exclusion,* p. 17, Baldassare, *Trouble in Paradise,* p. 22.

50. Peter Shergold, "'Reefs of Roast Beef': The American Worker's Standard of Living in Comparative Perspective," in *American Labor and Immigration History. 1877–1920s: Recent European Research,* ed. Dirk Hoerder (Urbana: University of Illinois Press, 1983), p. 101; Lester Thurow, "The Budget Catastrophe and the Big Lie Behind It," *Washington Post National Weekly Edition,* 15–21 October 1990. One poll showed that 75 percent of Americans favored government intervention to end poverty but that 50 percent, including 50 percent of the poor, thought that government poverty programs do not work (*Seattle Times,* 4 October 1985).

51. "Tracing the Billions," *Wall Street Journal,* 5 November 1990.

52. Edward Kane, *The S&L Insurance Mess: How Did It Happen?* (Lanham, Md.: Urban Institute Press, 1989); Lynn Doti and Larry Schweikart, "Financing the Postwar Housing Boom in Phoenix and Los Angeles,

1945–1960," *Pacific Historical Review* 58 (1989); Howard Grundfest, "And the S&Ls May Be Only the Beginning," *Washington Post National Weekly Edition,* 2–8 July 1990; *The Urban Institute Policy and Research Report,* Spring 1990; Robert Kuttner, "The Poor Don't Have to Get Poorer," *Washington Post National Weekly Edition,* 12–18 November 1990.

53. "How Did It Happen?" *Newsweek,* 21 May 1990; Kane, *The S&L Insurance Mess; The Urban Institute Policy and Research Report,* Spring 1990; "Blame for the S&Ls," *Washington Post National Weekly Edition,* 4–10 June 1990; Robert Sherrill, "S&Ls, Big Banks and Other Triumphs of Capitalism," *The Nation,* 19 November 1990; Jackson, *Crabgrass Frontier,* p. 300; Kathleen Day, "The S&L Hall of Blame," *Washington Post National Weekly Edition,* 2–8 July 1990; *Wall Street Journal,* 5 November 1990.

54. Grant Foundation, *The Forgotten Half,* p. 28; Baldassare, *Trouble in Paradise,* p. 51; *Journal of American History* (September 1990): 741; Leonard, Dolbeare, and Lazere, *A Place to Call Home,* p. 33; *The Olympian,* 9 August and 8 October 1989; Kirstin Downey, "Living on the Brink," *Washington Post National Weekly Edition,* 7–13 January 1991; "The Crushing Cost of Housing," *Washington Post National Weekly Edition,* 12–18 February 1990.

55. *Wall Street Journal,* 5 November 1990.

56. Sawhill, "Escaping the Fiscal Trap," pp. 21–22.

57. Allan Carlson, "The Family and the Constitution," *The Family in America* 3 (1989): 8.

Chapter 5

1. *The Olympian,* 21 November 1989, p. 1A; Alan Wolfe, *Whose Keeper? Social Science and Moral Obligation* (Berkeley: University of California Press, 1989), pp. 83–85.

2. *The Family: Preserving America's Future* (Washington, D.C.: White House Working Group on the Family, 1986), frontispiece.

3. John Howard, "The Contra-Family Forces in the Culture," *Vital Speeches of the Day* 55 (1 January 1979): 189.

4. Betty Friedan, *The Second Stage* (New York: Summit Books, 1981); Pat Schroeder, *The Great American Family Tour* (New York: N. Hall, 1988); Christopher Lasch, *Haven in a Heartless World: The Family Besieged* (New York: Basic Books, 1977); Jean Bethke Elshtain, "Feminists Against the Family," *The Nation,* 17 November 1979; Coalition of Labor Union Women,

"Strengthening Families," April 1988; AFL-CIO Executive Council, "Work and Family: Essentials of a Decent Life," 21 February 1986; Andy Rooney, "What Every Kid Should Have Growing Up," *Liberal Opinion Week*, 24 December 1990, p. 26.

5. *Newsweek*, 4 January 1988, p. 40; *Advertising Age*, 17 November 1988, p. 2; *Los Angeles Times*, 26 December 1988, p. G1.

6. Richard Cohen, "Wretched Excess, 1989," *Washington Post*, 20 August 1989; *Newsweek*, 28 August 1989; Alex Heard, "Gonna Party Like It's 1999," *Mother Jones*, November 1989, p. 29.

7. Paul Colford, "Back to the Future," *Newsday*, 15 December 1989, II, 2; Dan Olmsted, "The Boom in Tradition," *USA Weekend*, 12–19 November 1989; Associated Press stories in *The Olympian*, 27 January 1991, 30 January 1991, 10 February 1991, 24 February 1991, 4 April 1991; *USA Today*, 29 November–1 December 1991, p. 1A.

8. *The Olympian*, 7 January 1990; Melwyn Kinder, *Going Nowhere Fast* (New York: Prentice Hall, 1990); *USA Weekend*, 15–17 March 1991; *Newsweek*, 12 November 1990, p. 24, and 17 December 1990, pp. 50–56; Paul Pearsall, *The Power of the Family* (New York: Doubleday, 1990); Amy Saltzman, *Downshifting: Reinventing Success on a Slower Track* (New York: HarperCollins, 1991); *New York Times*, 3 April 1991; *The Olympian*, 4 April 1991; *Time*, 8 April 1991, p. 58.

9. *Newsweek*, 12 November 1990, p. 54; *Newsweek*, 17 December 1990, p. 53, *USA Today*, 29 November–1 December 1991, p. A1.

10. *New York Times*, 5 February 1986, p. A1; Rooney, "What Every Kid Should Have," p. 26.

11. Burton Bledstein, *The Culture of Professionalism: The Middle Class and the Development of Higher Education* (New York: Norton, 1976), pp. 56–57; W. Norton Grubb and Marvin Lazerson, *Broken Promises: How Americans Fail Their Children* (New York: Basic Books, 1982), p. 283.

12. Stephanie Coontz, *The Social Origins of Private Life: A History of American Families, 1600–1900* (London: Verso, 1988), pp. 106–11, 180–97.

13. Joyce Appleby, *Capitalism and a New Social Order: The Republican Vision of the 1790s* (New York: New York University Press, 1984); Sean Wilentz, *Chants Democratic: New York City and the Rise of the American Working Class* (New York: Oxford University Press, 1984); Alan Dawley, *Class and Community: The Industrial Revolution in Lynn* (Cambridge: Harvard University Press, 1976); Ruth Bogin, "Petitioning and the New Moral Economy of Post-Revolutionary America," *William and Mary Quarterly* 45 (1988): 403; Alan Trachtenberg, *The Incorporation of America: Culture and Society in the Gilded Age* (New York: Hill and Wang, 1982), p. 6; Roland

Berthoff, "Conventional Mentality: Free Blacks, Women, and Business Corporations as Unequal Persons, 1820–1870," *Journal of American History* 76 (1989): 760.

14. Jon Roper, "Ideas of Democracy in America and Britain," *Midwest Quarterly* 30 (1989): 292; Garry Wills, *Inventing America: Jefferson's Declaration of Independence* (Garden City, N.Y.: Doubleday, 1978), p. 164.

15. Robert Bellah et al., *Habits of the Heart: Individualism and Commitment in American Life* (New York: Harper & Row, 1986), p. 55; Berthoff, "Conventional Mentality," p. 757; David Leverenz, *Manhood and the American Renaissance* (Ithaca, N.Y.: Cornell University Press, 1989), pp. 78–81.

16. Merle Curti, *The Growth of American Thought* (New York: Harper & Row, 1943), p. 469; George Fredrickson, *The Inner Civil War: Northern Intellectuals and the Crisis of the Union* (New York: Harper & Row, 1965), pp. 40, 14.

17. Len Gougeon, *Virtue's Hero: Emerson, Antislavery, and Reform* (Athens: University of Georgia Press, 1990), p. 340.

18. Wolfe, *Whose Keeper?*, p. 19; Thomas Bender, *Community and Social Change in America* (New Brunswick: Rutgers University Press, 1978), pp. 87–94, 112; Richard Brown, "The Emergence of Urban Society in Rural Massachusetts, 1760–1820," *Journal of American History* 61 (1974); Stuart Blumin, *The Urban Threshold: Growth and Change in a Nineteenth-Century American Community* (Chicago: University of Chicago Press, 1976); Nathan Rosenberg and L. E. Birdsell, Jr., *How the West Grew Rich: The Economic Transformation of the Industrial World* (New York: Basic Books, 1986), p. 183.

19. Richard Sennett, *The Fall of Public Man* (New York: Basic Books, 1977), pp. 91, 338; Wills, *Inventing America*, p. 289; Bellah et al., *Habits of the Heart*, p. 40.

20. Mary Ryan, *Cradle of the Middle Class: The Family in Oneida County, New York, 1790–1865* (New York: Cambridge University Press, 1981), pp. 105, 143; Nancy Hewitt, *Women's Activism and Social Change: Rochester, New York, 1822–1872* (Ithaca, N.Y.: Cornell University Press, 1984), p. 22; Mary Ryan, *The Empire of the Mother: American Writing about Domesticity, 1830–1860* (New York: Haworth Press, 1982), p. 145. See also Carroll Smith-Rosenberg, "Beauty, the Beast, and the Militant Woman," and "The Cross and the Pedestal," in *Disorderly Conduct: Visions of Gender in Victorian America*, ed. Carroll Smith-Rosenberg (New York: Knopf, 1985); Lori Ginzberg, *Women and the Work of Benevolence: Morality, Politics, and Class in the Nineteenth-Century United States* (New Haven: Yale University Press, 1990).

21. Ryan, *Empire of the Mother*, p. 97; Ryan, *Cradle of the Middle Class*,

p. 153; John Higham, *From Boundlessness to Consolidation: The Transformation of American Culture, 1848–1860* (Ann Arbor: University of Michigan Press, 1969); Suzanne Lebscock, *The Free Women of Petersburg: Status and Culture in a Southern Town, 1784–1860* (New York: Norton, 1984), pp. xvi, 231; Kathryn Sklar, *Catharine Beecher: A Study in Domesticity* (New Haven: Yale University Press, 1973); Gerda Lerner, *The Majority Finds Its Past: Placing Women in History* (New York: Oxford University Press, 1979).

22. Fredrickson, *Inner Civil War,* p. 183.

23. Fredrickson, *Inner Civil War,* pp. 193–94; Sidney Harring, *Policing a Class Society: The Experience of American Cities, 1865–1915* (New York: Rutgers University Press, 1983).

24. Robert Gallman, "Trends in the Size Distribution of Wealth in the Nineteenth Century. Some Speculations," in *Six Papers on the Size Distribution of Wealth and Income,* ed. Lee Soltow (New York: National Bureau of Economic Research, 1969); Kevin Phillips, *The Politics of Rich and Poor: Wealth and the American Electorate in the Reagan Aftermath* (New York: Random House, 1990), pp. 159–60, 164.

25. S. J. Kleinberg, *The Shadow of the Mills: Working-Class Families in Pittsburgh, 1870–1907* (Pittsburgh: University of Pittsburgh Press, 1989); Herbert Gutman, "Persistent Myths about the Afro-American Family," *Journal of Social History* 5 (1971–72); Paul Worthman, "Working-Class Mobility in Birmingham, Alabama, 1880–1914," in *Anonymous Americans: Explorations in Nineteenth-Century Social History,* ed. Tamara Hareven (Englewood Cliffs, N.J.: Prentice-Hall, 1971); Lawrence Goodwyn, *The Populist Moment: A Short History of the Agrarian Revolt in America* (New York: Oxford University Press, 1978), p. 12.

26. Arthur M. Schlesinger, *Paths to the Present* (New York: Houghton Mifflin, 1949); Arthur M. Schlesinger, Jr., *The Cycles of American History* (Boston: Houghton Mifflin, 1986), pp. 24, 28; Alan Trachtenberg, *The Incorporation of America: Culture and Society in the Gilded Age* (New York: Hill and Wang, 1982), p. 81.

27. Russell Conwell, *Acres of Diamonds* (New York: Harper & Row, 1943), pp. 18, 21; Joseph Carter, *The 'Acres of Diamonds' Man* (Philadephia: University of Pennsylvania Press, 1981), p. 634; John Cawelti, *Apostles of the Self-Made Man* (Chicago: University of Chicago Press, 1965), pp. 180, 188; Mark Hellstern, "The 'Me Gospel': An Examination of the Historical Roots of the Prosperity Emphasis Within Current Charismatic Theology," *Fides et Historia* 21 (1989): 81.

28. Fredrickson, *Inner Civil War,* p. 213; Eli Zaretsky, "The Place of the Family in the Origins of the Welfare State," in *Rethinking the Family: Some Feminist Questions,* ed. Barrie Thorne with Marilyn Yalom (White Plains,

N.Y.: Longman, 1982), p. 205; Andrew Carnegie, *The Gospel of Wealth and Other Timely Essays* (New York: Doubleday, 1933), p. 15.

29. David Montgomery, *Beyond Equality: Labor and the Radical Republicans, 1862–1872* (New York: Knopf, 1967), p. 382.

30. Stuart Blumin, *The Emergence of the Middle Class: Social Experience in the American City, 1760–1900* (New York: Cambridge University Press, 1989), pp. 275–85; Margaret Marsh, *Suburban Lives* (New Brunswick: Rutgers University Press, 1990); Roland Berthoff, *An Unsettled People: Social Order and Disorder in American History* (New York: Harper & Row, 1971), p. 383; Thomas Bender, *Toward an Urban Vision: Ideas and Institutions in Nineteenth-Century America* (Baltimore: Johns Hopkins University Press, 1975), pp. 179–84; John Gilkeson, Jr., *Middle-Class Providence, 1820–1940* (Princeton: Princeton University Press, 1986); Iver Bernstein, *The New York City Draft Riots: Their Significance for American Society and Politics in the Age of the Civil War* (New York: Oxford University Press, 1990); Mary Ann Clawson, *Constructing Brotherhood: Class, Gender, and Fraternalism* (Princeton: Princeton University Press, 1989), p. 173 and passim; Mark Carnes, *Secret Ritual and Manhood in Victorian America* (New Haven: Yale University Press, 1989).

31. Berthoff, *Unsettled People*, pp. 411–17; Martin Marty, *Righteous Empire: The Protestant Experience in America* (New York: Dial Press, 1970), p. 182.

32. Barbara Cross, *Bushnell*; Horace Bushnell, "The Age of Homespun," in *Work and Play; or Literary Varieties* (New York: n. p., 1886); Marty, *Righteous Empire*, p. 149; Trachtenberg, *Incorporation*, p. 81; Berthoff, *Unsettled People*, pp. 236–37.

33. Ray Ginger, *Age of Excess* (New York: Macmillan, 1975), pp. 8, 27; Matthew Josephson, *The Robber Barons* (New York: Harcourt, Brace, and World, 1962); Trachtenberg, *Age of Incorporation*, p. 90.

34. "The Two-Class American Society," *The Phyllis Schlafly Report* 19 (1986): 1.

35. Conwell, *Acres of Diamonds*, p. 32; Horatio Alger, *Ragged Dick and Mark the Matchboy* (New York: Collier, 1962); Cawelti, *Apostles*, pp. 112–13.

36. Richard Sennett, *The Fall of Public Man* (New York: Knopf, 1977), p. 20.

37. Marty, *Righteous Empire*, pp. 153, 168, 187; Ryan, *Empire of the Mother*, p. 97.

38. Coontz, *Social Origins*, pp. 226–29, 235; Sklar, *Catharine Beecher*; Mary Ryan, *Women in Public: Between Banners and Ballots, 1825–1880* (Bal-

timore: Johns Hopkins University Press, 1990), pp. 37, 52–53; Conwell, *Acres of Diamonds,* p. 22.

39. Goodwyn, *Populist Moment;* Trachtenberg, *Incorporation of America,* pp. 90–91; Michael Haines, "Industrial Work and the Family Life Cycle, 1889–1890," *Research in Economic History* 4 (1979); John Cumbler, *Working-Class Community in Industrial America: Work, Leisure, and Struggle in Two Industrial Cities, 1880–1930* (Westport, Conn.: Greenwood Press, 1979).

40. Conwell, *Acres of Diamonds,* pp. 31, 19–20.

41. Henry Ward Beecher, *Lectures to Young Men* (New York: n. p., 1850), and *Royal Truths* (New York: n. p., 1866); William Gerald McLoughlin, *The Meaning of Henry Ward Beecher: An Essay on the Shifting Values of Mid-Victorian America, 1840–1870* (New York: Knopf, 1970), pp. 99, 113, 147, 176; Marty, *Righteous Empire,* p. 150.

42. McLoughlin, *Beecher,* pp. 115–16.

43. Jacob Riis, *How the Other Half Lives: Studies Among the Tenements of New York* (New York: Hill and Wang, 1957); Trachtenberg, *Incorporation of America,* p. 127; Boyer, *Urban Masses,* p. 127; *Wall Street Journal,* 9 October 1989, p. 1A; *Boston Globe,* 11 April 1991, p. 11A.

44. Boyer, *Urban Masses,* pp. 127, 131; Robert Bremner, "Introduction," in Anthony Comstock, *Traps for the Young* [1883], ed. Robert Bremner (Cambridge: Harvard University Press, 1967), p. xv.

45. Heywood Broun and Margaret Leech, *Anthony Comstock, Roundsman of the Lord* (New York: Literary Guild of America, 1927), pp. 139–40; Irving Stone, *They Also Ran: The Story of the Men Who Were Defeated for the Presidency* (Garden City, N.Y.: Doubleday, 1966), pp. 231–32; Shelley Ross, *Fall from Grace: Sex, Scandal, and Corruption in American Politics from 1702 to the Present* (New York: Ballantine, 1988), p. 121; *New York Times,* 8 October 1884; Calvin Trillin, "Dirty Talk and Protector of Public Morals," *Liberal Opinion Week,* 24 December 1990.

46. Paul Boyer, *Urban Masses and Moral Order in America, 1820–1920* (Cambridge: Harvard University Press, 1978), p. 146; David Ward, *Poverty, Ethnicity, and the American City, 1840–1925: Changing Conceptions of the Slum and the Ghetto* (New York: Cambridge University Press, 1989); Cawelti, *Apostles,* p. 183.

47. Philip Bruce, *The Plantation Negro as Freeman* (Williamstown, Mass.: Corner House Publishers, 1970), pp. 5, 10, 19, 64, 132, 145; Georgie Anne Geyer, "Jesse Ducks Black Youths' Call for Help," *The Olympian,* 8 March 1990, p. A7, and "Americans Must Be More Self-reliant," *The Olympian,* 18 January 1990, p. A8.

48. Michael Katz, *Poverty and Policy in American History* (New York:

Academic Press, 1983), p. 193; Anthony Platt, *The Child Savers: The Invention of Delinquency* (Chicago: University of Chicago Press, 1969); Linda Gordon, *Heroes of their Own Lives: The Politics and History of Family Violence* (New York: Viking, 1988), pp. 33, 42; Mimi Abramowitz, *Regulating the Lives of Women* (Boston: South End Press, 1988), p. 167.

49. *The Olympian,* 9 August 1989, 21 September 1989, 3 November 1989, 23 May 1990, 31 October 1991.

50. *The Olympian,* 12 February 1990; Mary Grabar, "Pregnancy Police: If You're an Addict It's Now a Crime to Give Birth," *The Progressive,* December 1990, pp. 22, 24; *New York Times,* 3 April 1991.

51. Katha Pollitt, "A New Assault on Feminism," *The Nation,* 26 March 1990.

52. Daniel Rodgers, *Contested Truths: Keywords in American Politics Since Independence* (New York: Basic Books, 1987), pp. 222–23.

53. Michael Ignatieff, *The Needs of Strangers* (New York: Cambridge University Press, 1985), p. 14; David Montgomery, *The Fall of the House of Labor: The Workplace, the State, and American Labor Activism, 1865–1925* (New York: Cambridge University Press, 1989); Walter Dean Burnham, *The Current Crisis in American Politics* (New York: Oxford University Press, 1982); Goodwyn, *The Populist Moment,* pp. 264–82.

54. *The Olympian,* 21 and 29 November 1989.

55. Rodgers, *Contested Truths,* p. 224.

56. Sennett, *Fall of Public Man,* p. 220; Bellah et al., *Habits of the Heart,* pp. 71–72.

57. Sennett, *Fall of Public Man,* pp. 219–20; Thomas Bender, *Community and Social Change in America* (New Brunswick: Rutgers University Press, 1978), p. 148; Bellah et al., *Habits of the Heart,* p. 281; Michael McGerr, "Political Style and Women's Power, 1830–1930," *Journal of American History* (December 1990): 870, and *The Decline of Popular Politics: The American North, 1865–1928* (New York: Oxford University Press, 1986).

58. Shelley, *Fall from Grace;* Michael Woodiwiss, *Crime, Crusades, and Corruption: Prohibitions in the United States, 1900–1987* (Totowa, N.J.: Barnes & Noble, 1988).

59. For various points of view, see *Newsweek,* 3 July 1989, p. 38; *U.S. News and World Report,* 11 September 1989, p. 23; Georgie Ann Geyer, "Adversarial Media Mislead Our Nation," *The Olympian,* 26 October 1989; Linda Witt, "Our Nation Can't Escape Blame for Those Elected," *The Olympian,* 14 April 1991; Mike Royko, "Hard to Separate Politics from the Trash," *Chicago Tribune,* 10 April 1991; George Will, "Kelly Labors in Sewers of Journalism," *The Olympian,* 14 April 1991; Larry Sabato, *Feeding*

Frenzy: How Attack Journalism Has Transformed American Politics (New York: Free Press, 1991); Suzanne Garment, *Scandal: The Culture of Mistrust in American Politics* (New York: Times Books, 1991).

60. Sennett, *Fall of Public Man,* p. 6; Joseph Featherstone, "Family Matters," *Harvard Educational Review* 49 (1979): 33.

61. Eli Zaretsky, "The Place of the Family in the Origins of the Welfare State," in *Rethinking the Family: Some Feminist Questions,* ed. Barrie Thorne with Marilyn Yalom (White Plains, N.Y.: Longman, 1982), p. 218.

Chapter 6

1. *American Medical News,* 11 March 1988, p. 1.

2. Marianne Jacobbi, "Your Wife May Never Wake Up," *Good Housekeeping,* June 1990, pp. 161, 214–17.

3. William Donahue, "Children's Rights: The Ideological Road to Sweden," *The Family in America* 2 (November 1988): 11.

4. "Forbidden Advice," *Washington Post National Weekly Edition,* 3–9 June 1991; Alexander Cockburn, "Out of the Mouths of Babes: Child Abuse and the Abuse of Adults," *The Nation,* 12 February 1990; John M. Johnson, "The Changing Concept of Child Abuse and Its Impact on the Identity of Family Life," in *The American Family and the State,* ed. Joseph Peden and Fred Glahe (San Francisco: Pacific Research Institute for Public Policy, 1986).

5. Elizabeth Pleck, *Domestic Tyranny: The Making of Social Policy Against Family Violence from Colonial Times to the Present* (New York: Oxford University Press, 1987), pp. 177, 197–98; Mimi Abramovitz, *Regulating the Lives of Women: Social Welfare Policy from Colonial Times to the Present* (Boston: South End Press, 1988), p. 358.

6. Claudia Mangel, "Licensing Parents: How Feasible?" *Family Law Quarterly* 22 (1988); *New York Times,* 9 December 1990.

7. Bradley Miller, "The Right's Nanny Agenda is Running for Your Life," *Washington Post National Weekly Edition,* 10–16 June 1991; Wendy McElroy, ed., *Freedom, Feminism, and the State: An Overview of Individualist Feminism* (Washington, D.C.: Cato Institute, 1986); Siegrun Fox, "Rights and Obligations: Critical Feminist Theory, the Public Bureaucracy, and Policies for Mother-Only Families," *Public Administration Review* 47 (1987): 438.

8. White House Working Group on the Family, *The Family: Preserving America's Future* (Washington, D.C., November 13, 1986), pp. 3, 4.

9. Mona Charon, "Family Is Issue Behind Gay Ordinance," *Tacoma News Tribune*, 9 July 1989.

10. George Catlin, *Letters and Notes on the Manners, Customs and Conditions of the North American Indians*, vol. 1 (New York: Dover, 1973), p. 122; James Adair, *The History of the American Indians* (New York: Johnson Reprint Corporation, 1925), p. 428; Baron LaHontan, *New Voyages to North America*, vol. 2, ed. Reuben Thwaites (Ann Arbor: University Microfilms, 1966), p. 463.

11. Leslie Howard Owens, *This Species of Property: Slave Life and Culture in the Old South* (New York: Oxford, 1976); Edmund Morgan, *The Puritan Family: Religion and Domestic Relations in Seventeenth-Century New England* (New York: Harper & Row, 1966), pp. 78, 88, 100, 142, 148; Eli Zaretsky, "The Place of the Family in the Origins of the Welfare State," in *Rethinking the Family: Some Feminist Questions*, ed. Barrie Thorne with Marilyn Yalom (White Plains, N.Y.: Longman, 1982), p. 197; John Demos, *A Little Commonwealth: Family Life in Plymouth Colony* (New York: Oxford, 1970), p. 183.

12. Morgan, *The Puritan Family*, p. 45; Julia Cherry Spruill, *Women's Life and Work in the Southern Colonies* (New York: Norton, 1972); Rhys Isaac, *The Transformation of Virginia, 1740–1790* (Chapel Hill: University of North Carolina Press, 1982).

13. Nancy Cott, "Eighteenth-Century Family and Social Life Revealed in Massachusetts Divorce Records," in *A Heritage of Her Own*, ed. Nancy Cott and Elizabeth Pleck (New York: Simon & Schuster, 1979), p. 110; Mary Ryan, *Cradle of the Middle Class: The Family in Oneida County, New York, 1790–1865* (New York: Cambridge University Press, 1983), pp. 24–43.

14. Michael Katz, *Reconstructing American Education* (Cambridge, Mass.: Harvard University Press, 1987), and "Origins of the Institutional State," *Marxist Perspectives* (Winter 1978): 6–22; Gerald Grob, *Mental Institutions in America: Social Policy to 1875* (New York: Free Press, 1973); David Rothman, *The Discovery of the Asylum: Social Order and Disorder in the New Republic* (Boston: Little, Brown, 1971), p. 237; Allen Steinberg, *The Transformation of Criminal Justice: Philadelphia, 1800–1880* (Chapel Hill: University of North Carolina Press, 1989); Barbara Brenzel, "Domestication as Reform: A Study of the Socialization of Wayward Girls, 1856–1905," *Harvard Educational Review* 50 (1980): 205, 208; Peter Tyor and Jamil Zainaldin, "Asylum and Society: An Approach to Institutional Change," *Journal of Social History* 13 (1979); Walter Trattner, *From Poor Law to Welfare State: A History of Social Welfare in America* (New York: Free Press, 1984).

15. Zaretsky, "The Place of the Family," p. 203; W. Norton Grubb and

Marvin Lazerson, *Broken Promises: How Americans Fail Their Children* (New York: Basic Books, 1982), p. 19. See also note 14.

16. Michael Grossberg, *Governing the Hearth: Law and the Family in Nineteenth-Century America* (Chapel Hill: University of North Carolina Press, 1985), p. 298.

17. Steven Mintz, "Regulating the American Family," *Journal of Family History* 14 (1989): 393; Grossberg, *Governing the Hearth,* pp. 259–68.

18. Jacobus tenBroek, *Family Law and the Poor,* ed. Joel Handler (Westport: Greenwood Press, 1971), pp. 47–50.

19. Mintz, "Regulating the Family," pp. 388, 395; Michael Grossberg, "Who Gets the Child? Custody, Guardianship, and the Rise of a Judicial Patriarchy in Nineteenth-Century America," *Feminist Studies* 9 (1983): 237, 247; Grossberg, *Governing the Hearth,* pp. 33–63, 237–43, 300; Eileen Boris and Peter Bardaglio, "Gender, Race, and Class: The Impact of the State on the Family and the Economy, 1790–1945," in *Families and Work,* ed. Naomi Gerstel and Harriet Gross (Philadelphia: Temple University Press, 1987), p. 135.

20. Christine Stansell, *City of Women: Sex and Class in New York, 1789–1860* (New York: Knopf, 1986), p. 210.

21. Maxwell Bloomfield, *American Lawyers in a Changing Society, 1776–1876* (Cambridge: Harvard University Press, 1976), p. 132.

22. William Graham Sumner, "The Forgotten Man," in *Social Darwinism: Selected Essays,* ed. Stow Persons (Englewood Cliffs, N.J.: Prentice-Hall, 1963), p. 129.

23. Grossberg, *Governing the Hearth,* pp. 136–46, 170–77; Mintz, "Regulating the Family," p. 396; Boris and Bardaglio, "Gender, Race, and Class," p. 142; Joan Hoff-Wilson, "The Unfinished Revolution: Changing Legal Status of U.S. Women," *Signs* 13 (1987): 8; Claudia Goldin, *Understanding the Gender Gap: An Economic History of American Women* (New York: Oxford University Press, 1990), p. 189.

24. Anthony Platt, *The Child Savers: The Invention of Delinquency* (Chicago: University of Chicago Press, 1969), p. 111.

25. Linda Gordon, *Woman's Body, Woman's Right* (New York: Grossman, 1976); James Mohr, *Abortion in America: The Origins and Evolution of National Policy* (New York: Oxford, 1978); Grossberg, *Governing the Hearth,* pp. 187 and 156–95.

26. Grossberg, *Governing the Hearth,* pp. 147–49; Michael Katz, *In the Shadow of the Poorhouse: A Social History of Welfare in America* (New York: Basic Books, 1986), p. 184.

27. Vandepol, "Dependent Children," pp. 224–25; Johnson, "Changing Concept of Child Abuse," p. 267; Trattner, *Poor Law to Welfare State,* pp.

71, 95; Michael Katz, *Poverty and Policy in American History* (New York: Academic Press, 1983), p. 235; Thomas Bender, *Toward an Urban Vision: Ideas and Institutions in Nineteenth-Century America* (Lexington: University Press of Kentucky, 1975), pp. 154–55.

28. Katz, *Shadow of the Poorhouse,* p. 77; Mimi Abramovitz, *Regulating the Lives of Women: Social Welfare Policy from Colonial Times to the Present* (Boston: South End Press, 1988), p. 167.

29. Peter Holloran, *Boston's Wayward Children: Social Services for Homeless Children, 1830–1930* (Rutherford, N.J.: Fairleigh Dickinson University Press, 1989); Vandepol, "Dependent Children," p. 227; Linda Gordon, *Heroes of Their Own Lives: The Politics and History of Family Violence, Boston 1880–1960* (New York: Viking, 1988), p. 42.

30. Katz, *Reconstructing American Education,* p. 116; Platt, *The Child Savers,* pp. 60, 176.

31. On the commitment of Progressives to these values, see Gabriel Kolko, *The Triumph of Conservatism* (New York: Free Press, 1963); Martin Sklar, *The Corporate Reconstruction of American Capitalism, 1890–1916: The Market, the Law, and Politics* (Cambridge, England: Cambridge University Press, 1988); Guy Alchon, *The Invisible Hand of Planning: Capitalism, Social Science, and the State in the 1920s* (Princeton: Princeton University Press, 1985); R. Jeffry Lustig, *Corporate Liberalism: The Origins of Modern American Political Theory, 1890–1920* (Berkeley: University of California Press, 1982); Edward Greenberg, *Capitalism and the American Political Ideal* (Armonk, N.Y.: M. E. Sharpe, 1985), pp. 83–92.

32. Katz, *Shadow of the Poorhouse,* pp. 120–21, 126; Rothman, *Conscience and Convenience,* p. 9.

33. Theda Skocpol, *Protecting Soldiers and Mothers: The Politics of Social Provision in the United States, 1870s–1920s* (Cambridge: Harvard University Press, forthcoming).

34. Susan Lehrer, *Origins of Protective Legislation for Women, 1905–1925* (Albany: State University of New York Press, 1987), p. 236; Boris and Bardaglio, "Gender, Race, and Class," p. 143; David Nasaw, *Children of the City: At Work and at Play* (New York: Oxford, 1985), pp. 138–206; Gordon, *Heroes of Their Own Lives,* p. 131.

35. Katz, *Shadow of the Poorhouse,* pp. 115, 128–29.

36. Ellen Ryerson, *The Best-Laid Plans: America's Juvenile Court Experiment* (New York: Hill and Wang, 1978); Mintz, "Regulating the Family," p. 398; Platt, *The Child-Savers,* pp. 69, 99, 135–45; John Sutton, *Stubborn Children: Controlling Delinquency in the United States, 1640–1981* (Berkeley: University of California Press, 1988); Susan Tiffin, *In Whose Best Interest? Child Welfare Reform in the Progressive Era* (Westport, Conn.: Greenwood Press,

1982), p. 286; Willard Gaylin et al., *Doing Good: The Limits of Benevolence* (New York: Pantheon, 1978); David Rothman, *Conscience and Convenience: The Asylum and Its Alternatives in Progressive America* (Boston: Little, Brown, 1980), pp. 363–64.

37. Rothman, *Conscience and Convenience,* p. 252.

38. Boris and Bardaglio, "Gender, Race, and Class," p. 142.

39. S. J. Kleinberg, *The Shadow of the Mills: Working-class Families in Pittsburgh, 1879–1907* (Pittsburgh: University of Pittsburgh Press, 1989), pp. 278–82; Gwendolyn Wright, *Building the Dream: A Social History of Housing in America* (New York: Pantheon, 1981), pp. 126, 127.

40. John Modell and Tamara Hareven, "Urbanization and the Malleable Household: An Examination of Boarding and Lodging in American Families," *Journal of Marriage and the Family* 35 (August 1973): 468–70; Wright, *Building the Dream,* pp. 125–26; Scott Davis, *The World of Patience Gromes: Making and Unmaking a Black Community* (Lexington: University Press of Kentucky, 1988), p. 147.

41. Mark Leff, "Consensus for Reform: The Mothers' Pension Movement in the Progressive Era," *Social Service Review* 47 (1973): 401, 412; Tiffin, *In Whose Best Interest?,* p. 132.

42. Gordon, *Heroes of Their Own Lives,* p. 75; Zaretsky, "Place of the Family," pp. 210, 215; Linda Gordon, "The New Feminist Scholarship on the Welfare State," in *Women, the State, and Welfare,* ed. Linda Gordon (Madison: University of Wisconsin Press, 1990), p. 19; Leff, "Consensus for Reform," pp. 410, 415.

43. Gwendolyn Mink, "The Lady and the Tramp: Gender, Race, and the Origin of the American Welfare State," in Gordon, *Women, Welfare, and the State;* Boris and Bardaglio, "Race, Gender, and Class," p. 143; Carol Joffe, *Friendly Intruders: Childcare Professionals and Family Life* (Berkeley: University of California Press, 1977), p. 6.

44. Abramovitz, *Regulating the Lives of Women,* pp. 210–314; Steve Fraser and Gary Gerstle, *The Rise and Fall of the New Deal Order, 1930–1980* (Princeton: Princeton University Press, 1989); Jill Quadagno, "Race, Class, and Gender in the U.S. Welfare State," *American Sociological Review* 55 (1990): 14–15; ibid., *The Transformation of Old Age Security: Class and Politics in the American Welfare State* (Chicago: University of Chicago Press, 1988); ibid., "Women's Access to Pensions and the Structure of Eligibility Rules: Systems of Production and Reproduction," *Sociological Quarterly* 29 (1988): 542; Eileen Boris, "Regulating Industrial Homework: The Triumph of 'Sacred Motherhood,'" *Journal of American History* 71 (1985): 749; Eileen Boris and Peter Bardaglio, "The Transformation of Patriarchy: The Historic Role of the State," in *Families, Politics, and Public Policy: A Feminist Dialogue*

on Women and the State, ed. Irene Diamond (New York: Longman, 1983), p. 87, and "Gender, Race, and Class," pp. 144–46.

45. Barbara Nelson, "The Origins of the Two-Channel Welfare State," in Gordon, *Women, the State, and Welfare,* p. 133.

46. Gordon, *Heroes of Their Own Lives,* p. 166; Elizabeth Pleck, *Domestic Tyranny: The Making of Social Policy Against Family Violence from Colonial Times to the Present* (New York: Oxford University Press, 1987), p. 197.

47. Francis Fox Piven and Richard Cloward, *Regulating the Poor: The Functions of Public Welfare* (New York: Vintage, 1971); Grubb and Lazerson, *Broken Promises,* pp. 27 and 44; Leff, "Consensus for Reform," pp. 413–14; Gordon, *Heroes of Their Own Lives,* p. 79; Andrew Hacker, "Getting Rough on the Poor," *New York Review of Books,* 13 October 1988, p. 12; Patricia Horn, "Creating a Family Policy," *Dollars and Sense,* January–February 1990; Laura Udesky, "Welfare Reform and Its Victims," *The Nation,* 24 September 1990; Hoff-Wilson, "Unfinished Revolution," p. 13.

48. Richard Mechel, *Save the Babies: American Public Health Reform and the Prevention of Infant Mortality, 1850–1921* (Baltimore: Johns Hopkins University Press, 1970); Abramovitz, *Regulating the Lives of Women,* pp. 324–28; Jean Bethke Elshtain, *Power Trips and Other Journeys: Essays in Feminism as Civic Discourse* (Madison: University of Wisconsin Press, 1990); William Graebner, *The Engineering of Consent: Democracy and Authority in Twentieth-Century America* (Madison: University of Wisconsin Press, 1987); Christopher Lasch, *Haven in a Heartless World: The Family Besieged* (New York: Basic Books, 1977); Nigel Parton, *The Politics of Child Abuse* (New York: St. Martin's, 1985).

49. C. Henry Kempe et al., "The Battered-Child Syndrome," *Journal of the American Medical Association* 181 (1962); Pleck, *Domestic Tyranny.*

50. Gaylin et al., *Doing Good,* p. 93; Abramovitz, *Regulating the Lives of Women,* pp. 313–14, 331–32; tenBroek, *Family Law,* pp. 198–202.

51. *Bowers* v. *Hardwick* 478, 186 (1986), discussed in Malcolm Feeley and Samuel Krislov, eds., *Constitutional Law* (Glenview, Ill.: Scott Foresman, 1990), pp. 903–7.

52. Mintz, "Regulating the American Family," p. 402; Martha Minow, "Changing Legal Conceptions of Family" (Paper presented to Wheaton College Conference on Families and Change, June 1990), and "Redefining Families: Who's In and Who's Out?" *University of Colorado Law Review* 62 (1991).

53. Rosalind Petchesky, *Abortion and Women's Choice* (Boston: Northeastern University Press, 1985), pp. 304–11.

54. Phyllis Beck, "A Balancing Act," in *Changing Families,* ed. Irving Sigel and Luis Laosa (New York: Plenum, 1983).

55. "Children Lost in the Quagmire," *Newsweek,* 13 May 1991; Beck,

"Balancing Act," p. 74; Pleck, *Domestic Tyranny,* p. 85; Mintz, "Regulating the American Family," p. 404; Bob Greene, "Sarah Gets a New Chance for Justice," *Liberal Opinion Week,* 4 March 1991, p. 29.

56. *Los Angeles Times,* 22 February 1989, p. 2A.

57. Linda Gordon and Allen Hunter, "Sex, Family and the New Right," *Radical America* 11 (1977): 23–24.

58. For the argument about subversion of parental authority, see Allan Carlson, *Family Questions: Reflections on the American Social Crisis* (New Brunswick: Transaction Books, 1988), p. xvii; Christopher Lasch, "Life in the Therapeutic State," *New York Review of Books,* 12 June 1980; James Dobson, *Straight Talk to Men and Their Wives* (Waco, Tex.: Word Books, 1982). For the preservation of patriarchy argument see Boris and Bardaglio, "The Transformation of Patriarchy," p. 85; Mary McIntosh, "The State and the Oppression of Women," in *Feminism and Materialism: Women and Modes of Production,* ed. Annette Kuhn and Ann Marie Wolpe (London: Routledge and Kegan Paul, 1978); Zillah Eisenstein, ed., *Capitalist Patriarchy and the Case for Socialist Feminism* (New York: Monthly Review Press, 1978); Barbara Ehrenreich and Deirdre English, *For Her Own Good: One Hundred and Fifty Years of the Experts' Advice to Women* (New York: Anchor, 1978); Kathy Ferguson, *The Feminist Case Against Bureaucracy* (Philadelphia: Temple University Press, 1984).

59. Allan Carlson, "How Uncle Sam Got in the Family's Way," *Wall Street Journal,* 20 April 1988, p. 2A, and "Is Social Security Pro-Family?" *Policy Review* (Fall 1987): 49; Nancy Folbre, "The Pauperization of Motherhood: Patriarchy and Public Policy in the United States," in *Families and Work,* ed. Gerstel and Gross, p. 494.

60. *Seattle Times,* 12 August 1991; Carol Brown, "Mothers, Fathers and Children: From Private to Public Patriarchy," in *Women and Revolution,* ed. Lydia Sargent (Boston: South End Press, 1981), pp. 258–59.

61. Molly Ladd-Taylor, *Raising a Baby the Government Way: Mothers' Letters to the Children's Bureau, 1915–1932* (New Brunswick: Rutgers University Press, 1986), p. 62 and passim; Joseph Featherstone, "Family Matters," *Harvard Educational Review* 49 (1979): 45; Gordon, *Heroes of Their Own Lives,* p. 105; Sherri Broder, "Informing the 'Cruelty': The Monitoring of Respectability in Philadelphia's Working-Class Neighborhoods in the Late Nineteenth Century," *Radical America* (July–August 1987): 34; Seth Koven and Sonya Michel, "Womanly Duties: Maternalist Politics and the Origins of Welfare States in France, Germany, Great Britain, and the United States, 1880–1920," *American Historical Review* 25 (1990): 1077, 1094, 1103.

62. Robert Nisbet, "Foreword," in Peden and Glahe, eds., *The American Family and the State,* pp. xxiii, xxvi.

63. Victor Ehrenberg, *The Greek State* (New York: Norton, 1964); W. K. Lacey, *The Family in Classical Greece* (Ithaca, N.Y.: Cornell University Press, 1968), p. 73; Sherry Ortner, "The Virgin and the State," *Michigan Discussions in Anthropology* 2 (1976); Ruby Rohrlich, "State Formation in Sumer and the Subjugation of Women," *Feminist Studies* 6 (1980); Georges Duby, *A History of Private Life, Vol. 2. Revelations of the Medieval World* (Cambridge: Harvard University Press, 1988); Roger Chartier, *A History of Private Life, Vol. 3. Passions of the Renaissance* (Cambridge: Harvard University Press, 1990); Wolfe, *Whose Keeper?*, p. 126.

64. Robert Wuthnow, *The Restructuring of American Religion: Society and Faith Since World War II* (Princeton: Princeton University Press, 1988); Albert Hirschmann, *Shifting Involvements: Private Interests and Public Action* (Princeton: Princeton University Press, 1982); Alasdair MacIntyre, *After Virtue: A Study in Moral Theory* (Notre Dame: University of Notre Dame Press, 1984), p. 33.

65. "What Price Privacy?" *Consumer Reports,* May 1991, pp. 356, 357; *Newsweek,* 3 June 1991; Daniel Mendel-Black and Evelyn Richards, "They Know Your Name, Bank and Cereal Number," *Washington Post National Weekly Edition,* 28 January–3 February 1991.

66. Featherstone, "Family Matters," p. 47; Fran Sussner Rodgers and Charles Rodgers, "Business and the Facts of Family Life," *Harvard Business Review* (November–December 1989): 128; Sheila Akabas, "Reconciling the Demands of Work With the Needs of Families," *Families in Society: The Journal of Contemporary Human Services* (June 1990).

67. Alida Brill, *Nobody's Business: The Paradoxes of Privacy* (Reading, Mass.: Addison-Wesley, 1990).

68. Grossberg, *Governing the Hearth,* pp. 293–95; Stephen Morse, "Family Law in Transition: From Traditional Families to Individual Liberty," in Virginia Tufte and Barbara Myerhoff, *Changing Images of the Family* (New Haven: Yale University Press, 1979), pp. 342–48; Rothman, *Conscience and Convenience.*

69. Jerold Auerbach, *Unequal Justice: Lawyers and Social Change in Modern America* (New York: Oxford, 1976).

70. Mary Ann Glendon, *Abortion and Divorce and Western Law* (Cambridge: Harvard University Press, 1987), pp. 99–100 and passim. See also Brill, *Nobody's Business;* Martha Fineman, "Dominant Discourse, Professional Language, and Legal Change in Child Custody Decisionmaking," *Harvard Law Review* 101 (1988).

71. Michael Woodiwiss, *Crime, Crusades, and Corruption: Prohibitions in the United States, 1900–1987* (Totowa, N.J.: Barnes & Noble, 1988), p. 1.

Chapter 7

1. Barbara Dafoe Whitehead, "The Family in an Unfriendly Culture," *Family Affairs* 3 (1990): 2; and "Two Languages of Family," *Atlanta Journal/Constitution,* 3 April 1990.

2. Susan Faludi, *Backlash: The Undeclared War Against American Women* (New York: Crown, 1991).

3. Christopher Lasch, *Haven in a Heartless World: The Family Besieged* (New York: Basic Books, 1977), p. xvi.

4. Edward Hoffman, "Pop Psychology and the Rise of Anti-Child Ideology, 1966–1974," *The Family in America* 5 (1991): 1; Allan Carlson, *Family Questions: Reflections on the American Social Crisis* (New Brunswick: Transaction Books,1988), p. 131.

5. Sylvia Hewlett, *A Lesser Life: The Myth of Women's Liberation in America* (New York: Warner Books, 1986), p. 333; Claudia Wallis, "Onward, Women!" *Time,* 4 December 1989.

6. Betty Steele, *The Feminist Takeover: Patriarchy to Matriarchy in Two Decades* (Gaithersburg, Md.: Human Life International, 1987), p. 3; Jane Crain, "The Feminine Mistake," *Chronicles,* March 1990, p. 36; Maggie Gallagher, *Enemies of Eros: How the Sexual Revolution Is Killing Family, Marriage, and Sex and What We Can Do About It* (Chicago: Bonus Books, 1989), pp. 56–57. On the retreat of some feminists, see Faludi, *Backlash.*

7. James Johnson, "Death Grief, and Motherhood: The Woman Who Inspired Mother's Day," *West Virginia History* 39 (1978); W. R. Higginbotham, "The Mother of Mother's Day," *San Francisco Chronicle,* 12 May 1985; "Mother's Day Origins and Tradition," *Triad Woman,* May 1985.

8. Indira Clark, "Mother's Day," *Woman's Compendium,* May–June 1987, p. 15. See also Louise Tharp, *Three Saints and a Sinner: Julia Ward Howe, Loyisa, Annie, and Sam Ward* (Boston: Little, Brown, 1956), p. 351; Laura Richards, *Julia Ward Howe, 1819–1910* (Dunwoody, Calif.: N. S. Berg, 1970), pp. 319, 345; Deborah Pickman Clifford, *Mine Eyes Have Seen the Glory: A Biography of Julia Ward Howe* (Boston: Little, Brown, 1979), p. 187.

9. James Johnson, "How Mother Got Her Day," *American Heritage* 30 (1979).

10. *Proceedings of the Sixty-third Congress,* sess. 2, res. 10–13 (Washington, D.C., 1914), p. 770; Johnson, "How Mother Got Her Day"; *Ladies' Home Journal,* 7 May 1914, p. 28.

11. E. Robert McHenry, ed., *Famous American Women: A Biographical Dictionary from Colonial Times to the Present* (New York: Dover, 1983),

pp. 209–10; Jane Hatch and George Douglas, *The American Book of Days* (New York: Wilson, 1978), pp. 439–40; Johnson, "How Mother Got Her Day," pp. 20–21.

12. Paula Fass, *The Damned and the Beautiful: American Youth in the 1920s* (New York: Oxford, 1977), p. 55; Barbara Laslett, "The Family as a Public and Private Institution: An Historical Perspective," *Journal of Marriage and the Family* 35 (1973): 482n4.

13. Claudia Goldin, *Understanding the Gender Gap: On the Economic History of American Women* (New York: Oxford, 1990), pp. 10–57; Nancy Cott, *The Bonds of Womanhood* (New Haven: Yale University Press, 1977), p. 67; Alan Dawley, *Class and Community: The Industrial Revolution in Lynn* (Cambridge: Harvard University Press, 1976); Mary Blewett, *Men, Women, and Work: Class, Gender, and Protest in the New England Show Industry, 1780–1910* (Urbana: University of Illinois Press, 1988).

14. Joan Jenson, "Cloth, Butter and Boarders: Women's Household Production for the Market," *The Review of Political Economics* 12 (1980); Christine Bose, "Household Resources and U.S. Women's Work," *American Sociological Review* 49 (1984): 476; Christine Bose, Roslyn Feldman, and Natalie Sokoloff, eds., *Hidden Aspects of Women's Work* (Westport, Conn.: Praeger, 1987); Barbara Bergmann, *The Economic Emergence of Women* (New York: Basic Books, 1986), p. 19.

15. Lynn Weiner, *From Working Girl To Working Mother: The Female Labor Force in the United States, 1820–1980* (Chapel Hill: University of North Carolina Press, 1985), pp. 83–84.

16. Andrew Cherlin, *Marriage, Divorce, Remarriage* (Cambridge: Harvard University Press, 1981), pp. 65–66; Claudia Goldin, *Understanding the Gender Gap: On the Economic History of American Women* (New York: Oxford, 1990), p. 159.

17. Susan Strasser, *Never Done: A History of American Housework* (New York: Pantheon, 1982), pp. 78–84, 102–3; Ellen Rothman, *Hands and Hearts: A History of Courtship in America* (New York: Basic Books, 1984), pp. 265–67.

18. Goldin, *Understanding the Gender Gap,* pp. 123, 159; Clair Brown, "Home Production for Use in a Market Economy," in *Rethinking the Family: Some Feminist Questions,* ed. Barrie Thorne with Marilyn Yalom (White Plains, N.Y.: Longman, 1982); Strasser, *Never Done,* pp. 242–62; Joann Vanek, "Time Spent in Housework," in *A Heritage of Her Own,* ed. Nancy Cott and Elizabeth Pleck (New York: Simon & Schuster, 1979), p. 503; Ruth Schwartz Cowan, *More Work for Mother: The Ironies of Household Technology from the Open Hearth to the Microwave* (New York: Basic Books, 1983).

19. Goldin, *Understanding the Gender Gap,* p. 138; Cindy Aron, *Ladies and Gentlemen of the Civil Service* (New York: Oxford, 1987); Winifred Wandersee, *Women's Work and Family Values, 1920–1940* (Cambridge: Harvard University Press, 1981); Susan Hartmann, *The Home Front and Beyond: American Women in the 1940s* (Boston: Twayne Publishers, 1982), p. 17; Edward Kain, *The Myth of Family Decline: Understanding Families in a World of Rapid Social Change* (Lexington, Mass.: Lexington Books, 1990), p. 98.

20. Robert Lynd and Helen Lynd, *Middletown: A Study in American Culture* (New York: Harcourt Brace Jovanovich, 1956 [1929]), p. 29.

21. Lois Scharf, *To Work and to Wed: Female Employment, Feminism, and the Great Depression* (Westport, Conn.: Greenwood Press, 1980); Mary Ryan, *Womanhood in America: From Colonial Times to the Present* (New York: Franklin Watts, 1975), p. 315; Ruth Milkman, "Women's Work and Economic Crisis: Some Lessons of the Great Depression," *Review of Radical Political Economics* 81 (1976): 80.

22. Milkman, "Women's Work and Economic Crisis," pp. 81–85; Glen Elder, *Children of the Great Depression: Social Change in Life Experience* (Berkeley: University of California Press, 1974).

23. Elyce Rotella, *From Home to Office: U.S. Women at Work, 1870–1930* (Ann Arbor: UMI Research Press, 1981); Kathy Peiss, *Cheap Amusements: Working Women and Leisure in Turn-of-the-Century New York* (Philadelphia: Temple University Press, 1986); JoAnne Meyerowitz, *Women Adrift: Independent Wage Earners in Chicago, 1880–1930* (Chicago: University of Chicago Press, 1988); Goldin, *Understanding the Gender Gap,* p. 117; Leslie Woodcock Tentler, *Wage-Earning Women: Industrial Work and Family Life in the United States, 1900–1930* (New York: Oxford, 1979).

24. Nancy Folbre, "The Pauperization of Motherhood: Patriarchy and Public Policy in the United States," in *Families and Work,* ed. Naomi Gerstel and Harriet Gross (Philadelphia: Temple University Press, 1987), p. 499; William Chafe, *The American Woman: Her Changing Social, Economic, and Political Roles, 1920–1970* (New York: Oxford, 1972), pp. 142, 183; Susan Hartmann, *The Home Front and Beyond: American Women in the 1940s* (Boston: Twayne Publishers, 1982), p. 21; Ryan, *Womanhood in America,* p. 317; Amy Kesselman, *Fleeting Opportunities: Women Shipyard Workers in Portland and Vancouver during World War II and Reconversion* (Albany: State University of New York Press, 1990).

25. Sheila Tobias and Lisa Anderson, "What Really Happened to Rosie the Riveter?" *MSS Modular Publications* 9 (1973); Ruth Milkman, *Gender at Work: The Dynamics of Job Segregation by Sex During World War II* (Urbana: University of Illinois Press, 1987); Hartmann, *The Home Front,* p. 24; Ryan, *Womanhood in America,* pp. 318–19; Goldin, *Understanding the Gender Gap,*

p. 120; Chafe, *The American Woman*, pp. 178–79; Kain, *The Myth of Family Decline*, p. 98.

26. Milkman, *Gender at Work*; Karen Anderson, *Wartime Women: Sex Roles, Family Relations, and the Status of Women During World War Two* (Westport, Conn.: Greenwood, 1981); Hartmann, *Home Front*, pp. 211–13; S. Gary Garwood et al., "As the Pendulum Swings: Federal Agency Programs for Children," *American Psychologist* (February 1989): 436; Carolyn Jones, "Split Income and Separate Spheres: Tax Laws and Gender Roles in the 1940s," *Law and History Review* 6 (1988): 296.

27. Chafe, *The American Woman*, pp. 218, 220.

28. Cherlin, *Marriage, Divorce, Remarriage*, pp. 50–51; Jane Adams, "The Decoupling of Farm and Household," *Comparative Studies in Society and History* 30 (1988): 477; Louise Lamphere, *From Working Daughters to Working Mothers: Immigrant Women in a New England Industrial Community* (Ithaca, N.Y.: Cornell University Press, 1987), p. 40.

29. Valerie Oppenheimer, *The Female Labor Force in the United States* (Berkeley: University of California Population Monograph Series, 1970); Alice Kessler-Harris, *Out to Work: A History of Wage-Earning Women in the United States* (New York: Oxford University Press, 1982), pp. 300–306; Cynthia Harrison, *On Account of Sex: The Politics of Women's Issues, 1945–1968* (Berkeley: University of California Press, 1988), pp. xi, 25, 90; William Chafe, *The Paradox of Change: American Women in the Twentieth Century* (New York: Oxford University Press, 1991), pp. 161–62, 188–89.

30. Bergmann, *The Economic Emergence of Women*, p. 35; Ryan, *Womanhood in America*, p. 277.

31. Steven McLaughlin et al., *The Changing Lives of American Women* (Chapel Hill: University of North Carolina Press, 1988), pp. 169, 183, 190.

32. Glen Cain, *Married Women in the Labor Force: An Economic Analysis* (Chicago: University of Chicago Press, 1966); William Bowen and T. Aldrich Finegan, *The Economics of Labor Force Participation* (Princeton: Princeton University Press, 1969); Susan Householder Van Horn, *Women, Work, and Fertility, 1900–1986* (New York: New York University Press, 1988), pp. 181–86, 207; Bergmann, *The Economic Emergence of Women*, p. 21.

33. Richard Easterlin, *Birth and Fortune: The Impact of Numbers on Personal Welfare* (New York: Basic Books, 1980).

34. Van Horn, *Women, Work, and Fertility*, pp. 171–72.

35. Van Horn, *Women, Work, and Fertility*, pp. 189, 198; Weiner, *Working Girl to Working Mother*, p. 93; Ryan, *Womanhood in America*, p. 330.

36. Susan Kleinberg, "Technology and Women's Work: The Lives of Women in Pittsburgh, 1870–1900," *Labor History* 17 (1976); Strasser,

Never Done; Stephanie Coontz, *The Social Origins of Private Life: A History of American Families, 1600–1900* (London: Verso, 1988), pp. 295–97.

37. Laslett, "The Family as a Public and Private Institution"; Van Horn, *Women, Work, and Fertility,* p. 211; Glenna Matthews, *"Just a Housewife": The Rise and Fall of Domesticity in America* (New York: Oxford, 1987), pp. 178–96.

38. James Davidson and Mark Lytle, "From Rosie to Lucy: The Mass Media and Changing Images of Women and Family," in *Women, Families, and Communities,* vol. 2, ed. Nancy Hewitt (Glenview, Ill.: Scott, Foresman, 1990), p. 211; Matthews, *"Just a Housewife,"* pp. 211–12, 221; Betty Friedan, *The Feminine Mystique* (New York: Norton, 1963).

39. Leila Rupp and Verta Taylor, *Survival in the Doldrums: The American Women's Rights Movement, 1945 to the 1960s* (New York: Oxford, 1987), pp. 18–23; Ryan, *Womanhood in America,* p. 341; Nancy Gabin, *Feminism in the Labor Movement: Women and the United Auto Workers, 1935–1975* (Ithaca, N.Y.: Cornell University Press, 1990); Sara Evans, *Personal Politics: The Roots of Women's Liberation in the Civil Rights Movement and the New Left* (New York: Vintage, 1980), pp. 3–23.

40. Glenda Riley, *Inventing the American Woman* (Arlington Heights, Va.: Harlan Davidson, 1987), p. 241; Jo Freeman, *The Politics of Women's Liberation: A Case Study of an Emerging Social Movement and Its Relation to the Policy Process* (New York: Longman, 1975); Evans, *Personal Politics;* Ruth Milkman, "Women Workers, Feminism and the Labor Movement Since the 1960s," in *Women, Work, and Protest: A Century of U.S. Women's Labor History,* ed. Ruth Milkman (New York: Routledge and Kegan Paul, 1985).

41. Suzanne Bianchi and Daphne Spain, *American Women: Three Decades of Change* (Washington, D.C.: Government Printing Office Special Demographics Analysis, 1984); Cherlin, *Marriage, Divorce, Remarriage,* pp. 52–53; Kathleen Gerson, *Hard Choices: How Women Decide About Work, Career, and Motherhood* (Berkeley: University of California Press, 1985).

42. Van Horn, *Women, Work, and Fertility,* p. 192; Barbara Ehrenreich, *The Hearts of Men: American Dreams and the Flight from Commitment* (Garden City, N.Y.: Anchor Press, 1983).

43. Cherlin, *Marriage, Divorce, Remarriage,* pp. 46–47; McLaughlin et al., *Changing Lives of American Women,* pp. 182–83.

44. Cliff Jahr, "Anita Bryant's Startling Reversal," *Ladies' Home Journal,* December 1980, p. 68.

45. McLaughlin et al., *Changing Lives of American Women,* pp. 90, 170, 179; Van Horn, *Women, Work, and Fertility,* pp. 199–201. Chapter 11 contains statistics about the rise in housing inflation and decline of real income during the 1970s.

46. Van Horn, *Women, Work, and Fertility*, pp. 172–73.

47. For an extended discussion of this point, see Faludi, *Backlash*.

48. Barbara Ehrenreich, *Fear of Falling: The Inner Life of the Middle Class* (New York: Pantheon, 1989), pp. 174, 177.

49. Daniel Rodgers, *The Work Ethic in Industrial America, 1850–1920* (Chicago: University of Chicago Press, 1979), p. 121; Alan Trachtenberg, *The Incorporation of America: Culture and Society in the Gilded Age* (New York: Hill and Wang, 1982), pp. 136, 130.

50. Richard Fox and T. J. Jackson Lears, eds., *The Culture of Consumption: Critical Essays in American History, 1880–1980* (New York: Pantheon, 1983); Daniel Horowitz, *The Morality of Spending: Attitudes Toward the Consumer Society in America, 1875–1940* (Baltimore: Johns Hopkins University Press, 1985), and "Periodization, Hegemony, and Method in the History of American Consumer Culture," *Maryland Historian* 19 (1988); Ronald Edsforth, *Class Conflict and Cultural Consensus: The Making of a Mass Consumer Society in Flint, Michigan* (New Brunswick: Rutgers University Press, 1987); Robert Lynd and Helen Lynd, *Middletown: A Study in Modern American Culture* (New York: Harcourt Brace Jovanovich, 1956), p. 88; Roland Marchand, *Advertising the American Dream: Making Way for Modernity, 1920–1940* (Berkeley: University of California Press, 1985), pp. 24, 234.

51. Rolf Lunden, *Business and Religion in the American 1920s* (Westport: Greenwood, 1988); John Cawelti, *Apostles of the Self-made Man* (Chicago: University of Chicago Press, 1965), p. 197; Susan Strasser, *Satisfaction Guaranteed: The Making of the American Mass Market* (New York: Pantheon, 1989); Larence Birken, *Consuming Desire: Sexual Science and the Emergence of a Culture of Abundance, 1871–1914* (Ithaca, N.Y.: Cornell University Press, 1988); Matthews, *"Just a Housewife,"* pp. 187–88; William Leach, "Transformations in a Culture of Consumption: Women and Department Stores, 1890–1925," *The Journal of American History* 71 (1984); Elaine Abelson, *When Ladies Go A-Thieving: Middle Class Shoplifters in the Victorian Department Store* (New York: Oxford University Press, 1989); Susan Benson, *Counter Cultures: Saleswomen, Managers, and Customers in American Department Stores, 1890–1940* (Urbana: University of Illinois Press, 1986).

52. Theresa Leininger, "Type-Cast: An Analysis of the Portrayal of American Women in Business Equipment Advertising, 1917–1929," *University of Cincinnati Forum* 15 (1988): 9–10.

53. Nancy Cott, *The Grounding of Modern Feminism* (New Haven: Yale University Press, 1987); Paula Fass, *The Damned and the Beautiful: American Youth in the 1920s* (New York: Oxford University Press, 1977), p. 55; Chafe, *The Paradox of Change*, p. 103.

54. Douglas Miller and Marion Nowak, *The Fifties: The Way We Really*

Were (Garden City, N.Y.: Doubleday, 1977), p. 119; William Chafe, *The Unfinished Journey: America Since World War II* (New York: Oxford University Press, 1986), pp. 144, 119; James Henretta et al., *America's History,* vol. 2 (Chicago: Dorsey, 1987), pp. 852–53; Elaine Tyler May, *Homeward Bound: American Families in the Cold War Era* (New York: Basic Books, 1988), pp. 166, 221.

55. J. Ronald Oakley, *God's Country: America in the Fifties* (New York: Dembner Books, 1986), pp. 267–90; Marty Jezer, *The Dark Ages: Life in the United States, 1945–1960* (Boston: South End Press, 1982), pp. 277–82; James Gilbert, *A Cycle of Outrage: America's Reaction to the Juvenile Delinquent in the 1950s* (New York: Oxford University Press, 1986), pp. 196–211; Thomas Doherty, ed., *Teenagers and Teenpics: The Juvenilization of American Movies in the 1950s* (Boston: Unwin Hyman, 1988); Landon Jones, *Great Expectations: America and the Baby Boom Generation* (New York: Ballantine Books, 1981), pp. 41, 49.

56. Lary May, ed., *Recasting America* (Chicago: University of Chicago Press, 1989), p. 5; Elizabeth Ewen, *Immigrant Women in the Land of Dollars: Life and Culture on the Lower East Side, 1890–1925* (New York: Monthly Review Press, 1985), p. 268; *New York Times,* 7 July 1985.

57. Ehrenreich, *The Hearts of Men,* pp. 42–51.

58. Helen Gurley Brown, *Sex and the Single Girl* (New York: Bernard Geis Associates, 1962), pp. 4, 112, 115, 28.

59. Stephen Fox, *The Mirror Makers: A History of American Advertising and Its Creators* (New York: Morrow, 1984).

60. Barbara Ehrenreich, *Fear of Falling: The Inner Life of the Middle Class* (New York: Pantheon, 1989), pp. 62–63; Ryan, *Womanhood in America,* p. 348.

61. Ella Taylor, *Prime-Time Families: Television Culture in Postwar America* (Berkeley: University of California Press, 1989), p. 44; Stuart Ewen and Elizabeth Ewen, *Channels of Desire: Mass Images and the Shaping of American Consciousness* (New York: McGraw-Hill, 1982), pp. 246–51.

62. May, *Homeward Bound,* p. 221.

63. Ruth Sidel, *On Her Own: Growing Up in the Shadow of the American Dream* (New York: Viking, 1990), p. 18.

64. My thanks to Charles Pailthorp, a former copyeditor at *People* magazine, for introducing me to this term.

65. Taylor, *Prime-Time Families,* pp. 45, 152–53; William Boddy, *Fifties Television: The Industry and Its Critics* (Urbana: University of Illinois Press, 1990).

66. Marjorie Williams, "MTV's Short Takes Define a New Style," *Washington Post,* 13 December 1989; Joanmarie Kalter, "How TV Is Shaking Up

the American Family," *TV Guide,* 23 July 1988; Taylor, *Prime-Time Families,* pp. 153, 157–59, 166; Paul Fahri, "The Broad View for Sales Goes Out the Window," *Washington Post National Weekly Edition,* 29 January–4 February 1990.

67. Benson, *Counter Cultures;* Lizabeth Cohen, *Making a New Deal: Industrial Workers in Chicago, 1919–1939* (New York: Cambridge University Press, 1990); Janice Radway, *Reading the Romance: Women, Patriarchy, and Popular Culture* (Chapel Hill: University of North Carolina Press, 1984); Fahri, "Broad View for Sales Goes Out the Window."

68. Kenneth Gergen, *The Saturated Self: Dilemmas of Identity in Contemporary Life* (New York: Basic Books, 1991); Stuart Ewen and Elizabeth Ewen, *Channels of Desire: Mass Images and the Shaping of American Consciousness* (New York: McGraw-Hill, 1982), pp. 268–69; Christopher Lasch, "The New Class Controversy," *Chronicles,* June 1990, p. 22; Carol Moog, *"Are They Selling Her Lips?" Advertising and Identity* (New York: Morrow, 1990), pp. 14–15, 113; Lawrence Cahoone, *The Dilemma of Modernity: Philosophy, Culture, and Anti-Culture* (Albany: State University of New York Press, 1988), p. 186; Christopher Lasch, *The Minimal Self: Psychic Survival in Troubled Times* (New York: Norton, 1984), pp. 19, 30.

69. Robert Bellah et al., *Habits of the Heart: Individualism and Commitment in American Life* (New York: Harper & Row, 1986); Lasch, *The Minimal Self,* p. 38.

70. Alan Wolfe, *Whose Keeper? Social Science and Moral Obligation* (Berkeley: University of California Press, 1989), p. 49; David Levine, *Economic Theory: The Elementary Relations of Economic Life* (New York: Routledge and Kegan Paul, 1978), p. 299; *USA Today,* 6 March 1991, p. 1A; Hilton Hotels 1991 Time Values Survey (Los Angeles, 12 March 1991).

71. Mavis Hethrington, Martha Cox, and Roger Cox, "Divorced Fathers," *Psychology Today,* April 1977, p. 42; Arlene Skolnick, *Embattled Paradise: The Family in an Age of Uncertainty* (New York: Basic Books, 1991), pp. 144–78.

72. Richard Sennett, *The Fall of Public Man* (New York: Knopf, 1977); Arlie Hochschild, *The Managed Heart: Commercialization of Human Feeling* (Berkeley: University of California Press, 1983), pp. 185–98; Ralph Turner, "The Real Self: From Institution to Impulse," *American Journal of Sociology* 81 (1976).

73. Christopher Lasch, *The Culture of Narcissism: American Life in an Age of Diminishing Expectations* (New York: Norton, 1978), p. 180; Hochschild, *The Managed Heart,* pp. 162–84, 195–96; Stanton Peele, *Love and Addiction* (New York: Signet, 1976).

74. Sennett, *The Fall of Public Man*, p. 10.

75. Robert Bellah et al., *Habits of the Heart*, pp. 56, 66.

Chapter 8

1. U.S. Department of Health and Human Services, National Center for Health Statistics, *Monthly Vital Statistics Report* 39 (May 1991); *Wall Street Journal*, 20 February 1990, p. B1; *Wall Street Journal*, 31 May 1990, p. B1; *Seattle Weekly*, 17 October 1990, p. 12; Gannett News Service release, 4 February 1991; *Newsweek Special Issue*, Winter/Spring 1990; Frank Macchiarola and Alan Gartner, eds., *Caring for American Children* (New York: Academy of Political Science, 1989), pp. 4–19; Sylvia Hewlett, *When the Bough Breaks: The Cost of Neglecting Our Children* (New York: Basic Books, 1991), p. 12; Nicholas Zill and Carolyn Rogers, "Recent Trends in the Well-being of Children in the United States and Their Implications for Public Policy," in *The Changing American Family and Public Policy*, ed. Andrew Cherlin (Washington, D.C.: Urban Institute Press, 1988), p. 39.

2. William Chafe, *The Paradox of Change: American Women in the 20th Century* (New York: Oxford University Press, 1991), pp. 220–22; *New York Times*, 7 June 1991, p. A18.

3. Dept. of Health and Human Services, *Monthly Vital Statistics Report* 39; *The Olympian*, 26 September 1991; *New York Times*, 30 January 1991; *New York Times*, 14 March 1991; *Seattle Times*, 26 September 1991, p. A12; *Los Angeles Times*, 23 March 1992, p. A3.

4. Elise Jones et al., *Teenage Pregnancy in Industrialized Countries* (New Haven: Yale University Press, 1986), pp. 37–66; Macchiarola and Gartner, *Caring for American Children*, pp. 14–19; *Los Angeles Times*, 23 March 1992, p. A3. See also notes 15 and 44.

5. *New York Times*, 31 August 1989, pp. C1 and C6; "The 21st Century Family," *Newsweek*, Winter/Spring 1990, p. 38; *U.S. News & World Report*, 21 August 1989, p. 13.

6. "The 21st Century Family," p. 39; *New York Times*, 4 July 1990, pp. 1, 10.

7. Howard Hughes, "Family Members in the Work Force," *Monthly Labor Review*, March 1990, p. 14.

8. Warren Sanderson, "Below-Replacement Fertility in Nineteenth-Century America," *Population and Development Review* 13 (1987); Stewart Tolnay and Avery Guest, "Childlessness in a Transitional Population: The

United States at the Turn of the Century," *Journal of Family History* 7 (1982); Heidi Hartmann, "Demographic and Economic Trends: Implications for Family Life and Public Policy" (Paper prepared for the American Council on Education, Women Presidents' Summit, Institute for Women's Policy Research, Washington, D.C., 5–7 December 1990), p. 9; Vivian Fox and Martin Quitt, *Loving, Parenting and Dying: The Family Cycle in England and America, Past and Present* (New York: Psychohistory Press, 1980), p. 33; Kain, *Myth of Family Decline,* p. 37; Dorrian Sweetser, "Broken Homes: Stable Risk, Changing Reasons, Changing Forms," *Journal of Marriage and the Family* (August 1985); Ben Wattenberg, *The Good News Is the Bad News Is Wrong* (New York: Simon & Schuster, 1985), pp. 283–84.

9. Kain, *Myth of Family Decline,* p. 127; John Gillis, "From Ritual to Romance: Toward an Alternative History of Love," in *Emotion and Social Change: Toward a New Psychohistory,* ed. Carol and Peter Stearns (New York: Holmes and Meier, 1988), p. 94; Martin Duberman, Martha Vicinus, and George Chauncey, eds., *Hidden From History: Reclaiming the Gay and Lesbian Past* (New York: NAL Books, 1989), p. 10; David Greenberg, *The Construction of Homosexuality* (Chicago: University of Chicago Press, 1988).

10. Sar Levitan, *What's Happening to the American Family?* (Baltimore: Johns Hopkins University Press, 1981), p. 66; Jack Larkin, *The Reshaping of Everyday Life, 1790–1840* (New York: Harper & Row, 1988); Susan Newcomer, "Out of Wedlock Childbearing in an Ante-Bellum Southern County," *Journal of Family History* 15 (1990).

11. Phillips Cutwright, "The Teenage Sexual Revolution and the Myth of an Abstinent Past," *Family Planning Perspectives* 4 (1972): 24, 26; Jane Lancaster and Beatrix Hamburg, eds., *Schoolage Pregnancy and Parenthood: Biosocial Dimensions* (New York: Aldine, 1986).

12. Howard Bahr, "Changes in Family Life in Middletown, 1924–77," *Public Opinion Quarterly* 44 (1980); James Mohr, *Abortion in America: The Origins and Evolution of National Policy, 1800–1900* (New York: Oxford University Press, 1978); Kain, *Myth of Family Decline,* p. 121; Ellen Dubois and Linda Gordon, "Seeking Ecstasy on the Battlefield: Danger and Pleasure in Nineteenth-Century Feminist Sexual Thought," *Feminist Studies* 9 (1973): 15.

13. Beth Bailey, "Sexual Containment" (Paper given at "Ike's America, a conference on the Eisenhower Presidency and American Life in the 1950s," University of Kansas, Lawrence, 4–6 October 1990), p. 2; John D'Emilio and Estelle Freedman, *Intimate Matters: A History of Sexuality in America* (New York: Harper & Row, 1988), pp. 65, 133–34.

14. Heidi Hartmann, "Changes in Women's Economic and Family Roles in Post–World War II United States," in *Women, Households, and the Econ-*

omy, ed. Lourdes Beneria and Catharine Stimpson (New Brunswick: Rutgers University Press, 1987), p. 37; Kingsley Davis, "The Future of Marriage," in *Contemporary Marriage: Comparative Perspectives on a Changing Institution,* ed. Kingsley Davis (New York: Russell Sage, 1986); Judith Blake, "Structural Differentiation and the Family: A Quiet Revolution," in *Societal Growth: Processes and Implications,* ed. Amos Hawley (New York: Free Press, 1979); Steven McLaughlin et al., *The Changing Lives of American Women* (Chapel Hill: University of North Carolina Press, 1988), pp. 5, 45, 188–89, 198–99.

15. McLaughlin et al., *Changing Lives,* p. 188; Doug Honig, "Altered States," *Pacific Northwest,* May 1987, p. 33; *The Olympian,* 29 May 1989.

16. Robert Wells, "Demographic Change and the Life Cycle of American Families," in *The Family in History: Interdisciplinary Essays,* ed. Theodore Rabb and Robert Torberg (New York: Harper & Row, 1973); Hewlett, *When the Bough Breaks,* p. 12; *Washington Post,* 16 December 1990; Kain, *Myth of Family Decline,* pp. 72–73; Philip Elmer-Dewitt, "The Great Experiment," *Time,* Fall 1990, p. 75.

17. Joseph Kett, "The Stages of Life," in *The American Family in Socio-Historical Perspective,* ed. Michael Gordon (New York: St. Martin's, 1978); John Modell, Frank Furstenberg, and Theodore Hershberg, "Social Changes and Transitions to Adulthood in Historical Perspective," in *Growing Up in America: Historical Experiences,* ed. Harvey Graff (Detroit: Wayne State University Press, 1987); Stephanie Coontz, *The Social Origins of Private Life: A History of American Families, 1600–1900* (London: Verso, 1988), pp. 258–63.

18. Viviana Zeliger, *Pricing the Priceless Child: The Changing Social Value of Children* (New York: Basic Books, 1985); Tamara Hareven, "The History of the Family and the Complexity of Social Change," *American Historical Review* 96 (1991): 106–8.

19. Martin Kohli, "The World We Forget: A Historical Review of the Life Course," in *Later Life: The Social Psychology of Aging,* ed. Victor Marshall (Beverly Hills: Sage, 1986); John Modell, *Into One's Own: From Youth to Adulthood in the United States 1920–1975* (Berkeley: University of California Press, 1989), pp. 18, 20–25, 79, 282; McLaughlin, *Changing Lives;* Barbara Vobejda, "Declarations of Dependence," *Washington Post National Weekly Edition,* 23–29 September 1991.

20. Sandy Parker, "More Young Adults Staying at Home," Gannett News Service, 25 August 1987; Modell, *Into One's Own,* pp. 275–76, 322–23; *New York Times,* 7 June 1991; Vobejda, "Declarations of Dependence."

21. Modell, *Into One's Own,* pp. 322–26; Jean Okimoto and Phyllis Stegall, *Boomerang Kids: How to Live with Adult Children Who Return Home*

(Boston: Little, Brown, 1987); *Newsweek Special Issue,* Winter–Spring 1990, pp. 54–55.

22. Joshua Meyrowitz, "The Adultlike Child and the Childlike Adult: Socialization in the Electronic Age," in Graff, ed., *Growing Up in America;* Neil Postman, *The Disappearance of Childhood* (New York: Delacorte, 1982).

23. Frances and Calvin Goldscheider, "The Intergenerational Flow of Incomes: Family Structure and the Status of Black Americans," *Journal of Marriage and the Family* 53 (May 1991); Andrew Cherlin, *Marriage, Divorce, Remarriage* (Cambridge: Harvard University Press, 1981), pp. 93–112; Cherlin, *The Changing American Family,* p. 4. For the argument that modern work for youth has lost the educational and social values it had in the past, see Naomi Greenberger and Laurence Steinberg, *When Teenagers Work: The Psychological and Social Costs of Adolescent Employment* (New York: Basic Books, 1986).

24. Sheila Zedlewski, *The Needs of the Elderly in the 21st Century* (Washington, D.C.: The Urban Institute Press, 1990); *Seattle Times,* 6 April 1988; *Newsweek,* 12 March 1990, p. 73; *Newsweek Special Issue,* Winter–Spring 1990, pp. 62–68; "Persons Needing Assistance with Everyday Activities," Bureau of the Census Statistical Brief, December 1990.

25. Abraham Epstein, *Insecurity: A Challenge to Americans: A Study of Social Insurance in the United States and Abroad* (New York: H. Smith and R. Haas, 1933); Michael B. Katz, *In the Shadow of the Poorhouse: A Social History of Welfare in America* (New York: Basic Books, 1986), pp. 121, 126, 244; Elaine Brody, *Women in the Middle: Their Parent-Care Years* (New York: Springer, 1990), p. 6.

26. Richard Louv, *Childhood's Future* (Boston: Houghton Mifflin, 1990), p. 301; Francine and Robert Moskowitz, *Parenting Your Aging Parents* (Woodland Hills, Calif.: Key Publications, 1990); William Booth, "Transitions," *Washington Post National Weekly Edition,* 29 July–4 August 1991; *Exploding the Myths: Caregiving in America* (Washington, D.C.: Subcommittee on Human Services of the Select Committee on Aging of the U.S. House of Representatives, Publication no. 99-611, January 1987).

27. *USA Today,* 3 September 1991; Nancy Hooyman and H. Asuman Kiyak, *Social Gerontology: A Multidisciplinary Perspective* (Boston: Allyn & Bacon, 1988), pp. 298–337; Elaine Brody, "Parent Care as a Normative Family Stress," *The Gerontologist* 25 (1985). I thank Judith Olmstead, researcher at the Washington State Department of Health Services, for directing me to these and other sources.

28. Terri Wades, "Corporate America Prepares for Eldercare," *Compass,* September 1990, pp. 18–19; E. Brody, "They Can't Do It All: Aging Daughters of Aging Mothers," *Generations* 7 (1982); P. G. Archbold, "The Impact

of Parent-Caring on Women," *Family Relations* 32 (1983); David Miller, "The 'Sandwich' Generation: Adult Children of the Aging," *Social Work* 26 (1981).

29. Ralph Nader, "Self-Impoverishment for Your Health," *Liberal Opinion Week,* 15 July 1991; *Dollars and Sense,* January–February 1988; *Newsweek,* 12 March 1990, pp. 73, 75.

30. John Edwards, "New Conceptions: Biosocial Innovations and the Family," *Journal of Marriage and the Family* 53 (May 1991); *Newsweek,* 5 November 1990; Jerrold Footlick, "What Happened to the Family?" *Newsweek Special Issue,* Winter–Spring 1990, p. 18; John Scanzoni, "Families in the 1980s: Time to Refocus Our Thinking," *Journal of Family Issues* 8 (1987); John Scanzoni et al., *The Sexual Bond: Rethinking Families and Close Relationships* (Newbury Park, Calif.: Sage, 1990).

31. Page Smith, *Daughters of the Promised Land: Women in American History* (Boston: Little, Brown, 1970), pp. 53–54.

32. Robert Padgug, "Sexual Matters: Rethinking Sexuality in History," in Duberman et al., eds., *Hidden From History;* Howard Gadlin, "Private Lives and Public Order: A Critical View of Intimate Relations in the U.S.," *Massachusetts Review* (Summer 1976): 306–19; John D'Emilio and Estelle Freedman, *Intimate Matters: A History of Sexuality in America* (New York: Harper & Row, 1988), pp. 166–67; Charles Rosenberg, "Sexuality, Class and Role in Nineteenth-Century America," *American Quarterly* 25 (1973): 39; John and Robin Haller, *The Physician and Sexuality in Victorian America* (Urbana: University of Illinois Press, 1974), p. 203; G. Barker-Benfield, *The Horrors of the Half-Known Life: Male Attitudes toward Female Sexuality in Nineteenth-Century America* (New York: Harper & Row, 1976), p. 159.

33. D'Emilio and Freedman, *Intimate Matters,* pp. 173–74; John D'Emilio, *Sexual Politics, Sexual Communities: The Making of a Homosexual Minority in the United States, 1940–1970* (Chicago: University of Chicago Press, 1983), p. 11; Carrol Smith-Rosenberg, "Sex as Symbol of Victorian Purity: An Ethnohistorical Analysis of Jacksonian America," *American Journal of Sociology* 84 (1978): 235–36; Daniel Scott Smith, "The Dating of the American Sexual Revolution," in *The American Family in Social-Historical Perspective,* ed. Michael Gordon (New York: St. Martin's, 1978), p. 434.

34. Paula Fass, *The Damned and the Beautiful: American Youth in the 1920s* (New York: Oxford University Press, 1979); Kathy Peiss, *Cheap Amusements: Working Women and Leisure in Turn-of-the-Century New York* (Philadelphia: Temple University Press, 1986); D'Emilio and Freedman, *Intimate Matters,* pp. 196, 226–27; John Kasson, *Amusing the Million: Coney Island at the Turn of the Century* (New York: Hill and Wang, 1978); Gadlin, "Private Lives and Public Order," pp. 304, 320–25.

35. Ellen Rothman, *Hands and Hearts: A History of Courtship in America* (New York: Basic Books, 1984), p. 289; Beth Bailey, *From Front Porch to Back Seat: Courtship in Twentieth-Century America* (Baltimore: Johns Hopkins University Press, 1989), pp. 13, 78.

36. D'Emilio and Freedman, *Intimate Matters,* pp. 240–41; Barbara Epstein, "Family, Sexual Morality, and Popular Movements in Turn-of-the-Century America," in *Powers of Desire: The Politics of Sexuality,* ed. Ann Snitov, Christine Stansell, and Sharon Thompson (New York: Monthly Review Press, 1983), p. 125; Modell, *Into One's Own,* p. 97; Chafe, *Paradox of Change,* p. 105.

37. Bailey, *Front Porch to Back Seat,* p. 77; David Halperin, "Is There a History of Sexuality?" *History and Theory* 28 (1989): 262–63; D'Emilio and Freedman, *Intimate Matters,* pp. 225–26, 274.

38. Gillis, "Ritual to Romance," pp. 96–97.

39. Lillian Faderman, *Odd Girls and Twilight Lovers: A History of Lesbian Life in Twentieth-Century America* (New York: Columbia University Press, 1990); Carroll Smith-Rosenberg, "The Female World of Love and Ritual: Relations Between Women in Nineteenth Century America," *Signs* 1 (1975); Anthony Rotundo, "Romantic Friendship: Male Intimacy and Middle-Class Youth in the Northern United States, 1800–1900," *Journal of Social History* 23 (1989): 20; John Farragher, *Sugar Creek: Life on the Illinois Prairie* (New Haven: Yale University Press, 1986), p. 153; Ruth Perry, review of *Western Sexuality* in *Journal of Interdisciplinary History* 18 (1987): 129.

40. Bailey, *Front Porch to Back Seat,* pp. 13, 15, 20, 58; JoAnne Meyerowitz, *Women Adrift: Independent Wage Earners in Chicago, 1880–1930* (Chicago: University of Chicago Press, 1988), p. xxiii; Modell, *Into One's Own,* p. 95.

41. Epstein, "Family, Sexual Morality," p. 127; Gadlin, "Private Lives and Public Order," pp. 322–23; Nancy Cott, *The Grounding of Modern Feminism* (New Haven: Yale University Press, 1990); Martha Vicinus, "Sexuality and Power: A Review of Current Work in the History of Sexuality," *Feminist Studies* 8 (1982).

42. D'Emilio, *Sexual Politics;* Allan Berube, *Coming Out Under Fire: The History of Gay Men and Women in World War II* (New York: Free Press, 1990); Faderman, *Odd Girls and Twilight Lovers;* Elaine Tyler May, *Homeward Bound: American Families in the Cold War Era* (New York: Basic Books, 1988), pp. 151–53; Michael Gordon, "From an Unfortunate Necessity to a Cult of Mutual Orgasm: Sex in American Marital Education Literature, 1830–1940," in *Studies in the Sociology of Sex,* ed. James Henslin (New York: Appleton-Century-Crofts, 1971); D'Emilio and Freedman, *Intimate Matters,* pp. 249–53, 282–88.

43. Steven Mintz and Susan Kellogg, *Domestic Revolutions: A Social History of American Family Life* (New York: Free Press, 1988), pp. 208–9; D'Emilio and Freedman, *Intimate Matters,* pp. 250–52, 306–60.

44. Freya Sonenstein, Joseph Pleck, and Leighton Ku, "Levels of Sexual Activity Among Adolescent Males in the United States," *Family Planning Perspectives* 23 (1991); *Washington Post National Weekly Edition,* 12–18 August 1991; *The Olympian,* 30 August 1991; James Patterson and Peter Kim, *The Day America Told the Truth* (New York: Prentice Hall, 1991), p. 103.

45. Morton Kondracke, "Washington Diarist," *New Republic,* 5 August 1991; *Newsweek,* 10 June 1991, p. 54.

46. Sonenstein et al., "Levels of Sexual Activity," p. 162; Ira Robinson et al., "Twenty Years of the Sexual Revolution, 1965–1985: An Update," *Journal of Marriage and the Family* 53 (1991); Jones, *Teenage Pregnancy,* pp. 38, 46–47; "Teenage Sexual and Reproductive Behavior in the United States," *Facts in Brief* (New York: Alan Guttmacher Institute, 1991).

47. Lillian Rubin, *Erotic Wars: What Happened to the Sexual Revolution?* (New York: Farrar, Strauss & Giroux, 1990); Doug Honig, "Altered States," *Pacific Northwest,* May 1987, p. 36; Modell, *Into One's Own,* pp. 291–93, 321–22; Bailey, *Front Porch to Back Seat,* pp. 141–43.

48. Judith Reisman and Edward Eichel, *Kinsey, Sex and Fraud* (Lafayette, La.: Huntington House, 1990), p. 114; Sonenstein et al., "Levels of Sexual Activity," p. 166; Wattenberg, *The Good News,* pp. 294–96; Andrew Greeley, Robert Michael, and Tom Smith, "A Most Monogamous People: Americans and Their Sexual Partners," National Opinion Research Center paper, 16 May 1989, p. 12; *Family Planning Perspectives,* June 1991.

49. Rubin, *Erotic Wars;* Linda Ellerbee, "What Your Kid Doesn't Know About Rape," *Liberal Opinion Week,* 2 September 1991; D'Emilio and Freedman, *Intimate Matters,* p. xi; *Newsweek,* 17 September 1990, p. 72; June Reinisch and Ruth Beasley, *The Kinsey Institute New Report on Sex: What You Must Know to be Sexually Literate* (New York: St. Martin's, 1990).

50. Jones et al., *Teenage Pregnancy,* pp. 60–61, 64, 223, 230; Hewlett, *When the Bough Breaks,* p. 103.

51. "Doing Something About Teenage Pregnancy," *Family Planning Perspectives* 17 (1985): 52; William Fischer, "An Integrated Approach to Preventing Adolescent Pregnancy and STD/HIV Infection," *Sex Information and Education Council Report* 18 (1990): 8.

52. D'Emilio and Freedman, *Intimate Matters,* pp. 323, 328–30.

53. Jonathon Schell, *History in Sherman Park: An American Family and the Reagan-Mondale Election* (New York: Knopf, 1987), p. 72; Marabel Morgan, *The Total Woman* (Old Tappan, N.J.: F. H. Revell, 1973).

54. Herbert Marcuse, *One Dimensional Man: Studies in the Ideology of Ad-*

vanced Industrial Society (Boston: Beacon, 1964); Michel Foucault, *The History of Sexuality,* trans. Robert Hurley (New York: Pantheon, 1978); Colin Gordon, ed., *Power/Knowledge* (New York: Pantheon, 1980).

55. Lawrence Birken, *Consuming Desire: Sexual Science and the Emergence of a Culture of Abundance, 1871–1914* (Ithaca, N.Y.: Cornell University Press, 1988), pp. 149, 153; Mirra Komarovsky, "Preface to the Second Edition," *Blue-Collar Marriage* (New Haven: Yale University Press, 1987), p. viii.

56. Lori Andrews, *Between Strangers: Surrogate Mothers, Expectant Fathers, and Brave New Babies* (New York: Harper & Row, 1989); Martha Field, *Surrogate Motherhood: The Legal and Human Issues* (Cambridge: Harvard University Press, 1989); Rita Arditti, Renate Klein, and Shelley Minden, *Test-Tube Women: What Future for Motherhood?* (London: Pandora Press, 1984); Andrea Bonnicksen, *In Vitro Fertilization: Building Policy from Laboratory to Legislatures* (New York: Columbia University Press, 1989); Gena Corea, *The Mother Machine: Reproductive Technologies from Artificial Insemination to Artificial Wombs* (New York: Harper & Row, 1985); Barbara Rothman, *The Tentative Pregnancy: Prenatal Diagnosis and the Future of Motherhood* (New York: Viking, 1986); Renate Klein, ed., *Infertility: Women Speak Out about Their Experiences with the New Reproductive Technologies* (London: Pandora Press, 1989); Gail Bronson, "Easier than Selling Soap," *Forbes,* 9 February 1987, p. 112.

57. Maris Vinovskis, *An 'Epidemic' of Adolescent Pregnancy? Some Historical and Policy Considerations* (New York: Oxford University Press, 1988), pp. 25–28.

58. *Seattle Times,* 23 April 1989; Jones et al., *Teenage Pregnancy in Industrialized Countries;* Karen Pittman and Gina Adams, *Teenage Pregnancy: An Advocate's Guide to the Numbers* (Washington, D.C.: Adolescent Pregnancy Prevention Clearinghouse, January/March 1988), p. 11; Hewlett, *When the Bough Breaks,* p. 41.

59. John Billy et al., "Effects of Sexual Activity on Adolescent Social and Psychological Development," *Social Psychology Quarterly* 51 (1988); Carol Webster and Felix D'Allesandro, *Teenage Mothers: A Life of Poverty and Welfare?* (Olympia: Washington State Institute for Public Policy, February 1991); "Teenage Mothers," *View,* July–August 1989, p. 17; Frank Furstenberg, Jeanne Brooks-Gunn, and Lindsay Chase-Lansdale, "Teenaged Pregnancy and Childbearing," *American Psychologist* 44 (1989): 315–18.

60. William Donohue, "Failed Formulas: Teen Pregnancy and the 'New Freedom,'" *The Family in America* 3 (1989): 1–8.

61. Colin Francome, *Abortion Practice in Britain and the United States*

(London: Allen and Unwin, 1986); *Seattle Times,* 3 March 1989; Jones et al., *Teenage Pregnancy;* Karen Pittman and Gina Adams, "What About the Boys? Teenage Pregnancy Prevention Strategies" (Washington, D.C.: Adolescent Pregnancy Prevention Clearinghouse, July 1988), p. 11; Lancaster and Hamburg, *School Age Pregnancy;* Frank Furstenberg, "Implicating the Family: Teenage Parenthood and Kinship Involvement," in *Teenage Pregnancy in a Family Context: Implications for Policy,* ed. Theodora Ooms (Philadelphia: Temple University Press, 1981), p. 143.

62. Donna Franklin, "Race, Class, and Adolescent Pregnancy: An Ecological Analysis," *American Journal of Orthopsychiatry* 58 (1988): 341–42.

63. Betty Bassoff and Elizabeth Ortiz, "Teen Women: Disparity Between Cognitive Values and Anticipated Life Events," *Child Welfare* 63 (1984): 127; "Adolescent Pregnancy: An Anatomy of a Social Problem in Search of Comprehensive Solutions" (Washington, D.C.: Adolescent Pregnancy Prevention Clearinghouse, January 1987), p. 5; Pittman and Adams, "Teenage Pregnancy," pp. 25–28; Franklin, "Race, Class, and Adolescent Pregnancy," pp. 348–49.

64. This fact has led to heated policy debates. Some observers object to the emphasis on preventing pregnancy rather than creating educational and job opportunities, pointing out that most teenagers who become pregnant have already dropped out of school. One recent longitudinal study of sisters from poor families found no differences in later poverty between women who gave birth as teens and their sisters who did not. A few researchers therefore suggest that, given the economic crisis of the black community, unwed teen motherhood is as effective a survival strategy for the poorest of the poor as marriage. Among poor black women, whose health deteriorates rapidly as they age, early childbearing may be associated with lower fetal and maternal death rates, as well as a more persistent commitment to work, than postponed childbearing; marriage by no means guarantees escape from poverty and may even worsen a woman's situation by increasing her chance of having closely spaced children, decreasing the likelihood of her returning to school, and cutting her off from support networks within her own family. Even in the poorest black communities, teens who have special resources or skills that make it feasible for them to escape chronic barriers to educational or economic achievement are discouraged from early childbearing. Arline Geronimus argues: "For those with less apparent chance of achieving upward mobility, early fertility may be one effective way to pursue personal and cultural survival and development." If so, however, it is effective only in the context of the incredible deprivation facing such women, and other researchers, most notably from

the Children's Defense Fund, have sharply contested this point. See Kristin Luker, "Dubious Conceptions," *The American Prospect* (Spring 1991); Ellen Coughlin, "Policy Researchers 'Shift the Terms of the Debate' on Women's Issues," *The Chronicle of Higher Education,* 31 May 1989; Arline Geronimus and Sanders Koreman, "The Socioeconomic Consequences of Teen Childbearing Reconsidered," *Research Reports* (Ann Arbor: Population Studies Center, 1990); Thea Lee, "Rational Expectations: A New Look at the Economics of Teen Pregnancy," *Dollars and Sense,* March 1989, pp. 10–11; Martha Hill, "Trends in the Economic Situation of U.S. Families and Children, 1970–1980," in *American Families and the Economy,* ed. Richard Nelson and Felicity Skidmore (Washington, D.C.: National Academy Press, 1983), pp. 9–53; *The Olympian,* 17 February 1990; Greg Duncan and Willard Rodgers, "Longitudinal Aspects of Childhood Poverty," *Journal of Marriage and the Family* 50 (1988): 1012; Catherine Chilman, "Feminist Issues in Teenage Parenting," *Child Welfare* 64 (1985): 232; *New York Times News Service,* 13 March 1990; Arline Geronimus, "On Teenage Childbearing and Neonatal Mortality in the United States," *Population and Development Review* 13 (1987): 256; *The State of America's Children, 1991* (Washington, D.C.: Children's Defense Fund, 1991), p. 95.

65. Judith Olmstead, "The New Family: Intergenerational Issues" (Washington State Department of Social and Health Services, Office of Research and Data Analysis, paper 07–41, May 1988); Eric Kingston, Barbara Hirshorn, and Linda Harootyan, *The Common Stake: The Interdependence of Generations* (Washington, D.C.: Gerontological Society of America, 1988).

66. Thomas Getzen, "Population Aging and the Growth of Health Expenditures" (Paper presented to the Association for Health Services Research, Tenth Annual Meeting, San Diego, California, July 2, 1991), pp. 8–9.

67. Glenda Riley, *Divorce: An American Tradition* (New York: Oxford University Press, 1991), pp. 164–68; Mary Ann Glendon, *The Transformation of Family Law* (Chicago: University of Chicago Press, 1989), p. 149.

68. The classic and much-quoted study of the ill effects of no-fault divorce is Lenore Weitzman, *The Divorce Revolution: The Unexpected Social and Economic Consequences for Women and Children in America* (New York: Free Press, 1985). This study is criticized in Stephen Sugarman and Herma Kay, eds., *Divorce Reform at the Crossroads* (New Haven: Yale University Press, 1990); and Faludi, *Backlash,* pp. 19–25. For "exit rules" see Alan Wolfe, *Whose Keeper? Social Science and Moral Obligation* (Berkeley: University of California Press, 1989), pp. 254–56; and Riley, *Divorce,* pp. 186–90.

Chapter 9

1. Stanton Peele, *The Diseasing of America: Addiction Treatment Out of Control* (Lexington, Mass.: Lexington Books, 1989), pp. 249–50; Alexander Cockburn, "Out of the Mouths of Babes: Child Abuse and the Abuse of Adults," *The Nation,* 12 Feburary 1990.

2. "99% of Child Abductions Involve Family," *USA Today,* 3 May 1990; Joel Best, "The Myth of the Halloween Sadist," *Psychology Today,* November 1985; J. Best and C. Horiuchi, "The Razor Blade in the Apple: The Social Construction of Urban Legends," *Social Problems* 32 (1985).

3. John Bradshaw, *Homecoming: Reclaiming and Championing Your Inner Child* (New York: Bantam Books, 1990); David Gelman, "Making It All Feel Better," *Newsweek,* 26 November 1990, pp. 66–67; Herbert Gravitz and Julie Bowden, *Recovery: A Guide for Adult Children of Alcoholics* (New York: Simon & Schuster, 1987).

4. *Seattle Post-Intelligencer,* 6 August 1989, p. A8; Christopher Lasch, *The Culture of Narcissism: American Life in an Age of Diminishing Expectations* (New York: Norton, 1979).

5. Susan Forward with Craig Buck, *Toxic Parents: Overcoming Their Hurtful Legacy and Reclaiming Your Life* (New York: Bantam, 1989), p. 7; Diane Baumriden and Black, "Socialization Practices Associated with Competence in Preschool Children," *Child Development* 38 (1967); E. Susman et al., "Child Rearing Patterns in Depressed, Abusive, and Normal Mothers," *American Journal of Orthopsychiatry* 55 (1985); Janet Miller et al., *Risk Assessment in Child Protection: A Review of the Literature* (Olympia: Washington State Department of Social and Health Services, 1987), pp. 56–59; David Gil, "The Political and Economic Context of Child Abuse," in *Unhappy Families: Clinical and Research Perspectives on Family Violence,* ed. Eli Newberger and Richard Bourne (Littleton, Mass.: PSG Publishing, 1985), p. 13; and *Violence Against Children* (Cambridge: Harvard University Press, 1970).

6. Lasch, *Culture of Narcissism;* Marie Winn, *Children Without Childhood* (New York: Pantheon, 1983); Landon Jones, *Great Expectations: America and the Baby Boom Generation* (New York: Coward, McCann, & Geoghegan, 1980); David Elkind, *The Hurried Child: Growing Up Too Fast Too Soon* (Reading, Mass.: Addison-Wesley, 1981); Ken Stout, "Bringing up Better Babies," *Mainliner Magazine,* October 1983; Peter Uhlenberg and David Eggebeen, "The Declining Well-being of American Adolescents," *The Public Interest* 82 (1986): 38.

7. Richard Lewine, "Parents: The Mental Health Professionals' Scape-

goat," in *Changing Families,* ed. Irving Sigel and Luis Laosa (New York: Plenum, 1983), p. 268.

8. M. J. Levy and L. A. Fallers, "The Family: Some Comparative Considerations," *American Anthropologist* 61 (1959): 649; Stephanie Coontz, *The Social Origins of Private Life: A History of American Families, 1600–1900* (London: Verso, 1988), pp. 7–21; Janice Stockard, *Daughters of the Canton Delta: Marriage Patterns and Economic Strategies in South China, 1860–1930* (Stanford: Stanford University Press, 1989). For more on the variety of family forms, see Jessie Embry, *Mormon Polygamous Families: Life in the Principle* (Salt Lake City: University of Utah Press, 1987); Lila Leibowitz, *Females, Males, Families: A Biosocial Approach* (North Scituate, Mass.: Duxbury, 1978), pp. 6, 8; Ifi Amadiume, *Male Daughters, Female Husbands: Gender and Sex in an African Society* (London: Zed Books, 1987); Kathleen Gough, "Is the Family Universal: The Nayar Case," in *A Modern Introduction to the Family,* ed. Norman Bell and Ezra Vogel (Glencoe, Ill.: Free Press, 1960), pp. 76–92; Evelyn Blackwood, "Sexuality and Gender in Certain Native American Tribes: The Case of Cross-Gender Females," *Signs* 10 (1984); Kate Mertes, *The English Noble Household, 1250–1600: Good Governance and Politic Rule* (New York: Oxford, 1988); Jean-Louis Flandrin, *Families in Former Times* (New York: Cambridge University Press, 1979), pp. 4–17; Russell Middleton, "Brother-Sister and Father-Daughter Incest in Ancient Egypt," *American Sociological Review* 27 (1962).

9. Jane Collier, Michelle Rosaldo, and Sylvia Yanagisako, "Is There a Family? New Anthropological Views," in *Rethinking the Family,* ed. Barrie Thorne with Marilyn Yalom (New York: Longman, 1982), p. 28; Leibowitz, *Females, Males, Families,* p. 21; Sylvia Yanagisako, "Family and Household: The Analysis of Domestic Groups," *American Review of Anthropology* 8 (1979); Martine Segalen, *Historical Anthropology of the Family* (New York: Cambridge University Press, 1986), pp. 14–18; Raymond Smith, "The Family and the Modern World System: Some Observations from the Caribbean," *Journal of Family History* 3 (1978): 353.

10. Esther Goody, "Parental Strategies: Calculation or Sentiment?: Fostering Practices Among West Africans," in *Interest and Emotion: Essays on the Study of Family and Kinship,* ed. Hans Medick and David Sabean (New York: Cambridge University Press, 1984).

11. Talcott Parsons and Robert Bales, *Family Socialization and Interaction Process* (Glencoe, Ill.: Free Press, 1955); Daniel Moynihan, *The Negro Family: The Case for National Action* (Washington, D.C.: U.S. Government Printing Office, 1965); Richard Sennett, *Families Against the City: Middle Class Homes of Industrial Chicago, 1872–1890* (Cambridge: Harvard University Press, 1984); Tamara Hareven, "Review Essay: Origins of the Modern Fam-

ily in the United States," *Journal of Social History* 17 (1983): 343; Linda Gordon, *Heroes of Their Own Lives: The Politics and History of Family Violence* (New York: Viking, 1988), p. 110.

12. Lloyd de Mause, ed., *The History of Childhood* (New York: Psychohistory Press, 1974), p. 51.

13. John Boswell, *The Kindness of Strangers: The Abandonment of Children in Western Europe from Late Antiquity to the Renaissance* (New York: Pantheon, 1988).

14. Deborah Luepnitz, *The Family Interpreted: Feminist Theory in Clinical Practice* (New York: Basic Books, 1988), pp. 109–49; Carl Degler, *At Odds: Women and the Family in America from the Revolution to the Present* (New York: Oxford University Press, 1981), pp. 86–87; John Demos, "Child Abuse in Context: An Historian's Perspective," in *Past, Present, and Personal: The Family and the Life Course in American History,* ed. John Demos (New York: Oxford University Press, 1986); E. P. Thompson, "Happy Families," *New Society,* 8 September 1977, p. 501. Anyone inclined to romanticize the strict discipline of colonial families, though, might read the tale of wife beating, adultery, and incest in Ann Taves, ed., *Religion and Domestic Violence in Early New England: The Memoirs of Abigail Abbot Bailey* (Bloomington: Indiana University Press, 1989).

15. John Demos, "The Changing Faces of Fatherhood: A New Exploration in American Family History," in *Father and Child: Developmental and Clinical Perspectives,* ed. Stanley Cath, Alan Gurwitt, and John Ross (Boston: Little, Brown, 1982), p. 426; Peter Stearns and Timothy Haggerty, "The Role of Fear: Transitions in American Emotional Standards for Children, 1850–1950," *American Historical Review* 96 (1991); Louisa May Alcott, *Little Men* (New York: Vintage, 1962), pp. 60–61; Degler, *At Odds,* pp. 92–93; Jan Lewis, *The Pursuit of Happiness: Family and Values in Jefferson's Virginia* (New York: Cambridge University Press, 1983), p. 179.

16. Viviana Zeliger, *Pricing the Priceless Child: The Changing Social Value of Children* (New York: Basic Books, 1985); Thompson, "Happy Families," p. 501; Allan Schnaiberg and Sheldon Goldenberg, "Closing the Circle: The Impact of Children on Parental Status," *Journal of Marriage and the Family* (November 1975).

17. Louise Tilly, "Individual Lives and Family Strategies in the French Proletariat," *Journal of Family History* 4 (1979); Medick and Sabean, *Interest and Emotion,* pp. 11–13.

18. John Demos and Sarane Boocock, eds., *Turning Points: Historical and Sociological Essays on the Family* (Chicago: University of Chicago Press, 1978), p. 573; Joseph Kett, "Curing the Disease of Precocity," *American Journal of Sociology* 84 (1978).

19. Ben Harris, "'Give Me a Dozen Healthy Infants': John B. Watson's Popular Advice on Childrearing, Women, and the Family," in *In the Shadow of the Past: Psychology Portrays the Sexes,* ed. Miriam Lewis (New York: Columbia University Press, 1984); Barbara Ehrenreich, *Fear of Falling: The Inner Life of the Middle Class* (New York: Pantheon, 1989), p. 86; David Nasaw, *Children of the City: At Work and at Play* (New York: Oxford University Press, 1985).

20. Rima Apple, *Mothers and Medicine: A Social History of Infant Feeding* (Madison: University of Wisconsin Press, 1987); Ilene Philipson, "Narcissism and Mothering: The 1950s Reconsidered," *Women's Studies International Forum* 5 (1982): 29.

21. T. S. Weismer and R. Gallimore, "My Brother's Keeper: Child and Sibling Caretaking," *Current Anthropology* 18 (1977).

22. "Day Care: Unhealthy Minds...In Unhealthy Bodies," *New Research: The Family in America* (November 1988): 2–3; Kenneth Labich, "Can Your Career Hurt Your Kids?" *Fortune,* 20 May 1991, pp. 40, 44; Bryce Christensen, "The Child Abuse 'Crisis': Forgotten Facts and Hidden Agendas," *The Family in America* 3 (1989): 4; Robert Fiala and Gary LaFree, "Cross-National Determinants of Child Homicide," *American Sociological Review* 53 (1988).

23. *The Olympian,* 12 January 1990; Susan Faludi, *Backlash: The Undeclared War Against American Women* (New York: Crown, 1991), p. 43; Fiala and LaFree, "Cross-National Determinants of Child Homicide"; Rosemary Gartner, "Family Structure, Welfare Spending, and Child Homicide in Developed Democracies," *Journal of Marriage and the Family* 53 (1991): 232, 238.

24. Andrew Cherlin, "The Changing American Family and Public Policy," in Cherlin, ed., *Changing American Family,* p. 10; Diane Scott-Jones, "Family Influences on Cognitive Development and School Achievement," *Review of Research in Education* 11 (1984): 276; Lois Hoffman, "Maternal Employment and the Young Child," in *The Minnesota Symposia on Child Psychology,* vol. 17, ed. Marion Perlmutter (Hillsdale, N.J.: Erlbaum Associates, 1984); Anita Shreve, *Remaking Motherhood: How Working Mothers are Shaping Our Children's Future* (New York: Viking, 1987), pp. 82, 100–104; Harriet Mischel and Robert Fuhr, "Maternal Employment: Its Psychological Effects on Children and Their Families," in *Feminism, Children, and the New Families,* ed. Sanford Dornbusch and Myra Strober (New York: Guilford Press, 1988), pp. 200–201.

25. Mischel and Fuhr, "Maternal Employment," pp. 193, 197.

26. Cynthia Epstein, "Toward a Family Policy: Changes in Mothers' Lives," in Cherlin, ed., *Changing American Family,* pp. 178–80; Barbara

Heynes and Sophia Catsambis, "Mothers' Employment and Children's Achievement: A Critique," *Sociology of Education* 59 (1986): 109; Mischel and Fuhr, "Maternal Employment," pp. 195, 197, 202; Hoffman, "Effects of Maternal and Paternal Employment," p. 386; Ellen Greenberger and Wendy Goldberg, "Work, Parenting, and the Socialization of Children," *Developmental Psychology* 25 (1989); Sandra Scarr, Deborah Phillips, and Kathleen McCartney, "Working Mothers and Their Families," *American Psychologist* 44 (1989); Elizabeth Managhan and Toby Parcel, "Determining Children's Home Environments: The Impact of Maternal Characteristics and Current Occupational and Family Conditions," *Journal of Marriage and the Family* 53 (1991): 427; Shreve, *Remaking Motherhood,* p. 143.

27. Jay Belsky, "Parental and Nonparental Child Care and Children's Socioemotional Development: A Decade in Review," in *Contemporary Families: Looking Forward, Looking Back,* ed. Alan Booth (Minneapolis: National Council on Family Relations, 1991), pp. 132–33; Faludi, *Backlash,* pp. 44–45; Jay Belsky, "Infant Day Care: A Cause for Concern?" *Zero to Three: Bulletin of the National Center for Clinical Infant Programs* (Washington, D.C.: U.S. Government Printing Office, 1986); Deborah Phillips et al., "Selective Review of Infant Day Care Research: A Cause for Concern!" *Zero to Three: Bulletin of the National Center for Clinical Infant Programs* (Washington, D.C.; U.S. Government Printing Office, 1987); Alison Clarke-Stewart, "Infant Day Care: Maligned or Malignant?" *American Psychologist* 44 (1989): 268–69.

28. Julius Segal, "10 Myths About Child Development," *Parents,* July 1989, p. 82; Michael Rutter, *The Qualities of Mothering: Maternal Deprivation Revisited* (New York: Jason Aronson, 1974), pp. 24–25, 75–77; Luepnitz, *The Family Interpreted,* pp. 181–95; Belsky, "Parental and Nonparental Child Care," pp. 126–28, 134; Jerome Kagan, *The Nature of the Child* (New York: Basic Books, 1984).

29. Sirgay Sanger, *The Woman Who Works, the Parent Who Cares* (Boston: Little, Brown, 1987), pp. 15–23; Lois Hoffman, "The Effects of Maternal and Paternal Employment," in *Families and Work,* ed. Naomi Gerstel and Harriet Gross (Philadelphia: Temple University Press, 1987), p. 384; Belsky, "Parental and Nonparental Child Care," p. 134; William Arney, "The Politics of Falling in Love With Your Child," *Feminist Studies* 6 (1980): 564.

30. Daniel Goleman, "New Research Overturns a Milestone of Infancy," *New York Times,* 4 June 1989; Clarke-Stewart, "Infant Day Care," pp. 267–68.

31. K. Young and E. Zigler, "Infant and Toddler Care: Regulations and Policy Implications," *American Journal of Orthopsychiatry* 56 (1986); Skold, "Feminists, Children and Child Care," pp. 128–29; Alison Clarke-Stewart,

Daycare: The Developing Child (Cambridge: Harvard University Press, 1982); Shreve, *Remaking Motherhood,* pp. 144–45.

32. Clarke-Stewart, "Infant Day Care," p. 268; *Los Angeles Times,* 4 December 1988; Michael Siegal and Rebecca Storey, "Day Care and Children's Conceptions of Moral and Social Rules," *Child Development* 56 (1985); M. Rubenstein and C. Howes, "Social-Emotional Development of Toddlers in Day Care: The Role of Peers and of Individual Differences," in *Early Education and Day Care,* ed. Sally Kilmer (Greenwich, Conn.: Greenwood Press, 1983). My research assistant, Paul Ortiz, a former child-care worker, points out that day-care children are under much closer observation, have more demands placed on them, and have fewer places to "cool out" or escape from confrontation than do children in their own homes, so that many studies purporting to show greater behavior problems are merely the result of greater scrutiny.

33. Edward Zigler and May Lang, *Child Care Choices: Balancing the Needs of Children, Families, and Society* (New York: Macmillan, 1991); R. Ruopp et al., *Children at the Center: The National Day Care Study* (Cambridge: Harvard University Press, 1979); Sandra Scarr, *Mother Care-Other Care* (New York: Basic Books, 1984); Shreve, *Remaking Motherhood,* pp. 60–61; Edward Zigler and Matia/Finn-Stevenson "Child Care in America: From Problem to Solution," *Educational Policy* 3 (1989); Mischel and Fuhr, "Maternal Employment," p. 194; Edward Zigler, "Shaping Child Care Policies and Programs in America," *American Journal of Community Psychology* 18 (1990): 188.

34. Labich, "Can Your Career Hurt Your Kids?"; James Kilpatrick, "Day-Care Bill Real Boon for Bureaucrats," *The Olympian,* 2 November 1989; Belsky, "Parental and Nonparental Child Care," p. 131; Zigler, *Child Care Choices,* pp. 70–76, 190–240.

35. Jean L. Richardson et al., "Substance Use Among Eighth-Grade Children Who Take Care of Themselves After School," *Pediatrics* 84 (1989); Labich, "Can Your Career Hurt Your Kids?" p. 44; *The Olympian,* 31 May 1990; "Latchkey Kids Do Better," *New York Times News Service,* 7 January 1990; James Brown, David Pratto, and Hyman Rodman, "Social Relationships as Determinants of Parental Satisfaction with Self-Care Arrangements for Children," *Journal of Clinical Child Psychology* 18 (1989): 8; Epstein, "Toward a Family Policy," p. 179.

36. *The Olympian,* 31 May 1990; Bryan Robinson, Bobbie Rowland, and Mick Coleman, *Latchkey Kids: Unlocking Doors for Children and their Families* (Lexington, Mass.: Lexington Books, 1986); Malcolm Gladwell, "Less Cause for Alarm," *Washington Post National Weekly Edition,* 28 May–3 June 1990.

37. Judith Wallerstein and Sandra Blakeless, *Second Chances: Men, Women and Children a Decade After Divorce* (New York: Ticknor and Fields, 1989); Clair Berman, *Adult Children of Divorce Speak Out* (New York: Simon & Schuster, 1991); John Beer, "Relation of Divorce to Self-concepts and Grade Point Averages of Fifth-Grade School Children," *Psychological Reports* 65 (1989); William Catton, "Family 'Divorce Heritage' and Its Intergenerational Transmission: Toward a System-Level Perspective," *Sociological Perspectives* 31 (1988): 418; Hewlett, *When the Bough Breaks*; Fred Moody, "The Case Against Divorce," *Utne Reader* (November–December 1989); George Pransky, *Divorce Is Not the Answer: A Change of Heart Can Save Your Marriage* (Bradenton, Fla.: Human Services Institute, 1990); Trish Hall, "Breaking Up Is Becoming Harder to Do," *New York Times*, 14 March 1991, p. B1.

38. Andrew Cherlin and Frank Furstenberg, "Divorce Doesn't Always Hurt the Kids," *Washington Post*, 19 March 1989, p. C3.

39. Cherlin and Furstenberg, "Divorce Doesn't Always Hurt"; Robert Emery, *Marriage, Divorce, and Children's Adjustment* (Beverly Hills: Sage, 1988); William Doherty, "Children and Divorce," *The Journal of Child Development* (April 1991); Constance Ahrons, *Divorced Families: A Multidisciplinary Developmental View* (New York: Norton, 1987); Robert Emery, "Interparental Conflict and the Children of Discord and Divorce," *Psychological Bulletin* 92 (1982); Marsha Kline et al., "The Long Shadow of Marital Conflict: A Model of Children's Postdivorce Adjustment," *Journal of Marriage and the Family* 53 (1991); Paul Allison and Frank Furstenberg, "How Marital Dissolution Affects Children: Variations by Age and Sex," *Development Psychology* 25 (1989): 546; B. Berg and R. Kelly, "The Measured Self-esteem of Children from Broken, Rejected and Accepted Families," *Journal of Divorce* 2 (1979); David Demo and Alan Acock, "The Impact of Divorce on Children," in Booth, ed., *Contemporary Families*, p. 185; Andrew Cherlin, "Longitudinal Studies of Effects of Divorce on Children in Great Britain and the United States," *Science*, 7 June 1991, pp. 1386–89.

40. Susan Krantz, "Divorce and Children," in Dornbusch and Strober, eds., *Feminism, Children, and New Families*, p. 250; Nancy Chodorow, *The Reproduction of Mothering: Psychoanalysis and the Sociology of Gender* (Berkeley: University of California Press, 1978); Sam Osherson, *Finding Our Fathers* (Glencoe, Ill.: Free Press, 1986); Robert Bly, *Iron John: A Book About Men* (Reading, Mass.: Addison-Wesley, 1990); Luepnitz, *The Family Interpreted*, p. 182. For an argument that Bly tends to blame women for much of this male suffering, see Fred Pelka, "Robert Bly and Iron John," *On the Issues*, Summer 1991. For alternative views on men's issues, see Andrew Kimball, "A Time for Men to Pull Together"; Warren Farrell, "Men as Success

Objects"; and Larry Letich, "Do You Know Who Your Friends Are?" *Utne Reader* 45 (May–June 1991).

41. Robert Haveman, Barbara Wolfe, and James Spaulding, "The Relation of Educational Attainment to Childhood Events and Circumstances," Institute for Research on Poverty Discussion Paper no. 908–90 (Madison: Institute for Research on Poverty, 1990), p. 28; Elaine Blechman, "Are Children With One Parent at Psychological Risk? A Methodological Review," *Journal of Marriage and the Family* (February 1982): 185; Ann Milne et al., "Single Parents, Working Mothers, and the Educational Achievement of School Children," *Sociology of Education* 59 (1986): 132.

42. Krantz, "Divorce and Children," pp. 257–58; Rie Bosman and Wiepke Louwes, "School Careers of Children from One-Parent and Two-Parent Families," *The Netherlands Journal of Sociology* 63 (1988): 122.

43. Demo and Acock, "Impact of Divorce," p. 170; Blechman, "Children with One Parent," pp. 186, 189; Joseph Guttmann, Nehemia Geva, and Sally Gefen, "Teachers' and School Children's Stereotypic Perception of 'the Child of Divorce,'" *American Educational Research Journal* 25 (1988).

44. Nan Marie Astone and Sara McLanahan, "Family Structure and High School Completion: The Role of Parental Practices," Institute for Research on Poverty Discussion Paper no. 905–89 (Madison: Institute for Research on Poverty, 1989), p. 38; Dornbusch and Gray, "Single-Parent Families," pp. 286–87, 292.

45. Joan Kelly, "Longer-Term Adjustment in Children of Divorce," *Journal of Family Psychology* 2 (1988); Faludi, *Backlash,* p. 26; Sara McLanahan, "The Two Faces of Divorce: Women's and Children's Interests," Institute for Research on Poverty Discussion Paper no. 903–89 (Madison: Institute for Research on Poverty, 1989); Martha Fineman and Anne Opie, "The Uses of Social Science Data in Legal Policymaking: Custody Determinations at Divorce," *Wisconsin Law Review* 1 (1987): 141n105; *Medical Tribune News Service,* 10 March 1991.

46. Blechman, "Children with One Parent"; James Coleman, "Families and Schools," *Educational Researcher* 16 (1987): 32–38, and Coleman, "The Corporation Versus the Family," *Innovation* 4, no. 5 (1988): 540; Colleen Johnson, *Ex Familia: Grandparents, Parents and Children Adjust to Divorce* (New Brunswick, N.J.: Rutgers University Press, 1988), pp. 162–83; Judith Stacey, *Brave New Families: Stories of Domestic Upheaval in Late Twentieth Century America* (New York: Basic Books, 1990).

47. Arlene Skolnick, "The Myth of the Vulnerable Child," *Psychology Today* 11 (1978): 58.

48. Donald Hansen, "Family-School Articulations: The Effects of Interac-

tion Rule Mismatch," *American Educational Research Journal* 23 (1986): 643.

49. Judy Dunn and Robert Plomin, *Separate Lives: Why Siblings Are So Different* (New York: Basic Books, 1991).

50. Jonathon Cobb and Richard Sennett, *The Hidden Injuries of Class* (New York: Knopf, 1972); Urie Bronfenbrenner, *The Ecology of Human Development: Experiments by Nature and Design* (Cambridge: Harvard University Press, 1979), pp. 269–70.

51. Douglas LaBier, *Modern Madness: The Emotional Fallout of Success* (Reading, Mass.: Addison-Wesley, 1986); Robert Karasek and Tores Theorell, *Healthy Work: Stress, Productivity, and the Reconstruction of Working Life* (New York: Basic Books, 1970); *The Olympian,* 8 May 1991; *University of California Wellness Letter* 6 (1990), pp. 4–5.

52. Karasek and Theorell, *Healthy Work; The Olympian,* 17 August 1989; Skolnick, "Vulnerable Child," p. 60; Susan Ostrander, *Women of the Upper Class* (Philadephia: Temple University Press, 1984), p. 84.

53. Daniel Goleman, "Older Men and Happiness," *New York Times News Service,* 24 February 1990.

54. Lois Hoffman, "The Effects of Maternal and Paternal Employment," in Gerstel and Gross, eds., *Families and Work,* p. 384.

55. Skolnick, "The Vulnerable Child," p. 58, and "The Family Revisited: Themes in Recent Social Science Research," *Journal of Interdisciplinary History* 4 (1975): 710; Jean MacFarlane, "Perspectives on Personality Consistency and Change from the Guidance Study," *Vita Humana* 7 (1964): 123.

56. Helen Keller, John Albert Macy, and Annie Sullivan, *The Story of My Life* (New York: Grossett & Dunlap, 1905). My thanks to Britt Nederhood, principal of Garfield School, for providing me with the other examples.

57. Donald Winnicott, "Communication Between Infant and Mother, Mother and Infant, Compared and Contrasted," in *Home Is Where We Start From,* ed. D. Winnicott (New York: Penguin, 1986), p. 144.

58. Richard Kagan, *Families in Perpetual Crisis* (New York: Norton, 1989).

59. *New York Times,* 21 December 1990; *The Olympian,* September 1989; Kenneth Dodge, John Bates, and Gregory Pettit, "Mechanisms in the Cycle of Violence," *Science* 250 (1990).

60. Leroy Pelton, "Child Abuse and Neglect: The Myth of Classlessness," *American Journal of Orthopsychiatry* 48 (1978); Eli Newberger, "The Helping Hand Strikes Again: Unintended Consequences of Child Abuse Reporting," and Newberger and Richard Gelles, "Family Violence: What We Know and Can Do," in Newberger and Bourne, eds., *Unhappy Families;* Dee Wil-

son, "Basic Information About Child Abuse and Neglect," Department of Social and Health Services, Olympia, Wash., January 1989; Joan Jones and R. L. McNeely, "Mothers Who Neglect and Those Who Do Not: A Comparative Study," *Social Casework: The Journal of Contemporary Social Work* (November 1980): 561; Miller et al., *Risk Assessment in Child Protection.*

61. Lois Forer, "Bring Back the Orphanages," *Washington Monthly,* April 1988; Bronfenbrenner, *Ecology of Human Development,* p. 144; Rutter, *The Qualities of Mothering;* Segal, "10 Myths."

62. Richard Gelles and Jon Conte, "Domestic Violence and Sexual Abuse of Children: A Review of Research in the Eighties," in Booth, ed., *Contemporary Families,* p. 331; Mary Pharis and Victoria Levin, "'A Person to Talk to Who Really Cared': High-Risk Mothers' Evaluation of Services in an Intensive Research Program," *Child Welfare* 3 (1991); Lisbeth Schorr, *Within Our Reach: Breaking the Cycle of Disadvantage* (New York: Anchor, 1988); James Garbarino, "Can We Measure Success in Preventing Child Abuse? Issues in Policy, Programming and Research," *Child Abuse and Neglect* 10 (1986); Edward Zigler, Nancy Rubin, and Joan Kaufman, "Do Abused Children Become Abusive Parents?" *Parents,* May 1988; Emmy Werner and Ruth Smith, *Kauai's Children Come of Age* (Honolulu: University of Hawaii Press, 1977); Emmy Werner and Ruth Smith, *Vulnerable but Invincible: A Longitudinal Study of Resilient Children* (New York: McGraw-Hill, 1982); Emmy Werner, "Children of the Garden Isle," *Scientific American,* April 1989.

63. *The Nation,* 20 May 1991, p. 653; Mary McGrory, "In Washington, Weapons Still Come Before Kids," *Washington Post,* 29 January 1991; Dornbusch and Gray, "Single-Parent Families," p. 280; Sheila Kammerman, *Child Care, Family Benefits, and Working Parents: A Study in Comparative Policy* (New York: Columbia University Press, 1981); *CDF Reports* 12 (1991): 2.

64. John Cotterell, "Work and Community Influences on the Quality of Child Rearing," *Child Development* 57 (1986); Keith Crnic et al., "Effects of Stress and Social Support on Mothers," *Child Development* 54 (1983); James Coleman, "Families and Schools," *Educational Researcher* 16 (1987): 20; Judith Omstead, "Informal Social Support: A Key to Family Support," Office of Research and Data Analysis, Washington State Department of Social and Health Services, May 1988; Benjamin Gottlieb, ed., *Social Networks and Social Support* (Beverly Hills: Sage, 1982), esp. pp. 108–9, 152, 187; James Whittaker and James Garbarino, *Social Support Networks: Informal Helping in the Human Services* (New York: Aldine, 1983).

65. Eleanor Leacock, "Montagnais Women and the Program for Jesuit Colonization," in *Women and Colonization: Anthropological Perspectives,* ed. Mona Etieinne and Eleanor Leacock (New York: Praeger, 1980), p. 31.

Chapter 10

1. On diversity among black families and teenagers, see Robert Hill et al., *Research on African-American Families: A Holistic Perspective* (Boston: William Monroe Trotter Institute, 1989); and Reginald Jones, ed., *Black Adolescents* (Berkeley: Cobb and Henry, 1989).

2. Gerald Jaynes and Robin Williams, Jr., eds., *A Common Destiny: Blacks and American Society* (Washington, D.C.: National Academy Press, 1989), pp. 27–28, 297–98; Walter Shapiro, "Unfinished Business," *Time,* 7 August 1989, p. 14.

3. Ronald Mincy, "Paradoxes in Black Economic Progress: Incomes, Families, and the Underclass," *The Urban Institute Discussion Paper,* February 1989; "Black Americans in City Hall," *Black Enterprise* 21 (1990): 149; Richard Marin and Dan Balz, "There's Still Room for Improvement in Racial Relations," *Washington Post National Weekly Edition,* 30 October–5 November 1989; *Wall Street Journal,* 22 August 1990.

4. Margery Turner, Michael Fix, and Raymond Struyk, *Opportunities Denied, Opportunities Diminished: Racial Discrimination in Hiring* (Washington, D.C.: Urban Institute Press, 1991); Marin and Balz, "Still Room for Improvement"; David Broder, "Who Will Face the Realities of Race?" *Washington Post National Weekly Edition,* 29 April–5 May 1991; U.S. Department of Health and Human Services report cited in *The Olympian,* 16 March 1989; James Comer, "Racism and the Education of Young Children," *Teachers College Record* 90 (1989); Jonathon Kozol, *Savage Inequalities* (New York: Crown, 1991); Christine Gorman, "Why Do Blacks Die Young?" *Time,* 16 September 1991.

5. *Atlanta Journal/Constitution,* 22 January 1989; *Dollars and Sense,* April 1990, p. 23; Douglas Massey and Nancy Denton, "Suburbanization and Segregation in U.S. Metropolitan Areas," *American Journal of Sociology* 94 (1988); *New York Times News Service,* 25 November 1990 and 11 January 1991; *Time,* 7 August 1989, p. 14; *The Nation,* 24–31 July 1989, p. 114; "The New Politics of Race," *Newsweek,* 6 May 1991.

6. *New York Times,* 9 October 1989; *Still Far from the Dream: Recent Developments in Black Income, Employment and Poverty* (Washington, D.C.: Center on Budget and Policy Priorities, October 1988); Morton Kondracke, "The Two Black Americas," *The New Republic,* 6 February 1989, p. 18; Jaynes and Williams, *Common Destiny,* pp. 6–8, 19, 28; *Wall Street Journal,* 22 August 1990; Bill McAllister, "The Plight of Young Black Men in America," *The Washington Post National Weekly Edition,* 12–18 February 1990; Fred Harris and Roger Wilkins, *Quiet Riots: Race and Poverty in the United States* (New York: Pantheon, 1988), p. 125.

7. *Kids Count* (Washington, D.C.: Center for Social Policy, January 1991); *New York Times,* 9 October 1989; U.S. Department of Health and Human Services report, *The Olympian,* 16 March 1989; David Ellwood, *Poor Support: Poverty in the American Family* (New York: Basic Books, 1988).

8. Robert Rector, letter to the editor, *Wall Street Journal,* 25 August 1989, p. A9; Georgie Ann Geyer, "Equality of Condition New Rallying Cry," *The Olympian,* 24 May 1990, p. 8A; Georgie Ann Geyer, "Jesse Ducks Black Youths' Call for Help," *The Olympian,* 8 March 1990, p. 9A.

9. Nicholas Lemann, "The Origins of the Underclass," *Atlantic Monthly,* June 1986, p. 35; Pete Hamill, "Breaking the Silence," *Esquire,* March 1988; Ismael Reed, "Living at Ground Zero," *Image Magazine, San Francisco Chronicle/Examiner,* 13 March 1988; Robert Samuelson, "Racism and Poverty," *Newsweek,* 7 August 1989; Daniel Moynihan, "Another War—the One on Poverty—Is Over, Too," *New York Times,* 16 July 1990; Morton Kondracke, "The Two Black Americas," *The New Republic,* 6 February 1989, p. 18.

10. Ken Auletta, *The Underclass* (New York: Random House, 1982); Working Seminar on the Family and American Welfare Policy, *The New Consensus on Family and Welfare: A Community of Self-Reliance* (Washington, D.C.: The American Enterprise Institute, 1987); *The Nation,* 24–31 July 1989, p. 120; George Will, "Work Ethic Our Best Tool to Fight Poverty," *The Olympian,* 31 May 1991.

11. Philip Bruce, *The Plantation Negro as a Freeman* (Williamstown, Mass.: Corner House, 1970); Herbert Gutman, "Persistent Myths About the Afro-American Family," *Journal of Interdisciplinary History* 6 (1975): 188. For a discussion of the falsified census figures Calhoun used to make his claims, see Stephen Jay Gould, *Hen's Teeth and Horses' Toes: Further Reflections in Natural History* (New York: Norton, 1984), pp. 303–9.

12. E. Franklin Frazier, *The Negro Family in Chicago* (Chicago: University of Chicago Press, 1932); Daniel Moynihan, *The Negro Family: The Case for National Action* (Washington D.C.: U.S. Government Printing Office, 1965); Bill Moyers, "The Vanishing Family: Crisis in Black America," CBS Special Reports, 1986.

13. William Wilson and Kathryn Neckerman, "Poverty and Family Structure: The Widening Gap Between Evidence and Public Policy Issues," in *Fighting Poverty: What Works and What Doesn't,* ed. Sheldon Danziger and Daniel Weinberg (Cambridge: Harvard University Press, 1986), p. 94; *U.S. News & World Report,* 3 July 1989; *Pathways to Success for America's Youth and Young Families,* William T. Grant Foundation Commission on Work, Family and Citizenship, November 1988, p. 25.

14. Pete Daniel, *In the Shadow of Slavery: Peonage in the South, 1901–1969*

(New York: Oxford University Press, 1973); Ronald Lewis, *Black Coal Miners in America: Race, Class and Community Conflict, 1780–1980* (Lexington: University Press of Kentucky, 1987); Leon Litwack, *North of Slavery: The Negro in the Free States, 1790–1860* (Chicago: University of Chicago Press, 1961); Herbert Shapiro, *White Violence and Black Response: From Reconstruction to Montgomery* (Amherst: University of Massachusetts Press, 1988); Stewart Tolnay and E. M. Beck, "Lethal Violence and the Great Migration, 1900–1930," *Social Science History* 14 (1990).

15. George Fredrickson, "Why Blacks Were Left Out," *New York Review of Books,* 12 October 1975; Gary Nash, *Forging Freedom: The Formation of Philadelphia's Black Community, 1720–1840* (Cambridge: Harvard University Press, 1988); Gutman, "Persistent Myths," p. 208; Shane White, "'We Dwell in Safety and Pursue our Honest Callings': Free Blacks in New York City, 1783–1810," *Journal of American History* 75 (1988); Shane White, *Somewhat More Independent: The End of Slavery in New York, 1770–1810* (Atlanta: University of Georgia Press, 1991); C. Vann Woodward, *Origins of the New South, 1877–1913* (Baton Rouge: Louisiana University Press, 1971); Sharon Harley, "For the Good of Family and Race: Gender, Work, and Domestic Roles in the Black Community, 1880–1930," *Signs* 15 (1990).

16. Joel Perlmann, *Ethnic Differences: Schooling and Social Structure Among the Irish, Italians, Jews, and Blacks in an American City, 1880–1935* (New York: Cambridge University Press, 1988); Stephen Thernstrom, *A History of the American People,* vol. 2 (New York: Harcourt Brace Jovanovich, 1989), p. 683; Stanley Leiberson, *A Piece of the Pie: Blacks and White Immigrants Since 1880* (Berkeley: University of California Press, 1980); Wilson, *The Truly Disadvantaged,* pp. 141–42; Theodore Hershberg et al., "A Tale of Three Cities," in *Philadelphia: Work, Space, Family, and Group Experience in the 19th Century,* ed. Theodore Hershberg (New York: Oxford University Press, 1981), pp. 470, 476–84; C. Vann Woodward, "The Crisis of Caste," *The New Republic,* 6 November 1989, p. 44; Douglas Massey, "American Apartheid: Segregation and the Making of the Underclass," *American Journal of Sociology* 96 (1990).

17. Peter Ripley, "The Black Family in Transition: Louisiana, 1860–1865," *Journal of Southern History* 41 (1975): 371; George Rawick, ed., *The American Slave: A Composite Autobiography,* vol. 1 (Westport, Conn.: Greenwood Press, 1972); Herbert Gutman, "The Slave Family and its Legacies," *Historical Reflections* 6 (1979): 195; Erna Hellerstein, Leslie Hume, and Karen Offen, eds., *Victorian Women: A Documentary Account of Women's Lives in Nineteenth-Century England, France, and the United States* (Stanford: Stanford University Press, 1981), pp. 231–33; Thelma Jennings, "'Us Colored Women Had to Go Through a Plenty': Sexual Exploitation of

African American Slave Women," *Journal of Women's History* 1 (1990).

18. Eugene Genovese, *Roll, Jordan, Roll: The World the Slaves Made* (New York: Pantheon, 1974); George Rawick, "The Black Family Under Slavery," in Rawick, ed., *The American Slave,* vol. 1, p. 79; Andrew Miller, "Social Science and the Heritage of African American Families," in *The 'Underclass' Debate and the Transformation of Urban America,* ed. Michael Katz (New York: Social Science Research Council, forthcoming); Andrew Miller, "Child Fosterage in the United States: Signs of an African Heritage" (Paper prepared for the National Annual Conference on the Black Family in America, Louisville, Kentucky, March 1991).

19. Eugene Genovese, "American Slaves and their History," *New York Review of Books,* 3 December 1970, and *Roll, Jordan, Roll,* p. 50; John Blassingame, *The Slave Community: Plantation Life in the Ante-Bellum South* (New York: Oxford University Press, 1972); Herbert Gutman, *The Black Family in Slavery and Freedom, 1750–1925* (New York: Random House, 1976), p. 500; Lawrence Levine, *Black Culture and Black Consciousness: Afro-American Folk Thought from Slavery to Freedom* (New York: Oxford University Press, 1977); Bonnie Thornton Dill, "Our Mothers' Grief: Racial Ethnic Women and the Maintenance of Families," *Journal of Family History* 13 (1988); Mary Beth Norton, Herbert Gutman, and Ira Berlin, "The Afro-American Family in the Age of Revolution," in *Slavery and Freedom in the Age of Revolution,* ed. Ira Berlin and Ronald Hoffman (Charlottesville: University Press of Virginia, 1983), p. 191.

20. Theodore Hershberg, "Free Blacks in Antebellum Philadelphia," in Hershberg, ed., *Philadelphia,* p. 374; James Horton and Lois Horton, *Black Bostonians: Family Life and Community Struggle in the Antebellum North* (New York: Holmes and Meier, 1979). For a poignant literary description of how black women's jobs as domestics have affected family life, even in the twentieth century, see Langston Hughes, "One Christmas Eve," in *The Ways of White Folks* (New York: Knopf, 1934).

21. Leith Mullings, "Uneven Development: Class, Race, and Gender in the United States Before 1900," in *Women's Work: Development and the Division of Labor by Gender,* ed. Eleanor Leacock and Helen Safa (South Hadley, Mass.: Bergin and Garvey, 1986), p. 53; Ira Berlin, Steven Miller, and Leslie Rowland, "Afro-American Families in the Transition from Slavery to Freedom," *Radical History Review* 42 (1988): 189–201; Ripley, "Black Family in Transition," p. 380; John Hope Franklin, *From Slavery to Freedom* (New York: Knopf, 1980); Leon Litwack, *Been in the Storm So Long: The Aftermath of Slavery* (New York: Knopf, 1979); Jacqueline Jones, *Labor of Love, Labor of Sorrow: Black Women, Work, and the Family from Slavery to the Present* (New York: Basic Books, 1985).

22. Herbert Gutman, "Persistent Myths About the Afro-American Family," *Journal of Interdisciplinary History* 6 (1975); Theodore Hershberg, "Free Blacks in Antebellum Pennsylvania," *Journal of Social History* 5 (1971–72); Paul Lammermeier, "The Urban Black Family of the Nineteenth Century: A Study of Black Family Structure in the Ohio Valley, 1850–1880," *Journal of Marriage and the Family* 35 (1973): 455; Shepard Krech III, "Black Family Organization in the Nineteenth Century: An Ethnological Perspective," *Journal of Interdisciplinary History* 12 (1982).

23. Elizabeth Pleck, *Black Migration and Poverty: Boston 1865–1900* (New York: Academic Press, 1979), pp. 194, 182; Gutman, *Black Family*, pp. 448–56, 521–26, 530.

24. Gutman, "Persistent Myths," pp. 205–7; Paul Worthman, "Working Class Mobility in Birmingham, Alabama, 1880–1914," in *Anonymous Americans: Explorations in Nineteenth-Century Social History*, ed. Tamara Hareven (Englewood Cliffs, N.J.: Prentice-Hall, 1971), p. 197; Ira Berlin and Herbert Gutman, "Natives and Immigrants, Free Men and Slaves," *American Historical Review* 88 (1983): 1194.

25. Rose Brewer, "Black Women in Poverty: Some Comments on Female-Headed Families," *Signs* 13 (1988): 339.

26. James Borchert, *Alley Life in Washington: Family, Community, Religion, and Folklife in the City, 1850–1970* (Urbana: University of Illinois Press, 1980); Pleck, *Black Migration and Poverty*, p. 196; James and Lois Horton, *Black Bostonians*; Jeanne Giovannoni and Andrew Billingsly, *Children of the Storm* (New York: Harcourt Brace Jovanovich, 1972); Edyth Ross, *The Black Heritage in Social Welfare, 1860–1930* (Scarecrow Press, 1978); Dorothy Height, "Self-Help—A Black Tradition," *The Nation*, 24–31 July 1989; Peter Holloran, *Boston's Wayward Children: Social Services for Homeless Children, 1830–1930* (Rutherford, N.J.: Fairleigh Dickinson University Press, 1989).

27. James Grossman, *Land of Hope: Chicago, Black Southerners, and the Great Migration* (Chicago: University of Chicago Press, 1989); Pleck, "A Mother's Wages," p. 499; Hershberg, "A Tale of Three Cities"; Michael Katz, *In the Shadow of the Poorhouse* (New York: Basic Books, 1986); Thernstrom, *History of the American People*, vol. 2, pp. 683–86; Stephanie Coontz, *The Social Origins of Private Life: A History of American Families* (London: Verso, 1988), chap. 8; *Washington Post National Weekly Edition*, 12–18 February 1990.

28. Gutman, *Black Family*, pp. 521–30; Jaynes and Williams, *Common Destiny*, p. 528; Henry Walker, "Black-White Differences in Marriage and Family Patterns," in *Feminism, Children, and the New Families*, ed. Sanford Dornbusch and Myra Strober (New York: Guilford Press, 1988), p. 99.

29. Carol Stack, *All Our Kin: Strategies for Survival in a Black Community* (New York: Harper & Row, 1974); Demetri Shimkin, Edith Shimkin, and Dennis Frate, eds., *The Extended Family in Black Society* (Chicago: University of Chicago Press, 1978); Joyce Aschenbrenner, *Lifelines: Black Families in Chicago* (New York: Holt, Rinehart & Winston, 1975); Joyce Ladner, *Tomorrow's Tomorrow: The Black Women* (New York: Doubleday, 1971); Paula Giddings, *"When and Where I Enter…": The Impact of Black Women on Race and Sex in America* (New York: William Morrow, 1984); Rosalyn Terborg-Penn and Sharon Harley, eds., *The Afro-American Woman: Struggles and Images* (Port Washington, N.Y.: Kennikat, 1978).

30. Jessica Daniel, "Cultural and Ethnic Issues: The Black Family," in *Unhappy Families: Clinical and Research Perspectives on Family Violence,* ed. Eli Newberger and Richard Bourne (Littletown, Mass.: PSG Publications, 1985), pp. 146–48. See also Robert Hill, *The Strength of Black Families* (New York: Emerson Hall, 1972); Joyce Ladner, ed., *The Death of White Sociology* (New York: Random House, 1973); Robert Staples, "The Myth of the Black Matriarchy," *Black Scholar* 2 (1970); Harriet McAdoo and Rosalyn Terborg-Penn, "Historical Trends in Perspectives of Afro-American Families," *Trends in History* 3 (1985); Andrew Miller, "Tangling with Pathology: Displacement and the Private Western Nuclear Family" (Typescript, Population Studies Center, University of Pennsylvania, 28 May 1991); Robert Taylor et al., "Developments in Research on Black Families: A Decade Review," in *Contemporary Families: Looking Forward, Looking Back,* ed. Alan Booth (Minneapolis: National Council on Family Relations, 1991), pp. 277, 280–81.

31. See, for example, James Comer, *Maggie's American Dream: The Life and Times of a Black Family* (New York: New American Library, 1988), and Allan Ballard, *One More Day's Journey: The Story of a Family and a People* (New York: McGraw-Hill, 1984).

32. Theodore Hershberg et al., "A Tale of Three Cities: Blacks, Immigrants, and Opportunity in Philadelphia, 1850–1880, 1930, 1970," in Hershberg, ed., *Philadelphia,* p. 480.

33. Jaynes and Williams, *Common Destiny,* pp. 6–7, 274, 294–97; Wayne Vroman, "Industrial Change and Black Men's Relative Earnings: Final Report" (Washington, D.C.: The Urban Institute, July 1989), p. 2; Robert Greenstein, "Losing Faith in 'Losing Ground,'" *The New Republic,* 25 March 1983, pp. 16–17.

34. Colin Greer, *The Great School Legend* (New York: Basic Books, 1972); Stephen Thernstrom, *Poverty and Progress* (Cambridge: Harvard University Press, 1964).

35. Nicholas Lemann, *The Promised Land: The Great Migration and How*

It Changed America (New York: Knopf, 1990); Jaynes and Williams, *Common Destiny*, pp. 9–13, 302; *Wall Street Journal*, 22 August 1989; John Bauman, *Public Housing, Race, and Renewal: Urban Planning in Philadelphia, 1920–1974* (Philadelphia: Temple University Press, 1987); James Zais, "The Housing of Families With Children," in *American Families and the Economy: The High Costs of Living*, ed. Richard Nelson and Felicity Skidmore (Washington, D.C.: National Academy Press, 1985), p. 311; Harris and Wilkins, *Quiet Riots*, pp. 108–9.

36. Maxine Baca Zinn, "Family, Race, and Poverty in the Eighties," *Signs* 14 (Summer 1989): 865; Harvey Bluestone, Bennett Harrison, and Lucy Gorham, "Storm Clouds on the Horizon: Labor Market Crisis and Industrial Policy," *Dollars and Sense* 115 (1986); Spencer Rich, "Black, White and Pink Slips," *Washington Post National Weekly Edition*, 2–8 September 1991.

37. William Wilson and Kathryn Neckerman, "Poverty and Family Structure: The Widening Gap Between Evidence and Public Policy Issues," in *Fighting Poverty: What Works and What Doesn't*, ed. Sheldon Danziger and Daniel Weinberg (Cambridge: Harvard University Press, 1986); *The Olympian*, 12 June 1987; *Pathways to Success for America's Youth and Young Families*, William T. Grant Foundation Commission on Work, Family and Citizenship, November 1988, p. 26; William Julius Wilson, "The Underclass: Issues, Perspectives, and Public Policy," *Annals, American Academy of Political and Social Science* 501 (1989): 184.

38. Elijah Anderson, *A Place on the Corner* (Chicago: University of Chicago Press, 1978); William Julius Wilson, *The Declining Significance of Race: Blacks and Changing American Institutions* (Chicago: University of Chicago Press, 1978), and *The Truly Disadvantaged: The Inner City, the Underclass, and Public Policy* (Chicago: University of Chicago Press, 1987); Paul Peterson, ed., *The New Urban Reality* (Washington, D.C.: The Brookings Institute, 1985); Jaynes and Williams, *Common Destiny*, p. 14; *Dollars and Sense*, April 1990, p. 6.

39. Douglas Massey and Mitchell Eggers, "The Ecology of Inequality: Minorities and the Concentration of Poverty, 1970–1980," *American Journal of Sociology* 95 (1990): 1183–86; Massey; "American Apartheid"; "Alternative Measures of Poverty" (Joint Economic Committee Report, Washington State Legislature, 18 October 1989); Douglas Massey and Nancy Denton, "Suburbanization and Segregation in U.S. Metropolitan Areas," *American Journal of Sociology* 94 (1988); Sidney Fine, *Violence in the Model City* (Ann Arbor: University of Michigan Press, 1989); Jaynes and Williams, *Common Destiny*, p. 310; Vroman, "Industrial Change and Black Men's Earnings," p. 1; John Kasarda, "Urban Industrial Transition and the Underclass," *Annals, AAPSS* 501 (1989).

40. Wilson, *The Truly Disadvantaged,* pp. 137–38; Massey and Eggers, "Ecology of Inequality," pp. 1178–79; Camilo Jose Vergara, "New York's New Ghettos," *The Nation,* 17 June 1991, and *The New American Ghetto* (Princeton: Princeton Architectural Press, forthcoming).

41. Loic Wacquant and William Julius Wilson, "The Cost of Racial and Class Exclusion in the Inner City," *Annals, AAPSS* 501 (1989). Jaynes and Wilkins cite research showing that even older, steadily employed men in the inner cities tend to be in industries that are no longer hiring. Lacking the social networks that refer people to jobs, they cannot help the young of their community in the same way that older men in white working-class communities can (*Common Destiny,* p. 321).

42. *Dollars and Sense,* April 1990, pp. 6–8; *Still Far from the Dream,* p. 11; Alex Kotlowitz, *There Are No Children Here: The Story of Two Boys Growing Up in the Other America* (New York: Doubleday, 1991).

43. *Time,* 29 August 1977, p. 14; "A Nation Apart," *U.S. News & World Report,* 17 March 1986; Lois Hoffman, "The Effects on Children of Maternal and Paternal Employment," in *Families and Work,* ed. Naomi Gerstel and Harriet Gross (Philadelphia: Temple University Press, 1987), p. 366; William Kornblum, "Who Is the Underclass?" *Dissent* (Spring 1991).

44. Wilson, *The Truly Disadvantaged,* p. 8; Wacquant and Wilson, "Cost of Racial and Class Exclusion," p. 25; Vergara, "New York's New Ghettos"; William J. Wilson, "The Ghetto Underclass and the Social Transformation of the Inner City," *The Black Scholar* (May–June 1988); Michael Katz, *The Undeserving Poor: From the War on Poverty to the War on Welfare* (New York: Pantheon, 1989), pp. 196–205, 234; Marian Wright Edelman, *Families in Peril: An Agenda for Social Change* (Cambridge: Harvard University Press, 1987), p. 73; *Dollars and Sense,* September 1989, p. 11; Harris and Wilkins, *Quiet Riots,* pp. 81–99; Patricia Ruggles, "Short- and Long-Term Poverty in the United States: Measuring the American 'Underclass'" (Washington, D.C.: The Urban Institute, June 1989); Richard Ropers, *Persistent Poverty: The American Dream Turned Nightmare* (New York: Plenum, 1991).

45. *Dollars and Sense,* April 1990, p. 7; Patricia Ruggles and William Martin, "Measuring the Size and Characteristics of the Underclass: How Much Do We Know?" (Washington, D.C.: The Urban Institute, December 1986); Ronald Mincy, "Is There a White Underclass?" (Washington D.C.: The Urban Institute, June 1988); *The Oregonian,* 28 October 1990; *New York Times,* 11 August 1990; *New England Journal of Medicine,* 26 April 1990; Michael Isikoff, "Contrary to Popular Belief," *Washington Post National Weekly Edition,* 4–10 March 1991; Evan Stark, "The Myth of Black Violence," *New York Times,* 18 July 1990; Clarence Page, "Black Crime and

the Chasm Between 'Correct' and 'Right,'" *Chicago Tribune*, 15 January 1991; Jaynes and Williams, *Common Destiny*, p. 22.

46. Mercer Sullivan, "Absent Fathers in the Inner City," *Annals, AAPSS* 502 (1989): 54, 58; Ron Haskins et al., "Estimates of National Child Support Collections Potential and Income Security of Female-Headed Families," Bush Institute for Child and Family Policy, Frank Porter Graham Child Development Center, University of North Carolina, 1985; Sandra Danziger and Norma Radin, "Absent Does Not Equal Uninvolved: Predictors of Fathering in Teen Mother Families," *Journal of Marriage and the Family* 52 (1990); Ann Nichols-Casebolt, "Black Families Headed by Single Mothers," *Social Work* 33 (1988): 309; Jerold Heiss, "Women's Values Regarding Marriage and the Family," in *Black Families*, ed. Harriette McAdoo (Beverly Hills: Sage, 1981).

47. Elijah Anderson, *Streetwise: Race, Class, and Change in an Urban Community* (Chicago: University of Chicago Press, 1990), and "Sex Codes and Family Life among Poor Inner-City Youths," *Annals, AAPSS* 501 (1989).

48. *CDF Reports* 12 (1991): 6; Anderson, "Sex Codes and Family Life," pp. 64–65, 76–78.

49. Robert Hayes, "Homeless Children," in *Caring for America's Children*, ed. Frank Macchiarola and Alan Gartner (New York: Academy of Political Science, 1989), p. 68.

50. Pleck, *Black Migration and Poverty*, pp. 198–200; Vonnie McLoyd, "Socialization and Development in a Changing Economy," *American Psychologist* 44 (February 1989); Alice Coner-Edwards and Jeanne Spurlock, eds., *Black Families in Crisis: The Middle Class* (New York: Brunner/Mazel, 1988); Katz, *Undeserving Poor*, p. 172.

51. Stack, *All Our Kin;* Elizabeth Higginbotham and Lyn Cannon, "Rethinking Mobility: Towards a Race and Gender Inclusive Theory" (Center for Research on Women Paper no. 8, Memphis State University, 1988), pp. 35–36.

52. Mary Jo Bane, "Household Composition and Poverty," in *Fighting Poverty: What Works and What Doesn't*, ed. Sheldon Danziger and Daniel Weinberg (Cambridge: Harvard University Press, 1986); Nichols-Casebolt, "Black Families Headed by Single Mothers," p. 310.

53. William Darity and Samuel Myers, "Does Welfare Dependency Cause Female Headship? The Case of the Black Family," *Journal of Marriage and the Family* (November 1984): 765; David Ellwood and Lawrence Summers, "Poverty in America: Is Welfare the Answer or the Problem?" in Danziger and Weinberg, eds., *Fighting Poverty;* Wilson and Neckerman, "Poverty and

Family Structure"; Grant Foundation, *Pathways to Success*, p. 25; Reynolds Farley and Walter Allen, *The Color Line and The Quality of Life in America* (New York: Russell Sage, 1987); Neil Bennett, David Bloom, and Patricia Craig, "The Divergence of Black and White Marriage Patterns," *American Journal of Sociology* 95 (1989): 692; Erol Ricketts, "The Origin of Black Female-Headed Families," *Focus* 12 (1989): 36.

54. Mark Testa, Nan Marie Astone, Marilyn Krogh, and Kathryn Neckerman, "Employment and Marriage Among Inner-City Fathers," *Annals, AAPSS* 501 (January 1989): 87, 90–91; Bennett et al., "Divergence of Black and White Marriage Patterns," p. 709.

55. David Ellwood and David Wise, "Youth Employment in the 1970s," in *American Families and the Economy: The High Costs of Living*, ed. Richard Nelson and Felicity Skidmore (Washington, D.C.: National Academy Press, 1983), pp. 63, 91, 100; Jaynes and Williams, *Common Destiny*, p. 281.

56. Greg Duncan and Willard Rodgers, "Longitudinal Aspects of Childhood Poverty," *Journal of Marriage and the Family* 50 (November 1988): 1012; Barbara Ehrenreich, "Two, Three, Many Husbands," *Mother Jones* (July–August 1986): 8.

57. Bane, "Household Composition and Poverty," pp. 214–15; *Still Far from the Dream: Recent Developments in Black Income, Employment and Poverty* (Washington, D.C.: Center on Budget and Policy Priorities, October 1988), p. 12.

58. Duncan and Rodgers, "Longitudinal Aspects," p. 1015.

59. Ronald Takaki, *Strangers from a Different Shore: A History of Asian Americans* (Boston: Little, Brown, 1989), pp. 474–75; Peter Kwong, *The New Chinatown* (New York: Hill and Wang, 1987); Thea Lee, "Trapped on a Pedestal," *Dollars and Sense*, March 1990; Henry Shih-Shan Tsai, *The Chinese Experience in America* (Bloomington: Indiana University Press, 1986), pp. 158–59, 188–90; Maxine Baca Zinn and D. Stanley Eitzen, *Diversity in American Families* (New York: Harper & Row, 1987), pp. 75–93; Maxine Baca Zinn, "Family, Race, and Poverty," *Signs* (Summer 1989); "Falling Further Behind," *Newsweek*, 19 August 1991; "Shortchanged: Recent Developments in Hispanic Poverty, Income and Employment," Center on Budget and Policy Priorities, November 1988, p. v; Gary Sandefur, "American Indian Reservations: The First Underclass Area?" *Focus* 12 (1989); Harris and Wilkins, *Quiet Riots*, p. 57. For references on the historical variety of Native American family traditions, see Stephanie Coontz, *The Social Origins of Private Life: A History of American Families, 1600–1900* (London: Verso, 1988), pp. 41–72.

60. *The Nation*, 26 March 1990, p. 410, and 20 November 1989, p. 597; *Tacoma News Tribune*, 29 October 1990; Michael Isikoff, "Contrary to Pop-

ular Belief," *Washington Post National Weekly Edition,* 4–10 March 1991; Joyce Beckett and Audrey Smith, "Work and Family Roles: Egalitarian Marriage in Black and White Families," *Social Service Review* 55 (1981); Julia Ericksen, William Yancey, and Eugene Ericksen, "The Division of Family Roles," *Journal of Marriage and the Family* 41 (1979).

Chapter 11

1. Charles Krauthammer, "An Epidemic No One Knows How to Cure," *Washington Post,* 28 June 1991; Richard Whitmore, "Education Declines Linked with Erosion of Family," Gannett News Service wire report, *The Olympian,* 1 October 1991, p. A2; Bryce Christensen, ed., *When Families Fail...The Social Costs* (Lanham, Md.: University Press of America, 1991); Lenore Weitzman, *The Divorce Revolution: The Unexpected Social and Economic Costs for Women and Children in America* (New York: Free Press, 1985), pp. 323, 343; National Advisory Council on Economic Opportunity, *Critical Choices for the '80s* (Washington, D.C.: National Advisory Council, 1980), p. 1; Samuel Preston, "Children and the Elderly: Divergent Paths for America's Dependents," *Demography* 21 (1984); *New York Times,* 29 January 1992, p. A14; E. J. Dionne, "The Idea of Equality Is Proving Unequal to the Demands of the Day," *Washington Post National Weekly Edition,* 7–13 May 1990, p. 13.

2. Richard Whitmore, "Way to Aid Education May Be to Aid Families," and "Marriage Helps End Poverty," Gannett News Service wire report, *The Olympian,* 24 June 1991, p. A2; Richard Whitmore, "Families Vital to Success," Gannett News Service wire report, *The Olympian,* 26 June 1991, p. A1.

3. *CDF Reports* 12 (1990): 10; Ann Rosewater, "Child and Family Trends: Beyond the Numbers," in *Caring for America's Children,* ed. Frank Macchiarola and Alen Gartner (New York: The Academy of Political Science, 1989), pp. 13–15.

4. "Mothers-Only Families" (Washington, D.C.: Government Printing Office/HRD–91–62, April 1991); Mary Jo Bane, "Household Composition and Poverty," in *Fighting Poverty: What Works and What Doesn't,* ed. Sheldon Danziger and Daniel Weinberg (Cambridge: Harvard University Press, 1986), p. 216.

5. Elizabeth Evanson, "Social and Economic Change Since the Great Depression: Studies of Census Data, 1940–1980," *Focus* 3 (Fall 1988): 4.

6. *Chicago Tribune,* 2 March 1991; Greg Duncan and Willard Rodgers,

"Longitudinal Aspects of Childhood Poverty," *Journal of Marriage and the Family* 50 (1988).

7. Lawrence Mishel and David Frankel, *The State of Working America, 1990–1991 Edition* (Armonk, N.Y.: M. E. Sharpe, 1991), pp. 7–8, 16, 186–87; Mark Littman, "Poverty in the 1980's: Are the Poor Getting Poorer?" *Monthly Labor Review* (June 1989): 14; Isabel Sawhill, "Poverty in the U.S.: Why Is It So Persistent?" *Journal of Economic Literature* (September 1988): 1088; Bane, "Household Composition," pp. 214–16; Richard Louv, *Childhood's Future* (Boston: Houghton Mifflin, 1990), p. 48; Greg Duncan and Willard Rodgers, "Lone Parents: The Economic Challenge of Changing Family Structures," Directorate for Social Affairs, Manpower and Education, Organization for Economic Cooperation and Development, paper 04, December 1987, pp. 13, 21.

8. Sheila Kammerman and Alfred Kahn, "The Possibilities for Child and Family Policy: A Cross-National Perspective," in Macchiarola and Gartner, eds., *Caring for America's Children*, pp. 84–86; "Testimony of Robert Greenstein, Director, Center on Budget and Policy Priorities," House Committee on Ways and Means, 13 March 1991 (revised April 1991), p. 2; Mishel and Frankel, *State of Working America*, p. 265.

9. Frances Dahlberg, ed., *Woman the Gatherer* (New Haven: Yale University Press, 1981); Marshall Sahlins, *Stone Age Economics* (Chicago: Aldine, 1972); Colin Turnbull, *The Forest People* (New York: Clarion, 1969).

10. Steven Eries, Martin Rein, and Barbara Wiget, "Women and the Reagan Revolution," in Irene Diamond, ed., *Families, Politics, and Public Policy* (New York: Longman, 1983), p. 100; Fred Harris and Roger Wilkins, eds., *Quiet Riots: Race and Poverty in the United States* (New York: Pantheon, 1988), p. 52; Steven Rose and David Fasenfest, "Family Incomes in the 1980s: New Pressure on Wives, Husbands, and Young Adults" (Washington, D.C.: Economic Policy Institute, Working Paper no. 103, November 1988); Mishel and Frankel, *State of Working America*, p. 6; *Utne Reader*, 10 September 1991, p. 18. Part of the increase in single-parent family poverty stems from the growth in never-married mothers, since divorced female heads of families actually have much lower rates of poverty than never-married heads of households (James Scanlan, "Comment," *Signs* 16 [1991]: 412), but this growth does not explain the increase in poverty on its own, because unmarried motherhood is far more closely associated with prior poverty than is divorce.

11. Mishel and Frankel, *State of Working America*, p. 82; Heidi Hartmann and Roberta Spalter-Roth, "Improving Employment Opportunities for Women" (Testimony before the U.S. House of Representatives Committee

on Education and Labor, 27 February 1991); *Washington Post National Weekly Edition,* 3–9 September 1990.

12. Sheldon Danziger and Peter Gottschalk, "Families with Children Have Fared Worse," *Challenge* (March–April 1986): 47; "The Decreasing Anti-Poverty Effectiveness of Government Benefit Programs: 1979–1987," Center on Budget and Policy Priorities Report, September 1988; Cliff Johnson, Arloc Sherman, and Stephen Shames, *Child Poverty in America* (Washington, D.C.: Children's Defense Institute, 1991); Mishel and Frankel, *State of Working America,* p. 181; Christopher Matthews, "The Struggling Class," *Liberal Opinion Week,* 9 September 1991.

13. *The Forgotten Half: Pathways to Success for America's Youth and Young Families* (Washington, D.C.: Youth and America's Future: William T. Grant Commission on Work, Family and Citizenship, 1988), pp. 16–18; Danziger and Weinberg, eds., *Fighting Poverty;* "Life at the Edge," *Consumer Reports,* June, July, August, 1987; *Seattle Times,* 12 June and 16 December 1987; "Family Incomes in Trouble," Economic Policy Institute Briefing Paper, October 1986, p. 14; Cynthia Rexroat, "Interim Report," Carnegie Corporation Joint Center for Political Studies, February 1989, p. 3.

14. *Forgotten Half,* p. 16.

15. Mishel and Frankel, *State of Working America,* pp. 197–224; *Forgotten Half,* pp. 26, 99; Luov, *Childhood's Future,* pp. 48–49.

16. Cliff Johnson and Andrew Sum, *Declining Earnings of Young Men: Their Relation to Poverty, Teen Pregnancy, and Family Formation* (Washington, D.C.: Adolescent Pregnancy Prevention Clearinghouse, May 1987), pp. 11–12.

17. Gregory Weeks, *Leaving Public Assistance in Washington State* (Olympia: Washington State Institute for Public Policy, The Evergreen State College, March 1991), p. 5. These figures are quite different from the national estimates made in David Ellwood, "Targeting 'Would-Be' Long-Term Recipients of AFDC," *Report to the U.S. Department of Health and Human Services* (Washington, D.C.: Mathematica Policy Research, 1986). Weeks suggests three reasons for this discrepancy. First, it may be a matter of timing, since Ellwood's data are from the 1970s and the Washington data from the 1980s. Second, geography may be involved: Washington state has fewer pockets of poverty, in which there are simply no jobs available for unskilled workers, than the nation as a whole. Third, Ellwood's methodology was biased toward explaining economic changes by marriage. If a woman who moved off welfare both got a job and married within a year, she was coded as having "married out" rather than worked her way out, even if she first got a job and left welfare and then married ten months later. I would like to

express my gratitude to Gregory Weeks for going over these figures and methodologies with me. On child support, see Freya Sonenstein and Charles Calhoun, "Survey of Absent Parents: Pilot Results Executive Summary," *The Urban Institute Project Report,* July 1988; and *Seattle Times,* 18 June 1989.

18. Frank Levy and Richard Michel, "An Economic Bust for the Baby Boom," *Challenge* (March–April 1986): 34.

19. "Shares of Total Family Wealth" (Press release, Joint Economic Committee, Congress of the United States, 21 August 1986); Frank Levy and Richard Michel, *The Economic Future of American Families: Income and Wealth Trends* (Washington, D.C.: The Urban Institute Press), pp. 9–11; Ferdinand Lundberg, *The Rich and the Super-Rich* (New York: Lyle Stuart, 1968); *Social Indicators, 1973,* compiled by the Social and Economic Statistics Administration (Washington, D.C.: U.S. Department of Commerce, 1973).

20. "Low-Wage Jobs and Workers: Trends and Options for Change," Institute for Women's Policy Research, 1990; Mishel and Frankel, *State of Working America,* pp. 1–2, 223; Susan Householder Van Horn, *Women, Work, and Fertility, 1900–1986* (New York: New York University Press, 1988), p. 157; Richard Easterlin, *Birth and Fortune* (New York: Basic Books, 1980); Frank Levy, *Dollars and Dreams: The Changing American Income Distribution* (New York: Russell Sage, 1987), pp. 137–38; Clifford Clogg and James Shockey, "Mismatch Between Occupation and Schooling," *Demography* 21 (1984); Levy and Michel, *Economic Future of American Families,* pp. 15–33; Barry Bluestone and Bennett Harrison, "The Great American Job Machine: The Proliferation of Low-Wage Employment in the U.S. Economy" (Study prepared for the Joint Economic Committee of the U.S. Congress, December 1986); Isaac Shapiro and Robert Greenstein, "Making Work Pay: A New Agenda for Poverty Policies," Center on Budget and Policy Priorities, 21 March 1989, pp. 3, 6; Sarah Kuhn and Barry Bluestone, "Economic Restructuring and the Female Labor Market," in *Women, Households, and the Economy,* ed. Lourdes Beneria and Catherine Stimpson (New Brunswick: Rutgers University Press, 1987).

21. *New York Times* News Service, 17 June 1991; Charles Tilly, *Short Hours, Short Shrift: Causes and Consequences of Part-Time Work* (Washington, D.C.: Economic Policy Institute, 1990); Richard Morin, "Moonlighting More, But Enjoying it Less," *Washington Post National Weekly Edition,* 7–13 October 1991.

22. Mishel and Frankel, *State of Working America,* p. xii; Sawhill, "Poverty in the U.S.," p. 1090; Sheldon Danziger and Peter Gottschalk, "Increasing Inequality in the United States: What We Know and What We

Don't," *Journal of Post Keynesian Economics* 11 (1988–89); Levy, *Dollars and Dreams,* p. 6; Sheldon Danziger, Peter Gottschalk, and Eugene Smolensky, "How the Rich Have Fared, 1973–1987," *American Economic Review* 79 (1989); *Washington Post National Weekly Edition,* 7–13 October 1991.

23. Levy and Michel, *Economic Future of American Families,* p. 64; Sylvia Ann Hewlett, *When the Bough Breaks: The Cost of Neglecting Our Children* (New York: Basic Books, 1991), p. 74.

24. Levy and Michel, "An Economic Bust," p. 34; Richard Michel, "Why Can't We Agree on What's Happening to U.S. Living Standards?" *The Urban Institute Project Report,* June 1979, p. 5; *USA Today,* 22 August 1989; L. S. Travianos, *Lifelines from Our Past: A New World History* (New York: Pantheon, 1989).

25. Mishel and Frankel, *State of Working America,* p. 77; Hartmann and Spalter-Roth, "Improving Employment Opportunities"; Ruth Needleman, "A World in Transition: Women and Economic Change," *Labor Studies Journal* 10 (1986); Heidi Hartmann, "Women's Work, Family Diversity, and Employment Instability" (Testimony before the U.S. Senate Committee on Labor and Human Resources, 7 January 1991).

26. Alan Wolfe, *Whose Keeper? Social Science and Moral Obligation* (Berkeley: University of California Press, 1989), p. 68.

27. Michel, "Why Can't We Agree?," p. 6; Levy and Michel, "Economic Bust," p. 37; *Washington Spectator,* 15 April 1990, p. 1.

28. "Working Mothers Are Preserving Family Living Standards," Joint Economic Committee, 99th Cong. 2nd sess., May 1986; *Seattle Post-Intelligencer,* 23 August 1989; *Seattle Times,* 4 September 1990; *Washington Post National Weekly Edition,* 25 June–1 July 1990; Mishel and Frankel, *State of Working America,* pp. 30, 47, 213; Rose and Fasenfest, "Family Incomes in the 1980s"; David Hauter, "Two-Income Families Worked Harder," *Honolulu Advertiser,* 17 January 1992, p. 1.

29. Levy, *Dollars and Dreams,* p. 123.

30. Heather Ross and Isabel Sawhill, *Time of Transition: The Growth of Families Headed by Women* (Washington, D.C.: Urban Institute, 1975), p. 171.

31. Arlie Hochschild with Anne Machung, *The Second Shift: Working Parents and the Revolution at Home* (New York: Viking, 1989); Heidi Hartmann, "The Family as the Locus of Gender, Class and Political Struggle: The Example of Housework," *Signs* 6 (1981); Trish Hall, "Time on Your Hands?" *New York Times,* 3 July 1991.

32. Rosewater, "Child and Family Trends," pp. 6–7.

33. *Washington Post National Weekly Edition,* 27 May–2 June 1991; *The Case for Comprehensive Unemployment Insurance Reform* (Washington,

D.C.: Center for the Study of Social Policy, March 1987); Hewlett, *When the Bough Breaks,* p. 47; Paul Taylor, "When Safety Nets Leave the Needy in Free Fall," *Washington Post National Weekly Edition,* 9–11 September 1991.

34. Katherine McFate, *Poverty, Inequality and the Crisis of Social Policy: Summary of Findings* (Washington, D.C.: Joint Center for Political and Economic Studies, 1991); M. Edith Rosell and Lawrence Mishel, "Shortchanging Education: How U.S. Spending on Grades K–12 Lags Behind Other Industrial Nations" (Economic Policy Institute Briefing Paper, Washington, D.C., 1989).

35. Study on Home Ownership for Joint Economic Committee of Congress, reported in *Seattle Times,* 8 October 1989; "Women and Housing Fact Sheet," Institute for Women's Policy Research, January 1989; Chris Tilly and Abel Valenzuela, "Down and Out in the City," *Dollars and Sense,* April 1990, p. 6; Center on Budget and Policy Priorities, news release, 10 July 1989, Washington, D.C.; *The Olympian,* 9 August and 8 October 1989; Mishel and Frankel, *State of Working America,* p. 231; Hewlett, *When the Bough Breaks,* p. 46; *Los Angeles Times,* 22 July 1989.

36. Hewlett, *When the Bough Breaks,* p. 34; *CDF Reports* 12 (1991); Maxine Baca Zinn and D. Stanley Eitzen, *Diversity in American Families* (New York: Harper & Row, 1987), pp. 113, 326; *Washington Spectator,* 1 November 1990, p. 3; Michael Specter, "Putting Little Hands to Profitable Work," *Washington Post National Weekly Edition,* 22–28 April 1991.

37. David Whitman, "The Rise of the Hyper-Poor," *U.S. News & World Report,* 15 October 1990, pp. 40–42; Patricia Ruggles, *Short and Long Term Poverty in the United States: Measuring the American Underclass* (Washington, D.C.: Urban Institute Press, 1989).

38. Peter Rossi and James Wright, "The Urban Homeless: A Portrait of Urban Dislocation," *Annals, American Academy of Political and Social Science* 501 (1989); Geoffrey Crowley, "Children in Peril," *Newsweek Special Issue,* Summer 1991, p. 21.

39. *The Forgotten Half: An Interim Report on the School-to-Work Transition* (Washington, D.C.: William T. Grant Foundation Commission on Work, Family and Citizenship, 1988), p. 25; *The Newsletter* (Center for Research on Women, Memphis State University) 7 (1988): 3; Levy, *Dollars and Dreams,* p. 6.

40. Mike Davis, "Los Angeles: Civil Liberties Between the Hammer and the Rock," *New Left Review* 170 (1988): 54, "Homeowners and Homeboys," *North Star Review* (Spring 1990): 2–3, and *City of Quartz: Excavating the Future in L.A.* (London: Verso, 1990); Robert Bellah et al., *Habits of the Heart:*

Individualism and Commitment in American Life (New York: Harper & Row, 1986), pp. 71–75, 335.

41. *Washington Post National Weekly Edition,* 29 July–4 August 1991; Robert Greenstein and Scott Barancik, *Drifting Apart: New Findings on Growing Income Disparities Between the Rich, the Poor, and the Middle Class* (Washington, D.C.: Center on Budget and Policy Priorities, July 1990); *Washington Spectator,* 1 August 1990, p. 3.

42. *Wall Street Journal,* 26 July 1989, p. A12; Rose and Fasenfest, "Family Incomes in the 1980s," p. 3; Rosewater, "Child and Family Trends," pp. 6–7; Greenstein and Barancik, *Drifting Apart; The Washington Spectator,* 1 November 1990, p. 2; Sally Reed and R. Craig Sautter, "Children of Poverty," *Kappan Special Report,* June 1990, p. K4; Kevin Phillips, *The Politics of Rich and Poor: Wealth and the American Electorate in the Reagan Aftermath* (New York: Random House, 1990), pp. 11–12.

43. Robert Reich, *The Resurgent Liberal (and Other Unfashionable Prophecies)* (New York: Times Books, 1989); Lester Thurow, "Tax Wealth, not Income," *New York Times Magazine,* 11 April 1976, pp. 32, 102; Robert McCartney, "The Economic Pulse," *Washington Post National Weekly Edition,* 30 September–6 October 1991.

44. Phillips, *Politics of Rich and Poor,* pp. 68–69; Michael Lewis, *The Money Culture* (New York: Norton, 1991).

45. Nikki Finke, "Lost Out Generation," *Los Angeles Times,* 8 January 1989; *Time,* 8 January 1986, p. 24; *Wall Street Journal,* 26 July 1989, p. A12; *Business Week,* 6 May 1991; *The Olympian,* 28 April 1991; Richard Cohen, "Greed, Inc.," *Washington Post National Weekly Edition,* 30 September–6 October 1991.

46. E. J. Dionne, Jr., *Why Americans Hate Politics* (New York: Simon & Schuster, 1991); Eric Ambler, *A Coffin for Dimitrios* (San Diego: University of California Press, 1977), p. 53.

47. Robert Blecker, *Are Americans on a Consumption Binge? The Evidence Reconsidered* (Washington, D.C.: Economic Policy Institute, 1990); Mishel and Frankel, *State of Working America,* p. 37; Robert Pollin, *Deeper in Debt: The Changing Financial Conditions of U.S. Households* (Washington, D.C.: Economic Policy Institute, 1990); Levy, *Dollars and Dreams,* p. 22; Lisa Collins, "Fewer Sons Will Top Dads' Jobs," *USA Today,* 22 August 1989, p. 1A.

48. *The Nation,* 18 June 1990, p. 845; Hewlett, *When the Bough Breaks,* p. 103.

49. James Coleman, "Families and Schools," *Educational Researcher* 16 (1987): 36; Ben Wattenberg, *The Good News Is the Bad News Is Wrong* (New

York: Simon & Schuster, 1985), p. 281; James Patterson and Peter Kim, *The Day America Told the Truth: What People Really Believe about Everything that Really Matters* (New York: Prentice Hall, 1991), pp. 31, 65–66, 155, 159–60, 171; Donald Kanter and Philip Mirvis, *The Cynical Americans: Living and Working in an Age of Discontent and Disillusion* (San Francisco: Jossey-Bass, 1989), p. 6.

50. Robert Reich, "Padding the Answer on Helping Education," *Washington Post National Weekly Edition*, 29 April–5 May 1991; Janice Castro, "Where Did the Gung-Ho Go?" *Time*, 11 September 1989; Richard Morin, "The Rich Are Different from You and Me," *Washington Post National Weekly Edition*, 28 October–4 November 1990; *Liberal Opinion Week*, 6 January 1992, pp. 3, 9; David Morris, "Rootlessness Undermines Our Economy as Well as the Quality of Our Lives," *Utne Reader*, May–June 1990, p. 88.

51. Phillips, *Politics of Rich and Poor*, pp. 78, 80; *Washington Post*, 13 August 1989; Thomas Edsall and E. J. Dionne, "A Tax Revolt of the People," *Washington Post National Weekly Edition*, 22–28 October 1990; Hewlett, *When the Bough Breaks*, p. 166; Christopher Matthews, "The Struggling Class," *Liberal Opinion Week*, 9 September 1991.

52. *Wall Street Journal*, 1 August 1989.

53. David Ellwood, *Poor Support: Poverty in the American Family* (New York: Basic Books, 1988), p. 103; Christopher Jencks and Kathryn Eidin, "The Real Welfare Problem," *American Prospects* (Spring 1990); Stephen Rose, *The American Economy Poster and Fact Book* (New York: Pantheon, 1987).

54. Quoted in Kanter and Mirvis, *The Cynical Americans*, p. 137.

55. Sanford Dornbusch and Kathryn Gray, "Single-Parent Families," and Margaret Crosbie-Burnett, Ada Skyles, and Jan Becker-Haven, "Exploring Stepfamilies from a Feminist Perspective," in *Feminism, Children and the New Families*, ed. Sanford Dornbusch and Myra Strober (New York: Guilford Press, 1988); Marilyn Coleman and Lawrence Ganong, "Remarriage and Stepfamily Research in the 1980s: New Interest in an Old Family Form," in *Contemporary Families: Looking Forward, Looking Back*, ed. Alan Booth (Minneapolis: National Council on Family Relations, 1991); Jean Giles-Sims and David Finkelhor, "Child Abuse in Stepfamilies," *Family Relations* 33 (1984); Lawrence Ganong et al., "A Meta-Analytical Review of Family Structure Stereotypes," *Journal of Marriage and the Family* 52 (1990); Art Levine, "The Second Time Around," *U.S. News & World Report*, 29 January 1990.

56. Wini Breines and Linda Gordon, "The New Scholarship on Family Violence," *Signs* 8 (1983); Sarah Begus and Pamela Armstrong, "Daddy's

Right: Incestuous Assaults," in *Families, Politics, and Public Policy,* ed. Irene Diamond (New York: Longman, 1983); Deborah Luepnitz, *The Family Interpreted: Feminist Theory in Clinical Practice* (New York: Basic Books, 1988), p. 225; Linda Gordon, *Heroes of Their Own Lives,* p. 230; Judith Herman with Lisa Hirschman, *Father-Daughter Incest* (Cambridge: Harvard University Press, 1981), p. 110.

57. James Maddock, "Healthy Family Sexuality: Positive Principles for Educators and Clinicians," *Family Relations* 38 (1989); Florence Rush, *The Best-Kept Secret: Sexual Abuse of Children* (Englewood Cliffs N.J.: Prentice-Hall, 1980); Henry C. Kempe, "Incest and Other Forms of Sexual Abuse," in *The Battered Child,* ed. Henry C. Kempe and Ray E. Helfer (Chicago: University of Chicago Press, 1980), p. 205.

58. John Demos, *Past, Present, and Personal: The Family and the Life Course in American History* (New York: Oxford University Press, 1986), p. 84; Collen McGrath, "The Crisis of Domestic Order," *Socialist Review* 43 (1979): 11.

59. Judith Stiehm, "The Protected, the Protector, the Defender," *Women's Studies International Forum* 5 (1982): 374; Breines and Gordon, "New Scholarship on Family Violence," pp. 495–96, 519.

60. Margaret Gordon and Stephanie Riger, *The Female Fear* (New York: Free Press, 1989); Linda Bourque, *Defining Rape* (Durham, N.C.: Duke University Press, 1989); David Gelman, "The Mind of the Rapist," *Newsweek,* 23 July 1990; David Lisak, "Sexual Aggression, Masculinity, and Fathers," *Signs* 16 (1991); Nancy Chodorow, *The Reproduction of Mothering* (Berkeley: University of California Press, 1978); Peggy Sanday, *Female Power and Male Dominance* (Cambridge, England: Cambridge University Press, 1981).

61. Vonnie McLoyd, "Socialization and Development in a Changing Economy," *American Psychologist* 44 (February 1989): 295, 297.

62. Hochschild, *The Second Shift;* J. Jill Suitor, "Marital Quality and Satisfaction with the Division of Household Labor Across the Family Life Cycle," *Journal of Marriage and the Family* 53 (1991); Hewlett, *When the Bough Breaks,* pp. 77–78, 212.

63. Andrew Hacker, "Farewell to the Family?" *New York Review of Books,* 18 March 1982, p. 39; Andrew Cherlin, "Review of *Contemporary Marriage,*" *Population and Development Review* 13 (1987): 352–53; Paul Amato and Bruce Keith, "Parental Divorce and Adult Well-Being: A Meta-analysis," *Journal of Marriage and the Family* 53 (1991): 56; James Coleman, "Families and Schools," *Educational Researcher* 16 (1987): 34, and "The Corporation versus the Family: Consequences for Persons," *Innovation,* no. 415 (1988): 540–45.

Epilogue

1. Edward O. Wilson, *Sociobiology: The New Synthesis* (Cambridge: Harvad University Press, 1975); Richard Dawkins, *The Selfish Gene* (New York: Oxford University Press, 1976); Christopher Lasch, "What's Wrong with the Right" and "Why the Left Has No Future," *Tikkun* 1 (1986): 96.

2. Jane Lancaster, *Primate Behavior and the Emergence of Human Culture* (New York: Holt, Rinehart & Winston, 1975); M. Kay Martin and Barbara Voorhies, *Female of the Species* (New York: Comumbia University Press, 1975); Richard Leakey, *Origins: What New Discoveries Reveal About the Emergence of Our Species and Its Possible Future* (New York: Dutton, 1977); Nancy Makepeace Tanner, *On Becoming Human* (New York: Cambridge University Press, 1988); Marshall Sahlins, *The Use and Abuse of Biology* (Ann Arbor: University of Michigan Press, 1976); Ruby Rohrlich Leavitt, "Peaceable Primates and Gentle People," in *Women's Studies: The Social Realities*, ed. Barbara Watson (New York: Harper's College Press, 1976); Frances Dahlberg, *Woman the Gatherer* (New Haven: Yale University Press, 1981); Eleanor Leacock, *Myths of Male Dominance* (New York: Monthly Review Press, 1981).

3. James Patterson and Peter Kim, *The Day America Told the Truth* (New York: Prentice Hall, 1991), p. 236; Dan Balz, "Actually, They're Mad As Hell," *Washington Post National Weekly Edition*, 10–16, June 1991; E. J. Dionne, Jr., *Why Americans Hate Politics* (New York: Simon & Schuster, 1991); Robert Bellah et al., *The Good Society* (New York: Knopf, 1991).

4. Naomi Weisstein, "'Kinde, Kuche, Kirche' as Scientific Law: Psychology Constructs the Female," in *Sisterhood Is Powerful*, ed. Robin Morgan (New York: Vintage, 1970), pp. 240–41; Urie Bronfenbrenner, *The Ecology of Human Development: Experiments by Nature and Design* (Cambridge: Harvard University Press, 1979), pp. 92–101, 121; Alan Wolfe, *Whose Keeper? Social Science and Moral Obligation* (Berkeley: University of California Press, 1989), pp. 42–44, 216–220; Craig Reinarman, *American States of Mind: Political Beliefs and Behavior Among Private and Public Workers* (New Haven: Yale University Press, 1987), pp. 221–22, 230; H. L. Mitchell, *Roll the Union On: A Pictorial History of the Southern Tenant Farmers Union* (Chicago: Charles H. Kerr, 1987; Harry Boyte, *Community Is Possible: Repairing America's Roots* (New York: Harper Colophon, 1984).

5. Kenneth Cooper, "52 Years of Giving Kids a Head Start," *Washington Post National Weekly Edition*, 30 April–6 May 1990; *Los Angeles Times*, 29 September 1989; *Youth Investment and Community Reconstruction: Street Lessons on Drugs and Crime for the Nineties* (Washington, D. C.: Milton S. Eisenhower Foundation, 1990); *Washington Post National Weekly Edition*,

28 January–3 February 1991; Lisbeth Schorr with Daniel Schorr, *Within Our Reach: Breaking the Cycle of Disadvantage* (New York: Anchor, 1988); *Poverty, Inequality, and the Crisis of Social Policy* (Washington, D. C.: Joint Center for Political and Economic Studies, 1991); *Newsweek*, 7 May 1990; *New York Times*, 13 September 1989; Hewlett, *When the Bough Breaks*, pp. 14, 28, 58–59, 166–80, 254–55; David Ellwood, *Poor Support: Poverty in the American Family* (New York: Basic Books, 1988).

6. T. Berry Brazelton, "Why Is America Failing Its Children?" *New York Times Magazine*, 9 September 1990, p. 90; Schorr, *Within Our Reach*, p. 305.

7. *Beyond Rhetoric: A New American Agenda for Children and Families* (Washington, D. C.: National Commission on Children, 1991), pp. 56–58; Emily Werner and Ruth Smith, *Vulnerable but Invincible: A Longitudinal Study of Resilient Children and Youth* (New York: McGraw-Hill, 1982).

8. "The Forgotten Half," *Phi Delta Kappan*, December 1988, pp. 287–88.

9. David Broder, "Now to Rescue Our Children," *Washington Post National Weekly Edition*, 11–17 March 1991; Marian Wright Edelman, "Kids First!" *Mother Jones*, May–June 1991, p. 76; *Dollars and Sense*, December 1989, p. 23; *American Priorities in a New World Era* (New York: World Policy Institute, 1989); Robert Fitch, "Money's There–Five Ways to Get It," *The Nation*, 29 October 1990; Michael Renner, "Swords into Plowshares," *Utne Reader*, May–June 1990, p. 44.

10. Marian Wright Edelman, *Families in Peril: An Agenda for Social Change* (Cambridge: Harvard University Press, 1987), pp. 31–32, 94–104; Hewlett, *When the Bough Breaks*, pp. 238–39, 263.

Select Bibliography

A GOOD overview of American family history can be found in Steven Mintz and Susan Kellogg, *Domestic Revolutions: A Social History of American Family Life* (New York: Free Press, 1988), or in Maxine Baca Zinn and D. Stanley Eitzen, *Diversity in American Families* (New York: Harper & Row, 1987). For other historical studies of family and gender roles in America, see Stephanie Coontz, *The Social Origins of Private Life: A History of American Families 1600–1900* (London: Verso, 1988); Nancy F. Cott and Elizabeth H. Pleck, *A Heritage of Her Own: Toward a New Social History of American Women* (New York: Simon & Schuster, 1979); Peter Filene, *Him/Her/Self: Sex Roles in Modern America* (Baltimore: Johns Hopkins University Press, 1986); Joseph Pleck, *The Myth of Masculinity* (Cambridge: MIT Press, 1981); Michael Gordon, ed., *The American Family in Social-Historical Perspective* (New York: St. Martin's, 1983); Arlene Skolnick, *Embattled Paradise: The American Family in an Age of Uncertainty* (New York: Basic Books, 1991); and William Chafe, *The Paradox of Change: American Women in the Twentieth Century* (New York: Oxford University Press, 1991).

On the history of courtship, see Beth L. Bailey, *From Front Porch to Back Seat: Courtship in Twentieth-Century America* (Baltimore: Johns Hopkins University Press, 1988), and Ellen Rothman, *Hands and Hearts: A History of Courtship in America* (New York: Basic Books, 1984). For the history and impact of divorce, see Glenda Riley, *Divorce: An American Tradition* (New York: Oxford University Press, 1991); Stephen Sugarman and Herman Kay, eds., *Divorce Reform at the Crossroads* (New Haven: Yale University Press, 1990); Andrew Cherlin, *Marriage, Divorce, Remarriage* (Cambridge: Harvard University Press, 1981); and Andrew Cherlin, ed., *The Changing American Family and Public Policy* (Washington, D.C.: Urban Institute Press, 1988).

On sexuality, see John D'Emilio and Estelle B. Freedman, *Intimate Matters: A History of Sexuality in America* (New York: Harper & Row, 1988); Barbara Ehrenreich, Elizabeth Hess, and Gloria Jacobs, *Re-Making Love: The Feminization of Sex* (New York: Doubleday, 1986); and Lillian B. Rubin, *Erotic Wars: What Happened to the Sexual Revolution?* (New York: Farrar, Straus & Giroux, 1990). An introduction to gay and lesbian history is provided by Lillian Faderman, *Odd Girls and Twilight Lovers: A History of Lesbian Life in Twentieth-Century America* (New York: Columbia University Press, 1990), and Jonathon Katz, ed., *Gay American History: Lesbians and Gay Men in the USA* (New York: Crowell, 1990). Elaine Tyler May covers 1950s family life in *Homeward Bound: American Families in the Cold War Era* (New York: Basic Books, 1988).

Youth and the life course are treated by John Modell, *Into One's Own: From Youth to Adulthood in the United States, 1920–1975* (Berkeley: University of California Press, 1989); Tamara Hareven, ed., *Transitions: The Family and the Life Course in Historical Perspective* (New York: Academic Press, 1978); John Demos, *Past, Present, and Personal: The Family and the Life Course in American History* (New York: Oxford University Press, 1986); and Joseph Kett, *Rites of Passage: Adolescence in America, 1790 to the Present* (New York: Basic Books, 1977). On the history of family violence, see Linda Gordon, *Heroes of Their Own Lives: The Politics and History of Family Violence, Boston, 1880–1960* (New York: Viking, 1988), and Elizabeth Pleck, *Domestic Tyranny: The Making of Social Policy Against Family Violence from Colonial Times to the Present* (New York: Oxford University Press, 1987).

Michael Katz has several books on the history of welfare and dependence in America. Books that contain useful information on families, gender roles, politics, and the state include Michael Grossberg, *Governing the Hearth: Law and Family in Nineteenth Century America* (Chapel Hill: University of North Carolina Press, 1985); Mary Ann Glendon, *The Transformation of Family Law* (Chicago: University Of Chicago Press, 1989); Linda Gordon, ed., *Women, the State, and Welfare* (Madison: University of Wisconsin Press, 1990); Alida Brill, *Nobody's Business: The Paradoxes of Privacy* (Reading, Mass.: Addison-Wesley, 1990); Mary P. Ryan, *Women in Public: Between Banners and Ballots, 1825–1880* (Baltimore: Johns Hopkins University Press, 1990); Nancy F. Cott, *The Grounding of Modern Feminism* (New Haven: Yale University Press, 1987); and Alan Dawley, *Struggles for Justice: Social Responsibility and the Liberal State* (Cambridge: Harvard University Press, 1991).

On families and women's work, see Christine Bose et al., *Hidden Aspects of Women's Work* (New York: Praeger, 1987); Naomi Gerstel and Harriet Gross, eds., *Families and Work* (Philadelphia: Temple University Press, 1987); Arlie Hochschild with Anne Machung, *The Second Shift: Working Parents and the Revolution at Home* (New York: Viking, 1989); Sanford Dornbusch and Myra Strober, eds., *Feminism, Children, and the New Families* (New York: Guilford Press, 1988); and Alice Kessler-Harris, *Out to Work: A History of Wage-Earning Women in the United States* (New York: Oxford University Press, 1982).

On African-American families, see Robert Hill et al., *Research on African-American Families: A Holistic Perspective* (Boston: William Monroe Trotter Institute, 1989); Herbert Gutman, *The Black Family in Slavery and Freedom, 1750–1925* (New York: Oxford University Press, 1976); and Jacqueline Jones, *Labor of Love, Labor of Sorrow: Black Women, Work and the Family from Slavery to the Present* (New York: Basic Books, 1985).

Recent figures on the socioeconomic status of children, youth, and families can be found in publications of the Children's Defense Fund, the Center for Budget and Policy Priorities, the William T. Grant Foundation, and the Urban Institute—all located in Washington, D.C.

Index